Negotiation

Corporate lawyers are rarely trained to negotiate. Yet negotiate they must, frequently.

This peer-reviewed book, dedicated to corporate counsel organizations worldwide, draws upon the latest negotiation teaching and the author's long in-house counsel experience, to provide you with the knowledge, skills, tools and techniques to:

- be a more creative negotiator;
- gain greater authority and control over process and outcome;
- add more value to your business; and
- know where to go for further inspiration.

With its wealth of examples and practical materials, this is a source of value for all in-house counsel, private practitioners, business managers, mediators, arbitrators and many others.

Negotiation

Things Corporate Counsel Need to Know but Were Not Taught

Michael Leathes

**With a Foreword by
Michael McIlwrath, GE Oil & Gas**

Published by:
Kluwer Law International B.V.
PO Box 316
2400 AH Alphen aan den Rijn
The Netherlands
Website: www.wklawbusiness.com

Sold and distributed in North, Central and South America by:
Wolters Kluwer Legal & Regulatory U.S.
7201 McKinney Circle
Frederick, MD 21704
United States of America
Email: customer.service@wolterskluwer.com

Sold and distributed in all other countries by:
Turpin Distribution Services Ltd
Stratton Business Park
Pegasus Drive, Biggleswade
Bedfordshire SG18 8TQ
United Kingdom
Email: kluwerlaw@turpin-distribution.com

ISBN 978-90-411-6734-7

e-Book: ISBN 978-90-411-6735-4
web-PDF: ISBN 978-90-411-8734-5

© 2017 Michael Leathes

All rights reserved. No part of this publication may be reproduced, stored in a retrieval system, or transmitted in any form or by any means, electronic, mechanical, photocopying, recording, or otherwise, without written permission from the publisher.

Permission to use this content must be obtained from the copyright owner. Please apply to: Permissions Department, Wolters Kluwer Legal & Regulatory U.S., 76 Ninth Avenue, 7th Floor, New York, NY 10011-5201, USA. Website: www.wklawbusiness.com

Dedicated to corporate counsel organizations worldwide, including:

American Bar Association, Sections of Business Law and Litigation, Corporate Counsel Committees
Arbeitsgemeinschaft Syndikusanwälte des Deutschen Anwaltvereins
Association of Caribbean Corporate Counsel
Association of Corporate Counsel
Association of Corporate Lawyers Sri Lanka
Asia Pacific Corporate Counsel Alliance
Associazione Italiana Giuristi di Impresa
Association Française des Jurists d'Entreprise
Australian Association of Corporate Counsel
Bendrovių & institucijų teisinikų asociacija (Lithuania)
Bolagsjuristernas Förening (Sweden)
Canadian Corporate Counsel Association
Commerce & Industry Group (UK)
Corporate Counsel Association of New Zealand
Corporate Counsel Association of South Africa
Corporate Counsel Forum of the International Bar Association
Corporate Counsel International Arbitration Group
Corporate Counsel Women of Color
Danske Virksomhedjurister
Eesti Juristide Liidu Ettevõtlusjuristide Uhendus (Estonia)
European Company Lawyers Association
Global Counsel Leaders Circle
Hong Kong Corporate Counsel Association
In House Counsel Worldwide
Indian Corporate Counsel Association
Indonesian Corporate Counsel Association
In-House Counsel Forum Korea
In-House Lawyers Association New Zealand Law Society

Instituto dos Advogados de Empresa (Portugal)
Institut des juristes d'entreprise (Belgium)
International Bar Association Corporate Counsel Forum
Japan In-House Counsel Network
Krajowa Izba Radców Prawnych (Poland)
Latin American Corporate Counsel Association
Legal Management Council of the Philippines
Malaysian Corporate Counsel Association
Mexican Company Lawyers Association
Nederlands Genootschap van Bedrijfsjuristen
Nigerian Bar Association Corporate Counsel Forum
Norges Juristforbund
Round Table Mediation und Konfliktmanagement der deutschen Wirtschaft
Russian Corporate Counsel Association
Seccion de Abogados de Empresa (Spain)
Singapore Corporate Counsel Association
Teollisuus Lakimiesten Yhdistys RY: Industrijuristföreningen (Finland)
The In-House Community (Asia and MENA)
The Pakistan In-House Lawyers' Forum
Udruga korporativnih pravnika; (Croatia)
Udruga Pravnika u Bankarstvu (Bosnia and Herzegovina)
Unie Podnikových Právníků České Republiky (Czech Republic)
and to
all internal lawyers listed in the Wolters Kluwer Directory of Corporate Counsel

About the Author

Michael Leathes spent his career as a corporate counsel with Gillette, Pfizer, International Distillers & Vintners and BAT based variously in Brussels, New York and London. His pro bono duties included board memberships of CPR Institute (2003–2006) and the International Mediation Institute (2007–2015).

Comments

This book was peer reviewed in draft, but if you have comments, suggestions, ideas or contributions that could be considered for the next edition, Michael Leathes would value hearing from you. He can be contacted at ML@MichaelLeathes.com and via www.MichaelLeathes.com, from where certain materials, such as the roleplay in Appendix 7 can be downloaded.

J'ai seulement fait ici un amas de fleurs étrangères,
n'y ayant fourni du mien que le filet à les lier

I have merely gathered a posy of other people's flowers,
only the thread that binds them is my own

Michel de Montaigne 1588

(Essais, Book III)

Drawing of Michael de Montaigne reproduced from Wikipedia

"Well don't just stand there - negotiate!"

This cartoon appeared in the magazine PUNCH, published from 1841 until 2002 and has been reproduced with permission of Punch Limited www.punch.co.uk.

Contents

About the Author		vii
Foreword		xiii
Preface		xvii
Abbreviations		xxi
Acknowledgments		xxiii
Chapter 1	Expectations	1
Chapter 2	Preparation	11
Chapter 3	Neuroscience	33
Chapter 4	Culture	53
Chapter 5	Leverage	77
Chapter 6	Communicating	93
Chapter 7	Process	119
Chapter 8	Disputes	137
Chapter 9	Ethics	177
Chapter 10	Techniques	191
Tomorrow		205
End Notes		211
Bibliography		215
Appendix 1	IMI Olé! Case Analysis and Evaluation Tool	219
Appendix 2	CPR Corporate Early Case Assessment Toolkit	233
Appendix 3	Article: Dealing With 'Selective Perception' and Bad-Faith Allegations in Commercial Settlement Discussions	253
Appendix 4	Article: Culture and its Importance in Mediation	259
Appendix 5	Singapore Arb-Med-Arb Clause and Protocol	281
Appendix 6	Mediation Suitability Scan	285
Appendix 7	Sample Roleplay	297
Index		303

Foreword

by Michael McIlwrath
Global Chief Litigation Counsel, GE Oil and Gas

A decade ago, I interviewed Michael Leathes for a podcast that I was hosting at the time called International Dispute Negotiation. It consisted of interviews with leaders in dispute resolution around the world. Unlike most of my other guests, who were happy to speak about themselves and their practices, Michael turned the tables on the interviewer.

He started *his* interview by asking me why my employer, General Electric, stood behind mediation as a form of dispute resolution, and why we had decided to invest both effort and money into the International Mediation Institute. IMI is a non-profit based in the Netherlands that Michael himself had co-founded to promote high standards of mediation around the world. I fumbled an answer on the spur of the moment about what mediation offers as a mechanism for resolving disputes.

But the real answer to Michael's question was actually much deeper, and it is only with the benefit of having read his book on negotiation these many years later that I can provide a fuller, better answer: traditional methods of resolving conflict are profoundly unsatisfactory and out of sync with the way business is conducted in the modern world. The speed of commerce, and the fluidity with which borders and time zones are crossed, and the virtual marketplaces where business is conducted, have long surpassed the ability of even the most efficient courts and arbitrators to keep up with the disputes that arise from them. And the gap is only getting greater with the passage of time.

Within this gap is a vast need for lawyers and business leaders to find solutions that may not be perfect, but that keep their deals moving instead of getting bogged down with the costs, distraction and uncertainty of litigation and arbitration. And they must do this while working seamlessly with counterparties from cultures and legal systems that may be identical one day and entirely alien the next.

What mediation offers is the opportunity to negotiate and find solutions for disputes and deals that rapidly and flexibly, allow businesses to keep moving. Through negotiation, mediation mirrors what already makes businesses thrive. I am sure this is why Michael ultimately found mediation so suitable for the businesses whose legal departments he successfully led over the years, and it is why we at GE have had such success in encouraging its use.

And yet negotiation, the core of mediation, is also a learned skill that is undervalued and underappreciated by both businesses and the legal community. When, nearly twenty years ago, I went about looking for negotiation training materials for myself and my colleagues, I assumed that law firms would have plenty for us to borrow. Instead, I could not find a single law firm where negotiation is systemically taught, and only one or two firms where any of the lawyers had even attended an external training.

This was confounding. As much as negotiation is a core skill in business, it is the foundation of what lawyers do. It is obviously called upon when we are in a "contract negotiation." But we are also in a negotiation when we appear in front of a judge or arbitrator, or at a mediation, or even when writing a letter to opposing counsel. We can never assume that our business partners will receive 100% of what they want, which is why they hire us lawyers. In fact, this was the reason I titled my podcast, "International Dispute Negotiation" because, at the end of the day, negotiation is deeply embedded in all forms of resolving disputes.

This is also the gap in skills that Michael's book begins to fill. I say *begins* because negotiation and by extension negotiation training are fields in their own rights that are not only rich, vast in their applications, but are also in rapid development and expansion as science reveals more about how people process information and reach decisions. It is probably a good thing that the "canon" of negotiation has yet to be written.

Therefore, while Michael's book aims to provide skills to the in-house counsel, it will also find a natural home in the offices of any law firm. In fact, lawyers who discover this book and embrace its teachings are bound to find they are more at ease in meetings with their business colleagues and more successful at their jobs, because negotiation is a language the business speaks.

To say that this book begins to fill a significant gap should not understate the breadth covered in the pages that follow, which is considerable. Michael provides insight on the importance of preparation, recent discoveries in neuroscience, problems that frequently arise in cross-cultural situations, and the ethical challenges that lawyer-negotiators face. He covers useful negotiation techniques and innovative methods that can yield high impacts, such as the use of impartial deal facilitators to aid in deal negotiations and not just to help parties resolve disputes.

And he also preaches to this choir when he writes about the low-hanging fruit by which in-house counsel can add enormous value to their businesses by promoting negotiating training. Indeed, the in-house lawyer imagined by this book is a true business leader who is fully engaged in the process of identifying and adding value, not just a lawyer relegated to the tasks of *docugotiation* or *litigotiation*, terms Michael has used for those who spend their time drafting terms in agreements and supervising disputes. The lawyer who reads this book should be one who wants to lead, innovate, inspire and increase value for their business or their client.

And I would be remiss with this introduction not to second Michael's suggestion of a greater emphasis on negotiation in law schools and professional legal development, and for a modern, global accreditation system – supported by businesses, law firms, and academia – for those who achieve objective standards of negotiation skills. It is a big idea, but it is one that would provide a substantial contribution to filling the current gap.

Of course, Michael Leathes has never been someone to traffic in small ideas. If the reader has neither the time nor the inclination to join in future initiatives associated with this big idea, they can rest assured that by the end of this book they will be a far more successful and appreciated counsel by their business colleagues or their clients than when they started reading Chapter 1.

Preface

This book is not a user guide to negotiation. There are exceptional books out there that set out to do that, many of them listed in the bibliography. Rather, it aims to inspire negotiation ideas and concepts from the standpoint of a lawyer employed by a company or other organization.

I have drawn this inspiration from two sources.

First, from the teaching of academics and trainers. In the many places that I have done so in the following pages, I have attributed the points mentioned to the sources I have used. Many of these points are well worth following up in their books.

I have also drawn from what I learned on the job as an internal lawyer for international companies. At an early stage, I was fortunate to be delegated with negotiating assignments. There were few negotiation skill books and courses forty or more years ago. You graduate from that School of Hard Knocks resolving never to make the same mistakes again, but negotiation is not a defined art or science. Never are two experiences the same. You learn as you go, trying not to make the same mistakes more than once.

We all need to make paradigm shifts in fast-changing times. Corporate counsel, whether employed in companies or government, can diversify from legal matters to delivering a wider value as negotiators; from managing to leading; from self-centered positions to mutual interests; from not accepting the inevitability of *Litigation As Usual* to finding creative strategies and processes to secure negotiated outcomes within and beyond the legal arena.

An important inspiration for negotiation is not a negotiation book, but one on team leadership. Getting It Done: How To Lead When You're Not In Charge is a 1998 book by Professor Roger Fisher and management consultant Alan Sharp. It was republished as Lateral Leadership: Getting It Done When You're Not The Boss, in 2004. It remains a great starting point. Fisher and Sharp identify many of the attitudes and skills that cause external deals to be impeded by internal politics and lack of leadership.

Preface

Corporate counsel are often in a perfect position to practice what Robert K Greenleaf, drawing on classic texts from the Zhou Dynasty, called *servant leadership,* and what the Danish conflict resolver Tina Monberg calls the Butterfly Effect in Serve to Profit: Butterfly leadership (2014).

Business schools (though, sadly, few law schools) teach negotiation skills and techniques, but more often as an elective than as a core subject. Most people emerge from business schools and law schools as instinctive positional bargainers expressing themselves in the form of wants and demands rather than needs and interests. They tend to be touchy about negotiation. Tunnel vision and a gladiatorial approach can block their ability to explore wider prospects and better opportunities.

Without realizing it, most are doing a disservice to the interests they represent, and to themselves. Today's market is driven more by quick and efficient outcomes. New ways of negotiating are gaining widespread acceptance because they are pragmatic, fast, optimize value and are more sustainable. Business leaders can no longer feel free to take silly risks with shareholders' assets. The premium now is on responsible leadership and management. That includes reputation enhancement, especially in this world where you can be made and destroyed on social media. It includes being a good party to do business with and securing certainty with minimum time, risk, cost and exposure. CEOs increasingly expect creative strategies for managing risks and costs and securing more effective outcomes.

Most of us know that, as corporate counsel, we have a wider responsibility than the one owed to the person or group to whom we report. It extends to our employers' shareholders and other stakeholders beyond the organization.

Some law firms and other service professionals, unconsciously or not, prioritize their income over a client's outcome. Realizing that this outmoded attitude has no viable future, many have moved on. Discerning external counsel, accountants and consultants know that to retain their ever more astute and demanding customer base, and to gain new business, they need to prove themselves as achievers of early results, as dealmakers, dispute avoiders and solution providers, and not just as good advisers, processors and litigators even if that means losing billings per case. This is also consistent with many modern Bar Rules.[1]

So the expectations on corporate lawyers have changed. The term *general counsel (GC)* implies the broader nature of the role, and not only of the most senior in-house lawyer. We are expected to be business and operational people who are lawyers, not lawyers with a business orientation.

Preface

I felt there was no point writing another negotiation book unless it makes an important point for internal counsel. Actually, seven important points, all of which emerge in more detail in the pages that follow. They are:

- Corporate and other internal counsel should not confine themselves to *docugotiation* and *litigotiation* – negotiating terms in agreements and settlements. Those who diversify as commercial negotiators outside the legal frame become true *general* counsel, empowered to lead, innovate, inspire and increase their value.
- Cross-cultural negotiations would lead to more effective outcomes if negotiators take more time to listen and truly understand the other party. Even though most people are not entirely stereotypical, understanding cultural frameworks is essential.
- Prepare better and faster by using openly available e-tools. Preparation is key, and the preparer is at the center of negotiations.
- The dynamics of neuroscience may make your eyes glaze over, but understanding the basics of brain science improves negotiation.
- Using a neutral facilitator to help the parties forge a more effective deal is a greatly under-used opportunity. By having a trusted impartial person take charge of the process frees everyone up to negotiate better. It should not be confined to dispute settlement.
- Legal education needs to include negotiation skills. Negotiation is a hard, not soft, set of skills and can be assessed. Accreditation should be offered to those who pass negotiation skills assessments.
- It is time for an international initiative, backed by top educators, businesses, professional service firms and professional bodies to set high-level global negotiation knowledge and skills standards, as well as an international code of negotiation ethics. An international negotiation institute would not provide training or other services but promote and encourage more and better education on negotiation in all main languages and cultures, treat negotiation as a hard skill, inspire more people to take negotiation courses and improve the quality and effectiveness of negotiated outcomes.

Michael Leathes, January 2017

Abbreviations

AAA	American Arbitration Association
ADR	Appropriate (or Alternative) Dispute Resolution
ATNAs	Alternatives To a Negotiated Agreement
BATNA	Best Alternative To a Negotiated Agreement
CEDR	Centre for Effective Dispute Resolution
CL	Collaborative Law
CISA	Centre for Interdisciplinary Sciences
CSR	Corporate Social Responsibility
DRB	Dispute Resolution Board
DSD	Dispute Systems Design
ECA	Early Case Assessment
EI	Emotional Intelligence
ENE	Early Neutral Evaluation
EQ	Emotional Quotient
GC	General Counsel
GPC	Global Pound Conference
HKMAAL	Hong Kong Mediation Accreditation Association Ltd
ICC	International Chamber of Commerce
ICCC	International Client Consultation Competition
IMI	International Mediation Institute
ISDS	Investor-State Dispute Settlement
JV	Joint venture
LAU	Litigation As Usual
MESO	Multiple Equivalent Simultaneous Offers
MCA	Music Corporation of America
NF	Negotiation Framework
OBE	Outcome-Based Education
ODR	Online Dispute Resolution
OECD	Organisation for Economic Co-operation and Development
O/S	Operating System
O/S 1	Emotional Operating System
O/S 2	Social Operating System
O/S 3	Rational Operating System
PATNA	Most Probable Alternatives To a Negotiated Agreement

Abbreviations

PEDR	Planned Early Dispute Resolution
PoN	Harvard Program on Negotiation
RATNA	Most Realistic Alternatives To a Negotiated Agreement
SI	Social Intelligence
SIAC	Singapore International Arbitration Centre
SIDRA	Singapore International Dispute Resolution Academy
SIMC	Singapore International Mediation Centre
SIMI	Singapore International Mediation Institute
6σ	Six Sigma
WATNA	Worst Alternative To a Negotiated Agreement
ZOPA	Zone of Potential (or Possible) Agreement

Acknowledgments

Like good negotiated outcomes, this book is a product of collaboration.

I have benefited from the writings of numerous leading negotiation teachers in business and law schools around the world. I have merely scratched the surface of their wisdom, ideas and experience. I urge you to read their books. They are packed with advice, fascinating examples, case studies and research work that prove their points. I only wish most had been available when I began my career. I am honored to have been given consent to feature material and extracts from some of their works.

I submitted the draft manuscript to an eclectic group of corporate counsel peers from different companies around the world, as well as some experienced negotiation and dispute resolution practitioners and skills trainers in different countries. All have contributed important insights and techniques that I felt needed to be captured and widely shared. The peer review group comprised:

Michael McIlwrath, Global Chief Litigation Counsel at GE Oil and Gas in Florence, Italy. Mike plowed through my chapters and provided a great variety of comments. He is one of the few corporate counsel to write a book to improve the field in which he mainly works – resolving disputes. He has been a source of inspiration for me for many years. I am honored that he has found time during a merger to contribute the Foreword.

Ute Joas Quinn, Associate General Counsel Exploration and Production at Hess Corporation in Houston, Texas provided critical steerage in relation to international corporate counsel needs and in many other ways.

Wolf Von Kumberg, until recently Associate General Counsel of Northrop Grumman, now a member of ArbDB, has given me several of the examples described in the following pages. As I write, he is Chair of the Board of Management of the Chartered Institute of Arbitrators, the world's largest professional body for dispute resolvers.

Karin Lutz, formerly Head of Fiscal and Corporate Affairs and Secretary of Gist-Brocades NV, has provided valuable ideas on numerous concepts and points and offered many practical improvements and suggestions.

Acknowledgments

Doug McKay, Vice President for Government Relations for Shell Asia Pacific provided a great number of suggestions for improving the content and flow from a non-lawyer's perspective. I wanted the book to be applicable to non-lawyers, and Doug has helped me with that goal.

Cyril Dumoulin, Senior Legal Counsel at Shell International, provided practical guidance that has been a great help in finalizing the manuscript.

George Lim SC, Co-Chair of the Singapore International Mediation Centre and **Professor Joel Lee**, Associate Professor of Law at the National University of Singapore offered many perceptive ideas.

Gigi De Groot, a senior consultant with Move Management in Stockholm, Sweden and former CEO of ITIM International, a leading trainer in intercultural management inspired by the work of Professor Geert Hofstede, kindly commented on the culture chapter.

Tony Eccles of Eccles & Lee in Hong Kong kindly provided additional guidance on aspects of the Culture chapter.

Jeremy Lack, a lawyer, mediator and arbitrator in private practice in Geneva, Switzerland specializing in deal facilitation and effective dispute resolution is a co-founder of Neuroawareness, an international neurobiology consultancy. **Dr. Olga M. Klimecki** is a psychologist and neuroscientist at the Centre Interfacultaire en Sciences Affectives (CISA). Both provided considerable material and guidance on the crucial neuroscience principles for Chapter 3, enabling complex science to be explained and illustrated in lay terms.

Corporate counsel **Leslie Mooyaart,** former General Counsel of KLM and of APM Terminals (Mærsk), **Deborah Masucci**, formerly head of the dispute resolution program at American International Group Inc (AIG), **Toe Su Aung**, formerly Head of Intellectual Property at BAT in London, and **Isabelle Hautot**, General Counsel International Expertise at Orange in Paris all reviewed and commented on the manuscript and gave strong encouragement to complete the task.

Jan Eijsbouts, former General Counsel and Director of Legal Affairs of AkzoNobel NV, a former co-Chair of the Corporate Counsel Forum, now Extraordinary Professor of Corporate Social Responsibility at Maastricht University and Chairman of the World Legal Forum foundation kindly provided much help, especially on Ethics Chapter 9.

Tina Monberg and Annette van Riemsdijk, respectively founders of mediationcenter A/S in Denmark and The New Resolution Group in the Netherlands, have been a constant source of compelling novel ideas many of which are captured in the book.

Manon Schonewille, a partner of the legal mediation office of Schonewille & Schonewille in Rotterdam, the Netherlands, has improved the text in many places, and allowed me to use her work on the value and practice of assisted negotiating as well as the material in Appendix 6.

Acknowledgments

Barney Jordaan, Professor of Management Practice: Negotiation, Conflict Management and Mediation at the Vlerick Business School in Belgium reviewed the book as a negotiation educator who is also a lawyer, having previously served as Professor of Law at the University in Stellenbosch in South Africa and offered numerous improvements.

Two experienced mediators provided me with valuable direct input. **Charles Middleton-Smith**, a leading London-based mediator and deal facilitator, assisted with comments on using neutrals in deal making. And **Martin Brink,** a well-known Dutch mediator, has provided thoughtful input on evaluative mediation and on other areas of the book.

I am also grateful to **Irena Vanenkova** and **Emma Ewart** of the International Mediation Institute (IMI) for their many suggestions, their encouragement throughout, and consent to use certain IMI materials.

Michel de Montaigne explained that he quoted other people in order to express himself more effectively, and I have followed his example, seeking their consent to draw on the inspiration they provided. I am especially grateful to the following, all of whom are named in the book:

The **American Arbitration Association** in New York City for agreement to quote from their Dispute-Wise study; **Bob Bulder**, Managing Director of Just Brands BV and business mediator **Willem Kervers** for allowing me to relate our deal facilitation experience; **CPR Institute** for agreeing to include their ECA Toolkit in Appendix 2 and the selective perception article in Appendix 5; **Professor Noam Ebner** of Creighton University and his four co-authors of You've Got Agreement: Negoti@ting via email; **Peter Child** of McKinsey & Company for allowing me to relate an illustration of cross-cultural negotiation behaviors; **Tina Monberg** and **Jeremy Lack** for consent to use their simplified diagram of the Glasl Escalator; **Professors Roy Lewicki** and **Robert Robinson** for permission to list the items from the Self-reported Inappropriate Negotiation Strategies (SINS) Scale; **Richard D. Lewis** of Richard Lewis Communications for agreement to use some of his culture diagrams; **Professor Erin Meyer** at INSEAD for permitting me to portray her amazing Culture Map; **Michael J. Roberts** for his excellent summary of why mediations work when negotiations fail; **Professor James Sebenius** of Harvard Business School for allowing me to list his six mistakes commonly made by negotiators; **Professor Richard Shell** at Wharton Business School for permission to relate his three schools of negotiation ethics; **Professor Richard Susskind** and **Matthew Lavy** for permission to quote from their working paper Likely Developments in ODR; **Sweet & Maxwell** for consent to feature in Appendix 4 a Chapter by **Professor Joel Lee** from Mediation in Singapore: A practical guide; **Geert Hofstede BV, The Hofstede Center**, Fons Trompenaars and **Charles Hampden-Turner** for supporting my requests to summarize their cultural dimensions; **Professor Roger Volkema** of Kogood Business School for approval to relate his categorization of leverage; and **Professor Michael Wheeler** at Harvard Business School for permission to use his memorable ethical conduct litmus test.

Acknowledgments

Most authors need to express their gratitude to their family for tolerating the endless stresses and strains involved, and I am no exception. My wife, Annette, applied her legendary Dutch tolerance in accommodating my unsocial hours and constantly acted as a sounding board. My brother-in-law, Nico van der Kleij, who spent many years in the publishing industry as a marketing director, guided me on manuscript preparation. Our offspring got stuck in too: Femke, a clinical psychologist in private practice, commented on the neuroscience, correcting over-simplifications; Tom, an internet entrepreneur with plenty of experience negotiating with lawyers and financiers, and Greg, a corporate international tax manager who frequently negotiates with lawyers and government agencies, both contributed from their different standpoints and experiences and helped me pitch to Generation Y millennnials.

Wolters Kluwer Law & Business were the ones that made it happen. Eleanor Taylor at Kluwer Law International challenged me when I expressed the idea of a non-legalistic book on negotiation aimed at corporate counsel, pointing out that the vision will remain a dream without the action of writing it. Gwen de Vries, Director of Publishing, backed my vision for the book and its somewhat unconventional approach. Monique Sasson was then assigned as my editorial adviser. Monique is an Italian Avvocato, and English Solicitor and a New York State Attorney, a dispute resolver with JAMS, co-Managing Editor of several of the Institute of Transnational Arbitration's publications and a respected author in her own right. Monique's guidance, creativity, flexibility, patience and encouragement have been pivotal. Mr. R. Srinivasan, Mrs. Pradhiba and the editing team at Newgen Knowledge Works in Chennai attended tirelessly to the task of getting the details right.

I sincerely thank them all; their collaboration and support made the book.

CHAPTER 1
Expectations

> The Power To Do More
>
> Dell Technologies slogan

Only rarely, it seems, does a leader make a public statement on the valued qualities of corporate counsel. It grabs your attention when made by the boss of one of the world's most admired and successful companies that employs hundreds of corporate counsel across numerous industries.[1]

On October 17, 2012, Jeffrey R. Immelt, Chairman and CEO of General Electric Company, was asked to introduce his then General Counsel, Brackett B. Denniston III, who was being honored at an event organized by the Pro Bono Partnership in New York for his leadership in voluntary legal services. Mr. Immelt delivered his remarks without notes:[2]

> There are three things I love about Brackett that I think great lawyers do. The first is that he is tough-minded. Today, you need a "yes" or "no". "Maybe's" don't cut it any more. Being surrounded by a legal leader and a legal team that is willing to get right there into the trenches with you and be accountable is unique and important, and Brackett does that. He is business savvy – let me tell you, in an organization in the world we live in today, no function sets the culture of the entire company the way the legal function does. You set the boundaries of who we can be; you define the field that we play on, and I couldn't do it without having a business savvy partner like Brackett Denniston, who not only is brilliant in the law but understands how engineering works, understands our aviation business, and is willing to get his hands dirty from the standpoint of running the company. And the third piece is – you have to have trust. Companies these days are so exposed, and there is no way we can run a company like GE unless we have trust – unless you have people around you that you can trust, that you know are going to do the right thing, and that you can just rely on their judgement – even, sometimes, when you don't like it, and you know it's the right thing to do. So – tough-minded, business-savvy, trust – that's Brackett Denniston.

Skills and competency as a lawyer were largely assumed.

Chapter 1

Earlier, writing in the Spring/Summer 2011 edition of the Hudson Institute's American Outlook magazine,[3] Mr. Immelt had used the same *tough-minded* adjective to describe Ronald Reagan, who had served as GE's Goodwill Ambassador prior to his political career. By *tough-minded* he meant: addressing problems realistically and with determination, intolerance of *"maybe's," "accountability"* and *"willingness to get right there into the trenches with you."* In The Other Kind of Smart (2009), Harvey Deutchendorf postulated seven habits of tough-minded leaders:[4] managing emotions; self-confidence; choosing whom to associate with wisely; facing one's fears and taking action; saying no when necessary; and being self-disciplined and independent.

Jeff Immelt's characterization of his GC's value raises the questions: how do GC's themselves interpret the competencies they need to meet the expectations of top management, and is negotiation one of them?

In July 2014, the Global Counsel Leaders Circle, a forum of senior corporate counsel and compliance officers, published a report[5] based on interviews with eight GCs, other internal counsel, two Board Chairs, an Audit Committee Chair, private practice lawyers and executive search firms. The report focused on corporate governance, and the following is an extract in a section on competency (presented in alphabetical order):

> In our discussions with legal chiefs and those who select them, as well as the top executives they work with, we compiled this list of competencies for GCs today: Advocacy aptitude and experience; business acumen; calm temperament; communications skills; crisis management ability; foresight and identification of trends; independence; integrity and good ethics; judgment; leadership competency; legal knowhow; management skills (including ability to involve and coordinate internal and external resources, as well as delegate); media awareness; **negotiation skills**; problem solving ability. [emphasis added]

Business acumen and a deep knowledge of the business is a need widely identified by internal lawyers. In their book The Generalist Counsel: How Leading General Counsel are Shaping Tomorrow's Companies (2013),[6] Prashant Dubey and Eva Kripalani interviewed many current and former corporate counsel, most of whom emphasized the importance of being valued by core commercial and other functions. Several of those quoted, such as Amy Shulman and Jeff Kindler, both former GCs of Pfizer Inc, had run businesses before being appointed as the company's GC.

In different ways, all the GCs interviewed indicated that business savviness entails much more than having had experience of business. It means being seen and felt to be business savvy – speaking the right language, expressing great ideas, making creative and helpful contributions, and being involved and adding timely value in the key issues. One visible measure of a GC's commercial acumen is running the legal function as a business, one that credibly produces a return on the overhead's investment, contradicting the widespread perception of internal lawyers as another dreaded cost center.

Trust is closely connected to savviness. Trust is partly related to depth and breadth of experience. Virgil had advised in The Aeneid in 19BC to *"trust one who has gone *through it."* Trust, as everyone is aware, takes time to build and is gained by being appreciated for exercising good judgment; by providing guidance that is reliable and typically not risk-averse, conventional and theoretical but, when circumstances allow, daring, pragmatic and innovative; by building a reputation for contributing a perspective that is broader than the legal aspects; and by not talking and writing like a lawyer except where legal-speak is essential to the issue, as it may be in dealings with other lawyers on technical issues, but is otherwise usually inappropriate.

HOW INTERNAL LAWYERS ARE PERCEIVED

There is some, but limited, research on how corporate counsel are valued within their organizations. In January 2014, researchers Lubomir Litov and Simon Sepe of the University of Arizona and Charles Whitehead of Cornell Law School, published the results of their empirical research in Lawyers and Fools: Lawyer-Directors in Public Corporations.[7] This found that in 2009, 43% of United States companies had at least one attorney as a member of their Board. The reasons may be related to necessity but the research also suggests that having a lawyer on a company's Board has a positive impact on the value of the company. Businesses are often exposed to more legal threats from regulation, and compliance has become a more significant issue. Legal monitoring and control increases value by reducing exposure to risk. For example, in September 2015, the US Department of Justice issued strict new guidelines[8] for public prosecutors and attorneys to increase the incidence of criminally charging individuals involved in corporate wrongdoing.

In 2013, The Global Legal Post, a London-based researcher and publisher that produces a magazine and blog of analysis and comment aimed at business lawyers internationally, presented The GC Excellence Report[9] based on survey results from 270 internal counsel. A further Report was published in 2015.[10] These Reports note the growing commercialization of the role of corporate counsel, but from a low base. Only 8.8% of those surveyed in 2013 were members of the Boards of their organizations, and, amazingly, only 20% aspired to become Board members. The 2015 Report, like the Arizona/Cornell research, emphasizes that increased regulation and litigation and the emphasis on compliance are main drivers of the development of internal lawyers.

While the role of corporate lawyers is clearly expanding and changing rapidly, the evidence suggests that the momentum originates more with outside pressures than the positive individual contributions that in-house lawyers can and should make to growing and improving stakeholder value. Corporate counsel face a daily dilemma: being practical and commercial and valued as a risk-taker while simultaneously protecting the business as a gatekeeper and ensuring compliance with laws, regulations and codes. These two responsibilities often conflict. Business colleagues tend to more easily remember the occasions when lawyers act to protect the business, rather than those where they use their skills to add value to it creatively. Internal lawyers therefore need a breakout strategy. They need to apply their skills and position to counter the perception that their role is only focused on keeping their business out of trouble. Negotiation is a prime way in which corporate lawyers can do just that.

WHY LAWYERS NEED NEGOTIATION SKILLS TRAINING

Lawyers, whether working as external or internal counsel, are rarely trained to negotiate, even though they have to negotiate frequently.

Most of us are natural skeptics. We tend towards pessimism, seeing problems before opportunities. We value factual evidence, definitions, analysis, winning, control and process. Our professional training and practice tends to be based on analytical capabilities, so most of us are likely to develop these skills more than others. When we negotiate, we are likely to adopt a fairly rigid positional approach based on rights and reasoning. Subconsciously, we tend to use our IQ more than our emotional intelligence (EI) or social intelligence (SI).

Business leaders tend to be different from lawyers psychometrically. Most are intuitively opportunistic, creative risk-takers and experimenters, otherwise they would most probably be in different jobs. They may see the downside but they focus on the upside. Daniel Pink asserted in A Whole New Mind (2006)[11] that business leaders apply more EI and SI than other groups of professionals.

For those of us lawyers employed by an organization, this creates a conundrum. How dominant should our analytical orientation be in our work and interactions with emotionally-savvy business people? Negotiation, requires considerable EI and SI in addition to IQ. To represent our organizations as lead negotiators, we need to negotiate commercially, not abandoning our legal instincts but adapting them with new skills and interacting well with EI-orientated business people.

Most newly-qualified lawyers are unlikely to have had formal training in negotiation. As Michael McIlwrath, Global Chief Litigation Counsel at GE Oil & Gas has explained, before GE began their international negotiation training program in around 2002, he canvassed many of GE's large international law firms, asking to borrow materials from their training courses. But he could not find a single firm that had a negotiation training program, and only a few had lawyers on their staff who had undertaken any negotiation training.

That was in 2002 and things are changing now. In recent years, in the Netherlands, for example, legal training includes training in early dispute resolution, including mediation. Some leading law firms are today putting new recruits from law school onto obligatory internal courses, some of which cram the curriculum of a typical MBA course into five or six weeks. This equips them far better to engage with clients and hit the ground running.

In-house law departments, however, may be reacting more slowly. GE was ahead of the curve. Some do have sophisticated business induction programs, but others, it seems, let new corporate counsel hires learn (and make mistakes) on the job, as I did.

As we will see in Chapter 3, negotiation is a skill and aptitude that firmly sits at the intersection of analytical, social and emotional capacities, and demands elements of each. Lawyers can capitalize on their analytical and rational nature if they also draw on their ability to navigate emotions and apply creativity to a roughly equal extent, depending on need.

Legal education in most countries is devoid of negotiation courses. Lawyers are primarily educated to apply knowledge of law and legal process to achieve desired ends. Legal process involves a defined series of steps, approaches and mindsets that are quite rigid and inflexible, which can constrain lateral moves outside the recognized limits of conventional process. This is true even when stepping outside the process into sometimes unfamiliar territory would be risk-free and could well lead to a more effective, safer and less costly result. Process can perpetuate an unhealthy comfort in habitual, tried & true ways of doing things that often take time, generate cost, incur risk, are inflexible and get nowhere.

At one point in my career, my in-house legal colleagues were responsible, for monitoring the trademark applications being filed by a major international competitor. When the team spotted a trademark application that was questionable, for example because it arguably resembled one of our own trademarks, they would automatically file a legal challenge, or opposition, regardless of whether the competitor's trademark application might impact on our business. Our competitors, not surprisingly, did exactly the same to us. This had been going on for decades, and no one could remember who started it. Once an opposition was filed, a stream of formal arguments and counter-arguments followed that took time and energy and incurred sometimes monumental legal and expert fees, often with no success. The strategy was more designed to harm the competitor, than to protect ourselves.

One day, we wrote to our competitor and proposed that, for a trial period, when we intended to oppose one of their trademark applications, we would contact them informally to explain, in general terms, why we would be doing so. We added that we would appreciate it if they extended the same courtesy to us. The competitor seemed to think it was a sensible idea, and agreed to follow suit. The number of oppositions filed by each company against the other almost halved overnight, along with the costs involved. More interestingly, the dialogue it opened up led to various negotiations for deals over trademark rights that significantly benefited both companies.

Post-qualification legal training in most countries also assumes trainees will pursue careers advising others, rather than assuming direct ownership of issues or problems, as internal counsel often have to do. It is assumed not only that lawyers advise clients, but also that clients will obligingly follow the advice given. Lawyers, like doctors, are therefore trained to develop a subconscious detachment from the issues on which they advise. That subtle and often invisible psychological separation can give the impression that the adviser is less engaged, even indifferent. Corporate counsel need to overcome these deficiencies in their approach by the way they think, speak and behave.

Language (such as referring to business colleagues as "clients," or the use of the personal pronoun "you" rather than "we") can easily suggest that the Law function regards itself as some kind of ersatz professional firm, that internal lawyers see their role as purely advisory, that they stand apart and do not partner with the business people and do not share the same stake in the problem. It can create a very negative impression. It suggests *not getting right there into the trenches with you.*

As a result of their training, and of their practice in law firms, lawyers naturally think in the linear terms of rights and liabilities, and win or lose. Lawyers are much more inclined than business people to approach a challenge as a battle to be won rather than a problem to be solved. They invariably set out on a quest for evidence, precise definitions and detailed analysis before they can begin to devise a game plan. This has its merits, especially when preparing for a negotiation, but also has its limits. The expectations of those who engage corporate lawyers are generally much more kaleidoscopic and geared to a multi-dimensional, multi-disciplinary, results-based approach to problem solving, in which gut-feel, rooted in knowledge and experience, predominates. Lawyers need to be trained to seek outcomes that leverage their analytical skills but also draw on their EI and SI to a much greater extent than their training and natural inclinations would encourage.

Outcome-Based Education (OBE) has gained momentum around the world in many areas of learning, but has had a disappointingly slow uptake in legal education in most countries, and has been implemented poorly in other countries . This is partly due to inadequate inclusion in existing curricula. OBE assesses students not just on their technical knowledge of inputs like textbooks and rules, but on the practicalities of whether they can achieve whatever result is required by applying wider skills that lie beyond conventional technical training. Legal education seems to have lagged behind accountancy, medicine, HR, project management and other disciplines in embracing OBE.

Change is happening, but slowly. Two reports in 2007 by the Carnegie Foundation for the Advancement of Teaching[12] and by a team under Roy Stuckey, Professor of Law at the University of South Carolina,[13] urged US law schools to broaden their range of courses. These recommendations are beginning to take root, especially in the US and the UK, but take-up is patchy and the pace of progress is slow.

Although business schools aim to impart more real-world skills, many still focus on traditional managerial skills, such as financial management, business strategy, economics, marketing, manufacturing and supply chain operations, statistics and business analysis. There are some important exceptions, but the core courses of most MBA programs are usually drawn from these areas. Many MBA courses do not feature negotiation as a core subject. Although, of course, some do, usually negotiation is an elective course, as negotiation is seen as a "softer" skill – harder to measure and assess.

Professors Robert Rubin and Erich Dierdorff at DePaul University's Kellstadt Graduate School of Business in Chicago conducted a study in 2009, which was updated in 2011, to determine the extent to which the core curricula of 373 business school MBA programs in the US were aligned with a managerial competency model derived from over 8,000 American business leaders.[14] Their analysis showed that most core MBA curricula emphasize analytical competencies such as administration and control, the task environment and managing logistics and technology. However, the competencies perceived as most critical by business leaders are the more creative skills, such as managing decision-making processes, human capital, strategy and innovation. The Kellstadt study noted that these are the very "soft" skill abilities least covered in required core MBA curricula. Decision-making, according to the Kellstadt study, was a core course in only 13% of MBA programs, even though negotiation is very much a decision-making skill.

As a result, many MBA graduates emerge from business school without having been trained or assessed in negotiation skills. In reality, business people can emerge from management training with as few taught negotiation skills as their lawyers. And yet, in the average company, the business people usually consider negotiation to be a core part of their role, largely because they consider themselves as the "owner" of all business-critical issues, and the lawyers as mere "advisers." Consequently, to the extent that the lawyers do negotiate, they most frequently confine themselves to doing so in esoteric legal environments involving other lawyers.

POST-QUALIFICATION TRAINING

The postgraduate Harvard Program on Negotiation (PoN) was innovative, inspiring and unique when introduced in 1983. Although the PoN remains one of the global leaders in negotiation training, other centers of learning, especially some business and postgraduate law schools, and also some dispute resolution trainers, have contributed to the wealth of knowledge, teaching and skills generated in the negotiation field. Others, including a few (but only a few) law schools, are now incorporating elements of negotiation training into core curricula.

But over the next few years, demand for these skills will increase as the expectations of businesses and professional firms crystallize and become increasingly geared to minimizing costly post-qualification training, and as graduates strive to maximize their employability. Business and law schools are likely to systematically incorporate negotiation skills into their standard mandatory curricula, driven by increased market demand for more OBE-trained professionals. *Adventure learning* is the term given to getting these skills played out in real environments and is described in detail in Venturing Beyond the Classroom (2010) edited by Christopher Honeyman, James Coben and Giuseppe De Palo, part of a project initiated by Hamline University to develop second generation negotiation teaching. Hopefully, adventure learning will become increasingly common in negotiation education.

Meanwhile, lawyers who have trained themselves to negotiate "on-the-job" need to ask whether their anecdotal exposure to negotiation is really enough to make them effective negotiators, and many will need to increase their negotiation knowledge and skills through training.

Chapter 1

MARKETING NEGOTIATION SKILLS INTERNALLY

Expectations can usually be met to some degree by smart marketing. Corporate counsel need to promote their skills and added value as broadly as possible. A good starting point is to recognize that internal law functions naturally suffer from an inbuilt perception problem. It is usually not a personal phenomenon (though it certainly can be) and most often arises from the conventional cynical view that business people, and the public in general, have of lawyers – that they are specialists rather than generalists, often more detached from the rough and tumble of the business than engaged in it, inclined to be more cautious than adventurous, and see their role as restraining freedom of action rather than enabling and encouraging it. Corporate lawyers with responsibility for the compliance area are especially exposed to the risk of being branded as naysayers and brakes on business momentum because, however creative they may be, the rigors of the discipline are largely inflexible.

There are many ways to address the negative image. They are usually there on or under the surface, in seriousness or in jest, and must not be brushed aside. Some corporate counsel regularly survey those they work with to tease out how they can improve and add more value. Being appreciated for having outstanding negotiating skills is one major area that can dramatically contribute to positive perceptions.

This potential of corporate counsel can be projected on both theoretical and practical levels.

On the theoretical level, it is tempting to pay little attention to our role profiles or job descriptions. They are usually hidden from view to all but our boss, a few colleagues and HR professionals. Neglecting job descriptions, or allowing them to become outdated or moribund, is a lost opportunity. Role profiles can be strong marketing tools when used creatively, for example in induction packs for new business managers. Having a website for the legal function is important for communicating the involvement and value of internal lawyers in the strategic development of the business, the purposes and breadth of the function, and for offering business people practically useful tools and information. Shrewd inclusion of negotiation, including negotiation skills training for business managers, can convey a highly business-tuned approach, and help dispel some of the outdated and negative imagery popularized by non-lawyers. Posting well-presented role profiles of each counsel or functional grouping on an intranet site can also help change perceptions, as can war stories and successes.

On the practical level, it should be possible to present the Law function as a value generator rather than a cost center. We must avoid being disingenuous, but values attributed to the involvement of internal lawyers can usually be measured, a substantial discount factor applied, and still arrive at a bottom line that shows the value we have added far exceeding our cost.

There are many examples. One would be to apply Six Sigma (6σ) principles to the Law function, or an area of the function's role, such as mergers and acquisitions, litigation, intellectual property, law firm management or compliance. 6σ is used by thousands of businesses worldwide as a methodology and a set of practices and tools for improving output quality by removing "defects," and can certainly be applied to staff support activities. The underlying precept is that all actions are parts of processes that can be defined, measured, analyzed and improved, combining to become "Critical To Quality" (CTQ) in business terms. Metrics are a central feature of 6σ and therefore provide a basis for demonstrating value of the activity being assessed.

6σ would have a clear application, for example, in dispute resolution. A major case being litigated or arbitrated can be viewed as a project, which, actually, is all it is in business terms. CTQs would include negotiating a resolution (and thereby achieving certainty) as quickly as possible, achieving a low-cost settlement when measured against the risks and costs of losing, preserving relationships and reputation, and minimizing management time. Litigation, in 6σ terms, can be classified a *defect* that can be *removed* through an early outcome. This can be presented conservatively, and therefore credibly, as value-generative on an individual case basis. For example:[15]

Cost Item	Legal Fees (USD)	Amount at Risk (USD)
Litigating the case	200,000	2,000,000
Negotiating a settlement	50,000	1,400,000
Avoidance costs	150,000	600,000
(Conservatively assume that just 33% of Avoidance Costs are attributable to Law function negotiation)		
Total Cost Avoidance	50,000	200,000

Total Cost Avoidance for dispute = USD 50,000 + USD 200,000 = USD 250,000

To boost the credibility, it can be useful to add what is not quantified, such as reputational benefits and preserving long-term relationships.

Many legal issues are akin to business processes. Lawyers can adapt systematic methods and principles for process improvement in manufacturing, logistics and project management such as 6σ and Lean (a Toyota-derived production system). In so doing, corporate counsel are appreciated for bringing business disciplines to their own field to the extent possible, making the task of meeting expectations much easier.

In Legal Design Lawyering: Rebooting Legal Business Model with Design Thinking (2016), Professors Véronique Fraser and Jean-François Roberge at Quebec's University of Sherbrooke warn of the danger posed by the mental maps instilled by legal training and involuntary adherence to prescribed process. These factors subconsciously direct lawyers how to behave in certain ways. Professors Fraser and Roberge have proposed the complementary development of a problem-solving competency called Legal Design Lawyering based on design theory which draws on the cognitive capacities of "knowing," "analyzing," "synthesizing" and "creating" to enable issues to be addressed more holistically and effectively. Although Legal Design Lawyering is a nascent concept, the modern demands of businesses and governments are likely to encourage its development and use internationally.

Chapter 1

DIVERSIFYING TO DELIVER

Demonstrating fine negotiating skills is a prime way to meet the expectations that modern business management increasingly have of their internal counsel at all levels. Negotiation offers corporate counsel two intrinsic values. First, you can demonstrate a competency that is ancillary to your main legal expertise or responsibility, for example mergers and acquisitions, contract management, litigation and arbitration, compliance, intellectual property, environmental issues or whatever. There is a further, even higher value – a corporate counsel who is perceived to be a good business negotiator per se transforms the perception of their commercial and other colleagues. You can be the obvious choice to lead the business negotiating team partly because of your legal ability but also, perhaps mainly, because of your competency as an effective negotiator.

There is a lot to think about as a negotiator. Preparation is paramount and is a natural responsibility for a corporate counsel to assume in many, if not most, mainstream negotiations. You get in early and can exert strategic influence on the course of the deal or settlement. It will benefit you and others to know how neurobiology and culture are likely to impact upon typical negotiating circumstances. You can bring the negotiating team to understand the changing spectrum of leverage as the negotiation progresses and to communicate well. A good negotiator will always be thinking about how to configure the process to the predicament, rather than the other way round, and to bring creative flair to the experience. The corporate counsel is perfectly placed to deploy dispute avoidance strategies, and bring unavoidable disputes to an early and beneficial outcome. And, crucially, to negotiate ethically. Ben Heineman Jr., a former GC of General Electric (1987–2003), points out in High Performance with High Integrity (2008) that internal counsel need to strike the balance between partnering the business units while guarding the company's integrity and reputation. These are complementary, not contrarian, responsibilities.

All these things need to be done using the right tools, processes and techniques. The following chapters aim to cover all these needs and opportunities. Let's explore them further.

CHAPTER 2
Preparation

By failing to prepare you are preparing to fail.

Benjamin Franklin

The lesson of rigorous preparation has been taught throughout history.

In the 5th Century BC, Sun Tzu, in The Art of War, denounced lack of preparation as the most heinous of crimes, and celebrated good preparation as the greatest of virtues. In the 1st Century, Seneca defined luck as something that happens when preparation meets opportunity. Michelangelo grumbled that if people knew how hard he had to prepare to gain his mastery, it would not seem so wonderful at all. In Henry V, Act 4, Scene 3, Shakespeare has the King giving the most famous pep talk in history to his overwhelmed army as they prepared for the unlikely English victory at Agincourt in 1415, explaining that *all things are ready if our minds be so.* President Lincoln is often credited with the remark that if he had eight hours to cut down a tree, he would spend the first six sharpening his ax, though the comment has more plausibly been traced to an Appalachian lumberjack in 1956. Napoleon admitted that it was not innate genius that suddenly and secretly enabled him to decide what he should do in unexpected circumstances, but thought and planning. In 1946, the first President of the International Standards Organization, Howard Coonley, accurately predicted that business leaders would in future be rated on their ability to anticipate problems rather than to meet them as they come. A stream of legendary American Football coaches, among them Michigan's Fielding Yost and Alabama's Bear Bryant, have perpetuated the pre-game mantra that *the will to win is worthless without the will to prepare.* And decorators the world over, when asked to name the ultimate secret behind a beautiful paint job, are certain to reply: *preparation, preparation, preparation.*

This increasingly busy world leaves most of us with less, or even no, prep time. We suffer from task saturation. Normality, in this constant state of un-readiness, is forcing us to rely on assumptions, instinct, hearsay, gossip and guesswork to get through the day. Negotiators who claim an intricate familiarity with the industry, subject matter or past experience, will often use this knowledge to compensate for a thoughtful and thorough analysis of the esoteric situation at hand. They may be deluding themselves.

I learned the importance of preparation through embarrassment. Almost forty-five years ago, about three months into my job as a junior counsel with Gillette, the GC decided I should gain familiarity with the business. One assignment was to spend a few days with a wholesaler's sales manager visiting retail stores. We went from one to another, discussing planned stock levels for different products, point-of-sale materials, upcoming advertising campaigns and credit terms.

On the afternoon of the second day, the sales manager suggested that as I had now witnessed how things are done, I should take the lead with the last customer on our visit list. It was a local chain of convenience stores and our appointment was with the owner in person. The sales manager had given 120 days credit terms for a limited period to help the stores through a difficult time, but now wanted to bring this down to 60 days. He asked me to take the lead. I had a weak grasp of the customer's sales levels of our products, no real understanding of their business model and did not spare a thought for their situation. I should have asked the sales manager these questions as we traveled to the meeting. But in the over-confidence of youth, I thought I could do it spontaneously, as the sales manager had appeared to do with the previous customers.

It turned into a humiliating experience. The owner of the stores, who thought I was a management trainee, took full advantage of the rookie that I was, agreeing to tighter credit but in return proposing new terms that sounded perfectly reasonable to me, including additional volume discounts. The new terms would have undone years of painstaking negotiations by the sales manager and his team. He took over from me, and wrapped up the discussion. I still fairly accurately recall the severe lecture he gave me in the car afterwards: *I threw you in deep because I expected you to fail and I was there to rescue the situation. In whatever you do, figure out your goals and stick to them, do not underestimate anyone, know more about them than they do about you, never assume, listen carefully, be patient, and leave a good feeling, as you may return.*

Fortunately, there is much we can do using available tools to reduce the time and effort needed for effective negotiation prep work, though all these tools demand discipline, initiative and care. Most of these time and energy savers can be adopted by anyone facing the prospect of any form of negotiation. With the right e-tools, you really can prepare on the fly.

To be their most effective, negotiators need to cover a lot of territory:

- be perceived appropriately by the other party;
- understand as much as possible about those you deal with;
- have the best possible information you can get;
- know your real leverage and focus on the other party's;
- think carefully about where the other side is coming from;
- distinguish between what they want and what they need;

- separate fact from fiction, and fairness from unreasonableness;
- know when to talk and when to walk;
- bring your own side along with you;
- know where best to turn for support;
- be skilled in listening, questioning and deep exploration;
- focus and do not let yourself be distracted; and
- generally be psyched up for the task.

PREPARING OURSELVES

The first impressions exuded by any negotiator, deliberately or accidentally, are among the uncountable things that really count. The vibes you transmit can have a huge impact on the way the negotiation is set up; how seriously you will be respected and trusted; who the other party puts forward to negotiate with you; their initial attitude and negotiating stance; how defensive, responsive, flexible, amenable or aggressive they are when they begin; and what expectations, realistic or imaginary, they may have. Your ability to negotiate successfully is partly related to how you handle what a management guru might call your *brand essence*.

All perceptions are kaleidoscopic. One of the loose colored beads in the negotiation cylinder is your persona, or what you want people to know of it. You can benefit from, and can equally be compromised or impeded by how you dealt with other parties in the past; how the other negotiator generally perceives the organization you represent; and by what the other party can find out about you, personally and as a professional. It is difficult, or too late, to change the first two of these, but the third is largely within your control. You can either neglect or craft your online persona, and the impressions that people draw from it. It is a basic, but common, error for negotiators to neglect their public *brand essence*.

We can also get it badly wrong without realizing it. For example, you often see external counsel claiming strong international competency and experience, while their bios are overwhelmingly domestic. Nonetheless, external counsel are generally far better placed than internal counsel to present themselves publicly. They also have an obvious incentive to do so, as they sell their knowledge and expertise in the open market. They all have law firm websites that promote their résumés, often citing their background, experience, awards, presentations, client lists and achievements. Yet many of these biographies fail to reveal their true personae. There are few videos embedded in their write-ups that would give people they later meet in negotiation a hands-on feel for their personalities, few links to articles they have written that give an insight into their beliefs, attitudes and convictions. Most professional litigators or arbitration counsel, for example, will extol their expertise in taking legal action for their clients, but give little away about their overall negotiation and settlement abilities. Perhaps they believe that to do so could be misconstrued as diluting the tough, me-no-compromise impression they think they need to cultivate, and their assumption of client expectation tells them to portray a win mentality rather than the versatility and pragmatism implied by the combination of a strong settlement and litigation track record.

Despite these common limitations, external counsel make better use of online marketing opportunities. Unlike external counsel, corporate lawyers usually operate behind the proverbial corporate or government veil. They tend to focus on internal PR as they do not have to sell themselves in the open market, and trying to do so could conceivably be frowned upon by their employer. The result, however, is that many corporate counsel are practically invisible at a public level, and there is little or no useful information about them for another party's negotiator to appreciate.

Corporate counsel therefore often overlook the value of their online presence. Anyone who keys in your name plus your organization is not likely to learn much, perhaps only a few one-liners on business and social networking platforms. Invisibility may not create a negative impression, but it can be a missed opportunity. The right kind of public information can generate a perception that will have a positive effect in any negotiations. We only get one chance to make that crucial first impression. Internet browsers provide that opportunity, if we take advantage of them. An important halo effect is created if you are seen publicly, via respected media, as an authority on a particular issue or field, even if the subjects covered do not have a direct bearing on, or are beyond the scope of, any prospective negotiation in which you are likely to be engaged.

One of the best ways of creating a controlled online profile is to publish articles and comments in professional blogs and other publications. There are now numerous quality forums in most fields that will gratefully accept thoughtful material and comment originating from the demand side – i.e. the organizations directly affected by, or involved in, particular issues. Once published, any browser will be likely to include a link to it when you are looked up online by potential negotiating partners. Where you have carved out an area of expertise for yourself internally, perhaps in a subject you feel passionately about and has a special value to your business, you have an opportunity to deliver presentations at seminars and conferences. Many of these can be made available online by conference organizers, and will also be picked up by search engines. The publishers of most blogs, articles and conferences will automatically link to the résumé you provide them, which can include your affiliations to membership organizations, such as a local, regional or global corporate counsel body, and many others. Being a member of professional or governmental committees or task forces indicates a desire to contribute to future development, and suggests peer-respected expertise and authority. Contributing online book reviews of appropriate publications will form part of your browser profile and do not take long to write. We should not over-egg our credentials, interests and external affiliations, but also not undercook them through silence and invisibility. Keep them updated. Allow photos of yourself where appropriate.

Unless there are exceptional circumstances, avoid claiming copyright on articles, speech texts and presentations, as that implies a commercial motive behind the effort and suggests an unwillingness to share. Media are more likely to republish works that are indicated as copyright-free, which in turn increases your online visibility. Articles that mention the name of your employer as part of your bio can feature a disclaimer that the views expressed are personal and do not necessarily represent those of any organization with which you are affiliated.

Online links can tell a prospective negotiating party many things about you. They show that you "exist" outside the safety of your own organization; that you have opinions on important issues; are considered a thought leader on certain matters; and evidently respected by peers at a cross-sector level. These impressions together generate perceptive conclusions, such as whether you appear likely to have the internal authority to influence your organization to back up statements and commitments you make in negotiations. They underpin your credibility.

Building and maintaining a visible online profile is useful for any corporate negotiator in any organization. It is not difficult to achieve. It is never too late to begin. Deciding on one or more focus areas relevant to your role, and then expressing interesting views publicly, can be challenging and enjoyable. The payback, though often intangible and, as Einstein might say, *uncountable*, will prove to be a good investment.

I have found that my title is also an important piece of my negotiating persona. Role titles are often historic and inherited. Most are designed to address internal relativities and distinctions, especially in hierarchical structures. Outsiders' perceptions will inevitably be influenced to some degree by the words used in your title on email signatures and cards. Outsiders rarely appreciate the internal subtleties. Internal titles that do not spin well externally need to be reconsidered, or some negotiators may be able to convince their boss to let them use a second, more authoritative, influential and descriptive title for external use.

Sorbonne Professor Eliane Karsaklian includes a toolkit in her book The Intelligent International Negotiator (2014) which, among other things enables you, through a questionnaire, to determine whether your personal behavioral style as a negotiator emphasizes an approach as amiable, driver or analytical. This can be a helpful aid when preparing yourself. If you know what elements your natural style accentuates, you can more easily adapt yourself to the demands of each negotiation you experience.

PREPARING THEM

We tend to assume that we have no control over the other side, and that we are powerless to prepare them for a forthcoming negotiation. But in most situations, there are things we can do that can have an influence on the framework for a negotiation before the interaction begins. Executed well, those investments can pay high dividends surprisingly fast, giving a strong yet subconscious sense of your leadership and control over the course of the negotiation.

Effective leaders subtly set atmospheres and agendas. A natural leader will be one who influences what happens next, without appearing overbearing or aggressive, or even perceived as pulling the strings. Influence that is not seen and felt to be controlling can be exercised in numerous ways. Who proposed that discussions take place – you, your external counsel, or the other party? How was that idea communicated? Who proposed or described the agenda, rationale, timing and location, and how were these things framed? Were they communicated off-the-record and verbally, and was it clear that the other party's input would be welcomed? How approachable people consider you to be largely depends on how implicitly sociable you project yourself. Are you exuding familiarity, hospitality, normality, informality and humanity between the lines? Or do you delegate these initial negotiation dance steps to outside counsel or others who may not convey an image of communicability and openness in quite the same way?

Doing these things yourself, communicating with the appropriate person in the other party, signals your quiet confidence. It suggests you are in control without that vibe being received negatively. It builds rapport and helps you influence how the other party reacts to you. Your initial projection indicates whether you are a decision maker or influencer, both of which can gain almost instant respect, or an implementer and technocrat, which may not. In turn, that can have a bearing on whom they put forward to engage with you in the negotiation, and what stance or attitude they adopt.

Although style is heavily dependent on cultural norms, many negotiations among lawyers are mainly positional in nature. If you strongly demonstrate from the outset that your style is a more problem-solving, less process-driven approach to negotiating, the other party is likely to be less positional to match you, even if they do so subconsciously. This can take time, so that your stylistic message comes across repeatedly. You may never truly know whether your approach worked, but getting a negotiation off in a way that the other party is on your plane, and not you on theirs, is a crucial, yet often ignored, prep task.

Soon after I joined one of my companies, I discovered that our relationship with an approximately similar-sized competitor was so bad that virtually all my business and legal colleagues spoke about the competitor in the most negative ways. The two companies were not on speaking terms and each had sued the other on numerous occasions at the slightest provocation, with dozens of lawsuits pending around the world. No attempt had been made to resolve any of these conflicts by negotiation because neither party would blink and propose talks. Arriving in the job from the outside, indeed from a company that enjoyed relatively civil relations with most of its competitors, I found this testosterone-charged, puerile situation untenable and self-defeating.

I called my senior team together. Did anyone have creative ideas for how we could break the vicious circle of mutual self-destruction? Some probably thought it a naïve question, but the current relationship was simply racking up huge litigation costs for little apparent benefit. Immediately one colleague piped up that we were sitting on an asset that we had owned for many years in a certain major country; the asset was redundant to us commercially, but the competitor needed it to protect themselves from third party unfair competition. The asset could not be used to harm us in any way, but we had never considered offering it to them out of pure spite. She explained details of this odd situation and how it had arisen. The asset in question really should belong to the competitor, but it had been expropriated by a government and eventually we had acquired it when we bought the nationalized company. It was perfect! What if we were to give the asset away to the competitor without seeking anything in return? Might the shock and awe that would ripple through the competitor provoke a change in attitude? Most agreed that it might, but would our own top management ever agree? A few of my colleagues thought it was madness.

I brought up the matter with the CEO. Transferring an asset to a competitor required Management Board approval. I explained the goal: to kick-start negotiations to settle a long string of lawsuits. I proposed not, in fact explicitly not, to attach any conditions to the asset transfer. The competitor would inevitably feel obliged to reciprocate but it would be clumsy and mercenary on our part to suggest what shape that reciprocation might take. The CEO was initially skeptical, given the identity of the competitor, but saw the fire in my eyes and came round to the idea. The Management Board subsequently agreed the strategy too.

I called the person who held the equivalent position to me in the competitor. He was a seasoned and streetwise corporate counsel, well-known and admired through his profile in industry associations, and it was easy to check out his credentials. He had a top academic background and had been a partner in a major international law firm in the past. He was startled by my call. I explained I had recently arrived in my company – he said he knew that, which I liked – and in reviewing the considerable number of legal issues between our companies I had learned about this important stray asset. Would he be interested in acquiring it? Silence. He asked how much. I told him, nothing; it was an historical anomaly which I felt needed correcting. More silence. Then more silence. Hello? He slowly, cautiously, said that he appreciated the thought, but tentatively asked what internal consents I needed to transfer this asset. I explained that Management Board approval was needed. He chuckled. Maybe, he said sarcastically, we can talk again once that approval was forthcoming. I told him OK, and that I'd call him back the following week (I did not say I already had the necessary approval).

The following week, I phoned him again and confirmed top management approval to transfer the asset for USD 1, but asked if he would just cover any minor legal costs we might incur. Silence, again. He said he was stumped for words and asked how I managed to pull it off. I simply explained that when the Management Board understood it would have been irresponsible to hold onto an asset that, while legally ours, rightfully belonged to someone else, and that it would not harm our interests if it were transferred, they agreed. Wouldn't any reasonable person reach the same conclusion? I remember him saying, with a perceptible hint of astonishment: *something's changed in your company*, to which I think I replied: *we all benefit from change.*

As it turned out, this simple occurrence empowered my team and me to negotiate a number of deals and litigation settlements with this competitor. It had positively altered the competitor's perception of us as individuals, and of my employer. And it bode well for me, too.

Chapter 2

PREPARING COUNSEL

There are advantages and pitfalls to relying on external counsel when preparing for negotiation. Proxy communications between parties, where each is represented by external lawyers, can be the only appropriate way to begin a dialogue, for example when litigation has begun and inflexible protocol or legal rules preclude direct contact. But external counsel are often inclined to take this too far in the interests of maintaining their control and involvement. It can lead to misunderstandings, complications, setbacks, even disaster. As Kenneth Cloke points out in Mediating Dangerously: The Frontiers of Conflict Resolution (2001), people often confuse debate and dialogue; debate is an argument, while dialogue is more what Ken calls *thinking together*. Lawyers are more schooled in debate than dialogue, so debate is what they intuitively do.

There is also the pervasive influence of hourly billing. While their clients are generally motivated by securing the earliest acceptable outcome, external counsel are also driven by earning the highest available income. The tension between outcome and income can in some cases lead to conflicts of interest. Everyone denies it, but everyone knows it is a risk factor.

As we noted in Chapter 1, few lawyers have been trained in negotiation. Most have acquired their negotiating skills on the job. Because of their training and professional practice, a typical lawyer's instinctive orientation is based on power, rights, evidence and process. This single-mindedness can be a great asset in the right context, such as intractable litigation and arbitration. But in a negotiating environment, a rigid rights-based approach channels each party's needs, concerns and goals through the legal prism. Too easily, a fairly straightforward negotiation morphs into a battle to be won by the strongest gladiator using the conventional weapons in a lawyer's arsenal, such as reliance on legal principles and intimidation skills.

Some negotiations clearly do require the deployment of a legalistic and positional, rights-based approach that can best be executed by aggressive outside counsel intent on beating the other party's lawyer into a groveling submission. But this is relatively rare. More common are negotiations where commercial and legal issues intersect, and where corporate counsel and their business colleagues lead, or at least share control with, external counsel.

As the party-based owner or co-owner of the issue, the internal counsel has a series of important decisions to take regarding the involvement of outside counsel. Should external counsel be up-front and openly involved, or operate behind the scenes? Is the external counsel route the only or best way to set up the negotiation, or could that be done more effectively by a business colleague, or by you, or jointly with the external lawyers? Who should be seen to be in control on your side – you or your external counsel, or the two of you together? These questions can affect how the other party handles the negotiation.

Whether you use your outside counsel visibly or privately, you need to ensure they are properly prepared, and to clarify who is in overall strategic and operational control. External counsel can be critical in developing arguments and implementing tactics, but these need to be part of a strategic framework. Sun Tzu's Art of War warned that *while strategy without tactics is the slowest route to victory, tactics without strategy is merely the noise that precedes defeat*. Outside counsel need clear directions on strategy, and in most situations that should come directly from internal counsel.

SYSTEMATIC AND SYSTEMIC PLANNING

Whether you are preparing to negotiate a new deal or resolve a dispute, planning systematically, and also systemically, will not only make the negotiation process easier, but also more successful.

Getting to Yes: Negotiating Agreement Without Giving In (1981) by Harvard Law School Professor Roger Fisher and the social anthropologist William Ury, advocated interest-based (also called integrative or win-win) negotiation, as opposed to rights and power-based approaches, to achieving agreement. It set off a domino drop of scholarly focus on collaborative problem-solving negotiation and conflict resolution coaching that prioritizes underlying interests and needs rather than claims and positions. Two years later, Harvard Law School, together with MIT and Tufts, initiated a research and teaching project that became the Program on Negotiation. As the 1980s unfolded, several leading negotiation experts involved with this movement broke new ground with articles and courses that advocated the importance of a systematic approach to interest-based outcome generation.

Probably because disputes are so adversarial and challenging to manage, the systematic approach first got applied to dispute management. Professors Ury, Jeanne Brett of the Kellogg School of Management and Stephen Goldberg of Northwestern University, published Getting Disputes Resolved: Designing Systems to Cut the Costs of Conflict (1988) which offered a range of methodical ways to address disputes using interest-based negotiation strategies.

Almost overnight, Dispute Systems Design, or DSD, became fashionable in conflict resolution, and has since become ingrained in many organizations to correct the previously ad hoc, haphazard, almost accidental approach to disputes that had prevailed in the past.

The basic DSD model is helpful in understanding the fundamentals of negotiation strategy in both deal and conflict scenarios. DSD centers on three main methods for resolving disputes: power, rights and interests. Power-based systems involve a clash of titans, as where a workforce union threatens strike action against an employer. They tend to occur when civil negotiations fail, and the parties descend into dysfunctional behavior. Rights-based approaches revolve around legal entitlements, arguments about rules and regulations, rights and wrongs and redressing the past. They are generally dominated by litigators and are highly positional. Interest-based negotiations are geared towards addressing the respective parties' needs. They have a collaborative, problem-solving character and are generally orientated more toward the future than simply redressing the past.

The Ury/Brett/Goldberg conception of DSD enunciated several new design principles for an outcome generation system and envisaged four critical stages. They are relevant not only to the resolution of disputes, but to negotiations in general. They include focus on interests, stakeholder consultation and feedback, and ensuring that all stakeholders are incentivized, skilled and supported in using the system. The four stages of a system can be broadly summarized as diagnosis and analysis; designing the system; implementing it; and post-outcome assessment.

Six years later, Professor Fisher and Harvard researcher Danny Ertl put out Getting Ready to Negotiate: A Step-By-Step Guide to Preparing For Any Negotiation (1995). This was soon followed by two dispute resolution professionals, Cathy Costantino and Christina Sickles Merchant who published Designing Conflict Management Systems: A Guide to Creating Productive and Healthy Organizations (1996). These works combined interest-based negotiation principles and DSD thinking, and enabled us to approach negotiations in more sensible, effective ways.

Fisher and Ertl's manual bills itself as *The Getting To Yes Workbook*. They point out that the extent of most people's prep work is usually highly self-centered and limited – to decide what they want and what they will settle for. This typically leads to a largely positional exchange on a narrow bandwidth of possibilities and deters negotiators from exploring creative options for mutual gain that are the hallmark of interest-based negotiations. As Fisher and Ertl put it, *positional preparation leads to positional negotiation*, and preparing only by making a list of demands and concessions is preparing for a poor negotiation.

Fisher and Ertl and Costantino and Merchant made a strong case for a structured, systematic approach to negotiation preparation, in both conflict resolution and deal making.

Fisher and Ertl proposed seven essential elements of a system to enable the negotiator to prepare. Each element employs checklists and forms to give the structure clarity. Those seven elements are: identifying interests (yours and, hypothetically, the other side's), possible deal options, alternatives to an agreement, legitimacy from external standards, the quality of communication with the other side, building relationships and mutual commitments.

Costantino and Merchant focus on the role of negotiation in conflict resolution, which is often assisted by a mediator in DSD. They stress the importance of stakeholder collaboration in the design of any system, and build their architecture around alternative dispute resolution (ADR) processes, especially mediation. They enunciate and explore six core elements for a good system design: whether to use ADR; if so, configure the process to the problem; include preventative ADR methods; ensure users have the knowledge and skills to make the right choices; simplicity and ease of use; and allowing users to control the method and to decide upon the mediator.

Preparation

What most parties fail to appreciate is that dispute resolution processes can generally be employed where there is no dispute. After all, the settlement of a dispute is just a deal, little different in its fundamental nature from a deal arrived at without the backdrop of a formal dispute. As discussed in Chapter 7, neutral facilitators can play an important role in deal making. Even arbitration, a process very different from mediation but, like mediation, almost exclusively used in dispute resolution, can be used to help negotiating parties who are not in dispute, but deadlocked, to break the impasse and move forward. So it is not only possible, but often wise and creative, to embrace DSD principles when negotiating deals.

There are also other important factors that need addressing in negotiation prep work. These include determining the deal's overall strategic framework; identifying your leverage and assessing how the other side may perceive it; the apparent leverage of the other side and how you and they evaluate its significance; overcoming reactive devaluation on both sides; the risks and benefits of uncertainty; deciding who needs to be consulted and who must endorse any deal; your mandate from your organization; tactical options; post-deal implementation and enforcement considerations; logistical matters and timing.

All these considerations need to be assessed when designing your own management framework to help you to prepare for a negotiation.

PREPARING A NEGOTIATION FRAMEWORK

For the corporate counsel, leading or being actively involved in the design and build of a negotiation framework is a powerful and smart way to demonstrate to all internal stakeholders the value that a lawyer can add in negotiation far beyond the technical legal arena.

As every negotiation is different, no single framework fits them all. Any effective Negotiation Framework (NF) needs to be adapted to each situation and be seen as a flexible instrument, capable of being updated and revised once the initial prep work is complete. Every NF is systemic and most of the NF's moving parts interlock with others. Approached properly, building and running a practical, user-friendly NF is an exciting task.

The secrets behind a good NF are structure, understanding, flexibility, brevity and specifics. Most can be captured in bullets, often as one-liners. Different stakeholders can be asked to contribute, enabling the NF to become a powerful collaboration platform, one that engages wide and active participation among internal stakeholders and with outside advisers. Set up the NF on a shared electronic platform to which each stakeholder can have access and, as appropriate, edit rights. Taking the initiative to construct the NF is invariably appreciated. As the initiator, you will usually be seen as overall editor, and may end up in a central, commanding or coordinating role in the ensuing negotiation.

To optimize the possible outcomes in the real world of negotiation uncertainty, there are at least twenty largely interrelated areas that can be included in a practical NF. There may be more, depending on the situation – for example, PR could be an issue, as could Tax, HR, Compliance, Operations and many others. In brief:

1. Goals

Defining in concrete terms what you (and, equally important, what you believe the other party) needs to achieve from a negotiation, and why, sounds like an obvious starting point, but quite often "goals" are expressed as vague and aspirational desires. Identifying the specific goals of a negotiation should predicate everything else. It's like going for a hike in a fog; you need a compass. There have been many studies emphasizing the importance of establishing negotiation goals. For example, in a 2002 article Goal Setting and Negotiation Performance: A Meta-Analysis,[16] DePaul University's Deborah Zetik and Alice Stuhlmacher summarize results from twenty-two research reports that convincingly demonstrate that when negotiators were given explicit and challenging goals, they achieved consistently better results than those with imprecise goals or none at all.

The late management consultant, Peter Drucker, developed the widely used acronym S-M-A-R-T as a way of configuring goals: they should be Specific, Measurable, Achievable, Realistic and Time-bound. The goals in a negotiation may be one or several but every good goal should be SMART-based and not an ambitious fantasy. Well-crafted and grounded goals set expectations, gain stakeholder commitment and enable outcome quality to be properly assessed after the event.

2. Strategy

Strategy is not a goal, nor even a collective noun for goals, but the overall framework or top-level roadmap to achieve the goals. A strategy should be realistic, and geared to the situation and any relevant policy frameworks. Strategies need not be complex. In fact, the simpler they are, the more stakeholders are likely to buy into them. As with goals, give reasons for strategies. It makes them more convincing.

3. Groundwork

Identify all major areas where relevant facts and issues that need flushing out can be explored. An action plan to cover all groundwork issues, assigning specific tasks together with a timeline for completion, will ensure that as little as possible is left to guesswork and assumptions. Capture evidence, if it could be needed for anchoring or other purposes, because it can evaporate all too easily. Give reasons for why tasks assigned to certain individuals are important to the negotiation so that they can see how their contribution fits into the bigger picture.

4. Stakeholders & Personalities

Press for clarity and transparency. Let everyone know who "owns" or has a decision-making or advisory responsibility in the negotiation; map out the extent to which different stakeholders should be involved in the negotiation and their inter-relationships; determine whether a negotiating mandate is needed and who will provide it; explain, if known, which stakeholders can be identified in the other party; and, also critical, spell out the precise roles of external advisors so they know what is expected of them.

Fisher & Ury's Getting To Yes rightly began with the proposition that often people complicate, impede and frustrate the achievement of outcomes. They emphasized the importance of separating people and issues, addressing each separately. The people element entails differing perceptions, the impact of emotions and communication difficulties. Negotiation styles differ considerably, but just because you do not like the other party's style does not necessarily mean they have evil intent. Do not reproach a snail for behaving like a snail, or even a rat for behaving like a rat. Personality considerations need careful and objective assessment before a negotiation begins. Scrupulously avoid unnecessary politics. Leave no one out.

5. Communications

Poor communications often lie at the root of negotiation problems. Failures in communication can be caused by many factors such as complex explanations, inability to listen properly, language, culture, aggression, grandstanding, and inadequate use of communication technology, internally and externally. Most can be fixed by thorough preparation.

In more complex negotiations, a private unified communications system accessible to all parties, which could include a dedicated space for shared drafts, due diligence records, key documents, relevant standards and laws and other materials can be a huge asset. Negotiators often do not take fullest advantage of IT tools, many of which cost little or are free. They can by used by a party privately, among its own stakeholders, or shared among the parties, for example an online deal room with due diligence materials and latest drafts. Communication is the subject Chapter 6.

6. Process

Too little, if any, attention is usually given to the negotiation process. It is generally assumed that each party will deal directly with the other, but using the same old process regardless of circumstances can be a major part of the problem in negotiation. There are often alternatives that are better suited to managing the dialogue effectively in one, several or all stages of the negotiation. Selecting the process most suited to the negotiation can dramatically improve outcome quality. Chapter 7 is dedicated to process.

7. Arguments & Persuasion

Lawyers, in particular, are schooled in the belief that good arguments win. Indeed they are important, and need to be expressed and presented well. The arguments against also need to be considered objectively and the answers prepared. However good your arguments may be, they are not necessarily going to persuade others to accept them. Persuasion is often more related to emotional intelligence (EI) and other factors. When preparing to articulate good arguments, the methods needed to make them persuasive must also be developed. Sometimes, the most compelling arguments are those you don't make, that remain unexpressed. It can help to think of persuasion in three distinct areas – business, personal and legal – and address each of them differently.

8. Positions & Interests

Each party's interests lie at the root of all negotiations. Good outcomes usually merge, dovetail or at least accommodate the respective parties' interests. How conscious the parties are of their real interests depends on several elements. Have they seriously focused on distinguishing between their wants and their needs? Are they credible? Have they prioritized them? Have they conducted the same analysis, hypothetically, with respect to the other party's interests, and to what extent is this assessment based on facts or assumptions? How do the needs of each side coincide and differ?

Positions are generally based on interests or needs, but often exaggerate, distort or camouflage them. Expression of positions can be helpful, if framed and explained skillfully, but can easily derail negotiations into intransigence, which can quickly impede negotiation and lead to loss of face, frustration, conflict and ultimately deadlock and negotiation failure. Have positions already been expressed by the parties? Do they signal the prospect of conflict? How can you ring-fence positions to enable an interest-based negotiation to progress?

In Negotiation: Strategy Style Skills (2010), Professors Nadja Alexander and Jill Howieson persuasively warn negotiators about focusing too passionately on either positional or interest-based bargaining, and instead reconcile the dichotomy between the two with a "constructive model," advocating an ingenious "negotiation navigation map." Pointing out that interest-based negotiation only works optimally when all parties adopt it, and that interest-based negotiators can be exploited by savvy positional bargainers, the navigation map they present is a personal framework that negotiators can use privately. It begins by identifying as neutrally as possible all key perspectives and goals, to the extent that they can be identified, then focusing on the people aspects, including indirect stakeholders, moving on to the respective interests of the parties and how they are likely to be reflected in communication patterns, ending with a recitation of possible options, including ATNAs (see point 12 below) and positions.

9. Information

Knowledge is power. What information do you have? What more do you need to increase your leverage and improve your ability to negotiate effectively, and how can you get it? What information is the other party likely to have, and not to have, or to have misinterpreted? How does each party value the different elements of the negotiation based on the information they have at their disposal?

10. Bias

A bias is an irrational cognitive inclination or prejudice. A biased reaction could be for or against a particular fact, proposal, argument, belief, person or group. Bias is common in negotiation, and there are several different kinds. Rolf Dobelli's bestseller The Art of Thinking Clearly (2013) identifies eighteen types of bias. In negotiations, reactive devaluation occurs when negotiators provoke a negative bias and response from the other side simply by how they frame a proposal and by the fact that it originates with them. Appreciating the impact and negative power of bias, the different kinds of bias and the consequences and risks involved, can help avoid or minimize potential points of resistance.

11. Anchors

Anchors are an important tool in the art of persuasion. Fisher and Ertl describe anchors as legitimacy, by which they mean independent or external standards, criteria or references against which a desired point can be fairly and objectively assessed and which give the matter a rational and appropriate context. There are also other, more subtle, anchors that are not necessarily external but which can improve the fertility of the negotiation terrain, such as the first offer. Having a set of anchors to support the goals, even if they are not ultimately communicated to the other side, gives negotiators more confidence and a clear advantage. It helps prevent over-reaching and exaggerated claims that merely risk deadlock.

The most powerful anchor is often the first one to be dropped, for example the first offer. In Negotiation Genius: How to Overcome Obstacles and Achieve Brilliant Results at the Bargaining Table and Beyond (2007), Professors Deepak Malhotra and Max Bazerman of Harvard Business School (HBS) mention that many negotiators hesitate to make the first offer, preferring to let the other party do so. Malhotra and Bazerman emphasize that the first offer is often the most crucial and valuable anchor and predicates much of the remainder of the negotiation. Figuring it out in advance is a vital component of a negotiation framework, even if you have yet to decide whether to be the first to drop an anchor.

See Chapter 5, on Leverage, for more on anchors and first offers.

12. ATNAs

All negotiators need to be conscious of their backup or Plan B if the negotiation does not lead to agreement. Negotiators call them Alternatives To a Negotiated Agreement, or ATNAs. Consider three kinds of ATNA in order to visualize your walk-away situation. Your BATNA and your WATNA are your Best and Worst Alternatives To a Negotiated Agreement and lie at the extreme ends of the scale. Each can vary according to uncertain issues. Your PATNA (or RATNA) is your most Probable (or the most Realistic) ATNA. The PATNA can be close, on the spectrum of alternatives, to either the BATNA or the WATNA or can be somewhere in the middle. Having a weak BATNA (where your WATNA is also your BATNA, or close to it), suggests that attempting to negotiate may not be a viable option. Capitulation, or retreat in order to strengthen your BATNA, may be the wisest course.

ATNAs are discussed in more detail in Chapter 5.

13. ZOPA

The Zone of Potential Agreement (ZOPA) is the area where the underlying interests of the parties overlap. A negotiated agreement is generally possible somewhere within the ZOPA range. Although the exact ZOPA limits only usually emerge during or right at the end of a negotiation, an approximate or theoretical ZOPA can often be envisaged in advance, depending on the hypothetical assumptions you make about the other side's interests. The ZOPA, if it can be worked out, becomes a target range.

ZOPAs are explored in Chapter 5.

14. Hurdles

Envisaging areas of potential deadlock enables negotiators to separate high-and low-hanging fruit that in turn can determine the most appropriate tactics and options. Some hurdles are very obvious; others may be camouflaged to the point of invisibility by hidden agendas, or for other reasons. Assumptions can be dangerous, but being as well prepared as possible for potential hurdles will enable you to avoid or overcome them more easily.

15. Options

The most likely and practical options that can emerge from a negotiation are usually those from which the parties each derive advantage.

Negotiators naturally focus more on what they need from a negotiation and instinctively concentrate less on the other party's needs. This can be a grave error. An option where you secure a benefit and the other party incurs a consequential loss, the so-called zero sum gain, can often be counterbalanced by trading it for an option, possibly unrelated, in the other direction. It may be something worthless to you, but valuable to the other party. A well-prepared negotiator will have thought about potential options for mutual gain. They can be useful for trading.

16. Leverage

A crucial factor in any negotiation, leverage is whatever has an impact on the other party that can influence them to agree. Leverage can take many forms, can be overt or implicit, theoretical or real, existing or prospective. Figuring out in advance who has what bargaining power, and assessing its relative strength in the eyes of the other party, is a vital preparatory exercise. You need to consider how to strengthen your own leverage in the eyes of the other party, and how to reduce their perception of their own leverage. Chapter 5 is devoted to leverage and related mechanisms.

17. Tactics

Tactics are not strategy. They are interconnected, as tactics reflect and implement strategy. The boundaries between the two can sometimes become indistinct and the temptation to confuse them needs to be resisted to avoid the risk that a tactic runs away with itself and leads to an uncontrolled and irreversible change of strategy.

The tactics deployed by the parties directly impact on any negotiation. Depending on whether the style of the negotiation is competitive or collaborative, or a mixture of the two, tactics can have a positive or problematic effect. Some tactics are predictable and originate from how each party approaches the negotiation. Others are reactions to the other side's behavior. You need to consider what approaches to take, the relative merits of each option, how you should execute them and what effects they may have. Tactics can frame the character of a negotiation, including whether it is positional or problem-solving in nature, as well as the mindset and attitudes of the other party.

Identifying the relevant objective criteria that you may need to use in a negotiation is a good way to begin thinking about tactics, because if they are rooted in persuasive benchmarks they are more likely to work than if they are perceived as trickery.

18. Financials

Financial objectives and constraints play a controlling part in most major negotiations. How will different options affect the financial integrity of the deal? No matter whether money is being spent or received, should a model be used during the negotiation to analyze the financial implications when parameters change. If so, who will construct and be responsible for it? Where financial aspects are not at the heart of the deal, what will be the negotiating role of those who control monetary consequences?

19. Legals

Relevant legal issues can take many forms. For NF purposes, they need to be expressed in non-technical language and in summary form so that non-lawyer stakeholders can appreciate their place in the negotiation. Legal issues, like financials, need to be fully understood and accommodated in advance by all stakeholders. Separate the core substantive legal issues from the drafting, process and recordal aspects.

Chapter 2

20. Closure and Execution

It pays to have clear ideas at the outset about how a deal can best be closed, what resources will be needed, who will be responsible, when they should be engaged and the steps that need to be taken to implement the deal. Rudyard Kipling observed that: *Nothing is ever settled until it is settled right.*

This comprehensive Negotiation Framework is simple in principle, and the content needs to be kept clear, comprehensible and concise in practice if it is to work across all stakeholders. Different elements will not necessarily have the same bearing on the negotiation as others. In most cases, it helps to assign time-bound responsibilities to named individuals to ensure that assignments get done, and to keep track of progress. Although it may appear that some tasks have a higher priority, the key, as Stephen R. Covey wrote, is *not to prioritise what may be on your schedule but to schedule your priorities*. So if you have too little time to prepare, pick out the most crucial elements, and focus on them first.

DISPUTES

An exceptionally high proportion of disputes that end up in courts and arbitration tribunals in most jurisdictions settle before a judgment or an award is given. Pre-judgment settlement rates vary not only by country but often by virtue of the type of case, government and judicial or arbitral policy on encouraging settlement, and when dispute managers start settlement negotiations. Excluding cases where one party needs to establish a legal precedent, or secure a deterrent effect, or where revenge, recrimination or a kamikaze party are involved, litigation and arbitration can be seen as a procedural, even as a tactical, precursor to settlement, and as a particular form of positional negotiation.

In her book The New Lawyer: How Settlement is Transforming the Practice of Law (2008), Professor Julie Macfarlane explains how 21st Century lawyers need to operate at the intersection of conflict and collaboration. These are complementary, not contradictory, notions. All too often, lawyers, particularly litigators or arbitration counsel, take a linear perspective – conflict or collaboration, but not both simultaneously. This helps them focus on the crusade of winning, rather than on the task of resolving the matter as quickly as possible. External litigation counsel often default into gladiatorial mode, where their strengths lie. The aim is to win and if a settlement is the end game, then it should occur at the end of the process when, in theory, you are at your strongest but after all the costs, time and effort have been expended. A strident litigious stance can be a strength when the strategy demands increased leverage and force of argument, or extracting new information from the opposing litigant. But it can also be a weakness, blinding litigators from pursuing early resolution options and missing golden opportunities to secure the most practical outcome needed. The more a dispute escalates, the harder it is to resolve. Conflict and collaboration need to be kept in balance.

Alternative (or Appropriate) Dispute Resolution or ADR is usually meant to mean mediation or some other settlement process. But there is nothing *alternative* about negotiation; it should normally be the *primary* process to resolve disputes. The real *alternative*, the option that arises when negotiations fail, is litigation or arbitration. Many corporate counsel feel that the term ADR needs to be reframed.

Corporate counsel are generally salaried. Their main motivation is to resolve disputes, eliminating risk, saving cost and reducing time. Resolving a dispute by negotiation requires a different mindset, strategy and tactics from resolving it in a court or tribunal. As internal counsel, it helps when we adopt a bifurcated approach to disputes, supporting the progression of litigation and arbitration, which can strategically be part of a well-considered positional pre-negotiation tactic, while simultaneously, and with equal energy, planning and preparing for settlement negotiations. A conflict management system following the principles of DSD can help corporate lawyers to apply these two approaches, and to decide how to balance them.

EARLY CASE ASSESSMENT

Early Case Assessment (ECA) is a vital risk management precaution as well as a sensible cost containment exercise. There are now electronic ECA tools on the market. Many result in a snapshot analysis and are not particularly strategic. A good ECA tool needs to raise the questions and issues needed to assess the other party's case objectively, focus on all the potential dispute resolution options, and show how to approach each, and with what consequences. Many ECA systems tend to emphasize measurable factors, such as cost of time and money. Although important, a broader analysis is also needed. Fortunately, there are strategically-orientated case evaluation tools in existence, and internal counsel can use them to stay on top of fast-changing developments.

Two ECA tools are included, with consents, in Appendices 1 and 2 as examples of the tools available.

Olé!, the online evaluation tool available as a free download from the International Mediation Institute,[17] can be completed online or downloaded as a Word document and is not jurisdiction-specific. (Appendix 1)

CPR Institute's ECA Toolkit is a comprehensive analytical guide for new ECA users but also includes a summary for more experienced users. It is geared to US disputes, but can be adapted by the user for application to disputes anywhere. (Appendix 2)

Any good ECA tool should lend itself to being shared in conference with external counsel, so that a joint approach can be forged, and cover at least the following elements:

Chapter 2

1. Basic Facts of the Dispute

Summarize key facts, claims made and positions taken by each side both formally and off-the-record. Consider which stakeholders have most to gain or lose as a result of the case, and how far the dispute has escalated.

2. Case Analysis

An aid to analyzing the future interests of both sides separately from the positions taken to date. The analysis should also focus on the historic and prospective costs for both sides.

3. Strategy Analysis

List questions that can impact on the strategy behind the dispute.

4. Financial Loss Analysis

Identify the financial impact of the claims made in the dispute by each side.

5. SWOT Analysis

Assess the Strengths, Weaknesses, Opportunities and Threats for each side.

6. BATNAs, WATNAs and PATNAs

Identify the best, worst and probable outcomes if the dispute does not settle.

7. Way Forward Options

A scorecard for comparing the relative attraction of the alternative ways forward for the dispute.

8. Future Strategy Summary

Summarize the strategy for each dispute looking to the future, and identify the action steps and options to implement them.

9. Ongoing Review

An option to reconsider the strategy depending on certain trigger events.

10. Performance Measurement

Identify how to measure success.

Using even a basic ECA tool will help you to improve your preparation for the management of a dispute, and its resolution. An ECA tool can be dovetailed into a Negotiation Framework with ease, and some of the sections coincide.

Checklists for negotiation preparation, value creation and implementation feature in Built To Win: Creating a World-class Negotiation Organization (2009) by Hallam Movius and Lawrence Susskind. Checklists are valuable in both deal making and dispute resolution negotiations to ensure that all issues have been addressed, and to allocate tasks and responsibilities.

IN A NUTSHELL

- Preparation is a most crucial task for anyone involved in negotiation.
- Effective preparation puts you in control of your own behavior, and, to some extent, the attitudes, approaches and actions of others.
- If you assume the initiative to take charge of preparation, you will often be warmly welcomed, because others are unlikely to want to do this on a thorough, systematic basis, even though the effort is invariably highly valued. You become empowered to extend your role beyond the legal area, and legitimately become your negotiation team's linchpin, the one to whom the business, other functions and stakeholders will increasingly defer. By taking a broad systematic approach, you can quickly be perceived as the de facto orchestrator of the negotiation, the one that knows the score across all angles, an indispensable member of the negotiation team.
- Design a conflict management system.
- Develop a Negotiation Framework.
- Consider using an Early Case Analysis tool.
- Exert a tight control on external counsel, if retained. Use them tactically in negotiation, and always ensure they know the limits of their role and the expectations you have of their performance.

CHAPTER 3[18]
Neuroscience

Of the modes of persuasion furnished by the spoken word there are three.

The first depends on the personal character of the speaker;

the second on putting the audience into a certain frame of mind;

the third on the proof, or apparent proof, provided by the words spoken.

Aristotle, *Rhetorica* treatise – Book 1 Chapter 2

Negotiation is the art of persuasion. In any dialogue, just below the surface, sits a complex web of unexpressed, often latent forces and factors that persuaders need to understand, as they may have the power to achieve or kill the outcome. The neuroscience behind every negotiation easily escapes attention, but a basic appreciation of it can vastly improve the effectiveness of our persuasive abilities and enable us to achieve better results.

We should begin with Aristotle's treatise *Rhetorica*, written in the 4th Century BC. Aristotle developed the simple and brilliant idea of three interrelated modes of persuasion – ethos, pathos and logos. The ethos mode is an appeal to the audience's character such as their sense of integrity and authority; pathos is directed to their mindset and emotions and logos is targeted at their reasoning and logic.

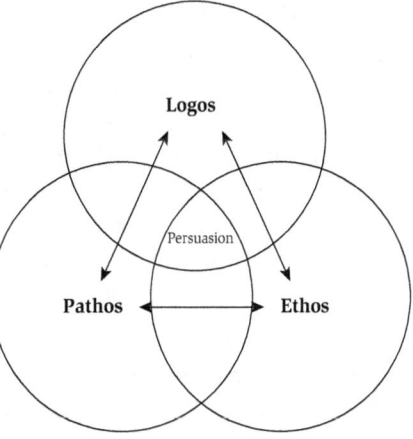

Chapter 3

Neuroscientists at the Centre for Affective Sciences (CISA) in Switzerland conduct research to understand how emotions and social patterns of behavior may be affecting decision-making when people are in situations of stress or conflict. A CISA group under Professor David Sander and Dr. Olga Klimecki, which includes two dispute resolution professionals, François Bogacz and Jeremy Lack, have developed a model known as "Tri-O/S" to help non-scientists understand how the plasticity of the brain determines the patterns of behavior that may lead to conflict escalation if they are not identified and managed. The model includes dispute resolution tools and techniques. From this Tri O/S Model, which echoes Aristotle's ethos, pathos, logos model, we can see how our choice of negotiation behavior can itself impact on human behavior and the possible outcomes we can achieve.

For example, there is empirical research,[19] reported by Judge Andrew Wistrich and Professor Jeffrey Rachlinski in How Lawyers' Intuitions Prolong Litigation (2013) that suggests many people, in particular lawyers, are prone to making cognitive errors by rejecting offers that, in hindsight, should have been accepted, and about when and whether to settle, resulting in delaying settlement negotiations until late in a dispute's life cycle.

In order to appreciate how this works, we need to understand the basic functioning of the brain, and how the prospect of disagreement, deadlock and conflict typically affects thought patterns in negotiation.

THE BRAIN'S THREE OPERATING SYSTEMS

Oxygen and glucose are limited resources in the brain. Our brain receives a maximum of 20% of the body's total oxygen and glucose at all times, and it has to be efficient in how it uses and allocates them. Many things are related to how oxygen and glucose are consumed throughout the brain at different times, including our behavior and therefore our negotiation performance.

Computers, which require electricity, are a perfect analogy. Like computers, we each have our "hardware" – our brain and its extensions. We also have three different operating "software" systems. They are the emotional operating system ("O/S 1"), the social operating system ("O/S 2") and the rational operating system ("O/S 3"). We know when we try to run two different computer operating systems simultaneously, such as Apple and Microsoft, on the same piece of hardware, that the electricity flows in different ways, and that the computer is likely to develop glitches and malfunctions. Our brains work that way too.

Our three operating systems run in parallel, but the emotional and social systems (O/S 1 and O/S 2) often limit our third system (O/S 3), which is our ability to be rational or cognitive. These three operating systems tend to behave in limited ways when faced with the stress of negotiating, particularly where conflict is a possibility or the stakes are high. They can consequently restrict or expand the range of solutions we visualize.

Let's first consider each of these three operating systems to see how they can affect our judgment and decision-making abilities in stressful situations. Then we can assess how they combine and how we may be able to control them more efficiently and become more effective negotiators and persuaders as a result.

THE EMOTIONAL OPERATING SYSTEM (O/S 1)

A key purpose of emotions in the human brain seems to be to allow us to do very rapid relevance detection, or what emergency room physicians call "triage," when managing an emergency situation. Before we think consciously, O/S 1 decides where in the brain to allocate oxygen and glucose, and to prepare for situations of fear or reward. When faced with a new stimulus, do you need to allocate your resources to be in "fight," "flight" or "freeze" mode? What do you need to be ready for? O/S 1 rapidly prepares us for action or inaction, fight or flight, mobilizing the rest of our body's resources according to what it emotionally deems to be a potential risk or reward. All this happens in milliseconds.

This triage by the brain is "subconscious" or "pre-conscious." It is not something we are aware of. It explains why we are often startled by unconscious stimuli, jumping at something that we have not consciously seen or heard. A person can self-regulate and consciously manage this behavior, but only after becoming aware of their emotions. This will usually happen several hundred milliseconds after the first emotions were felt.

Imagine walking into a negotiation and, to your surprise, the other party's external counsel, an intimidating dinosaur of a litigator, immediately goes on the offensive: *"Your behaviour has been outrageously duplicitous and downright dishonest. The right word is racketeering. We see no point in continuing. You are nothing but a bunch of no-good sleazebags. We are going to sue."* His face is red as he throws a sheaf of papers articulating a legal claim across the table, clumsily spilling his coffee in the process.

O/S1 kicks in before the tirade is over. You are likely to have an instantaneous emotional reaction. Your first thought may be to respond with equal or greater invective, or get up, walk out and slam the door.

As much as we may want to believe to the contrary, there is no such thing as not having an emotional response in a negotiation situation. If we look at a linear time scale for reacting to a stimulus, we have two basic responses: an "away mode" for avoiding or confronting risks and danger (fear), and a "towards mode" attracted to satisfaction and pleasures (reward). Whether we realize it or not, this first phase operates within 0 to 350 milliseconds, and our emotional system is already filtering and influencing all our sensory perceptions before we are capable of conscious thought.

This extraordinary activity takes place in our brain's limbic systems, and in particular in the amygdala, two small almond-shaped areas in the center of our brain. They are responsible for rapid relevance detection, and have almost instantaneous connections to the rest of the brain. They not only assess fear, but also reward. And the amygdala are involved in more than just emotional responses. They are responsible for triggering, at lightning speed, a pre-conscious flow of oxygen and glucose. Consciousness, and our ability to reorientate that energy flow, only happens in the 400 + millisecond range, well after the stimulus was first experienced and unconsciously diagnosed by our amygdala.

Our brains filter everything through emotions, even if this is unconscious. Most of the time we are simply unaware of it. Only when we have a sufficiently high level of emotional arousal do we become aware of our feelings. But we need to gain this awareness before we can attempt to "self-regulate" our feelings, and this involves O/S 3. Self-regulation takes time, patience and practice, all of which in turn consumes a lot of glucose and oxygen.

Back to our example of the over-bearing lawyer. If you recognize that your brain has just performed a fight, freeze or flight triage, you are well-positioned to self-regulate your reaction. For example, you might burst into laughter, though that might inflame things. Or you may think about how to reconnect emotionally, socially or cognitively with the other party's counsel by taking a napkin to mop up his coffee, and saying in a non-confrontational tone: *Thank you for reminding us of why we are here and what the parties' alternative is if we fail to reach an agreement.*[Now turning to the lawyer's client] *Perhaps we could start by exploring what we might all achieve together if we begin by focusing on the potential market opportunities that brought us here today?* [Still looking at the other party, not their lawyer] *And then we can certainly get into the legal issues later.*

To understand how self-regulation works, think back to the famous incident of US Airways Flight 1549 from New York LaGuardia to Charlotte, NC on January 15, 2009. Ninety-five seconds after take-off, as many of us know from media reports at the time, pilot Chelsey B. Sullenberger's bestseller Highest Duty: My Search for What Really Matters (2010) and the movie adaptation Sully (2016) starring Tom Hanks, the Airbus A320 at an altitude of less than 3,000 feet during its ascent, flew into a large flock of Canada geese. The acrid smell of burning birds instantly filled the flight deck. Both engines, which had been generating 18 tonnes of thrust to propel the 68 tonne-jet upwards at a steep angle, vibrated severely, then abruptly stopped. Simultaneously Captain Sullenberger, with over forty years of piloting planes, had never seen anything like it, even in the simulator. Both engines failing together at very low altitude is virtually unprecedented in modern aviation. Afterwards, Captain Sullenberger reported: *I knew I had seconds to decide on a plan and minutes to execute it. I was aware of my body. I could feel an adrenaline rush. I'm sure that my blood pressure and pulse spiked. But I also knew I had to concentrate on the tasks at hand and not let the sensations in my body distract me.*

The Captain and First Officer immediately applied the mantra of their training. *Aviate, Navigate, Communicate.* Heading Northwest, they were flying over one of the most densely populated areas in the world. At

such a low level, they calculated that gliding back to LaGuardia, or on to another runway, like Teterboro in New Jersey, was too risky. Just 21 seconds after the bird strike, *Captain Cool*, as New York Mayor Bloomberg subsequently dubbed him, reported the situation to an incredulous controller at LaGuardia. Thirty-two seconds later, he decided that a water landing in the Hudson River was reachable, and was their only option. "Water landings" are usually a euphemism for catastrophic crash landings from which few or none live to tell the tale, but in this instance all 150 passengers and 5 crew survived without serious injury.

Flight simulators train pilots not to panic when things go wrong. Their natural reflexes in cases of an aircraft spinning out of control, or a sudden drop in altitude or loss of power, are at first like those of any other human being. But after spending enough hours in simulators, where they are put through extreme positions of stress, they no longer panic or freeze like the rest of us. They are able to continue to function rationally, using checklists they have been taught to go through in crisis situations. Long exposure to simulator training enables pilots to self-regulate and stay focused, going through their checklists and protocols even while a plane may be experiencing potential or even inevitable disaster conditions. Oxygen and glucose continue to be allocated to, and consumed by, parts of their brains that function more rationally than emotionally. This demonstrates our brain's wonderful plasticity. It proves that our patterns of behavior can be changed or controlled. With enough practice, we can generate new patterns of thinking and self-regulate better in moments of high emotion, stress or crisis.

There is also a less appealing aspect. We tend to cruise in "autopilot" mode, responding emotionally to some stimuli and discarding others, while being unaware of them. We tend to lack insights into our behavior, and reject the notion that emotions may be influencing our ability to think rationally. The fact is, to be human is to be emotional, and to be emotional is to be human: "*I feel, therefore I am, and I am, therefore I feel,*" to misquote Descartes. Emotions will always create biases and cloud our rational capacities pre-consciously. Once O/S 1 is activated, an "away" or "fear" mode is likely to be more dominant, last longer, and take greater precedence over a "towards" or "reward" stimulus.

THE SOCIAL OPERATING SYSTEM (O/S 2)

Like meerkats, elephants, dolphins, gorillas and most other members of the animal kingdom, we humans are social and gregarious, even if some of us appear not to be. O/S 2 is another rapid and pre-conscious triage system that is also modulated by the amygdalae. Just as in O/S 1, we have the "away mode" for fear and the "towards mode" for reward. However, we have also evolved with two fundamental patterns of social behavior that are pre-consciously managed by O/S2 and drive "pro-social" or "anti-social" behavior, as well as seeking comfortable status levels. These modes subconsciously diagnose whether, at any moment, we are in an "in-group" or an "out-of-group" environment, and our status within our group or in a given set of circumstances.

When we meet people, we behave differently based on whether we unconsciously perceive them as belonging to our clique or tribe, or to another. This suggests an uncomfortable propensity for humans to discriminate unconsciously based purely on first impressions, which can be unconsciously influenced by previous exposure to certain cultures, or to the stereotypes we may have of them.

If our "in-group" mode has been triggered, we have an intuitive ability to understand one-another's feelings without words. The non-verbal behavior of another person in our group does not require much, if any, explanation. We pick up on one-another's emotions intuitively, like sadness, joy and excitement, without any need for words. We even tend to *mirror* them. There is an automatic system of empathy that is triggered whenever we feel "in-group."

When we feel "out-of-group," this empathy system in the brain is switched off or is less active. We tend to stop resonating with others, become indifferent to their emotions and suffering, are intuitively less inclined to address their needs and become more likely to develop a negative bias.

An example of how O/S 2 is distinct from O/S 1 relates to how we reflect one-another's behavior when "in-group" but not when "out-of-group." When we are in "in-group" mode, shared neural networks, sometimes called *mirror neurons*, which have been identified in animals though not yet in humans, are believed to be activated. These cause us to mimic behavior that we see in others without realizing it. If you yawn, then I am likely to yawn too, assuming we are both "in-group." This can trigger a contagious effect throughout a room. We have this ability to connect to each other unconsciously and to experience one-another's sensations when we activate our "in-group" scripts of social behavior.

Oxytocin is a chemical social modulator that is part of the O/S 2 system. It is a primitive neuropeptide that we secrete and is sometimes, though misleadingly, called the "trust hormone." Oxytocin does create trust but augments either an "in-group" script (which leads to confidence and comfort) or an "out-of-group" script (which can result in aggression and caution). Pregnant women secrete high levels of oxytocin. In fact, oxytocin can even induce labor. A mother's oxytocin is usually passed onto her infant, when it suckles. The baby ingests oxytocin through its mother's milk, creating a strong neurochemically-induced bond between mother and infant.

We can increase our oxytocin levels (in controlled experiments) using nasal sprays. When people are primed to think of one-another as "similar" or "in-group" in social experiments, inhaling oxytocin leads to more cooperative and pro-social behavior. But when people are primed to think of one-another as "dissimilar," or as belonging to opposing or competing teams, sniffing oxytocin leads to more aggressive and competitive behavior. So oxytocin is not simply a trust hormone – it can also be an aggression hormone. It seems to enhance basic patterns of "in-group" (pro-social) or "out-of-group" (anti-social) behavior, depending on the circumstances.

Many things can also influence our oxytocin levels. Chocolate and dopamine are examples. Touching or hugging induces oxytocin release, with pro-social effects when coming from a welcome and "in-group" source, but can also induce an "out-of-group" script when unwelcome.

In a 2007 study reported by Californian researchers Paul Zak, Angela Stanton and Sheila Ahmadi, people were each given an amount of money, asked to sniff a substance and encouraged to invest the money with a stranger. Those who sniffed a placebo placed up to a third of the money with the stranger. Participants who inhaled a little oxytocin invested around 80% with the stranger.[20]

It is possible to create pro-social feelings and in-group bonding in negotiations by triggering common social patterns when we gather together with others, for example by sharing a meal. Australian dispute resolver Joanna Kalowski, makes a point of serving freshly-baked pastries at the start of her negotiation sessions. Ken Cloke, Director of the Center for Dispute Resolution in Santa Monica, is among many leading conflict management practitioners who encourage mirroring of body language as a way of promoting collaborative behavior.[21]

The words and terms we use can have a similar effect. Referring to the other party as "the other side" or "opponents" may unconsciously trigger "out-of-group" behavioral scripts. On the other hand, referring to them, and thinking of them conceptually, as "negotiation partners" in a joint process can unconsciously trigger "in-group" scripts. These are unconscious patterns of social plasticity, and participants' abilities to empathize with one another are things that we can influence by activating or deactivating these patterns. They are important concepts to bear in mind when negotiating.

The danger of both "in-group" and "out-of-group" programming is that whichever has been unconsciously activated through O/S2 can affect our cognitive abilities and how O/S 3 will function.

If an "in-group" or "similar person" pattern in our brain was first activated when we met someone, we are likely to unconsciously assume that this person is similar to us, and project our own biases and preferences onto them. We are more likely to assume or envisage that whatever works for us will work for them. On the other hand, when we meet a person who has unconsciously been labeled by our brains as "out-of-group" or "dissimilar," we do not naturally project our own preferences onto them. We are likely instead to stereotype the "other." This all happens pre-consciously, whether "in-group" or "out-of-group," based on what we have been told by others or read in the media.

Whether we perceive one-another as "similar" or "dissimilar" is because our brains make rapid social triage judgments and perceive everything through stereotypes. It is human nature to do so and it is one of the dangers inherent in the way our brains

Chapter 3

function. To be human is to be biased. The good news is that, thanks to the brain's plasticity, we can consciously act to minimize these sub-conscious reactions if we choose to do so, and re-trigger "in-group" patterns of pro-social behavior.

Labeling, and dividing people into "in-group" and "out-group" is something negotiators can control in the interests of securing an optimal conversation. A better and more sustainable outcome can be reached through joint dialogue, focusing on interests, rather than positional rhetoric and trying to impose outcomes. This underscores the importance of early relationship-building in any negotiation. The journey can lead to a better destination.

THE RATIONAL OR COGNITIVE OPERATING SYSTEM (O/S 3)

Daniel Kahneman's Thinking Fast and Slow (2011) describes many issues with respect to O/S 3, the system we use when thinking rationally. He compares our brains to the engine of a hybrid vehicle. They function most efficiently when using as little oxygen and glucose as possible, conserving resources we may need later. O/S 3 is slower and prefers to take mental shortcuts and follow rapid pathways of pre-defined thinking to conserve whatever limited oxygen and glucose resources are left in our brains after our emotional and social systems have kicked in. Much of our thinking is what Kahneman refers to as "system one" or "fast" thinking. Matthew Lieberman, a professor in the Psychology Department at University of California Los Angeles, refers to this as the "X mode" of rational thinking. He means refle$\underline{x}$ive or reactive rational thought processes, not those that are emotional or social, both of which are pre-conscious but unconsciously stored patterns of rational thinking (such as when we speak in our mother tongue and use semantic memory to find words).

Our brains want to connect the dots, even when we are not conscious of them doing so. For example, when we try to interpret the phrase: *"I can aulaclty uesdtannrd tihs satnecne"* our brains can immediately read: *"I can actually understand this sentence,"* despite the jumbled letters. This happens because our rational brain does not try to read the whole word, but skims onto the first and last letter in each word, assuming the rest. The brain conserves energy by not needing to read all the letters in between. The words make sense to us so long as the first and last letters are in the right place. That is an example of Lieberman's X system or Kahneman's rapid system one.

The power of the brain in connecting dots has its limitations. The brain fills gaps where it thinks they should be filled. This can often mean that perceptions will be enhanced, modified or expanded beyond all recognition of the initial event. In fact, it can influence people to see and perceive things that do not exist, a phenomenon is called pareidolia. Benjamin Disraeli, during his time as British Prime Minister, was making a profound point that negotiators do well to remember when he remarked that: *Like all great travellers, I have seen more than I remember and remember more than I have seen.*

Take, for example, the famous "Man's Face on Mars" that some claimed was evidence of civilization on the Red Planet:

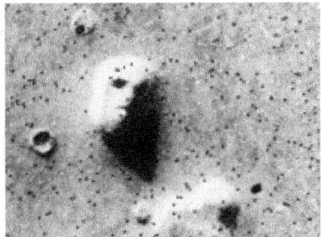

NASA has repeatedly explained to the public that the "face" is just a rock formation. But the image provokes pure pareidolia. The brain has a natural desire to see a recognizable pattern, and one type of pattern it is always seeking is facial recognition. The brain will, if it can, interpret rocks to look like something it knows well. To reassure the public that there really is no mountain carved like a human face on Mars, pictures taken of the same object from different NASA spacecraft between 1976 and 2001 with increasingly higher definition show that the facial pattern dissolves as resolution increases, and the brain is then no longer fooled.

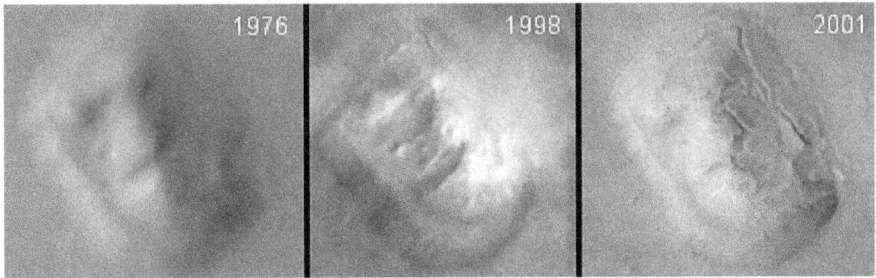

http://science.nasa.gov/science-news/science-at-nasa/2001/ast24may_1/.

There are analogies to pareidolia in negotiating. In any debate or dialogue, we automatically seek familiar patterns. We do so through the prism of our own backgrounds, training and inclinations. If we trust someone, we are likely to look for reasons to trust those with whom they are associated. If we can develop mutual levels of trust during a discussion, the negotiation is likely to be more successful. So where there are multiple issues, some of which are easier to agree than others, it can help to encourage not only trust, but also Kahneman's rational thinking habit *system one* or Lieberman's *X-mode*, when it comes to the tougher points if the parties have already covered the easier issues and agreed on them. That is why an early focus on "low-hanging fruit" is one of the techniques covered in Chapter 10.

Chapter 3

The other system is what Lieberman calls the C system and Kahneman labels "system two" or "slow thinking." The "C" denotes what Lieberman called "refle<u>c</u>tive" as opposed to "refle<u>x</u>ive" thinking. It is generally more demanding in terms of oxygen and glucose consumption, so our brain tries to avoid using it when thinking rationally by unconsciously adopting the rapid "X mode" instead. The C system is what we need to use when we want to think deeply and optimally.

In negotiations, we generally need to be reflective and not reflexive. It is better to understand which rational thought processes we are using when reaching a decision, especially in situations of stress and conflict. For example, try calculating in your head "24 x 17" without using an aid like a pencil, paper or calculator. Mathematicians apart, most of us find this simple multiplication hard to do. Breaking it down into steps, using rapid patterns of thinking that are familiar from using a piece of paper and a pencil, makes solving the equation easier. We immediately pull faces as we try to concentrate, visualizing the carryforward of numbers from one column to another. Thinking cognitively or rationally in this way is tiring. We crave a piece of paper and pen or calculator because it is so difficult to keep numbers in our heads, while also keeping a mental track of columns.

The word for this is heuristics – quick, easy and practical, but not necessarily technically accurate, ways to connect dots, rather than deep or slow thinking, because it is a lot easier than starting on a blank page. We unconsciously store and use a series of rapid heuristics when we think rationally and problem-solve, often finding that we have skipped over major pieces of data when reaching our decisions. This is one of the reasons why confirmation bias is common in negotiation; we tend to perceive and retain whatever is consistent with our heuristics.

On the other hand, some situations are so complex that we cannot consciously keep track of all the different lines and columns of data that need to be computed in order to make the right decision. In highly complex situations where large amounts of information may need to be analyzed, our intuitive X system of thinking may be better than our deeper C system, but it is important in either case to know which thinking system has been used, and to evaluate it in a number of ways.

So, when making decisions, we unconsciously prefer to use our X system rather than our C system. It is an unpleasant reality we have to face, especially in high impact negotiations or when important decisions need to be taken. Even judges and lawyers, it seems, have a tendency to use rapid heuristics and mental shortcuts when identifying relevant facts and passing judgment on people.

Professor Shai Danziger at the Tel Aviv University School of Management showed in a 2011 paper in the Proceedings of the US National Academy of Sciences how judges tend to think in X mode as opposed to C mode. Listening to complex legal reasoning is likely to drain cognitive resources, which in turn can have a significant impact on the interpretation of evidence and pleadings.

Attention span was identified as being the most important unconscious variant for eight Israeli judges while conducting over 1,000 prisoner parole hearings. One can speculate on the factors that might have the greatest influence on whether an Israeli judge would grant parole to a prisoner: such as whether the crime was minor or serious. Or personal biases of the judges based on whether the prisoner was young or old, Arab or Jewish or male or female. Remarkably, the answer was none of the above. Danziger's research indicated that the depressing factor influencing whether a prisoner was granted parole was: *time of day*.

When the judges had last eaten or taken a break was more likely to affect their willingness to grant parole. The proportion of favorable decisions seemed to increase and fall, depending on meals and breaks, rather than on the legal or cognitive merits, attributes or specific circumstances of each prisoner's individual case. There were three peak periods during the day when paroles were being granted. They coincided with times when the glucose levels of each judge's brain was at its highest (although the paper does not mention glucose as the principal reason for these variances). Their abilities to concentrate and think deeply, however, were depleted more rapidly after each peak, as the day wore on. Prisoners who were heard long after the ingestion of food (late in the morning, in the middle of the afternoon or at the end of the day) were less likely to be granted parole. A glucose-depleted judge would seem to favor the *status quo* and not grant release at those times. If asked, however, it is likely that each judge would be convinced they were making the same rational quality of decisions at all times of the day.

Corroboration for these findings came in 2016 in a study conducted for the US National Bureau of Economic Research (NBER) by Naci Mocan and Ozkan Eren, respectively Chair of Economics and Associate Professor of Economics at Louisiana State University (LSU). They studied the expected and actual performance of LSU's football team, the Fighting Tigers, in games played between 1996 and 2012. They then plotted criminal cases before Louisiana judges involving over 8,000 juvenile first-time offenders. They found that in days following an unexpected loss by the Fighting Tigers, the average custodial sentence handed down was 7% higher than usual, which doubled in the case of judges who were LSU alumni. When the Fighting Tigers predictably won or predictably lost, however, this had no significant effect on sentencing practice. In their paper to the NBER,[22] Professors Mocan and Eren noted: *The results are important for a number of reasons... They provide evidence of reference-based preferences in an environment where the decision-makers are uniformly highly educated, and when the decisions in question should have been bound by institutional restrictions and ethics. Specifically, application of the relevant legal principles to the facts of the case is expected to eliminate arbitrary and capricious decisions by judges. Yet, we find that the severity of sentences handed down by judges are impacted by the results of a football game for those judges who are more likely to be emotionally attached to the team. This finding underscores the importance of emotional cues in decision making even in a high-stake environment.*

Unlike our muscles, our brains may not let us know when they are tired. When we exercise, our muscles build up lactic acid and become sore, so we know when to give them a rest. Our brains receive no such signals. We often do not know when our brains are less able to process complex issues, as we will have moved into X mode. We do this constantly, when reading, writing or listening to other people.

Understanding sleep patterns, what and when people last ate and when they took a break may have a major impact on negotiations, in addition to how stressed they are, or whether they feel "in-group" or "out-of-group."

AN EXAMPLE

Years ago, new in my job in London, my phone rang. It was an external counsel in New York City. He introduced himself and explained he had been representing us in a case that had been dragging through the courts for over ten years. We had apparently terminated a distributor, allegedly without cause, and the distributor had claimed millions in damages. The case was due to go to trial the following month. The lawyers for both sides had met at a social event at the Yale Club and agreed the time was right for a settlement negotiation. *Was I up for it?* I was asked.

I'm always up for a negotiation, was my reply – even though I was completely unaware of the situation, having joined my employer just a few weeks earlier. I was told to stand by for a call from a mediator that the two lawyers were recommending and that the other party had already agreed. I decided not to second-guess my own lawyer. I had never met him, or even heard of him, before his call. Instinct told me to trust him, and so did practicality – I had too many other things to do at that moment. After all, he was "in-group."

My phone rang the next day, this time it was the mediator on the line. He exuded a pleasant but direct and authoritative air. He said something along the following lines: *OK, I've been appointed your mediator. Are you willing to come to New York on the 14th of next month to resolve this? And I mean come with authority to sign if you reach agreement? The other side will be represented by their President and you seem to be some way down the pecking order in your outfit, so I need to know that you come able to bind your people. Can that be arranged?*

I told him that so far I had only flipped through the file a few hours earlier but that the answers were affirmative – yes, I'd come to New York and, yes, come with my employer's authority to settle.

The next bit surprised me at the time: *Good. Now listen up. The way I deal with warriors is always the same. I want you and the guy on the other side, and one representative of your lawyers, to meet me for dinner on the evening before. I'll book a fancy restaurant. Each of you will pay 50%, including my meal ticket and my fee. OK? But there's a condition. We don't talk business over dinner. Not a word. I want you two to get to know one another. We'll talk business the next day. OK?*

I thought it a good idea and agreed. I spoke to my external counsel and made an appointment to see him the day before the negotiation in order to prepare, and we would then go along to the dinner together.

The dinner was in a private room. The President of the distribution company, whose name was Gene, was already there, a tanned, elegant Italian-American, an impeccably dressed man in his 60s with strong laughter lines radiating from his eyes.

He didn't wait to be introduced. *Hiya Michael, great to meet you* he said, advancing to meet me in the doorway. His handshake crushed my right metacarpals. His attorney was noticeably less affable, but didn't seem to be a Rottweiler. The mediator was not what I imagined; more engaging, not as high-handed as his telephone manner.

We had a drink standing up, then sat down to eat. The conversation jumped around, from our families and backgrounds, through culture, the Presidential election, political events in South Africa and the city crime wave. The dialogue was mainly, I realized, between Gene and me.

We got to the mains plate, still talking, often joking. Gene looked straight at me: *I like you, Michael, I really do. You know something, I'll be damned if we can't do business together tomorrow, you and me. Huh?* It was a rhetorical question. I looked at the mediator, remembering his prohibition on talking shop. He looked at me with a kindly expression but the only signal I think I saw was a very slight shrug of the shoulders. I could have imagined it. I turned to Gene. *Well, I like you too, Gene. And like you I have come to try and do a deal.*

Gene nodded, paused, then frowned: *There are a few things that have been blocking progress, you know. Like difficulties. Know what I mean?*

Obviously, Gene wanted to talk. You could have heard a pin drop on the plush carpet. The lawyers exchanged glances, but said nothing. The mediator didn't move and I glanced at him as if to say – *is this permitted?* but still no signal whatsoever. I turned to Gene. *Which difficulties, Gene?*

He drew breath to answer but the mediator intervened and cut him off. *Guys* (we were all men), *if you want to discuss this now, that's OK with me, but let me propose a few little ground rules.* He went on to explain principles of confidentiality, that nothing said should be used in litigation and that we could continue tomorrow where we left off tonight. We all nodded. *I apologise for interrupting, Gene. Go ahead,* he said.

We settled the case that evening. The mediator applied a very light touch. The attorneys, who knew one another well, were brilliant settlement enablers. They made proposals to embellish the core discussion. They moved places to sit together, confusing the servers of the desert and coffee. As Gene and I talked, they constructed a memorandum of understanding that we signed as the restaurant was closing for the night.

Back at my hotel, I pinched myself, wondering if I had been dreaming. Thinking it over, the change drivers were the meal, the convivial atmosphere, the steerage of the mediator, and the proactivity of the attorneys as merchants of mutual gain. And, most important of all, the relationship between the principals, a factor I only truly understood after reading Professor Michelle LeBaron's thought-provoking book Bridging

Troubled Waters (2002) which emphasizes and vividly explains the heart and soul aspects of negotiation and which inspired me to freely leverage my personality before and during negotiations.

I had not really focused on oxytocin at the time, nor any neuroscience principles. The experience reflected the words of Philip K. Howard, author of The Death of Common Sense: How Law is Suffocating America (1994):

> We should stop looking to law to provide the final answer.... Law cannot save us from ourselves.... We have to go out and try to accomplish our goals and resolve disagreements by doing what we think is right.... Let judgment and personal conviction be important again.

CONNECTING THE THREE OPERATING SYSTEMS: THE TRI-O/S MODEL

CISA in Geneva and the consultancy Neuroawareness are researching methods for how the three operating systems can be managed to design negotiation processes and improve cognitive outcomes. This is work-in-progress at the time of writing but the researchers are hoping to show that it is possible to design and combine optimal negotiation processes, particularly in tense and stressed situations.

Recent research indicates that the same parts of the brain seem to be involved in different ways in all three systems. So when one operating system is activated, it impacts on the others. Networks of the brain or neural patterns of thinking that are consuming more oxygen and glucose at any given time are likely be more active in influencing decisions than others that are comparatively deprived of oxygen and glucose at that moment. Switching between them is not easy.

There is a certain logic to this. Think of a very angry person. If you ask them to "be logical," or "be rational," or even to "calm down," they are likely become even more resentful. This is because the emotional network that is currently active and dominant is that of outrage, so asking them in effect to reallocate glucose to other parts of their brain, and switch on rational cognitive thinking, is something they find practically impossible to achieve at that specific moment. Getting oxygen and glucose to be redistributed and consumed in different neural networks in the brain will take time.

The best thing to do, when that happens in a negotiation, is to take a break, change the subject or try a "soft re-boot" to activate a strong heuristic that is often available and accessible. In Getting Past No: Negotiating With Difficult People (1991), William Ury talks about *going to the balcony*, by which he means resisting impulsive reactions, detaching yourself from the heat of the moment, and re-evaluating before re-engaging. In many ways, this is mindfulness. Trying to become aware of our emotional, social and rational ways of thinking at a particular moment in time is what Bogacz and Lack call *"Neuroawareness."*

Like the Israeli and Louisiana judges, we tend to overlook the fact that fatigue, glucose and oxygen levels of all participants really seem to matter. Yet we tend not to focus on this. Are the participants tired or rested? Have they slept enough? What did they eat?

Did they get proper food or were they rushed? What is their mood? Have they just had an argument with a friend or colleague? Has their sport's team just unpredictably lost a game? Did they have a pleasant or positive experience that morning, walking through nature or seeing a sunrise? Such apparently trivial details may have the greatest impact on the patterns that will be active when people meet one another to negotiate. These may well be things that are outside your control, and it may not be fruitful to try, but simply being aware of them can prove useful to understand why certain techniques work better sometimes than others.

First impressions may occur in seconds, but can have long-lasting and unconscious influences and consequences. How often, when organizing a negotiation, do we concern ourselves with the pro-social impacts we should trigger when we first meet? It may seem silly to focus on such details, but they can affect a negotiation's outcome as much as the quality of the arguments raised. Gene's warm and friendly behavior when we first met in New York clearly affected me, and I believe my engaging response affected him. Was it manipulation? I did not think so at the time. It needs to be appropriate and authentic. It is easy to detect fake or artificial behavior, which of course can have precisely the opposite effect of building up anti-social rather than pro-social patterns.

During negotiations to resolve the student takeover of Columbia University's Hamilton Hall in 1996, mediators Carol Liebman and Carlton Long ordered Deli refreshments. While negotiating, normal eating schedules ceased for all of the participants. Liebman and Long reported[23] that when negotiators had not eaten for a long time, their morale dropped, they became pessimistic, and it was difficult to consider new options. After experiencing the surge of energy provided by food, they made progress, before going downhill again. There are benefits for all parties to eat at the same time or together, and to do so regularly. Whether they should eat in separate rooms or together is something that has not been given much attention.

People often come to negotiations quite stressed and anxious to achieve specific outcomes or goals. They can all be under a lot of pressure to perform. Their O/S 1 and O/S 2 systems are likely to kick in first and establish the patterns by which any glucose and oxygen left in their brains can be allocated to their O/S 3 system. The rational system is always last in line, picking up whatever limited brain resources, crumbs or patterns of thought that O/S 1 and O/S 2 have left available. Like Danziger's judges, their minds may be stuck on the status quo of the solutions they envisaged prior to the negotiation, rather than opening up to optimal outcomes based on the interests of all of the parties involved using flexible and creative new thought patterns.

One challenge facing negotiators is that our O/S1 is fueled by selective perception – that is, our bias towards facts and arguments that we see as supporting our interests, beliefs and goals. This is often called confirmation bias. Even though it may be rationally inappropriate, we develop strong attachments to our positions, and devalue the other party's positions and arguments, unconsciously causing us to stick more rigidly to our positions. The way this works is quite dramatically illustrated in a 2004 article by Michael McIlwrath of GE entitled Dealing with Selective Perception and Bad Faith

Chapter 3

Allegations in Commercial Settlement Discussions, a report on the results of a GE internal negotiation course. This article is reproduced with permission in Appendix 3.

The three operating systems are like cogs in a clock. Intersections and polarities seem to exist. O/S 1 comprises two polarities: the *"away"* mode when people are affected by stress, fear or anxiety, and the *"towards"* mode, when people feel safe or perceive a reward. They are at different ends of a spectrum.

O/S 2 also consists of two polarities: "in-group" and "out-of-group" scripts, and notions of status (whether another person is likely to be dominant or trustworthy).

O/S 3 can also be perceived as containing two polarities: rigid, pre-set patterns of cognitive thinking (e.g., the X mode heuristics, which are easier to access) and dynamic, new creative patterns of rational thinking that require deeper thought (such as the C mode, which may be more difficult to access or inaccessible if the other social systems are already too active).

A zone of intersection can be identified as an optimal area that negotiators may want to target for interest-based negotiations:

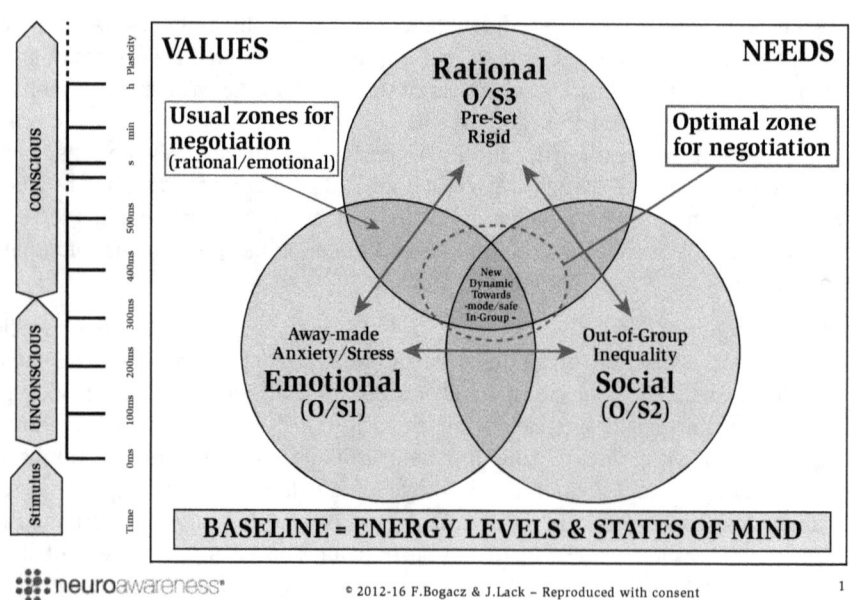

HOW TRI-O/S CAN BE USED TO IMPROVE NEGOTIATION SKILLS

The three operating systems appear to converge at a point where people can feel safe, motivated by possible rewards, being "in-group," feeling comfortable with their status, and where they can more easily think differently. But this optimal state will not necessarily be activated if the participants are feeling tired, stressed or "out-of-group."

Creativity, for example, draws greater oxygen and glucose to certain parts of the cortex, but it is unlikely that participants can get these resources to the right place to enable them to co-create new solutions if they are tired, stressed, poorly fed and distrustful of one another, which of course is a common starting situation in many important negotiations.

PRACTICAL STEPS TO ACHIEVE THE ZONE OF CONVERGENCE

There are many practical things you can do when approaching a negotiation to improve dialogue quality, for example by easing the parties into the space where "in-group" patterns of social behavior, co-creation and the ability to consider all interests provide a basis for moving forwards:

Process design: Process can easily be part of the problem confronting negotiators. Conventional methods of negotiating should gradually be replaced by more creative options that naturally guide the participants into the concentric target zone of collaborative problem-solving. But seasoned professionals who have developed their preferred, if not entrenched, dialogue and persuasion styles can find this a difficult concept to accept. Conventional negotiation styles require the parties not only to negotiate the substance, but also to manage the process through which their communication and dialogue is conducted. They are unlikely to think about the emotional and anti-social patterns they might activate because they are focused on the substance. This can greatly exacerbate an already difficult negotiation and unnecessarily turn it into adversarial experience.

In the New York negotiation with Gene related a few pages back, a very simple process entailing a mediator in the room with the parties and their lawyers, all sharing a meal before negotiating, worked wonders. The process was convened by the mediator. But Gene and I and our respective external counsel were able to allow our natural personalities to predominate, under the watchful eye of the neutral person, which enabled us to concentrate on the negotiation and how to reach a mutually beneficial outcome, encouraged, even enabled, by the mediator (it was he, after all, who insisted that we eat first and talk later).

We tend to be unimaginative when considering negotiation process design options, even if they cross our mind. Most of us simply show up and rely on our self-inflated view of our leverage and powers of persuasion. But where negotiations are likely to be positional, tense, difficult or unpredictable, or very likely all of the above, we need to maximize the chances of starting off in the Tri O/S Target Zone. Chapter 7 covers negotiation process design in more detail and presents widely tried and tested ways to approach negotiation from a process perspective by focusing on the Tri-OS target zone of convergence to achieve more successful outcomes.

Formalities: In the preparation phase explored in Chapter 2, consider who should attend the negotiation, where or how it should take place, and what the environment should be. How do we prepare participants socially for a first meeting? Should the meeting happen in an office or off-site location? If we cannot meet physically, what electronic communication medium should we use? If meeting face-to-face, our turf or theirs? Should there be a dress code? Casual or formal? What about food: will meals be eaten together or separately? Should we discuss the menu or at least enquire about dietary preference? Should we stay over at the same venue or only meet there? What proactive steps can be taken when we first meet in person? How can we encourage optimal listening that activates beneficial emotions and motivates positive relationships? How can we best avoid reactive devaluation where we reject offers purely based on who made them? How do we encourage joint "ownership" of the outcome?

Language: Nomenclature and labels are important. They trigger positive, if unconscious behavior. Often in negotiations, especially where a conflict has arisen or the prospect of a dispute is hovering over the parties, the negotiators are likely to allocate responsibility or blame at one another. We frequently negotiate in a triangular pattern, where people are stressed, fearful, distrusting and primed through language not to empathize. Thinking and speaking using terms, like "sides," "us vs. them," "plaintiff," "claimant," "defendant" or "respondent," primes "out-of-group" and anti-social behavior. Referring to the participants or their advisors as "our opponents" or "opposing counsel" does not encourage "in-group" behavior. Asking for a "position paper" is hardly likely to prompt discussion on interests (have you ever heard anyone ask for an "interests paper"?). Lawyers who think they are entering a positional process are more likely to interrupt, fence and point score. While they focus on past facts, claimed rights and applicable laws (which is where their strengths lie), the participants' interests, emotions, relationships, social patterns and cognitive states of mind tend to be sidelined, practically consigned to irrelevancy.

Words matter. In 2006, Dr. Benedetto De Martino at the University of Cambridge conducted a now famous experiment where people were put into fMRI brain-scanning machines and told they had been given a fifty-pound note. One group was informed they could "keep £20" or that they could gamble, at low odds, to keep the £50. The other group was told they could "lose £30" or gamble, with equally low odds, to keep the £50. The only rational difference between these two groups were the words "keep £20," and "lose £30" as the two propositions are mathematically identical. If the rational O/S 3 thinking system were to guide decision-making in both groups, the decisions should be the same in both groups. However, the behaviors exhibited by each group were very different, and the results showed that the decision was in fact pre-determined by the O/S 2 system. Since "keep" is a safe word, there is no triggering of fear but of safety, and the brain's pre-frontal cortex is enabled and activated upon hearing the word "keep." Oxygen and glucose can be detected as being consumed in this area within a few milliseconds, before cognitive O/S 3 thinking kicks in. It is a pre-conscious, rapid way of thinking. Most people in this group did not gamble. With the other group, because "lose" is a fear word, the fMRI scans showed that the amygdalae in the participants' O/S 2 systems were first activated. The activation of the amygdalae led to a different cascade of networks in this group's way of thinking, one that was more willing to take risks. The result was that most people in this second group chose to gamble. All because of a single word, and how it triggered pre-conscious thought that, in a way, "hijacked" the O/S 3 system before it could be aware of how these words had unconsciously affected their cognitive abilities to think rationally.

This simple experiment helps us consider how to frame negotiation offers. Is an offer more likely to be accepted if expressed as a *"keep"* or as a *"lose"* proposition? In the statement: *"Here is my fantastic offer, take it or leave it"* the last five words negate the perception of autonomy or choice, and the possible true benefits of the offer, no matter how good it may actually be. It simply increases pressure and distrust. This is because fear, a sense of unfairness, social exclusion or being potentially deprived of autonomy, are sentiments that are likely to dominate and prevent a proper assessment of the substantive merits of the offer. Also, who communicates the offer may sometimes have far greater impact than the substance of the offer itself.

Using appropriate language, such as "negotiation partners" rather than the "other side," or "we" as opposed to "they," may seem trivial, but choice of language and process can make an enormous difference.

IN A NUTSHELL

- Understanding the basics of the Tri O/S model, the role of glucose and oxygen and how the brain's software operates is useful for dealing with the pressures of negotiating.
- Consider aiming for the notional zone of convergence between the three O/S systems, where people can feel safe, motivated by possible rewards, "in-group" and with comfortable status levels, and where they can think dynamically, cooperatively and seek options for mutual gain.
- There are numerous, practical, everyday things that negotiators can do to achieve this zone of convergence.
- Focus on setting up the negotiation process around the people and circumstances, rather than, as usually happens, forcing the negotiators to implement a conventional, default process.

CHAPTER 4
Culture

A riddle, wrapped in a mystery, inside an enigma

Winston Churchill, struggling to understand the behavior of Russia

When Amerigo Vespucci returned to Florence from the so-called New World in around 1500, he famously reported that the place was populated by *barbarians*, defined by him as those who *would not eat at fixed times but as often as they pleased*. Had this disparaging comment been made more widely known at the time, perhaps the people might not have adopted his first name for that of their Continent and country. No doubt Vespucci himself would have been mortified had he guessed that, 500 years later, there would be over 1,000 international burger outlets in his homeland, and that McDonalds would engage in a public bunfight with his city's Mayor over plans for a restaurant in the Piazza del Duomo.

Culturology is the multi-dimensional science of understanding the values, beliefs, assumptions, attitudes, interests, experiences, ways, practices and habits that we share with groups of others, and that strongly influence our own, and others' behavior. Culture governs how negotiators understand, communicate and conduct themselves when operating across cultures. Most aspects of our cultures are subconscious, but have a profound impact on how we interpret information and act when negotiating, as well as on the outcomes we achieve. The consequences can be pleasurable and successful, irritating and disastrous. Culture is just as often a source of contention as it is of harmony.

People assume that the influence and consequences of culture arise only when dealing with people from another country or region. This is no longer the case. Most of us live in multi-cultural societies in which, even in local negotiations, we regularly engage with people whose cultures differ from our own. Many countries are no longer culturally homogeneous, and some, like the US, really never have been, despite the melting pot syndrome.

Chapter 4

Cultures cross geographic and political boundaries. Many people have more than one culture, having been raised and educated in several places. Then there is the overlay of organizational cultures. Some are tightly controlled and limit individual empowerment; others encourage responsible risk-taking, where people have freedom to apply their discretion and where one-off failure is not reprimanded. Some organizational cultures are governed by processes and rules; others are results driven. To add to the complexity, management guru Charles Handy identified at least four types of organizational culture that he called power, role, task and person cultures, each interacting differently with personal cultures.

Being acutely inter-culturally aware, having an insight into how and why people from other backgrounds think and act differently, and having the basic knowledge to behave and communicate cross-culturally, is vital when negotiating. It does not mean that everyone will conform to a personal cultural stereotype, nor does it mean that you need to go native and unnaturally take on cultural characteristics of those around you. And nor does it mean that every behavior has a cultural root. Respecting the other party as an individual, regardless of culture, while having a basic understanding of cultural dynamics, makes for much better negotiating.

CULTURAL UNDERSTANDING

Many distinguished researchers and educators have devised frameworks to help us understand how cultures inter-relate. Conspicuously, but perhaps not surprisingly, most culturology researchers and writers seem to be Westerners. This, in itself, reflects a cognitive cultural norm. In The Geography of Thought: How Asians and Westerners Think Differently and Why (2003), Richard E. Nisbett, Professor of Social Psychology at the University of Michigan, pointed out that Westerners tend to be obsessed with categorizing things because this enables them to decide what rules to apply and what logic to use when problem solving. Conversely, Asians are less inclined to classify everything because the wider contextual considerations they instinctively take into account are more complex and do not lend themselves to being grouped in convenient categories. Professor Nisbett observed that logic plays a somewhat lesser role in problem solving in Asian than in Western cultures.

There seems to be something important, perhaps even dangerous, wrapped up in this observation. Research to date on cultures has focused on identifying differentiating factors that enable Westerners to understand other cultures and their effect on human interaction. This simplified approach has proved important to help Westerners understand core principles and become more culturally aware and sensitive. However, the risk it creates is that it leads to insights gained through a Western prism. These include theoretical stereotyping, with less attention given to how the stereotypes can be affected by the context of the situation, the impact of organizational norms, and by the several cultural environments in which a person worked or was educated. In addition, facework and guanxi (which, as explained later, are not exclusively Asian phenomena) are crucial for a proper understanding of many cultures.

Although it is easy to criticize the largely Western analysis of cultural paradigms, negotiators find it enormously helpful to be sensitized to the ways researchers have been classifying cultural characteristics, and how the different dimensions intersect and interact. Professor Clifford Geertz, the leading Princeton anthropologist, warned that cultural analysis is intrinsically incomplete, and suggested that the deeper the analysis, the more incomplete it becomes. Culture can be much more dynamic and complex than the principles suggest, and, as most culturologists readily concede, research in the area is still developing and shaping our views. But we should be acutely aware of the principles generated by research to date, keep them top of mind when negotiating, and learn to be more tolerant.

CATEGORIZATIONS

The late American anthropologist Edward T. Hall is widely recognized as the progenitor of cross-cultural communication for homing in on the distinction between high context and low context cultures in his classic work Beyond Culture (1976).

Dutch social psychologist Professor Geert Hofstede, working for IBM as a management trainer in the late 1960s and early 1970s, generated a mass of data on inter-cultural dynamics and introduced a way of categorizing cultures based on six axes or principles: individualism/collectivism, power distance, degrees of uncertainty avoidance, long-term orientation, masculinity/femininity and indulgence/restraint. These are presented in his various books including Culture's Consequences (1983, 2001) and Cultures and Organizations: Software of the Mind (1993 and subsequent editions).

Dutch/French management consultant, Fons Trompenaars, has also researched heavily in this area, developing Hofstede's frameworks for classifying cultures into seven dimensions. He explains these in Riding the Waves of Culture: Understanding Diversity in Global Business (1997, 2012), co-authored with Charles Hampden-Turner.

Richard D. Lewis, a British cross-cultural skills trainer, identified a three-part classification of cultural stereotypes: Linear-Active, Multi-Active, Re-Active or a hybrid form of them. His books, When Cultures Collide (1996) and Cross-Cultural Communication: A Visual Approach (1999, 2008), are instructive.

Michele Gefland, Professor of Psychology at the University of Maryland and Jeanne Brett, Professor of Management and Organizations at the Kellogg School of Management co-edited The Handbook of Negotiation and Culture (2004), which deals comprehensively with the theories surrounding the intersection of culture and negotiation. Professor Brett is also the author of Negotiating Globally: How to Negotiate Deals, Resolve Disputes and Make Decisions Across Cultural Boundaries (2001).

Joel Lee, Associate Professor of Law at the National University of Singapore and Teh Hwee Hwee, Deputy Registrar of the Supreme Court of Singapore, edited a revealing book entitled An Asian Perspective on Mediation (2009). As mediation is a prime form of assisted negotiation, their book, very much written from an Asian standpoint but also taking note of Western cultural categorizations, has many suggestions for how assisted negotiation can be improved using cultural phenomena.

Erin Meyer, Professor of Organisational Behaviour at the INSEAD business school in Paris, has written one of the most recent works, The Culture Map: Decoding How People Think, Lead and Get Things Done Across Cultures (2014). In this very useful and readable offering, drawing on the work of leading culturologists and her own research, Professor Meyer constructs a handy and practical model for assessing and comparing cultures based on eight scales or characteristics that can be viewed simultaneously.

The principles, concepts, theories and models described by these thought leaders are important for negotiators to understand. This can only be done properly by reading their books. Any negotiator will greatly improve their abilities by understanding their classification frameworks.

Stereotyping has both merits and risks. The risks can be minimized by keeping all the main classifications in mind while remembering the limitations and dangers of over-simplification, and that the real world is much more complex than the categories suggest. It is always the case that individual personality, life experiences and situational factors can result in exceptions and deviancies from any stereotypical norm. For example, lawyers are likely to have developed a rules-based culture that qualifies their culture of origin, though cultural attitudes towards those rules can vary greatly. On the plus side, the main accepted classifications are easy to remember, and help us anticipate likely cultural relativities before we start negotiating. Actually, knowledge of even the most accepted classifications, far from being dangerous, will elevate our consciousness of cultural aspects in any given interaction and give us both strategic and operational advantages when negotiating.

EDWARD HALL'S CONTEXT INDEX

How people from different backgrounds instinctively interpret and apply the wider contextual setting in which communications or events occur is fundamental to the art of negotiation. "Context" was meant by Edward Hall to mean the framework and surrounding circumstances that may have a bearing on the situation at hand. Hall drew an axis, with high-context cultures at one end, and low-context cultures at the other, with many others at different points in between.

High-context cultures are those prevalent in most of Asia, Africa, parts of Latin America, the Middle East, Russia, Eurasia and the sub-continent – in other words, most of the world. Over millennia, these cultures have distilled and ingrained norms that draw heavily from the relevant background, including relationships, many of them founded on trust, harmony and consensus over long time frames. High contexters are instinctively intuitive, implicit and generally indirect in how they communicate, enabling and expecting others to interpret between the lines. High contexters expect those with whom they communicate to, as Erin Meyer puts it, *read the air*. They want to know and trust the people they are dealing with before doing business. Tone of voice, written words, pictorial depictions and non-verbal signals all rank highly in communication patterns, as do humility, respect and apology. High contexters ascribe special significance to the timing of communications, as well as the identity of the person communicating and also what happened prior to the communication. They tend to rely on what legal documents and laws intended, the spirit of the text, and not just the literal interpretation of the drafting.

Low-context cultures, typified in North America, Australasia and northern Europe, rely much less on background, are typically more literal, direct and explicit, do not rely so heavily on trust and often fail to appreciate what is not being said outright. Low contexters rank the individual above the community, and place a premium on factual knowledge and logic. Although low contexters may begin with pleasantries, they keep them brief and want to knuckle down to business and reach finality quickly. Closure and contracts are crucial in low context cultures, setting out, often in excruciating detail, concise action steps, time lines and responsibilities that are meant to be interpreted very literally. They expect contracts to be as clear and explicit as possible to enable them, in the event of a later confusion or disagreement, to fall back on what was agreed when the contract was signed. Low contexters rely mainly on the letter of the law, even if circumstances change, and give less credence to what they perceive to be the vague, uncertain and unrecorded spirit or intention behind it. They are uncomfortable with ambiguities and want to resolve them before a deal is done, not later. Their written agreements therefore tend to be complex, imagining every conceivable scenario that might occur – a so-called lawyers' field day.

Somewhere in-between come the Southern and Eastern European and many Latin American cultures with characteristics drawn from the two extremes, though adapted and manifested in different ways.

This sweeping categorization is punctuated with copious exceptions and qualifications, but is a useful way of thinking about likely negotiating practices and how contracts are viewed and negotiated.

To illustrate the diversity, in a lecture at College of Marin, just north of San Francisco, a Japanese manager is quoted explaining his culture's communication style to an American: *We are a homogeneous people; we do not have to speak as much as you do; when we say one word, we understand ten; you have to say ten words in order to communicate one.*

GEERT HOFSTEDE'S SIX CULTURAL DIMENSIONS

Hofstede's classification of cultures, based on his IBM research, began with the four different dimensions of power distance, individualism-collectivism, uncertainty avoidance and ego/social (originally called masculinity-femininity). Subsequent research with other culturologists led him to consider two further dimensions: long-term-short-term orientation and indulgence-restraint. In different ways and to varying degrees, they all have a relevance to negotiators.

Power Distance

Hofstede defines power distance as the extent to which less powerful people in a given society accept and expect that power is divided unequally in favor of others. A high power distance rating indicates a strong and established status-orientated hierarchical structure that is accepted by those who are controlled at the lower levels of the hierarchy by those in positions of power at the upper levels. A low power distance number suggests that people at the bottom are more willing, and welcome, to challenge and question those in power, and strive towards a redistribution of power and a flatter hierarchy. In organizations based in low power distance cultures, it can be hard for outsiders to tell who has the real power to decide.

Individualism-Collectivism

Hofstede devised the individual-collective dimension to indicate the extent to which people are integrated into groups and have a sense of belonging with those groups. Those that are well-integrated in groups are considered collectivist, whereas those that are less tightly associated or committed to a particular group are classified as individualistic, both in nature and behavior.

In collectivist cultures, shared in-group interests prevail, and members of the group loyally support one another, particularly when dealing with an out-group party or in conflict situations. In negotiations, collectivist parties are much more likely than individualistic societies to consult the group to secure consensus before committing, and much less likely to assume authority to commit without prior group endorsement or approval. Negotiations with collectivists rarely involve a sole decision maker, and even when they do, that person will usually emphasize their need to refer back to a group before finally committing.

Uncertainty Avoidance

Tolerance for ambiguity differs greatly among cultures. A high level of intolerance to ambiguity indicates that a particular culture prizes certainty and has developed rules and procedures designed to ensure clarity, maximize predictability and avoid surprises. People from these cultures have a voracious appetite for detailed information, and they often have many laws, regulations and other rules, even if they do not always comply with them. A lower score on this dimension suggests that the culture is more tolerant of unexpected events, is therefore more flexible, can accommodate changing circumstances more easily, and is generally more able to adapt than those at the higher scoring end.

Ego/Social (Masculinity/Femininity)

This index acquired the masculinity-femininity tag in the early 1970s when, in some cultures, diversity had a different definition than today. Hofstede intended it to illustrate distinctions that draw parallels with animalistic behavior. So-called masculine cultures are those that are more egocentric, assertive, materialistic and grandstanding by nature, whereas cultures that Hofstede labeled "feminine" are more social, collaborative, compromising and polite. This dimension is now often called ego/social or some another politically-correct descriptor.

Long-Term/Short-Term Orientation

The long/short term orientation index measures openness to change. Cultures at the low, short-term end of this scale usually have long, rich histories and carefully handed-down traditions that ascribe great value to precedent, beliefs and conventions. They can have difficulty departing from them even when problems arise as they tend to value the significance of the past more than that of the future, which can produce a more short-term view of the future.

Cultures at the high, long-term, end of the scale may also have rich histories but often less stable ones, are less constrained by the past and are generally more free and able to challenge tradition and status quo. They are therefore more able to adapt quickly to new circumstances and view the need to solve problems as paramount. They can be less focused on "why," and more interested in "how."

Indulgence-Restraint

Indulgent societies are considered to be those that are hedonistic and open to relatively unrestricted enjoyment of life. There are few social limits on self-gratification, other than the norms of criminal law to protect from anti-social behavior, damage or harm. At the other end of this axis are restraint cultures where society and law limit, often severely, the gratification of human needs and emotions, usually because of a range of powerful inherited beliefs, practices and traditions.

Many of Hofstede's dimensions can be used to understand different negotiation situations. In Culture Shock! Sweden (2009), Charlotte Rosen Svensson graphically describes what happened when Volvo and Renault were negotiating a possible cooperation for their truck businesses. The first round of negotiations between the French and the Swedes broke down. When Volvo's negotiators were asked why, they said that they could not get a word in edgeways because the French dominated the negotiations with endless talking. Their Renault counterparts, asked the same question, said the Swedes were silent and uncommunicative during the negotiations.

Hofstede explains this contradiction using uncertainty avoidance dimensions. French culture has a lower tolerance for ambiguity than Swedish culture, so French negotiators prefer to talk more, often using long sentences that emphasize their knowledge and expertise. Swedes tend to view communication from a different perspective; once someone has spoken, a stereotypical Swede will wait for a natural pause, allow some seconds to accord respect for the speaker, think about how to reply, and only then offer a comment. Talkative cultures can quickly misinterpret pauses as a nil response, feel uncomfortable with silence, and so keep talking.

The Hofstede Centre offers an online tool[24] to enable you to measure almost any country's national cultural stereotype on the six cultural dimensions. It also includes The Culture Compass, a tool for assessing your own cultural values and likely behaviors.

RICHARD LEWIS' THREE-DIMENSIONAL "ACTIVES" SCALE

Richard Lewis' research has led him to group cultures on an interesting and easily-understood three-dimensional model: linear-active, multi-active or reactive:

Linear-Active

People from linear-active cultures are inclined to do one planned thing at a time, and are diary-driven. Linear-actives are decisive, comfortable speaking first, can be confrontational and accept conflict situations as inevitable. They consider themselves pragmatic, no-nonsense debaters and negotiators. Logic prevails over emotions in the quest to achieve fast outcomes, if necessary conceding on some points to get a deal done.

Multi-Active

Multi-active cultures thrive on flexibility. They are relatively emotional, sometimes theatrical, and strongly people-orientated, placing a high value on relationships. They feel uncomfortable with discord and conflict and much prefer diplomacy and dialogue. They easily initiate conversation and are impulsive. They think about, and do, several things at once, listening and talking simultaneously, and are expert at improvisation.

Reactive

Reactive cultures are masters at the art of listening. While concentrating intently on what is being said to them, reactives may exhibit dynamic listening skills, sometimes using body language, such as head nodding, to signify that they have understood a point (though have not necessarily agreed with it). Reactives prefer to hear and assess what someone is saying, and then think carefully about it, before considering how to respond. They are typically polite, avoid interrupting and value silence and amiability. Reactives are natural compromisers if that is what it takes to maintain harmony.

The potential mismatch between these three cultural extremes is clear. Linear-actives can be seen by multi-taskers and reactives as inflexible, even obstinate, arrogant, rough or impolite. Multi-actives are less driven by agendas and schedules, and therefore can be perceived by linear-actives and reactives as chaotic and unpunctual. Linear-actives are often diary-driven, wanting to get to the point quickly so they can move to closure and progress to the next challenge, much to the frustration of reactives who need time and space to build trust. Linear-actives are likely to prefer discussing issues in the order of a specific agenda, which has, in their eyes, a methodical flow; multi-actives are much more inclined to disregard order and explore issues as they arise, jumping around pre-determined agendas. Reactives will usually go with the flow, listening to understand, but engaging in only a modest amount of two-way communication. Each can find the other's style annoying, even exasperating, stretching patience all round. Linear-active negotiators dislike exchanges that go off on tangents while multi-actives thrive off-piste. Reactives focus first on understanding, and only then responding. It takes all kinds to make the world go around.

Richard Lewis shares many experiences in his books and lectures. One memorable story concerns negotiations between an American and a Finn. The American had heard that it would be tough to negotiate with "ice-cold" Finns. By the time they got to negotiating price, the American was already feeling uncomfortable due to the inscrutable Finn's frequent bouts of silence. The American quoted his price. The Finn sat impassively, not reacting. The American became more nervous. Misreading the wall of ice on the other side of the table, he dropped his price. The Finn remained unresponsive. The American took a deep breath, endured the silence for another few seconds and then felt he had to speak: "*OK, I can make you a special price*" and lowered it once more. The Finn, now feeling very uncomfortable, opened his mouth slowly and began "*Well....*" But before he could continue, the American blurted out: "*Look, OK, OK, this really is my final offer and is the best I can possibly do*" and dropped the price further. The Finn looked at the American, took another deep breath, imperceptibly nodded and simply said "*OK.*"

After the deal was done, the Finn expressed astonishment to his colleagues that he was able to get the product so cheaply without uttering a word. He would have been perfectly comfortable paying the first price quoted, but the American did not even give him the opportunity to accept! Finns are typically in the Reactive category. The American stereotype is firmly in Richard Lewis' Linear-Active camp.

Many cultures exhibit blends of these stereotypical characteristics. Richard Lewis has a model depicting the inter-relationship between typical cultures based on the Actives categorization:

Chapter 4

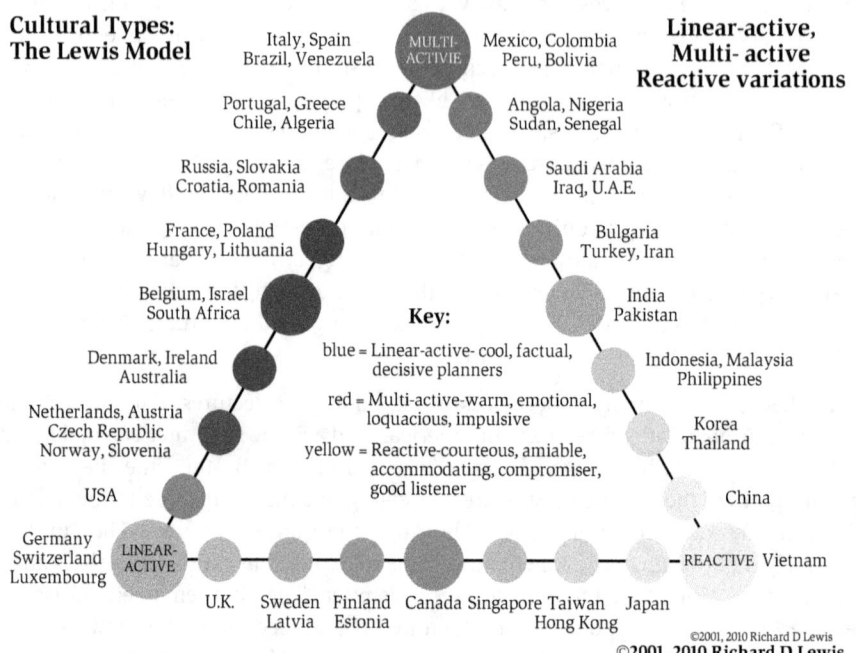

Richard Lewis has also applied his three dimensions into a series of diagrams that depict how people from different cultural backgrounds typically might be expected to behave in five areas: how they communicate and negotiate during meetings; their listening habits; audience expectations during presentations; leadership styles; and management language. These diagrams, covering over seventy cultures, are set out in his book Cross-Cultural Communication: A Visual Approach (1999, 2008). While not intended to be taken too literally, it is an indispensable fund of reference for any negotiator. Many people find the diagrams quite revealing, even hilarious, especially when seeing how their own cultural styles are depicted, probably because of the implicit and inconvenient truths they surface.

Three of the diagrams, featuring negotiation styles in Germany, Japan and Hispanic America, cultures at the three corners of Actives triangle, give a flavor of the approach taken:

Culture

National Communication Patterns
– Germany –

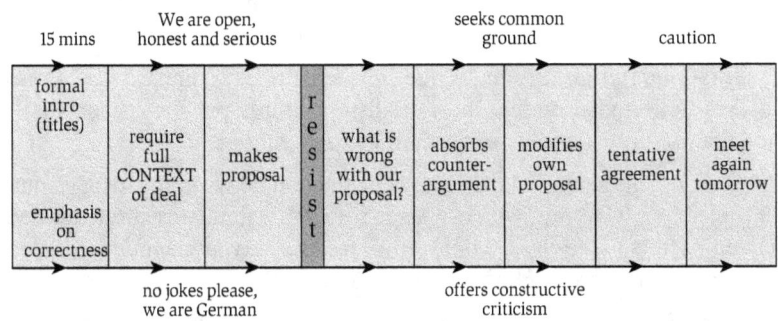

"die Wahrheit ist die Wahrheit"

© 2001, 2009, Richard D. Lewis

National Communication Patterns
– Japan –

© 2001, 2009, Richard D. Lewis

National Communication Patterns
– Mexico –

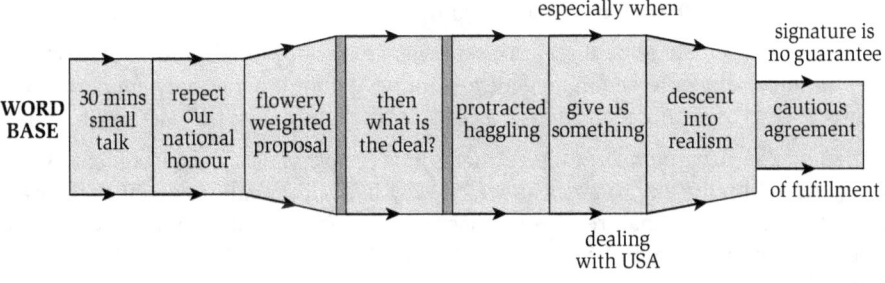

© 2001, 2009, Richard D. Lewis

FONS TROMPENAARS' SEVEN DIMENSIONS

In Riding the Waves of Culture: Understanding Diversity in Global Business (1997, 2012), Fons Trompenaars and Charles Hampden-Turner ("Trompenaars") developed five cultural dimensions, originally proposed by the American sociologist Talcott Parsons researching in the 1950s, and added two of their own. Most of these dimensions have slightly esoteric titles, but all are well worth noting by negotiators.

Chapter 4

Universalism-Particularism: Universalists pursue what they perceive to be correct and right. It may not be the only or proper way, but if they consider it to be valid, they stick to it. Particularists will adapt according to the relationships involved and any applicable circumstances that they want to see addressed.

Individualism-Communitarianism: This dimension is similar to Hofstede's Individualism-Collectivism index. Individualistic cultures put the person first while communitarianists more readily represent the group interest.

Neutral-Affective: This axis plots the relative distinction between the focused quest for achieving objectives (Neutral), which tends to restrict or eliminate extraneous issues as complicating factors, measured against the acceptability of emotional expression (Affective) as a normal part of human interaction.

Specific-Diffuse: Specific cultures tend to restrict negotiations to the situation at hand, with the relationship aspects viewed as transitory and superficial. Diffuse cultures are based on the relationship between the parties, where emphasis is given to building a trusting and mutually respectful connection for the long term.

Achievement-Ascription: Cultures can be orientated in different ways in relation to how individuals are assessed. Achievement cultures apply much greater weight to track records of past accomplishments, while ascription cultures give greater weight and respect to intensely personal characteristics, such as age, position or title, connections, network and gender. When negotiating, this can cause friction; ascriptive negotiators can have difficulty accepting positions and arguments communicated by young middle-ranking achievers, however expert and persuasive they may be. Conversely, achievement-based negotiators become frustrated when their ascriptive negotiation partners need to refer repeatedly to some authority in their organization that may not seem to be involved in the negotiation. When achievers express irritation or frustration with ascriptive negotiators, it can be interpreted as disrespectful, even insulting, and this seed can germinate into serious dissent.

Attitudes to Time: Some cultures prize knowledge and appreciation of factors in the past as important criteria for judging the future, while others apply much greater significance to assessing the actual prospects for the future than the past might imply.

Attitudes to the Environment: Culture affects how people view the environment. Some are governed by the environment in which they live and breathe, as well as their attitudes to people and to nature. The approach of others is more influenced by addressing their own individual interests, desires and needs. Trompenaars illustrates this dimension by reference to the explanations some cultures give as to why they wear ear pods when listening to music; the Japanese do so in order not to disturb others, while Westerners are more likely to say they wear them to avoid being disturbed by others.

Trompenaars takes these basic dimensions to a further level, ranking national cultures in different ways under each one, illustrating the danger in assuming an over-simplistic interpretation of cultural dimensions.

These cultural characteristic scales are easy to understand. None of the researchers ever intended them in any way to be judgmental, or be interpreted as sexist, racial, religious or politically incorrect. The scales merely express stereotypical relativities and comparisons to help communicators consider how they act and communicate and how they interpret others' behavior when interacting with those positioned differently on any of the dimension scales. They therefore have an important influence on how people relate to one another, and how they negotiate successful outcomes.

When one scale is assessed in relation to another, or several others, the situation starts to become much more complex but can create valuable insights into negotiation behaviors. In an article[25] in McKinsey Quarterly, Peter N. Child of McKinsey & Company quotes Jean-Luc Chéreau, former CEO of French hypermarket group Carrefour's business in China: *When I arrived..., my former boss told me I was lucky: I was set for the first year because he had already signed five contracts for five new stores. Then I started talking with one of our Chinese partners who had signed those contracts, and nothing seemed to be happening. Finally, my assistant told me, "Just because he signed a 20-year contract two years ago with your former boss, a person who is not you, does not mean he will respect the contract." That was a big shock to me; the contract was notarized and everything. But we started to renegotiate article by article. Five years later, during the Asian crisis, I invited this same partner to my office and said, "Just because I signed a contract with you does not mean I will respect it. We are in a crisis." So he said, "Fine," and we started to renegotiate, to reduce the rent. It was these very interesting experiences that showed me that we are in another world. If you come to China with preconceived ideas after having been successful in Europe or the U.S., you make mistake after mistake.*

Trompenaars' Universalism-Particularism and Specific-Diffuse dimensions can help us to understand these differences.

Trompenaars Hampden-Turner Consulting is a business now owned by KPMG. Their website at www2.thtconsulting.com includes a suite of open culture tools that anyone can use, including a questionnaire-based intercultural awareness profiler.

MICHELE GEFLAND & JEANNE BRETT

Professors Gefland and Brett's Handbook of Negotiation and Culture (2004) includes contributions from over thirty leading experts in culture or negotiation or both. Most of the subject matter chapters, such as those on cognition, emotion and communication, are paired, one on negotiation, the other on cultural aspects. Like the other books mentioned, this is essential reading for anyone serious about negotiating across cultures.

ERIN MEYER

Erin Meyer's The Culture Map (2014) is one of the most recent offerings on cultural comparisons, and one of the most comprehensible, dramatic and useful. Her ingenious and simple "map" enables us to plot several stereotypical national cultures on a one-page diagram so that their relative similarities and differences can be compared at

Chapter 4

a glance across eight dimensions. Like any mapping exercise, more detail adds complexity, but the Meyer map easily lends itself to a clear comparison of up to six different cultures at a time.

Professor Meyer's eight dimensions reflect but re-assign the categories developed by those that have preceded her. She uses non-technical, self-explanatory terminology and her dimensions are all directly relevant to negotiating qualities. The Meyer eight mapping dimensions are:

Low Context	**Communicating**	High Context
Direct negative feedback	**Evaluating**	Indirect negative feedback
Egalitarian	**Leading**	Hierarchical
Consensual	**Deciding**	Top down
Task-based	**Trusting**	Relationship-based
Confrontational	**Disagreeing**	Avoids confrontation
Linear time	**Scheduling**	Flexible time
Specific	**Persuading**	Holistic

An example of a Meyer Culture Map featuring the stereotypical cultures of France, Germany, China and Japan looks like this:

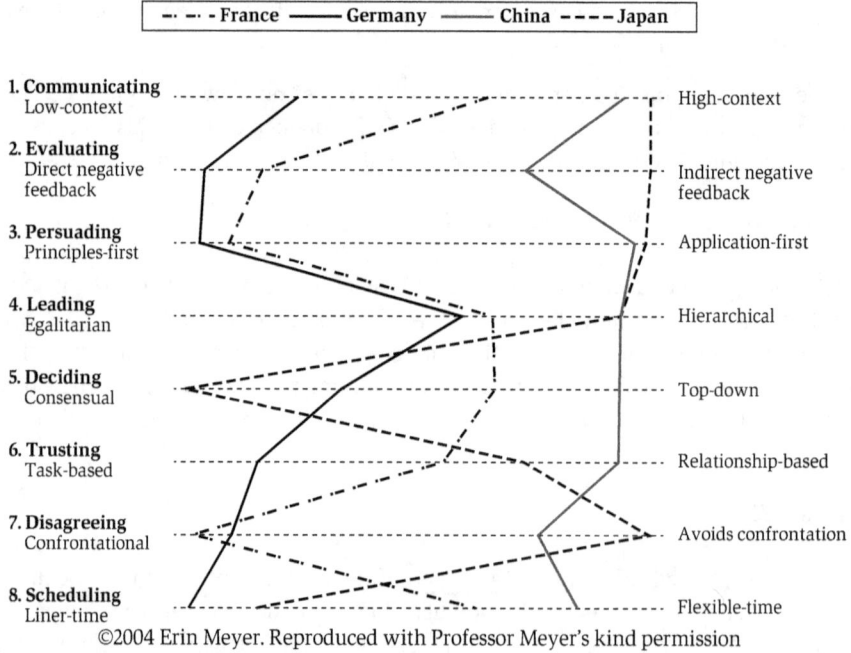

©2004 Erin Meyer. Reproduced with Professor Meyer's kind permission

Professor Meyer's Culture Map enables us instantly to compare not only each of these cultures with the other three, but also to highlight how different two European and two Asian cultures are to one another, and as between the Asian and European cultures more generally.

The Culture Map contains examples of national cultural stereotypes along each dimension. Professor Meyer's website at www.erinmeyer.com includes a tool to determine similarities and differences between several national cultural stereotypes using the eight dimensions. The website also enables you to complete a twenty-five-section questionnaire to self-assess your own positions on The Culture Map and determine how you may differ from your own stereotypical national cultural norm. This is a really useful tool to elevate cultural awareness. Ideally, get someone who shares the cultural credentials of your negotiating partners to complete the questionnaire to give you all an understanding of the main areas of common and uncommon cultural ground that might be expected to influence the progress of a negotiation. It's a fun thing to do.

FACEWORK

In different ways, face permeates all cultures. Intangible yet powerful, invisible yet palpable, and invaluable yet frequently discounted, face is one of the most important elements of human nature. It can be lost, shared, fed and starved, as well as given, asserted, saved and restored, but cannot be bought, sold, licensed or stolen. Face is so complex, with such a multi-dimensional character, differing in application across many cultures, that dictionaries struggle to explain it, with words like respect, image, honor, dignity and prestige, none of which reveal its true meaning. In 1943, the Chinese intellectual Lin Yutang concluded: *Face cannot be translated or defined*.

Professor Stella Ting-Toomey at the Department of Human Communication Studies at California State University at Fullerton has offered a model for face in an article: Intercultural Conflict Styles: A Face Negotiation Theory (1988, subsequently improved and revised). Professor Ting-Toomey's model describes face using two intersecting dimensions that she calls the positive-negative face axis, and the self-other face axis.

Positive face is the need for autonomy or inclusion. Most people require elements of both, depending on their broader cultural framework and the situation at hand. Individualistic cultures generally need more autonomy than inclusion, while collectivist cultures need more inclusion than autonomy. The extent to which people in mainly collectivist cultures need privacy is a negative face phenomenon.

Self-face refers to the inclination, typically manifested by individualistic cultures, towards respect for themselves. At the opposite end of the spectrum, collectivist cultures are more orientated towards concern for others, especially their "in-groups," which can be in preference to, or even to the exclusion of, self-face.

Combining elements of both these dimensions, Professor Ting-Toomey overlaid her positive-negative/self-other framework with four main face needs – face restoration, face saving, face assertion and face giving:

Chapter 4

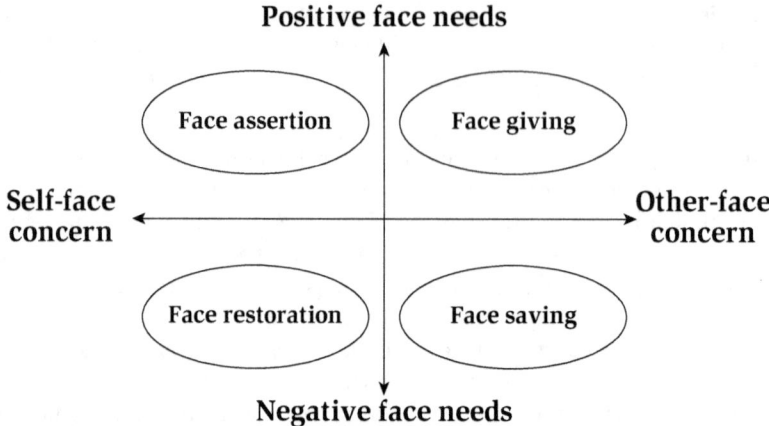

Face restoration is the protective need to give oneself autonomy, space and freedom. It presents itself most frequently at the outset of negotiations, while the parties are weighing up one another, being positional and generally unwilling to trust the other with information for fear that it may be misused or not reciprocated.

Face saving is the need to protect or restore the face of another person, such as your negotiating partner. If you perceive that loss of face, or the prospect of loss of face, on the part of the other party may be a hurdle or blockage in a negotiation, thoughtful strategies to deal with that issue could deliver meaningful progress.

Face assertion involves addressing your own need to convey respectful inclusion and association, which can be done in many ways, including being pleasant, reasonable, open, unaggressive and understanding, and through active listening.

Face giving is the need to support the other person's need for inclusion and association, genuinely and with sincerity. You can give face by gratuitously honoring someone, providing them with an expression of public respect, celebrating their achievements, avoiding criticism, appropriate but not over-the-top exaggeration, complimenting and emphasizing positive aspects such as hard work and intellectual vigor, treating the other person as an expert and generally showing deference. A properly-given apology can be a very effective face giving act.

Politeness Theory has gained considerable recognition in the West, having been postulated by anthropologists Penelope Brown and Stephen Levinson of the Max Planck Institute for Psycholinguistics in the Netherlands in their book Politeness: Some Universals in Politeness Usage (1987). They identified various facework strategies that threaten negative or positive face and that have potentially serious consequences. Examples include warnings, allegations and ultimatums, as well as straight talk, bluntness and insistence. The effect of these face-threatening acts will usually prompt lack of co-operation, such as unwillingness to agree or to share information. When conveying difficult messages, a strategy of indirect, polite and civilized expression, for example by artful framing and camouflaging the message in the form of a rhetorical question, is likely to be face-neutral and non-confrontational, and therefore much more effective when communicated to a person or group likely to have positive face needs.

Professor Ting-Toomey's framework can be used as a guide by negotiators to identify what kind of face factors may be involved in any given dialogue and how they can best be managed.

INTERSECTING STATUS, BELONGING, COMMUNICATION AND FACE

In an article entitled Culture and Its Importance to Mediation (2015), Professor Joel Lee assessed the interplay of power distance, collectivism-individualism, communication and facework in a negotiation context. Professor Lee illustrates how a negotiating party's degrees of power distance (status) and collectivism-individualism (belonging) can help you decide which communication and facework strategies might be most appropriate. A copy of this article is included in Appendix 4.

CULTURE OF RELATIONSHIPS

According to legend, when a pupil asked: *"Master, is there a single word that may serve as a rule of practice for all one's life?"* Confucius replied: *"Is not Reciprocity that word?"* Reciprocity is part of what in China is called 關係. Its pinyin transcription is *guanxi* and is pronounced something like *gwan-shee*. This hugely meaningful term in Chinese, like face, escapes a precise definition. Reciprocity, or mutual obligations, are part of guanxi, but so too is trust, the power of relationships, respect and networks. Guanxi is more a way of life and is therefore a way of business. Non-ethnic Chinese, or *gweilos*, who negotiate contracts with Chinese cultures, are unlikely to develop a state of full guanxi with their partners, but there are elements that foreigners can aspire to achieve over time. Guanxi is a direct manifestation of high-context, reactive, Confucian-based cultures.

Where relationships matter so much that they can make the difference between doing and losing a deal, those from low-context, linear-active, universalist, particularist, egalitarian, confrontational cultures, such as North America and Northern Europe, need to adapt their approach to negotiating. Instead of doing the deal first and forging the relationships later, they need to reverse the order, spending what, to them, may be inefficient hours, days, weeks or longer building the relationships, creating the trust, and establishing a semblance of guanxi before getting down to the deal.

When the deal is done, care should be taken over how it is memorialized in a contract. Pressing the <Print> button to spew out a long, complex, Western-style agreement from a precedent file littered with perceptually pejorative terms like "breach," "damages," "failure to perform," "liability," "dispute" and "insolvency," and insisting on your own law to govern the contract, is likely to scream lack of trust. It can destroy whatever guanxi may have been banked to date.

A simpler Memorandum of Understanding (MoU) or deal sheet, not favoring one side over the other but finely balanced, unlegalistic, and in artfully diplomatic language, may be a much wiser approach, even if it is simply a milestone document and not technically binding. Instead of a boilerplate dispute resolution clause, guanxi can be created by including an Amicable Resolution (avoiding the word "dispute") clause, where each party formally agrees to submit to mediation any "difficulties," "challenges" or "hurdles" that may arise, or failing that, conciliation or arbitration, in order to preserve the relationship. Lawyers are trained to express themselves clearly and completely, but in negotiation, especially in the early phases, ambiguity can sidestep problems cropping up too early to manage conveniently.

Guanxi is not unique to Confucian-based cultures. Several aspects of guanxi are evident in many other cultures. Philotimo in Greek culture is an example. Derived from *filos* (friend) and *timi* (honor), philotimo is the product of the Plato and Aristotle teachings of integrity, virtue, empathy, respect, trust and commitment. Greeks, whether born and raised in their homeland or abroad, instinctively value philotimo characteristics in non-Greeks. Negotiators who are not Greek can develop highly valuable relationships with Greeks by exhibiting philotimos attributions. They will be trusted more quickly and be more able to create a desire in their negotiating partners for a sustainable deal.

ORGANIZATIONAL CULTURE

Like any society, organizations have their own cultures. They do not replace societal cultures but need to be considered by negotiators, both in understanding their own organizational culture, which can easily be taken for granted, and the culture of the other party's organization. The interplay between the organizational cultures needs to be understood in order to appreciate how they can modify and even override the national stereotypical cultural norms and create problems and opportunities in a negotiation.

Geert Hofstede has researched organization cultures.[26] Based on the available data, he devised six autonomous organizational dimensions, and The Hofstede Center added two semi-dependent dimensions:

    Means v. Goals orientated
    (focus on how things are done or on what can be achieved)
    Internally v. Externally driven
    (doing things right or driven by customer needs)
    Easy v. Strict work discipline
    (loose or disciplinarian structure)
    Local v. Professional
    Local (short-term internal focus or long-term external focus)
    Open v. Closed system
    (whether outsiders are included (open) or excluded (closed))
    Employee v. Work orientated
    (degree to which employee interests prevail over work)
    Degree of acceptance of Leadership Style
    (employee alignment with leaders)
    Degree of identification with the organization
    (employee alignment with organization).

The first four of the Hofstede organizational dimensions can be especially helpful to negotiators. They can help us to figure out whether our negotiation partner is likely to have real authority to influence or commit their organization. They can also be helpful in understanding the other party's motivations or behavior. Does, for example, the other party's organization operate a command and control structure that results in a culture of blame or are its employees more likely to be flexible and creative in seeking options for mutual gain because their organization operates within a culture of innovation and experimentation?

Part III of Cultures and Organisations: Software of the Mind (2010) by Hofstede, Hofstede and Minkov is an interesting revelation of many typical, traditional organizational cultures.

In 2006, two professors at the University of Michigan, Kim Cameron and Robert Quinn, developed a quick online psychometric tool called the Organizational Culture Assessment Instrument (OCAI)[27] to enable business and other group cultures to be identified, and, if appropriate, modified. It revolves around four ways of indicating organizational effectiveness, namely clan, adhocracy, hierarchy and market. Going through the analysis can help you better understand your organization and assess what to retain and what to consider changing. However, organizational culture is something you need to work with rather than try to change, as John Weeks, Professor of Leadership and Organizational Behavior at the IMD Business School in Lausanne amply illustrates in Unpopular Culture: The Ritual of Complaint in a British Bank (2004).

BEHAVIOR

Although everybody knows that any two cultures can differ radically in how they interpret acceptable behavior, almost everyone, regardless of culture, finds it difficult to adapt properly. What we each accept as normal, those from other cultures may consider inappropriate or disrespectful. How we are each neurologically constructed, our *cultural software* as Hofstede calls it, can make adaptation a real challenge, even at a relatively superficial level.

Take, for example, the ritual of exchanging business cards. In many Eastern cultures, cards represent not only someone's identity but also their status, and have facework implications. Cards are presented with both hands, with the text orientated towards the receiver, often accompanied by a slight bow, for example in Japan. The card should be received with both hands and perhaps with a reciprocal bow, and be studied carefully and respectfully. If preceding a meeting, it is appropriate for negotiators to lay the cards on the table before them, at least for the initial session.

Most Westerners know all this, but how many negotiators go to the trouble of having the local language translation printed on the reverse of their card, and to present that side to the receiver? This is a mark not just of convenience but, crucially, of respect and sensitivity.

Chapter 4

In each culture, there are many important and seemingly trivial cultural behaviors that need to be respected. Whenever a negotiator is due to interact with someone from an unfamiliar culture, whether at home or abroad, it is important to spend time focusing on their likely cultural behaviors and to be prepared to apply and respond to them.

Ian McDuff, former Professor of Law at the Singapore Management University and now a Teaching Fellow at the Centre for ICT Law at Auckland Law School, related a story in one of his lectures about a Somalian mediator trained in New Zealand. Back in Somalia he used his training to mediate between two rival clans. The first group was asked to tell their story and express their view. Once they finished the mediator said: *"Thank you, I now understand your point of view. Can we hear party B?"* Party B then asked for a break. When they returned, they were armed and angry and threatened to open fire. They felt the mediator had already acknowledged party A's position simply by saying *"I understand."* That language may have worked perfectly well in New Zealand, but was far too explicit in Somalia. He should have rephrased to say something like: *"I hear you."*

Indispensable guides include Roger Axtell's bestselling Gestures: Do's and Taboos Around the World (1991) and his Dos and Taboos of Humour Around the World (1999). Also Kiss, Bow or Shake Hands: Doing Business in More Than 60 Countries (1995) by Terri Morrison and Wayne Conaway, and Building Cultural Competence: Innovative Activities and Models (2012) edited by Darla Deardorff and Kate Berardo.

LANGUAGE

Everyone knows that communicating is a pathway covered by the tripwires of miscomprehension. This applies not only when negotiating parties use a bridge language, or lingua franca, but also when parties share the same mother tongue. All cultures have developed words and expressions that do not mean what they say literally. When George Bernard Shaw reputedly observed that England and America are *two countries separated by a common language*, he was not merely referring to interpretation of words and phrases, but to the cultural drivers that create that result. When communicating, high contexters can be surprisingly direct, and low contexters can use expressions that are astonishingly indirect.

It's amazing how easily people can be misunderstood. The British, for example, although low context and quite direct, can camouflage well:

When the British Say...	*Others Understand...*	*But the British Mean...*
How very interesting	They are intrigued	What a lot of nonsense
With the greatest respect	They hold me in high esteem	You're an idiot
That's not bad	They rather like it	It's awful
We have a few small comments	They agree with most of it	We disagree with most of it

Culture

When the British Say...	Others Understand...	But the British Mean...
That's a bit of a problem	They have a minor issue with it	It's a fundamental problem
Ah, by the way	It's a minor issue	My core demand is...
It has been well drafted	They like my wording	The substance is unacceptable
We're sorry to say that...	They feel a little disappointed	No way. Never. Forget it
It's rather disappointing that...	They feel a little disappointed	We are deeply insulted
I hadn't thought of that...	They like my creativity	It's a non-starter
That's a brave position to take...	They think I'm courageous	It's totally insane
Shall we go for lunch?	They are hungry	This meeting is a waste of time

Theoretically, this comes as a surprise. British culture is so low-context that one might expect from that categorization that the British typically say it how it is. Often they do, but, like all cultures, they do not always conform to the stereotype and can be far more obtuse than people expect. Likewise, high context Asians, for example, who low contexters might expect to communicate in code, can be breathtakingly direct.

Most cultures have similar communication snares. It is important for listeners to ensure they are not misunderstanding words and non-verbal signals by taking them too literally, and to watch and not just listen.

A NEGOTIATOR'S NEGOTIATION CULTURE

There are two basic, even primitive, cultural approaches to the art of negotiation. Some negotiators choose a more hands-on, functional, problem-solving stance, while others naturally project a more open and creative style. The implications of each can be quite dramatically different. That difference between the two suggests, as Warren Bennis has described in On Becoming a Leader (1989), the distinction between a managerial style and a leadership style. Adopting one style or the other can influence how the other party reacts and can therefore define the character of the negotiation process.

Borrowing from Bennis' comparisons of managers and leaders, the contrast in fundamental negotiating cultures can be summarized succinctly:

Functional Culture	Leading Culture
Competent, safe pair of hands	Inspirational
Administers, Maintains	Innovates, Develops
Focus on structure	Focus on outcome
Hesitates to take risks	Seeks sensible risks

Chapter 4

Functional Culture	Leading Culture
Narrow, short-term risks	Wide, long-term view
Asks: How? When?	Asks: What? Why?
Hates the competition	Respects the competition
Eye on bottom line	Eye on horizon
Maintains status quo	Challenges status quo
Follows familiar path	Invents better ways
Protects against blame	Dares to experiment
Addresses problems	Addresses opportunities
Glass half empty	Glass half full
Does things right	Does the right things

Effective negotiators will have the versatility to apply both these cultural perspectives simultaneously, with, generally, the Leading approach more evident to negotiating partners than their Functional competence.

FIRST IMPRESSIONS LAST

In Harry Potter and the Order of the Phoenix (2014), J.K. Rowling expressed what parents have been advising their children for centuries: *A good first impression can work wonders.* We all know this to be true, and it is one of those things that transcends cultures because it is a human, indeed an animal, trait.

A good first impression is particularly crucial in negotiation. Research by Alexander Todorov, a Professor of Psychology at Princeton, indicates that judgments we make after one tenth of a second exposure to someone new, correlate highly with judgments we make about them over a much longer time period. This suggests that initial impressions are not only formed quickly, but also that they endure. While it is impossible to negotiate in milliseconds, the fact remains that the initial contacts, whether in person or electronically, are crucial to a successful outcome.

One of the first impressions that should always be made when negotiating cross-culturally is to convey a genuine appreciation for a negotiating partner's culture. This can normally be done indirectly, but consciously. Consider the impact of the following initial exchange when a Western visitor arrives in Hong Kong to start talks about a new deal:

> Host (smiling): *Welcome to Hong Kong! We are delighted to meet you. You had a comfortable and uneventful journey, hopefully?*
> Visitor (smiling, skating over the fact that the trip over the Pacific was characterized by constant turbulence and a sleepless night): *Well, thank you. I am equally delighted to meet you, too. My flight was very easy indeed as I took the opportunity to travel with Cathay Pacific, which certainly justifies its reputation as one of the best in the world. Thank you so much for*

> *your thoughtfulness in sending a car to meet me on arrival and take me to my hotel, despite the wonderful train service. The taxi line was long with tourists eager to savour the wonders of this amazing city, and it was extremely welcome.*
>
> Host (feeling some pride, but not showing it): *You are most welcome. Hopefully you had time to rest up a little? However good the trip, the jetlag can be tough.*
>
> Visitor (feeling exhausted and aching for some sleep but not showing it): *Yes, thank you, I did. The hotel is excellent and the welcome and service are impeccable. I specially arrived yesterday morning to steal a chance to experience Hong Kong again. Wow, I had a ball immersing myself in the museums...*

What did this simple initial interaction convey? Both parties had the opportunity to engage on a personal level in a dialogue that would have continued, enabling each to get the measure of the other. Politeness prevailed, negativity was absent. The Westerner will have picked up the vibe of Asian hospitality and genuine concern for welfare. The host will have read the foreigner's interest in local culture and positive reaction to the flag-carrying airline. Each party will have begun their relationship giving some face to the other, opening up a little on a personal level. Those initial minutes are confirming their immediate tenth-of-a-second impressions.

The significance extends deeper. Low contexters, such as Westerners, negotiating in high context societies, must avoid the mistake of getting down to business too quickly, and allow time for a level of familiarity, comfort, trust and respect to be generated. It would not be unusual for this process to last for hours, even, possibly, several days. It is a cardinal error for a Westerner to broach the business at hand before the other party signals their readiness to do so. It would be a mistake to pull papers from a bag, or draw a pen, displaying impatience to get down to business, and important to feel very comfortable with purely contextual exchanges for a much longer period than the customary five-minute exchange of pleasantries that might be the norm with people sharing common cultural credentials. The early investment of time applied to relationship-building is fundamental in such cross-cultural negotiations, and will pay major dividends at a later stage. More haste, less speed.

A WORD OF WARNING

All culturologists emphasize that their dimensions are guidelines, no more and no less. Many people and groups do not conform to the stereotypes in some situations, and sometimes hardly at all. Professor Joel Lee, for example, warns:

> *Generalizations are useful in that they give us shortcuts through which we can more easily navigate in our world. However, the sin is to forget that they are generalizations, and that the map is not the territory.*

Chapter 4

Organizational cultures can also complicate expectations, resulting insignificant diversions from theoretical norms. To be forewarned is to be forearmed.

IN A NUTSHELL

- Never negotiate monoculturally when dealing with people from other cultural backgrounds, including those who may share your nationality.
- Know the main cultural dimensions to sharpen awareness of where other cultures typically fit in relation to your own, and how that interaction may change the way negotiations work.
- The Lewis diagrams and the Meyer Culture Map help negotiating teams to focus on the differences and similarities that are likely to be encountered, but there may be exceptions and deviations from the norm.
- Understand the principles of guanxi and face and build them into negotiating style and processes.

CHAPTER 5
Leverage

You can get further with a kind word and a gun

than you can with a kind word alone

Al Capone

Canadian Professor Laurence J. Peter, author of The Peter Principle in 1968, likened competence to truth, beauty and contact lenses, as all are in the eye of the beholder. He could just as easily have said the same about leverage. You only ever have true leverage when the other party thinks your negotiating power exceeds theirs. It's not what you think that matters, it's what the other party perceives.

Regardless of negotiating skills, few things have a greater influence over the outcome of a negotiation than leverage. The right leverage, skillfully deployed, enables you to persuade someone to accept or act in a way they might not otherwise agree or do. Badly executed leverage forces you into too much compromise. Absence of leverage results in capitulation.

Just as Sun Tzu revealed that the art of war is the art of deception, so the art of negotiation is the art of perception. Leverage can be used, misused or wasted. It can be gained, improved, concealed, exaggerated, marketed, weakened, lost and destroyed. It can also be real, obvious, invisible, assumed, debatable and even imaginary. How the parties use and perceive their own and the other party's leverage are the key factors. Leverage is more than the actual strength of your position or argument compared to that of the other party. Leverage is highly susceptible to circumstances and attitudes, and can change in a flash. Keeping leverage under constant review throughout a negotiation, and how you use your own leverage and deal with the other party's, will influence the outcome.

Chapter 5

LEVERAGE DEFINED

Leverage can come in so many forms that it is hard to construct anything more than a generalized definition. In The Art of the Deal (1989), Donald Trump wrote: *Leverage is having something the other guy wants, or better yet needs, or best of all simply cannot do without...[but] that isn't always the case, which is why leverage often requires imagination and salesmanship. In other words, you have to convince the other guy it's in his interest to make the deal.*

G. Richard Shell is Professor of Legal Studies and Business Ethics and Management at the University of Pennsylvania's Wharton School. His book, Bargaining for Advantage: Negotiation Strategies for Reasonable People (2001, 2006) includes a useful test for leverage: *Ask yourself...which party has the most to lose from no deal. The party with the most to lose has the least leverage; the party with the least to lose has the most leverage; and both parties have roughly equal leverage when they both stand to lose equivalent amounts should the deal fall through.*

Professor Shell groups leverage into three types, which he calls positive, negative and normative. Positive leverage is when one party is able to deliver something another party wants or needs. Negative leverage is where one party can threaten another party with consequences they would not want. Normative leverage is related to anchors, such as standards, precedents, facts or authorities that another party would find difficult to deny. Of the three, negative leverage is the trickiest and riskiest. But all three can be strengthened or weakened by attitudinal, financial, egoistical and emotional factors, and by status quo, time, publicity and context.

Roger Volkema, Emeritus Associate Professor of Management at the Kogod Business School at the American University in Washington DC is the author of Leverage: How To Get It & How To Keep It In Any Negotiation (2006). It is an insightful and readable analysis of negotiation leverage. Professor Volkema categorizes leverage in four ways: Active, Blind, Potential and Unknown. Active leverage is where all the parties are aware of the leverage, though they may not perceive its consequences in quite the same way. Blind leverage is where the party with the leverage is unaware of it, but the burdened party is fully aware. Potential leverage is the opposite of Blind leverage; the burdened party is unaware of it but the party that has it knows it. Unknown leverage is leverage that exists, but that none of the parties are yet aware it exists.

Both of these basic ways of thinking about leverage are valid. Classifying leverage is not just an academic exercise but enables us to make better decisions on the quality and consequences of each party's relative negotiating strength and to determine whether stronger leverage is needed. The classifications help you to consider how to boost your own leverage. They also emphasize that one way to strengthen your leverage is by finding ways to weaken the other party's, for example by casting credible doubt on their arguments, positions, options or other circumstances they have taken for granted.

UNDERSTANDING LEVERAGE

Your earliest memories can be the most impactful, unforgettable and formative. I was fortunate enough to experience the power of all three of Professor Shell's leverage types and all four of Professor Volkema's, in a single negotiation very early in my career, though I did not fully realize it at the time.

While a student, I was on a temporary internship in the small regional legal department of an international technology company. The event that occurred while I was there taught me several things at once: you never have no leverage in a negotiation (otherwise there would be no negotiation to be had); that you can increase your leverage with thought and creativity by improving your position and by weakening the other party's; that timing is everything; and that ethical standards are not just the interpretation of written words in formal codes but something you live and breathe.

The following facts are true, though to save the blushes of certain people in case they are still living, I have masked a few irrelevant details.

My employer was plaintiff in a pending patent case in an appeal court in a European country. The defendant was a prominent local competitor in that market and regionally. The competitor had been producing and marketing a product using our patent without a licence. We had, several years earlier, sued for an injunction and damages. The competitor's defense was that our patent was invalid because its claims were not novel, and therefore there was no infringement. The Court had appointed an independent expert, a professor at a leading local university, to advise on whether our patent disclosed a novel invention and therefore whether we had a valid and enforceable patent.

After months of inaction, and just as my internship began, our corporate counsel responsible for the case received a phone call from the external lawyer. He announced the good news that the Court-appointed expert had contacted him to say that he had written his opinion, would file it with the Court by the end of the month, and that the opinion confirmed the validity of our patent. The internal lawyer rejoiced out loud. We all heard a scream of *"Yippeee"* echoing in the corridor. The company needed the injunction to protect its market, to recover damages to compensate for lost profits, and to warn off anyone thinking about infringing the patent in the future. The expert's opinion would enable the Court to rule in our favor.

When the reaction subsided, the external lawyer calmly continued. He agreed it was great news, the result of much hard work advocating complex technical details. Unapologetically, he explained that in his jurisdiction, Court experts and academic staff were paid very little; that in litigation, many experts relied on disputing parties to make up the difference between the small fixed scale fees laid down by law for Court experts and the real costs of their time and expertise at normal commercial rates. The judges all knew this, and turned a blind eye. It was an unofficial subsidy system. He said that, in this case, the difference amounted to the equivalent of about USD 30,000 (in today's money). Before my speechless colleague could utter a word, the external lawyer, as if

Chapter 5

reading his mind, reassuringly added that it was not a bribe to influence the opinion because it had already been written, though he acknowledged that it had yet to be formally submitted to the Court. On the mechanics of payment, the lawyer proposed that he would add USD 30,000 for his rendered services, and that he would then settle up with the Court-appointed expert.

The internal counsel, wisely or because he was too stunned, did not react, other than to ask a few questions, and told the lawyer we would call him back the following day. The lawyer urged us not to delay. Time, he said, was of the essence.

The legal department was small – the regional GC and two legal managers (and, for the next few weeks, one rather green summer intern). We gathered together, with me joining them to take notes for the record. The seasoned GC took it in his stride, but he was visibly angry. I remember he stood up, paced the room and said something like: *We are being held to ransom. We have two options, both completely unacceptable. Either we pay what must be interpreted as a thinly-disguised bribe, violate our Code of Conduct and win the case, or we refuse to play ball, in which case the expert will no doubt reverse his opinion, get paid by the local defendant, and we will lose the case to corruption. We need a third option, one that gives us the ability to handle this situation effectively from both legal and ethical standpoints. Suggestions?*

One of the internal counsel thought we should instruct our external lawyer to report his conversation with the expert to the Court in writing. The GC predicted that this would not work because, as the external lawyer had already pointed out, and it was probably true, this was common practice in the jurisdiction in question, and as the lawyer had almost certainly facilitated this kind of thing before, he would never expose himself and others to scrutiny by going public. In any case, there was no evidence, and he would certainly not be inclined to trigger a major public incident with one of the country's leading academics, compromising his personal standing and practice.

The other legal manager, thinking aloud, wondered if we could just go public with the story at our own initiative and denounce the judicial system as corrupt. Having spoken the words, she immediately admitted that, in the absence of any proof to counter the inevitable howl of denial (including from our own local operating company), this would lead nowhere but embarrassment. It could also prejudice our other cases before the Courts.

Then she came up with another idea for generating leverage. She suggested telling the external lawyer to contact the professor and say we were surprised to receive this request, and wanted to send a representative to meet him, alone, to discuss the matter, without indicating whether we would accept the demand or not. The representative would capture the conversation with the expert using a concealed recording device, which had just come onto the market, and hopefully the demand would be caught on tape. The recording would be our leverage to ask the expert to submit his opinion to the Court without any payment being made. Cloak and dagger. As a rookie, I loved it and remember sitting on the edge of my chair, transfixed.

The GC liked the essence of the idea and asked for the risks to be weighed up. What if the external lawyer refused to play ball and declined to set up a meeting with the expert because he would lose direct control over the matter? What if he paid the professor anyway and just invisibly loaded future fees to claw back the cost? What if the nascent recording machine let out a whine of static or some other give-away noises at an inopportune moment? What if the tape or battery ran out early? What if the expert changed his opinion as a recriminatory act? What if...?

Each of the problems was analyzed. In the end, the GC thought the idea was the best anyone could come up with, and that the risks were more or less manageable, certainly better than the consequences of doing nothing, which was the only other viable option. However, he said it was not appropriate to allow the expert to retain his appointment and issue his opinion to the Court. His integrity had now been compromised as his opinion may well have been influenced by the prospect of earning money, and he might twist the facts to allege undue influence by us over the outcome. We could expose ourselves to blackmail. After a long discussion, the GC gave the go-ahead, but on five conditions.

First, the goal of the exercise must be to restore due process in the litigation by creating the leverage to persuade the Court expert to resign his appointment, using whatever reasons he wished, such as the complexity of the issues, and to recommend to the Court that a panel of three experts, one of whom should be from a university in another European country, be appointed in his stead.

Second, we verify that making an undisclosed recording of a conversation would not violate any laws, local or otherwise. If it turned out to be technically illegal, the next best alternative would be to send two representatives for corroboration purposes, though it would still then be our word against the expert's, and much weaker leverage.

Third, that our external counsel should not be told that the conversation would be recorded, or the real purpose of the meeting with the expert.

Fourth, that our representative should not negotiate with the Court expert, but merely ask him to repeat the conversation with our lawyer, and then return to base so that we could all hear the recording and decide how and when to deploy the next step.

Finally, the representative should be a respected outside security consultant, someone professionally able both to handle the conversation and to make the recording. It was agreed that he or she would be given a temporary position in the company's Finance team in case the lawyer or expert ran a credential check. I was asked to write up the meeting notes immediately.

I remember my heart was pounding with excitement.

A phone call to an external lawyer in another firm quickly confirmed that undisclosed recordings were not illegal in that jurisdiction, though it was unclear whether the Courts would accept taped evidence. As we would not need the recording in Court proceedings, this was not a major concern. An experienced security consultant was engaged and accepted her brief.

Chapter 5

The external lawyer was contacted and told that we wanted a representative to meet the professor alone. He rejected this idea initially, saying that it would breach protocol. However, he admitted it was not illegal if the representative did not attempt to influence the substance of the expert's opinion. We instructed him to comply. He agreed to set up an appointment for our representative to meet the professor. We gave the lawyer the name of a person in our Accounts department, and it was agreed she would meet the professor outside a well-known city landmark on a certain day and time and they could decide where to go and talk.

They met as arranged. Once seated comfortably in a booth at the far end of a busy family restaurant, our representative charmingly began by saying she had been dropped into the matter with little background, and would be very grateful if the professor could please explain, from the beginning. The professor obliged, detailing his role at the University, his occasional advisory work for Courts, tribunals, the government and international agencies, and leading up to the patent infringement case. He produced, but did not hand over, some papers that he identified as his expert opinion that would be filed with the Court shortly. He said it represented several weeks' intensive research and his professional charge would have been the present day equivalent of USD 20,500. He asked to receive this amount in cash. Our representative asked a few questions, such as whether he meant USD 30,000 (to which the professor confirmed he did not) and said she would report back and someone would be in contact in a few days.

Back in the office, we listened to the recording, and made a transcript. It was not perfect, as some early parts of the conversation were drowned out by the clanking of cutlery, nearby laughter and the general background noise of a busy eating place, but it was easily good enough to understand the entire story, how much fee was requested, by whom and why.

My colleague called our external lawyer, who had already left us several anxious messages. He explained that our representative had recorded the conversation, and that Company policy excluded involvement in this kind of unethical practice, however common it may be. He told the lawyer that we wanted him to contact the professor in person, explain that the conversation in the restaurant was on tape, and say that under no circumstances would we make any payment, however small. External counsel was told to advise the professor to resign his appointment as Court expert in the case and suggest that the Court consider recommending that a panel of three qualified experts, one a foreign expert, be appointed in his place having regard to the technical complexity. We asked the lawyer to do this immediately. No overt threats were made of what might happen if the professor did not act appropriately. This was left to the external counsel's imagination. There was also no mention of the amount the expert had requested, and how this differed from the number given to the Company by the lawyer. External counsel was deeply unhappy, probably enraged, but he had no option but to do as his client had instructed. He complied.

Days later, the professor duly tendered his resignation from the case. After my internship ended, I learned that three experts were appointed by the Court. A year or so after that, the new expert panel came to the conclusion that the patent was valid, and eventually the Court ruled in the Company's favor.

The Company handled the situation with its external counsel deftly. Without saying they knew that he had inflated the sum requested by the expert, the Company suggested that he might like to make a USD 30,000 donation, in his own name, to a local anti-corruption charity that the Company identified, and to send the Company a copy of the cleared cheque. The Company transferred all its legal work to another firm.

As this case demonstrated, the balance of leverage is a highly dynamic phenomenon that can quickly tip one way or another during a negotiation. Leverage assessments must therefore be made continuously as more and new information comes to hand.

The case also illustrated the perception factor. No warnings or threats were needed, no arm twisting took place. Just enough information to trigger a reappraisal by the other party. Sometimes your strongest points are those you never have to express.

Decades later, I could finally extract the lessons this experience taught me in negotiation terms, with the benefit of the thinking expressed by Professors Shell, Volkema and other negotiation gurus.

Positive leverage/Active leverage: The expert thought he could deliver the key thing the Company needed, a favorable opinion on the patent's validity, and that this carried a value that the Company would pay for. Both parties knew this, even though they perceived the leverage in very different ways. This positive/active leverage drained away from the expert the instant he learned the Company had recorded the conversation. The expert presumably realized he could have lost his Chair, reputation and other things if the tape ever became public.

Negative leverage: The Company built itself into a defensive position where it could more than counter the expert's positive leverage by being able to disparage the expert publicly if necessary.

Normative leverage: Clearly, as evidenced by the expert's insistence on a cash payment, the Company had the leverage that such a payment, if made, would be illegal. Of course, this cut both ways as it would have been illegal both for the expert to receive a bribe and for the Company to have paid one. The balance of risk, however, was not on the expert's side because it was illegal even to ask for a bribe, though he evidently reckoned, wrongly as it turned out, that since the demand was made in a phone call to a respected local lawyer, and such demands were common practice, there was no way he could be found out.

Blind leverage: The Company initially had blind leverage over its external lawyer in this situation. The lawyer was fully aware that he had inflated the demand made by the expert by USD 9,500, which was unethical, but at the time he evidently assumed that there was no way the Company could ever discover it. The Company was blind to its leverage until its representative met the expert and learned the true level of the expert's demand, when it instantly turned into powerful active leverage.

Chapter 5

Potential leverage: At the moment the Company listened to the tape, the internal counsel knew they had potential leverage over both the expert and the external counsel. The next question was how best to convert it into active leverage by making the other party, or parties in this case, aware of the leverage and to perceive it in the way intended.

Unknown leverage: From the moment that the representative conducted her lunchtime conversation with the expert until, a day later, when the internal counsel listened to the tape, the leverage was unknown. It was short-lived in this case, quickly turning into positive/active leverage, but information in the hands of one or both parties, and the ability to know how to use that information, is what converts unknown leverage into something useful.

INCREASING LEVERAGE BY ALTERING PERCEPTIONS

All this goes to show that leverage is multi-dimensional and perception-based. You can increase your leverage simply by changing how the other party views it. You may be able to do this directly or indirectly. Sometimes the indirect approach can be the most effective. There can be several or numerous fulcrums of leverage and they can change over time as new information comes to light and fresh events occur. Leverage can be a seesaw, and also an illusion.

Reactive devaluation happens when people ascribe less significance and value to something that favors the other party more than themselves, or even anything that originates from the other party. The other side of that coin is that we naturally tend to overvalue anything that favors our own wants and needs or that originates from ourselves. Instinctive bias, either way, can easily result in unrealistic and dangerous miscalculations.

Negotiators need to begin by reality-testing their perceptions about their own leverage. You need to assume that, just as you are naturally inclined to exaggerate the significance and value of your leverage, and downplay that of the other party, so the other party will most likely be doing the same thing in reverse. You may need to reassess your leverage more realistically, and then find ways to make the other party re-evaluate theirs.

The perception problem is particularly acute with lawyers and legal arguments. Legal training and practice is directed at improving your own arguments while contradicting and weakening those of the other party. Litigation and arbitration are entirely based on primitive win-lose strategies. Where legal opinion and argument represents a major element of the leverage, parties can very easily get stuck in the delusional rut of believing their own hype. The late David Shapiro, a hard-nosed New York litigator-turned-mediator used to say: *Parties come to me in love with their legal case; my job, as a mediator, is to break up that romance.*

ATNAS

Your ATNAs are your *Alternatives To a Negotiated Agreement*. Since the concept came to wide public attention following publication of Getting To Yes by Professors Roger Fisher and William Ury in 1981, experts commonly advise negotiators to know their "Best Alternative to a Negotiated Agreement" or BATNA. This helps determine not only the value of the deal to you but also the point at which you are better off walking away from a negotiation and pursuing other options. Knowing your, and figuring out the other party's, alternatives to a deal enables you to consider carefully the interplay of everyone's needs and interests, many of which may be undisclosed. Unlike wants and positions, which are usually disclosed and exaggerated, needs and interests may well be less apparent and implicit. You often need to be good at spadework to unearth them.

BATNAs need to be kept in perspective. A frequent error made in defining a BATNA is to idealize it as the best theoretical, or best possible, alternative. Negotiators tend to fall into an overly optimistic trap when configuring their BATNA. An ideal BATNA may be a great aspirational target, and may be achievable, but it may depend on any number of variables and involve genuine risks. In practice, such a BATNA may be an unlikely scenario. You need to strive for it, but will you consider you have failed if you walk away from your negotiation and are then unable to realize your BATNA?

To put your BATNA into perspective, it helps to consider your WATNA, or Worst Alternative To a Negotiated Agreement. Your WATNA or disaster scenario, helps you to focus on how badly you need the deal, which in turn helps determine leverage. What is the most unfavorable thing that could happen if your deal fails to materialize? What is the cost or consequence of not doing this deal? How likely is that possibility? What are the relative prospects of the BATNA as opposed to the WATNA? If you weigh the risks of achieving your BATNA against those of ending up with your WATNA, you are likely to focus somewhere in between the two with a more *realistic* ATNA, or RATNA. This does not mean that you should limit yourself to your RATNA, but at least it would define what currently would be an acceptable agreement.

Once you have carried out the BATNA-WATNA-RATNA exercise for yourself, it is important to repeat it, hypothetically, wearing the shoes of the other party. Because you are unlikely to know all the facts that they are weighing up, there are real dangers in relying too heavily on your ATNA analysis from their perspective. They may have a smoking gun that they are carefully camouflaging. Or they may have an Ace of Spades they have yet to reveal. Nonetheless, keeping these things in mind, constantly thinking about the other party's situation as well as your own, helps you perceive everyone's leverage more accurately and to appreciate the interplay of bargaining power between the parties.

The ATNA analysis is one that needs to be kept under constant, sometimes daily or even hourly, review. New information and perceptions usually emerge during the negotiation. They can come from the other party, your own constituency, or from outside sources and circumstances. They can radically change the ATNA assessments for better or worse. Also, new and unpredictable ideas may be expressed that might change the structure or complexion of the prospective deal, meaning that the ATNAs could be very different from how you originally conceived them.

Flexibility is the watchword of ATNAs.

ZOPA

The ZOPA is the Zone Of Potential Agreement. An ATNA analysis may also do something else. It can help you work out an approximate, and possibly even an accurate, ZOPA, based on each party's needs and interests. A ZOPA that emerges from the interplay of the superficial positions the parties have taken, and what they say they want, is likely to be theoretical and illusory, so it needs to be based more on interests. A negotiation's ZOPA defines the approximate perimeter of the real negotiation field and the area where leverage can be applied.

In so-called distributive negotiations, where there is a fixed pie to be divided between the parties, usually over money or money's worth, there may be a very small ZOPA and possibly none at all. In such zero-sum-gain negotiations, parties are unwilling to disclose much information to the other and the negotiation is typically very positional and orientated towards respective "wants." Anchors and alternatives become especially important, and are often the subject of discussion in a negotiation dance routine. It can be hard to establish how much each party is willing to give, and wishes to take, and whether there is a crossover between the parties' needs that would represent the ZOPA.

Integrative negotiations are very different. A negotiation is integrative when the situation offers a range of potential options for mutual gain, and by coinciding those options, the parties can benefit more than if they did not do a deal. Those benefits are not necessarily financially orientated. For example, one or all parties may need to save face, or create a precedent or not risk an adverse one, or secure an apology, promise, change of conduct or some other non-monetary benefit. Integrative negotiations offer more scope for creativity, and the ZOPA may be easier to establish, or guess at, and may also be broader, than in purely distributive situations.

If a ZOPA can be worked out, the parties can make maximum use of their leverage. Where the ZOPA is unknown, or a wild guess, it is often much harder to estimate whether, when and how best to use leverage. Negotiations outside the ZOPA range, or in the absence of a ZOPA range, become much more tactical and opportunistic. To progress into a ZOPA range, you need to ask questions and be prepared to give some information in return so that the other party can also perceive a ZOPA. As more information is shared, the ZOPA becomes more concrete to all parties, and the outcome moves closer.

A good way to define a negotiation's ZOPA, aside from the obvious technique of asking as many questions as possible, is to search for areas of common ground or resolve peripheral differences (so-called low-hanging fruit) that reduce the breadth of likely disagreement. Picking low hanging fruit simplifies the negotiation. It is normally possible to agree on issues of secondary or marginal importance conditional on striking an agreement on the core issues, so they sit on the shelf as prizes if the main deal can be cut. The ZOPA gradually emerges from the fog of negotiation confusion and leverage comes into sharper focus. Finding areas of common ground also builds a psychological momentum for agreement, improves the parties' relationship and encourages the mutual drive for consensus on the major matters under discussion.

There are two different types of ZOPA: theoretical and actual, and two forms of each: declared and latent.

Theoretical ZOPAs are constructed from bargaining positions. A seller may ask for 10,000 and the buyer may offer 5,000. These are the theoretical upper and lower limits of the ZOPA. If a deal is to be made, it is more than likely to be inside this range.

Actual ZOPAs are the intersection range between what each party is willing to agree. So if a seller is willing to accept 6,000 and the buyer is willing to pay 7,000, the actual ZOPA is the intersection between the two, which has a ZOPA range of 1,000. Unlike theoretical ZOPAs, where each party is likely to be aware of the other's ZOPA limit, actual ZOPAs are usually undeclared, or latent, until the last moment. But the other party's actual ZOPA limit can be guessed at, or can be made conditional on other points.

The theoretical ZOPA determines the outer limits of the negotiation. Leverage comes into its own to move the theoretical ZOPA towards the actual ZOPA.

In Good For You, Great For Me: Finding the Trading Zone and Winning at Win-Win Negotiation (2014), Professor Lawrence Susskind of MIT surveys many effective techniques negotiators can use to steer the other party into their ideal ZOPA range, or what he calls your "trading zone."

ANCHORS

Reference points, commonly called anchors, are used in negotiations to influence responses to arguments, positions, demands and refusals. When deployed shrewdly, the "anchor effect" is an important and special kind of leverage. Laboratory and real world studies illustrate that the anchoring effect can be subconscious. Many people deny being influenced by anchors because they often do not realize the psychology behind their response, as explained in Chapter 3. It is similar to the subliminal effect of offers, positioning and packaging played out daily to influence buying decisions in supermarkets, car showrooms and many other environments. You just don't consciously realize you are being anchored in the art of persuasion.

For example, urinals in the male restrooms at Amsterdam's Schiphol airport have a decal of a realistic-looking fly located near the drain holes. Practicality, liberality and frugality being hallmarks of Dutch culture, the fly is not modern art, but is there for a good reason: to reduce cleaning costs. Research shows that men instinctively, and with astonishing accuracy, pee on anything that might wash away. Locating a fly in the

Chapter 5

deepest part of the bowl dramatically minimizes splashback. The Schiphol urinal fly is a physical anchor. Its presence configures people's behavior, usually without them realizing they are being influenced.

Nobel Prize winner Daniel Kahneman, Emeritus Professor of Psychology at Princeton, developed theories about why and how we use anchors in decision making. His best-seller Thinking Fast and Slow (2011) referred to in Chapter 3, describes research that indicates the anchoring effect. One experiment[28] was conducted by researchers at the University of Arizona in 1987. Two groups of experienced real estate brokers were invited to review the sales particulars of a house that was already on the market in Tucson, Arizona that had been professionally appraised at a value of USD 74,900. The ten-page sale particulars given to both groups were identical except for one thing: the USD 74,900 appraisal value. The particulars given to Group A mentioned that the appraised value was USD 65,900 while the particulars given to Group B indicated that the figure was USD 83,900.

The participants in both groups were asked to visit the house armed with the detailed particulars, and then complete a form indicating how they would assess the value of the house, the correct listing price, the likely purchase price and the lowest acceptable offer the seller should consider.

When asked later, the participants in both groups, having an average experience of over five years in real estate valuation in the Tucson area, were emphatic that the appraisal figure they had been given had no effect whatsoever on their valuations. However, the results indicated otherwise. Group A valued the house much lower than Group B, and the ratio of the two differences, the "anchoring index," was substantial at 41%. Professor Kahneman concluded that the only possible explanation for the valuation differences between the two groups was the anchoring effect of the declared appraisal value.

Anchors offer maximum leverage when they can be substantiated, justified or credibly explained. You have a work of art that you want to sell for at least 100,000, so you make an appointment with a dealer. After examining the item, the dealer asks your price. You say that you bought it at an auction ten years earlier at a cost of 90,000, producing a copy of the bill of sale, and adding that market appetite for this genre of antique has not decreased over that time, but if anything may have increased. You state your price as 100,000. By making the first offer supported by a credible explanation and showing the receipt, you have dropped a viable anchor. Assuming the dealer is interested in the work and would acknowledge that the market has not declined in ten years, you are more likely to get an offer closer to your 100,000 than if you did not substantiate the historic market value, or if you waited for the dealer to make an offer using a buyer's anchor.

Because people are likely to be influenced by believable anchors, they can be important leverage tools. Conversely, if your anchor is arbitrary, subjective or excessive, it is less likely to be taken seriously. Your bluff may be called, or the other party may walk away or ask you to make a new offer that is more reasonable, or may put forward their own counter-anchor supported by a rationale. Whatever, an unreasonable or unsupportable anchor, like no anchor at all, enables the other party to steal the leverage initiative. Bargaining on the basis of another party's anchor, or surrendering any part of your leverage, generally weakens your position.

First offer strategy is addressed by Professors Margaret Neale and Thomas Lys in Getting More of What You Want: How the Secrets of Economics and Psychology can Help you Negotiate Anything in Business and Life (2015). They point out that when you make the first offer, you are invariably being aspirational and delivering an optimistic assessment of the possible outcome. But the party receiving the first offer is focusing in the opposite direction, on their reserve position, that is, the lowest offer they would consider accepting. If you drop the first anchor by making the first offer, you focus the other party away from their floor and onto your ceiling.

If, in a price or value-driven negotiation, you kick off first with an anchor, you will set one of the limits for the theoretical ZOPA, and, if it is a credible proposition, you are likely to provoke a response from the other party that will establish the other ZOPA limit. Their theoretical ZOPA limit is likely to be closer to yours than if you had waited and allowed them to drop the first anchor.

That can also lead to deadlock, however. Then the course of the negotiation is likely to be influenced by which anchor is the more credible, and how that credibility can be manifested.

In the early 1980s, I was a member of a small corporate negotiation team that met with representatives of the revolutionary Iranian Government. The meeting took place in Austria, and at the insistence of the Iranians the location was their Consulate in Vienna. I recall the magnificent tall ceiling, silk wallpaper and a huge portrait of Grand Ayatollah Khomeini surveying the French-polished antique table with a steely gaze. The aim of the negotiation was to resolve a case that my employer had filed with the Iran-US Claims Tribunal in The Hague, established in 1981 in the wake of the Hostage Crisis in 1980 and the seizure of Iranian assets, to recover the value of our expropriated Iranian operating company.

As the meeting was taking place on territory of the Revolutionary Government of Iran, we were cordially invited to present our arguments first. We began with an anchor, a copy of an audit report of our Tehran subsidiary's operations that had been routinely prepared during the final months of our ownership by one of the large international accounting firms. The audit had assessed the net worth of the subsidiary at X million, and on top of that we claimed loss of the net present value of future income from the subsidiary's operations. The Iranian negotiators politely and impassionately listened to our explanation, but did not open the audit report, which lay untouched before them on the table. When we had finished, the lead Iranian negotiator, with some ceremony, discarded his unopened copy of our audit, and passed to us a document in Persian that he said was an audit by the Ministry of Finance of the Revolutionary Government. He simply remarked that this audit, carried out more recently, indicated that our former subsidiary that the Government had since "inherited" had a negative net worth of Y,

Chapter 5

and that we should be the ones providing compensation by having the temerity of leaving the Iranian Republic with a costly liability.

Unsurprisingly, the negotiation on that day did not progress. Sometime later, the case settled close to our audit-backed claim because we had the more credible BATNA, which was to pursue our claim in the Tribunal in The Hague. Anchors that lack the force of credibility, or are less robust than those presented by the other party, generally weaken your position.

For that reason, many negotiation specialists point to a natural human reluctance to "shoot first." For example, in their book, The First Move: A Negotiators Companion (2010), Professors Alain Lempereur and Aurélien Colson suggest that most people prefer not to be the first to drop an anchor. They give two risk-related reasons for this. First, the danger of being overly optimistic and therefore appearing unreasonable to the other party. Second, the opposite, by being overly pessimistic and having their proposal snapped up by the other party, leaving potential value on the table. By encouraging the other party to be first to drop an anchor, so the argument goes, there is at least a prospect that you may be pleasantly surprised and able to react accordingly. If all parties feel this way about anchoring, and no one is willing to anchor first, a standoff ensues.

Although this instinctive hesitation to drop the first anchor is explainable, it is risk-averse, and you need confidence to overcome it. My rule is that negotiators should generally try to anchor as soon as they have gathered sufficient information to enable them to state a claim that is as far above their WATNA as it is possible to get while retaining genuine credibility for their anchored claim. This emphasizes the importance of pre-negotiation preparation in order to greatly reduce the first-to-anchor risks, and secure the leverage and persuasive benefit of getting the other party to negotiate from your anchor, not theirs.

Where the other party beats you to it, and drops an anchor that is nowhere near your own perception of reasonableness, think fast how to respond. You could challenge them to justify their anchor, but that can cause them to entrench and become unwilling to move away from it, which can lead to deadlock. Another response is immediately to table your best possible anchor and explain your justification for it, stimulating a discussion on your rationale rather than theirs. Alternatively, change the subject and move the discussion away from the unreasonable anchor.

IN A NUTSHELL

- Leverage is a perceptive phenomenon. Neuroscience and psychology play a very important role. You can increase your leverage simply by influencing how the other party sees it in the context of how they see their own.
- Understand the different types of leverage to enable you to analyze more effectively the relative bargaining strengths of the parties.
- Be aware of reactive devaluation. Engage in reality-testing.

- Work out your ATNAs, not just your BATNA but also your WATNA and above all your RATNA.
- Focus on the ZOPA. Seek information to establish the ZOPA as accurately as possible.
- Keep your analysis of leverage, including ATNAs and ZOPA, under constant review.
- Develop credible anchors. Use them as needed.
- Identify your potential leverage in how you can satisfy the other party's needs and assess the best way and time to use it.

Chapter 6
Communicating

> *The single biggest problem in communication*
>
> *is the illusion that it has taken place*
>
> George Bernard Shaw

Sometime around 60AD, Seneca explained that the meaning of communication is *to understand as well as to be understood*. Stephen Covey, in his best-seller The 7 Habits of Highly Effective People (1989), emphasized the sequence. The Fifth Habit is: *seek first to understand, then to be understood*.

Communication is double-sided. You communicate not only when you speak or write but when you hear and interpret what is not said or written and how you behave in response. Communication is passive and active. Passive communication is gathering information by listening and comprehending, often through open questioning. Active communication is about conveying information and ideas by word, behaviour and action.

Negotiation and communication are inseparably intertwined. The quality of a negotiation is directly related to the quality of the spoken, written and non-verbal communication flow. A great negotiation depends on great dialogue. Negotiations also do not just happen face-to-face; a lot of professional negotiating is done by email and other e-communication media, frameworks that offer different opportunities and pitfalls from traditional face-to-face negotiating. Let's first focus on face-to-face negotiating, and then explore how e-communication changes the frame.

NEGOTIATION PLATFORM

Where interactions have been bad during the build-up to formal negotiations that are likely to be difficult, take the initiative to press the communications reset button. Perhaps the purpose of the negotiation is to try and settle a conflict, or colleagues or external counsel have been fencing with the other party, or tensions are running high for some other reason. Even where the negotiating parties have no relationship history prior to negotiating, it is critical to kick off with good communications and to set up an appropriate and positive negotiation platform.

Most successful negotiations require a bedrock of patience, respect, decency, politeness and courtesy, at least on a superficial level, even where the parties are deadlocked or in conflict, and even when some participants are cantankerous or objectionable. Your behavior to repair or reinstate any of those missing elements, for example through small acts of unexpected thoughtfulness, can work wonders, provided your motives are not misinterpreted. The effect can be particularly dramatic if you are likely to surprise the other party. For example, simple gestures like arranging for a chauffeur to collect the party from the airport for transfer to their hotel sends a welcome signal. Try planning the timing of the negotiation in such a way that you can first invite the other party to dinner or lunch to generate a positive interaction. There are numerous ways to create communication platforms, but they need deliberate and thoughtful effort.

Building a negotiation platform in whatever way is appropriate to the circumstances does something else. In a subtle way, your initiative gives you an element of authority and control that does not threaten the other party. On the contrary, they are likely to appreciate it.

KICKING OFF

Allow time for banter and socializing. It may seem like lost time to low contexters, but is never wasted as it helps to build rapport. Never express impatience or frustration at this point. Wait for the other party to indicate when they are ready to start negotiating more formally. Their reticence may be cultural and their desire to assess and bond may be strong.

Having clear negotiation goals is always essential, even if the intention is merely to engage in negotiations about negotiations. An agenda agreed in advance can be a hindrance as well as a help, depending on the situation.

The advice offered by some negotiation specialists is mono-cultural. As discussed in Chapter 4, some cultures are naturally uncomfortable with rigidity and may feel they are being railroaded when the other party proposes an agenda or moves too quickly. Most cultures feel less threatened by a common general goal, especially when it is expressed in aspirational terms. Consider the possible cultural implications when planning negotiations.

Where an agenda is likely to be helpful and well-received, take care to phrase it in objective terms and resist language, order and implications that are loaded or imply bias. Consider who will attend, and who among those present has decision-making power and influence. For example, where the parties will be accompanied by external counsel, do you really want them running the dialogue? The answer may be yes, for example where the issues are highly legal-technical, or your relationship with the other party is poor while that between the external counsel is more amenable. But consider also whether the negotiation risks degenerating into polarized positions if the external counsel start trading blows and scoring points across the table. External counsel are instinctively motivated to grandstand on their clients' behalf, but is that productive in the situation at hand? Perhaps it is the right thing to do – to get the positions on the table at the outset – but then for the lawyers to back off and let the owners of the issues lead the interaction. Control your external counsel. Legal issues are almost always positional in nature and inhibit exploration of options for mutual gain. Listen to the advice you are given, but do not necessarily follow it. Follow your gut instincts.

It is usually best to configure negotiations so that the other party talks first, assuming they are willing to do so, but not necessarily if they are likely to get straight to the point and make the first offer. Letting the other party speak first enables you to listen and question, assess their leverage and consider ways forward that may previously have been invisible.

PASSIVE COMMUNICATION: LISTENING

Listening is more than just hearing, especially in a negotiation setting. It has two main purposes: to comprehend and to challenge. Your non-verbal signals usually disclose your listening purpose. When the party conveying information feels you are listening in order to understand, you are developing your relationship with them, and the information flow spontaneously increases. This is particularly true when your whole body exhibits your active listening, for example by echoing and mirroring the speaker. Active listening is an important part of passive communication. If you listen in order to defend, rebut and react, the speaker is likely to pick up your signals, and the quality and style of the interaction may well change. Taking notes, for example, in order to argue your view can inhibit active listening because your non-verbals indicate you are writing, not apparently engaging with the speaker. You can overcome any negative impressions your non-verbal signals may have conveyed by summarizing and reframing what you heard, referring to your notes, and seeking confirmation that you understood correctly.

Active listeners are those whose behaviors, in particular non-verbal signals, make it evident to the speaker that the listener has not just heard what is being said, but sees what they mean. Displaying attentiveness through physical behavior, like matching and mirroring the speaker's physical stance, politeness, empathy, clarifying questions, positive tonal sounds like "uh-ha," perhaps occasional note taking when doing so shows you are recording something said, avoiding distractions and maintaining concentration, all convey the impression that the speaker is being respected and understood. A dialogue is developing and a relationship is building.

It usually helps to summarize, and possibly to reframe, what you have understood using positive and equivocal language, without any judgmental overlay, and invite confirmation that your understanding is correct. Robert Mnookin, Professor of Law at Harvard Law School and Chair of the Program on Negotiation calls this *"looping"* in his book Bargaining With The Devil: When to Negotiate, When to Fight (2010). Looping creates a series of links between what the speaker says, what the listener understands, what the listener summarizes back to the speaker, and finally the speaker's confirmation that the listener understood correctly. A virtuous circle or loop of comprehension. *Think Loop* is a great motto.

Listening for what is not being said is more difficult but can be even more revealing and important. A speaker's non-verbals and carefully chosen words can suggest that more information may be available with a little encouragement. Active listening and receptive behavior can provide some of that encouragement by building trust with the speaker and lowering their guard, as can follow-up clarificatory questioning. Taking a break together by going for a walk changes the dialogue environment and capitalizes on informality. Philosophers' one-liners often capture the point: Friedrich Nietzsche wrote that *all truly great thoughts are conceived by walking*. Two people in step together in the same direction, occasionally exchanging comments about things they encounter, is a very different experience from the formality of sitting across a meeting room table, however familiar that may be. Musings and off-the-record remarks are easier to express when the speaker is not looking at, or being watched by, the listener.

True active listening can be very difficult to pull off. In a negotiation setting, the task involves more than convincing the speaker that we are taking their words seriously and genuinely striving to understand what they are saying, and doing so because we want to. Intellectually, we must also try to manage the probable clash between our own views, factual knowledge, interests, positions and beliefs and those of the person we are listening to. Project manager and facilitator David Fraser extols the virtues of *mindful listening* in his book Relationship Mastery: A Business Professional's Guide (2015).

Psychologists call this phenomenon cognitive dissonance. The contradictions that surface can range from mildly uncomfortable to highly stressful. While actively listening, seeking new insights from the speaker, we are simultaneously struggling mentally to reconcile the differences between what we think and believe and what we are hearing and understanding. Perhaps we are being told things that we know to be untrue, or that we strongly disagree with, or that are offensive, humiliating or patronizing. There is a natural urge to hit back, defend, correct and explain.

The experience of listening, struggling with the cognitive dissonance that often arises from the new information that we are taking on board, and managing our own biases, actually enables us to become more creative. It takes effort. If we consciously use the new information creatively, we can start to envisage new options that may not have occurred to us before. We may revise our own thinking, or generate new possibilities or fresh approaches to the goal of the negotiation. To flush them out, we usually need more information. Which is where artful questioning comes in.

PASSIVE COMMUNICATION: QUESTIONING

In his book Value Negotiation: How to Get the Win-Win Right (2010) Horatio Falcão, Professor of Decision Sciences at INSEAD, points out that *information asymmetry*, the gap between the information available to the parties and their understanding of it, or the imbalance of information between the parties, is what causes many negotiation problems. People tend to fill the gaps with assumptions, guesswork, rumor and hearsay, but if only they would engage in effective questioning, they would more easily be able to replace conjecture with knowledge. In Negotiation (2003), one of the Harvard Business Essentials series, this crucial information gap is referred to as the *negotiator's dilemma*.

Questioning is an exploratory exercise. Good dialogue through smart questioning can improve your preparation and strengthen leverage. You need to be sincere in how you go about it if you want to tease out new insights and information, overcome pushback and get past any roadblocks.

There are lots of different types of questions and, in negotiation, it is important to master them all. I like to think of questions as tools. Different instruments for different jobs. Questions can perform a range of tasks depending on how they are phrased and the purposes behind them.

Open questions do not invite a specific response, leaving the answerer to choose how to reply and with what level of detail. Use open questions for diagnosis, and when you are looking for general context or insights to help you address the rationale behind something. Open questions can also exert a subtle influence because the person answering subconsciously feels more comfortable, more in control, and less challenged through cross-examination. It may be an illusion of control, but it often works in the questioner's favor. People tend to be less defensive and also less aggressive when being asked open questions. Open questioning helps you understand positions more clearly, and to begin to dig into the needs, concerns and fears that underpin them.

There is an endless stream of appropriate open questions, such as:

"Could you tell me about…?"

"What do you think about…?"

"How do you feel about…?"

"How did that happen…?"

"What's your take on…?"

Some of the most effective open questions begin with, or pivot around, a single interrogative: *Why?* or *Why not?*

"Why?" begins the sentence construction of all children as soon as they can talk. Often, "why?" and "why not" are sentences in themselves. As we all know, children's "why?"

questions can be so innocent and basic that they are difficult to answer. Kids find the responses to their "why?" and "why not?" questions formative and revealing. Negotiators can find them revealing too.

Why? questions can be difficult both to ask and to answer in negotiations. Depending on how they are asked, they can be interpreted as quite aggressive, suggesting irritation or annoyance or implying cynicism, challenge, doubt, interrogation, sarcasm or a fishing expedition. To encourage helpful answers, most people soften these questions with pleasant, genuine tones and additional wording, such as: "Can you help me understand why...?" and, as a follow-up: "Ah, yes, I'm starting to understand where you're coming from more clearly, but why...?"

The answers to "Why?" questions are revealing because they tend to elicit responses based on feeling and behavior as well as logic and facts. "Why?" questions dig deep. So it helps to phrase the question to encourage expression of practice, reasons, beliefs, passions and purposes. Do not avoid *why?* type questions about strategic, policy, emotional or philosophical areas. They can explain a lot and reveal hidden anxieties that you may be able to address without compromising on your needs. For example, the answer may reveal that someone has been hurt or harbors a grudge, which might be addressable with a sincere apology. Avoid assuming you know the answer; you may very well be wrong.

Clarifying questions and requests are natural follow-ups to open questions:

"Could you elaborate on...?"

"I'd like to learn more about..."

"What did you mean by...?"

Closed questions are specific, using more probing interrogatives such as when?, what?, who?, where? and how?. Their aim is targeted and functional. They invite a shorter answer, such as yes or no, and are more investigative, designed to understand particular matters or opinions. People tend to be more guarded when asked closed questions because their freedom in answering is restricted. They find it harder to be evasive or to bluff.

EFFECTIVE ANSWERING

Most negotiation books, courses and materials focus on the art of effective questioning but equally important is art of effective answering. In any dialogue, you are not the only one asking the questions. When you provide answers, you do, of course, have to be truthful and not mislead. Your answers may strengthen your leverage by weakening how the questioner views their own leverage. Or they may have the opposite effect.

As a lawyer, you will be bound by whatever rules of professional conduct govern your professional status. Ethics could be relevant when confronted with uncomfortable questions and situations. But those rules and your own standards of integrity do not necessarily mean that you need to disclose everything that may conceivably be relevant to the question. Most people will try to bluster their way around difficult questions by trying to change the subject, or to reframe the question before answering. Responding to part of the question, pretending to answer the question by actually addressing a different one, or responding with a question of your own, are all common politician tactics. Sometimes they work, but they risk diluting trust, which in turn creates suspicion and causes people not to cooperate, or to do so with caution. Chapter 9 deals more comprehensively with negotiation ethics.

In Beyond Winning: Negotiating to Create Value in Deals and Disputes (2000), Professors Robert Mnookin and Scott Peppet, respectively at Harvard and Colorado law schools and Andrew Tulumello of the Gibson Dunn law firm, address how lawyers may react when asked a question they really do not want to answer. They point out, not surprisingly, that you should prepare yourself for the most awkward questions that may be asked, and then prepare your answers. Share these Q&As with your colleagues so that the team is singing the same tune. Cluster those to which the straightforward or complete answer would damage your interests or dilute your credibility. Decide on appropriate responses. Sly evasion suggests embarrassment, guilt or something to hide, so the best avoidance is almost always an honest sidestep, one that offers a credible explanation for not answering. For example:

"I am really not in a position to answer that right now because..."

"Can I ask you the same question because...?"

"I wish I knew enough to address that..."

"I need to check on some points before I can respond to that"

or humor, which can break the tension of the moment.

One potential approach, suggested by Mnookin, Peppet and Tulmello, is to address the problem that the question presents, for example that the other party is effectively inviting or enticing you to lie. Turn round the question and ask the other party how they would react if you asked them a similar question, which you have avoided doing up to that point. Say that this kind of questioning is not helping to move the discussion forward and the last thing either party should do is to be economical with the truth. This approach will not work in all situations, but is worth keeping in mind.

ACTIVE SPEAKING

Communicating persuasively with clarity, sensitivity, credibility and conviction, giving reasons for your proposals, sounds obvious but is a vital yet tricky skill. It needs to draw on all three of the brain's operating systems described in Chapter 3 on all three of the listener's modes of ethos, pathos and logos. Active speakers often prefer short sentences, one per point, because brevity is less complex and has more impact. Avoid monologues; they suggest bluffing. Pause between sentences, allowing the listener to absorb or interject. Welcome interruptions, but rewind and recover the flow afterwards. Give examples, short stories and other anchors to illustrate and support, and to appeal to the listener's emotions. Repeat key points several times, always briefly.

Many TED Talks offer excellent examples of active speaking, among them Simon Sinek's on How Leaders Inspire Action, viewed over 5 million times at the time of writing. He gives three inspiring examples (Apple, Martin Luther King and the Wright Brothers) to prove his points. His sentence construction holds attention. On average every three minutes in his eighteen-minute TED talk, Simon repeats his core message: *"People don't buy what you do, they buy why you do it."*

Good active speakers avoid aggression, dispel fear and doubt, project fairness and optimism, emphasize the positives in any situation, and make it very clear that they personally believe what they are saying. This way, they encourage collaboration by making their listeners feel safe, a sentiment they may not have been expecting, and which helps to trigger the zone of convergence of the brain's three cognitive operating systems described in Chapter 3. When people feel safe they are much more likely to trust and cooperate, trading value and compromises in pursuit of a mutually acceptable deal.

NON-VERBAL COMMUNICATION

Sub-conscious non-verbal signals are an external expression of internal feelings, and like words, they can easily be read and interpreted.

In a 2016 interview with the athlete video platform Unscriptd, Andre Agassi, former World No. 1 tennis player and eight-time Grand Slam champion, explained how he overcame the challenge of beating Boris Becker in the 1990s. His story memorably illustrates the importance of non-verbal signalling in negotiation:

Tennis is about problem solving... and you can't problem-solve unless you have the ability or the empathy to perceive all that's around you. The more you understand what the problem is through other people's lens, the more you can solve [things] *in life and in business.*

Boris Becker, for example, beat me the first three times we played, because his serve was something the game had never seen before. Well, I watched tape after tape of him, and stood across from him three different times, and I started to realise he had this weird tick with his tongue... He would go into his rocking motion, his [service] *routine, and just when he was about to toss the ball he would stick his tongue out. And it would either be right in the middle of his lip, or it would be to the left corner of his lip. If he was serving and he put his tongue in the middle of his lip, he was either serving up the middle or to the body, but if he put it to the side, he was going to serve out wide.*

The hardest part wasn't returning his serve; the hardest part was not letting him know that I knew this. So I had to resist the temptation of reading his serve for the majority of the match, and choose the moment when I was going to use that information on a given point to execute a shot that would allow me to break the match open. That was the difficulty [I had] *with Boris. I didn't have a problem breaking his serve. I had a problem hiding the fact that I could break his serve at will because I just didn't want him to keep that tongue in his mouth – I wanted it to keep coming out!* [Agassi went on to win nine of their next eleven matches.]

So I told Boris about this after he was retired… I couldn't help but say: "By the way, did you know you used to do this, and give away your serve?" He just about fell off the chair, and he said: "I used to go home all the time and tell my wife, it's like he reads my mind, and little did I know that you were just reading my tongue!"

In the early 1970s, Dr. Albert Mehabrian, now Professor Emeritus of Psychology at the University of California, Los Angeles, published the results of studies indicating that certain forms of face-to-face communication comprise 7% words, 38% tone of voice and 55% physiology. These findings have been misunderstood and widely misrepresented ever since, distilled in the vernacular to suggest that 80% to 90% of communication takes place through the medium of what is metaphorically called "body language." I do not buy this. If it were true, you could watch a movie in mute mode or in any completely unfamiliar language and understand 93% of the dialogue. Perhaps it's just me, but I find this impossible. Professor Mehabrian's studies focused on the interpretation of emotional preferences, what people liked and disliked, not on risks, desires, needs, hopes or other sentiments.

Nonetheless, there is no doubt that non-verbal signals are a major part of the communication matrix. Quite how much is impossible to say, and is affected by lots of variables like culture and context, but it is fair to conclude that a significant proportion of emotional expression is communicated non-verbally. This means that signals not expressed verbally are crucial for negotiators to read, and to read accurately. It is an important area because there is far more emotion in professional and business life than most people realize. In fact, business, like politics, is highly emotive and provokes strong feelings in those involved.

In his book Bargaining With the Devil: When to Negotiate, When to Fight (2010), Professor Mnookin quotes many examples of mega-negotiations where emotion played a dominant role. His examples cover not only the emotional rapport between the parties but also how they behaved toward one another and to the outside world, and how they approached the deals they negotiated and the disputes that erupted.

One commercial instance he mentions is the infamous software dispute between global competitors IBM and Fujitsu, in the late 1980s and 1990s. Mnookin, then a professor at Stanford Law School, was asked to be an arbitrator in the dispute, a role that morphed into a hybrid of arbitration and assisted negotiation. One of the points he makes, in a thirty-seven-page revealing chapter devoted to this case, is that when the dispute began, the two corporations saw each other as not just enemies, but in satanical terms. Demonization is a common emotional stance among competitors. Fujitsu and IBM each deeply mistrusted and felt betrayed by the other. Professor Mnookin quotes extreme invective used by both the Americans and, very unusually, by some of the Japanese people involved. The bottom line remains that because emotion and feelings play a major role in negotiation, the Mehabrian findings are important, even if the percentages should be interpreted with a pinch of salt.

Emotion is not the only sentiment conveyed non-verbally in a readable manner. Tone of voice, even noises, can carry clear meaning, and can often be interpreted more easily than physiological features.

At a large conference in Kuala Lumpur a few years ago, I arrived late and took a seat on the front row in a session led by Professor Joel Lee of the Faculty of Law at the National University of Singapore. He is one of the foremost thinkers and researchers in assisted negotiation and its cross-cultural aspects. His subject that day was non-verbal communication. To illustrate the impact of voice tone, he happened to pick on me, as one of the closest members of the audience to the stage, and asked me to close my eyes. With over 200 people watching intently, I closed my eyes and after a few moments of silence, I heard him scream aggressively, at very close range: *"Michael, you bastard!"* (he was either a phenomenal actor, or had chosen this highly public moment to convey a deep contempt he harbored that had previously escaped my attention). He then told me to open my eyes and explain how I felt about what I had just heard. I said I felt under attack, insulted, shocked and saddened, especially coming from him, someone I admired as one of the best brains in the field.

Professor Lee then asked me to close my eyes again. Ten seconds elapsed. The silence in the lecture hall was deafening. Almost inaudibly, I heard him say, in a sensuous, almost seductive, way: *"Michael, you bastard"* (now convincing me it was all an act!), then asked me to open my eyes and explain my reaction to this second delivery of the same three words. Unsurprisingly, it was the opposite of the first.

Tonality strongly impacts interpretation, especially when combined with facial and other physical expressions. A lot of negotiation takes place over the phone, and when it does, we need to rely on tone to understand fully what is being said.

Professor Lee summarized his thoughts on this fascinating area in a post on the Kluwer Mediation Blog.[29] In it he suggests some ways in which tone of voice helps negotiators to interpret underlying meaning. For example, with many English speakers, an upward inflection at the end of a sentence suggests that a question is being posed, or something that may be negotiable, whereas a downward inflection may indicate a command that does not invite further discussion. This is not always the case, however. Many English speakers from Northern Ireland, for example, habitually end sentences with an upward inflexion. Another example is the use of tonal changes in certain parts of a spoken sentence, with an upward tonal inflection, or a louder or softer delivery for a few words suggesting a different intention to the rest of the sentence.

In their book Mastering Negotiations Through Body Language and Other Nonverbal Signals (2015), Greg Williams and Kristin Williams-Washington urge negotiators to use non-verbal signaling to capitalize on their underlying likability, regardless of the toughness of the negotiation taking place, since these signals help build rapport in difficult conditions. Professor Lee, in an earlier blog post,[30] suggested that consciously using non-verbal characteristics to match or mirror your negotiating partner can aid the generation of rapport. Simple rapport-building practices like respectfully and subtly adopting another person's seating stance, or gestures, or nodding at the speed at which the other is speaking, can create a positive atmosphere.

Learning the basic principles of interpreting another person's physiological behavior is a good investment for negotiators, though there are obvious dangers in jumping to conclusions too quickly. There are many books and websites on this subject. One informative guide is What Every Body is Saying: An Ex-FBI Agent's Guide to Speed-Reading People (2008) by Joe Navarro. With separate sections for different parts of the body, Navarro explains possible meanings behind common Western behaviors. However, as he would readily agree, some of these fail to transport across cultures. While a Westerner may nod their head to indicate agreement, a Japanese head nod is more likely to indicate that the listener has heard the speaker but does not necessarily suggest agreement with what is being said. A native of India may rock their head from side to side to signify "yes," but a Westerner may interpret this action to mean uncertainty. Raising the shoulders and lowering the neck indicates sorrow or apology in some cultures, but in France it suggests uncertainty, or lack of knowledge. So physiological signals can easily be misread, and need to be interpreted in light of culture and other contextual signals.

Just as important, perhaps even more so, is the challenge of regulating the non-verbal signals you send to the other party. The books on non-verbal communication listed have useful tips on communicating messages in negotiation contexts. Carol Kinsey Goman, author of The Nonverbal Advantage: Secrets and Science of Body Language at Work (2008) has many suggestions, such as having your hands palms-down when speaking to display confidence, and speaking early in the negotiation process indicates engagement in the dialog. Other experts have similar suggestions. The corporate counsel negotiator may wish to resist the temptation to do what most lawyers do, which is instinctively to extract papers from a case or bag before the negotiation begins. Communicate a different non-verbal message by having no papers before you for as long as possible. Although papers are inevitable when negotiating the wording of a contract, for example, only produce them when needed, not in anticipation of need.

One of the most watched TED Global talks, with 38 million views, was given in June 2012 by the social psychologist Amy Cuddy, an Associate Professor at HBS, entitled Your Body Language Shapes Who You Are.[31] Subtitled in forty-five languages, Professor Cuddy explains why our non-verbals affect how others see us, as well as our perceptions of our own confidence and power, giving many examples in the process. By regulating our body signals, we are able to reduce internal stress levels, increase our influence and be more successful negotiators. Your mindset is often revealed by your non-verbals, and your non-verbals can also influence your mindset.

Chapter 6

EMOTIONAL INTELLIGENCE

Effective communicating in negotiation demands effective handling of emotions – your own as well as those of others. In short, EI which we touched upon in earlier chapters.

The ability to recognize, manage and apply emotions first attracted the EI label in the 1960s. It was not until the 1980s that the discipline really crystallized in a program developed at Tufts University called Project Spectrum. This was a study aimed at assessing children's education, led by Howard Gardner, Professor of Cognition and Education at the Harvard Graduate School of Education and author of Frames of Mind: The Theory of Multiple Intelligences (1983). Other social psychologists built on this work, including Peter Salovey, now President of Yale University and Professor John Mayer at the University of New Hampshire. Together with Dr. David Caruso, an EI trainer at Yale, they worked to define five areas that together make up EI. Psychologist Daniel Goleman then refined these areas for popular attention in his international bestseller Emotional Intelligence: Why It Can Matter More Than IQ (1995).

The five components of EI as presented by Goleman are self-awareness, self-regulation, motivation, empathy and social skills.

Self-awareness is recognizing and monitoring your feelings as they arise and properly understanding the effect they may have on other people.

Self-regulation is the ability to manage your feelings so that you can express them appropriately.

Motivation, in the EI context, is the marshalling of emotions in pursuit of a goal.

Empathy is the ability to recognize and be sensitive to the feelings and emotions of other people when making decisions.

The social skills element involves the capacity to manage the emotions in others and therefore the ability to develop relationships effectively and persuasively.

Although EI is now widely discussed, people still misconstrue what it is. In a 2009 post in the Psychology Today blog,[32] Professor Mayer felt it necessary to set the record straight by pointing out that EI is not agreeableness, optimism, happiness or calmness. These may be characteristics of EI, but are not what researchers define as EI.

Just as you can test your own IQ, you can also measure your EI and your ability to manage emotional information. This can be done online through a number of professional assessment organizations such as Multi-Health Systems Inc[33] which uses the comprehensive and validated Mayer-Salovey-Caruso Emotional Intelligence Test (MSCEIT). Goleman developed a shorter test that is not as comprehensive but is useful as an indicator of your EI and is cost-free from various organizations' websites such as the management consulting firm Hay Group.[34] These assessments, like the Myers-Briggs and other personality assessments, are valuable tools to promote a sharp awareness of your EI strengths and shortcomings and help you to improve your negotiating skills.

Although EI is a topic of great interest, its practical effect on communication and negotiation is more difficult to determine with certainty. The Harvard Program on Negotiation Daily Blog[35] reported on a US-Korean study[36] involving 200 participants that tried to establish whether EI impacts on negotiation outcomes, especially building trust, the parties' wish to work together in the future and mutual gain. The study found that higher EI correlated with greater rapport, trust and willingness to work together. But this particular study, which involved students and used a points system to measure the value of the deals they struck, could not find a clear correlation between EI and the quality of negotiated outcomes.

Some observers have expressed caution that, in some situations, high EI levels may actually impact negatively on negotiated outcomes because high EI individuals may find it harder to be tough-minded in negotiations and can therefore find themselves being exploited. Although this seems like a real problem, as with any other risk, awareness can enable you to manage it through discipline, sticking to your goals, knowing your ATNAs and always giving reasons when unable to compromise. I personally happen to score highly in EI tests, but have rarely been conscious of having been exploited in a deal, or feeling I have given too much away, except in my early career. If anything, just based on my own anecdotal experience and entirely unscientifically, I am convinced that higher EI helps generate improved outcomes especially in joint venture (JV) and other negotiations where the sustainability of the deal and the continuing relationship between the parties are crucial factors. EI can soften difficult and intractable parties if you also use it to drive your goal achievement.

Legal training and practice almost everywhere relies on the application of dispassionate norms, such as rules, facts, logic, risks, positions and rational argument, to achieve results. Most external counsel behave true to this type – relatively formal, impassive and temperate. Just as you can spot a police officer in plain clothes at 100 paces, you can generally identify a lawyer in the blink of an eye. Some would argue that they have to maintain this accepted aura of professionalism, despite masking their true personality, owing to the strictures of ethics, convention, protocol and liability.

This is not to imply that lawyers lack emotion, just that most tend naturally to allow its expression in a tactical way rather than as a personal asset. In reality, emotional undercurrents run deep in legal practice. Lawyers are expert in believing the veracity of their own arguments. Litigation lawyers that practice before juries are skilled in the art of emotional persuasion. Nonetheless, when negotiating on behalf of a client, many external counsel have difficulty liberating their persona from their professional convictions and inhibitions.

Corporate counsel are far less constrained by these implicit restrictions. Being a party, or one of the party's team, the internal counsel often has a greater interest in building a relationship with the other party, for which effective use of EI is critical. This is another reason why internal counsel should always consider carefully what involvement or role, if any, external counsel should have during planned negotiations.

Chapter 6

I recall a difficult negotiation with a JV partner. My company had financed the venture and the other party had contributed the technical expertise as well as marketing and sales. Profits were split 50–50. The twenty-year relationship had become strained in the period leading up to the negotiation because the business began performing poorly. We wanted to dissolve the venture, but leave the door open to a possible future collaboration. The negotiation was about how to divide up the JV's rights and assets, which both parties wanted to use independently once the JV dissolved.

The other party's external counsel pulled out a copy of the JV agreement, entered into over twenty years earlier, and did most of the talking. She said that her client's engineers and other experts were the ones that had developed the IP rights and the intrinsic value, and their individual names were on all the patents even though they had been assigned to the JV. She was extremely positional, saying the only arrangement she could possibly envisage was that the rights would be assigned to her client when the JV dissolved, and that the most my company would receive would be a non-exclusive, royalty-bearing license. It was a demand, her idea of an anchor, not a proposition for discussion. We did not agree, proposing to leave the JV as an IP owning but non-operational company that would continue to license the patents to both parties and on a royalty-free basis. The talks became acrimonious and legalistic and the parties' external lawyers argued interminably, ultimately arriving at a positional deadlock from which neither would back down. Communications stopped. The air was acrid.

I ran into the other party's internal counsel at a conference dinner a week or so later. We had always got on well, but this time I sensed a greater distance. Without mentioning the JV, I proposed that we skip the dinner and find a nearby restaurant. I'll buy this time, you buy next time, I suggested. He hesitated, studied my eyes, smiled and nodded. He knew exactly what I had in mind. We were both managing our emotions. As we entered the first restaurant we came upon, we noticed a full suit of armor in the lobby, with the visor dropped into the fight position. *"Gladiators!"* he exclaimed, *"shall we go elsewhere?"* We laughed, both of us envisioning our external counsel locked in mortal combat. *"Oh, let's have a drink and drown them."* After we sat down and ordered, I asked: *"Shall we go off the record, strictly between us, no reporting back?"* He winked: *"No other way to go forward."*

We admitted we should not have left the negotiation in the hands of unrestrained warriors. Inevitably, it degenerated into an arcane fight over poorly-drafted words in a dusty contract signed by former managements of both parties. It was backward-looking, and we needed a forward-facing solution. We agreed it would make sense if we each explain what our respective companies needed out of the situation, and why, and then brainstorm some future-orientated solutions. I spoke first, being totally honest. He reciprocated. It turned out that each company had completely different business interests in the IP rights; there would be no competition, and neither need have any commercial fears about the other. Before we got onto the desert, we had mapped out a potential solution that left the patents in the dormant JV until they expired, with each party taking a royalty-free non-exclusive license and sharing royalties charged to third parties.

Looking back, all five of the components of EI played a role in breaking the deadlock. Each party had been concerned that the other would be a competitor and sought to limit the downside. Emotions were running high, stirred up by the invective of two external counsel unable to agree and stumbling over words in an old agreement. As internal counsel, we had the flexibility and self-confidence to trust one another with information that could break the deadlock. We both wanted to find a solution based on a fair mutual gain outcome. We built on our relationship to discover that our companies would be exploiting different market segments, and that our initial concerns were unfounded.

In negotiations that are likely to be particularly strained, perhaps because of an acrimonious history, high stakes, the imminent threat of litigation or the presence of difficult personalities, anything that can ease tensions and promote some degree of relaxation to encourage the release of latent EI should be valuable. There are several simple ways to do this.

As suggested in Chapter 3, eating together is one proven method. One researcher who has conducted some studies on this fascinating subject is Professor Lakshmi Balachandra at Babson College in Massachusetts, a business school specializing in entrepreneurship. In an article[37] in the Harvard Business Review, Professor Balachandra presented the results of experiments in which 132 MBA students were asked to perform a roleplay in which their task was to negotiate the final terms of a JV involving a potential value of between USD 38 million and USD 75 million. Some of the students were asked to share a meal while negotiating, either in restaurants or in meeting rooms, while others were not given that opportunity. There was a clear and substantial correlation between those that ate together while negotiating and the most mutually profitable negotiated outcomes. Those who negotiated in restaurants achieved value 12% higher, and those eating in conference rooms achieved 11% higher value than those who did not eat together at all. The researchers were convinced that it was the act of negotiating while eating together that made the difference. But to be sure, the experiment was run again to compare results when all the negotiators were asked not to negotiate but to complete a jigsaw puzzle. The puzzle participants all performed about the same. Interesting, but why?

In The Choreography of Resolution: Conflict, Movement and Neuroscience (2013) edited by Michelle LeBaron, Carrie MacLeod and Andrew Floyer Acland, the view is persuasively expressed that anything parties can naturally do together in a synchronized way can generate subconscious empathy and a heightened degree of openness because they tend to set off mirror neutrons in the participants' brains. Sharing a meal has a certain synchronicity, and can have that effect, as can walking together while taking a break, and this can create implicit and unspoken bonds. When you think about it, the results of Professor Balachandra's experiments are not really surprising.

Chapter 6

TENSION RELEASE: HUMOR

Appropriate humor in the form of witticisms, irony and amusing anecdotes can be a great tension-breaker and point-maker. Professor John Forester at Cornell University has observed the negotiation impact of humor, in the form of perceptive and imaginative responses during the course of communication. He notes[38] that negotiation humor can acknowledge historic issues, disrupt expectations of parties and encourage new actions and relationships while avoiding being clumsy, insensitive, disrespectful or forceful. Relatively safe ground is humor directed at the preposterous situation in which all the parties find themselves, self-deprecating humor and remarks that strike a chord in the minds of the party to whom they are expressed but who would never have spoken them openly. Ed Brodow, author of Negotiation Boot Camp: How to Resolve Conflict, Satisfy Customers and Make Better Deals (2014) quotes an occasion when a US diplomat, arriving in Pyongyang to negotiate the release of an American pilot shot down over North Korea, asked: *"Well, is he OK? Does he still have his fingernails?"* This was met by a long moment of stony silence, after which the North Korean delegation burst into fits of laughter. It was a bit risky, but proved to be an effective tension breaker.

However, humor does not necessarily travel well, and can sometimes do more harm than good. Much depends on the cultural situation, the facial and other physical expressions that accompany it, as well as tone, timing and content. Telling a funny short story or anecdote that bears a relevance to the matter at hand can be an effective way to communicate a reality that may be awkward or seen as hostile to express openly.

TENSION RELEASE: VENTING

Unless they are dispute settlements, few negotiations, especially those that are collaborative in nature, are focused on the past. Even distributive negotiations are related to the present, not the past. Yet a party may come to a deal negotiation with serious hang-ups about the past, perhaps because they feel wronged. Unless they have the opportunity to vent these feelings, progress can be slow or stall.

Researchers and skills trainers are divided on the value of encouraging or allowing a party to vent their anger and frustrations. Most of the literature on the subject originates in the individualistic cultures of North America and northern Europe, yet cultural issues can drive the need to vent and how it is expressed. There is no universal, reliable guidance on this issue because it is circumstance-driven. When a party gets emotional and upset, I have usually tried to give them the opportunity to express themselves, and to convey a degree of empathy for their anxiety. I have generally tried to do this by making it apparent that I will not take it badly, however severe the message. This was a way to exert control. To prevent emotional outbursts leading to meltdown, it is important to display sincere compassion and resist the temptation to argue, strike back, hint at ridicule or convey any negativity. Take it calmly and make it clear that you genuinely understand their feelings. Half apologize: *"I'm sorry you feel that way."* Or acknowledge: *"I know exactly how you feel."* Or share: *"Something similar once happened to me..."* Consider accurately repeating and reframing what you heard. Such engagement helps contain the underlying feelings and restore equilibrium. To do otherwise risks creating a vicious circle and adding fuel to the fire.

Controlled venting can release tensions, clear the air and enable negotiators to move forward. It can be better to let it happen than bottle it up, but always take care – in Negotiating the Nonnegotiable: How To Resolve Your Most Emotionally Charged Conflicts (2016), Professor Daniel Shapiro at Harvard Medical School/McLean Hospital warns that venting can just as easily reinforce anger as release it.

TENSION RELEASE: APOLOGIZING

Lawyers hate apologies. Somewhere or somehow, instinct tells them, liability lurks. That may, indeed, be so on occasion, but far less often than lawyers assume. When expressed with sincerity, apologies can be cathartic for both the injured party and the perpetrator of the words or act that has caused offense, hurt or loss of face. Appropriate apologies expressed in the right way cost nothing but humility, and have the power to remove important blockages to the progress of a negotiation.

A spontaneous apology or expression of regret, communicated from the heart, is an act of EI because the perpetrator is openly recognizing the offense and is empathizing with the injured party. Apologies can restore the perpetrator's integrity and face, and reconcile parties' emotions.

Deborah L. Levi, a Boston litigator and mediator who tragically died of breast cancer aged 34, left an important legacy for negotiators throughout the world with her award-winning article in the NYU Law Review on The Role of Apology in Mediation.[39] Deborah identified four general categories of contrition and apology in the context of dispute settlements, but they apply equally to deal making:

- tactical (acknowledging the victim's suffering in order to gain credibility and influence the victim's bargaining behavior);
- explanation (attempting to excuse the offender's behavior and make the other party understand that behavior);
- formalistic (capitulating to the demand of an authority figure); and
- happy-ending (accepting responsibility and expressing regret for the negative act).

Deborah suggested that apologies may play less of a role in commercial disputes because she felt that business relationships are impersonal and financially orientated, and because they are characterized, in her experience, by the heavy-handed and dispassionate role of litigators. While external counsel may bristle at the very idea of apologies, fearing the implication of admission of liability, business issues are generally just as emotive and temperamental as interpersonal matters. Whatever your view and experience, any negotiator contemplating the possibility of offering an apology as a way to break through impasse or improve the quality of dialogue will find Deborah's article helpful. Legal implications should certainly be considered, but artful wording can often overcome them.

One of the key defects identified in the wake of the 9/11 outrage was the problem that emergency responders – police, fire and ambulance services – encountered in communicating with one another. A project was launched to correct this glaring and dangerous deficiency. It was important technically and also from national security and public confidence perspectives.

The challenge was given to a leading US technology company. Among the elements needed to complete the project was a major technology that had been developed by an Asian company. The US company had already worked on another project with the Asian company and had obtained a license for the use of their technology, which it felt also covered the 9/11 project. But when the Asian company saw its technology being used on the 9/11 project, it strongly objected, saying that the previous license was specific to another deal and did not cover the 9/11 assignment. It threatened an injunction to prevent the US company from using the Asian technology for the 9/11 project.

The Americans felt they had a good position on the license issue. But a delay on the 9/11 project, given its high profile and security importance, was untenable. The dispute had to be resolved immediately. The Asian company felt that the Americans had acted dishonorably and the Americans needed to dispel that notion. The matter was so critical that the American company's CEO proposed a meeting with the Asian company's President.

The first thing the American CEO did was to address the Asian President directly. He said something like: *"We apologize if you are under the impression that we have misappropriated your technology. That was never our intent."* The words were sincere. Technically, he was not apologizing for having misappropriated the technology, but for having given the impression that misappropriation had taken place. Nonetheless, because of the way it was delivered, this apology was enough to get the two sides talking again. They were then able to negotiate an extension to the license to cover the 9/11 project and potentially other projects in the future.

The deal delivered mutual gain. The Americans now had broad licensed use of the technology and the Asian company had a major long-term partner for these and other projects. The opposite result might have occurred had the lawyers controlled a backward-facing strategy, which might have resulted in a lawsuit over the interpretation of the original license. Perhaps a pyrrhic victory would have been won, but it would have been practically valueless.

FRAMING AND REFRAMING

Framing is the term given by negotiators to how the scope and content of a matter is defined and expressed. Issues are the value-creating drivers in any negotiation, whether they are few or many. How they are framed influences how they are discussed. Most negotiations involve many frames, starting with why the negotiation is taking place, to the things that need to be discussed, and to the details of the final agreement. Negotiations involve a constant ebb and flow of framing and reframing until agreement is reached.

A good analogy is the picture frame. In existence since art began in caves and on rocks, in one form or another picture frames have two main functions: to present the image in the best possible way, and to protect it.

Framing issues in a negotiation is similar. You frame an issue how you would like it to be viewed. Your framing may also be protecting an interest you have in the issue.

The significance of framing propositions and statements began to attract wide attention from about 1981, when the late Professor Amos Tversky, working together with Daniel Kahneman, published studies to support their Prospect Theory on how people manage risk and uncertainty. They are related in Kahneman's Thinking Fast and Slow (2011). The bottom line, as political spin doctors have long known, is that the type of response that you get to a proposition is influenced by how you present it, just as the quality of an answer you get often depends on the quality of the question you ask.

A critical frame involves what the negotiation is about in the first place. Most framing is selective. In a broad sense, an opening line could be the suggestion "to meet for a coffee," indicating a quasi-social occasion with the potential of addressing a more substantive issue. Many negotiations are preceded by a negotiations-about-negotiations phase. It can be very short, when one party proposes negotiations to the other, or a third party makes a proposal to talk. Exactly how the idea of negotiation is expressed, and sometimes who the proposer is, can determine whether a meeting of minds takes place. Where the concept and purpose of the negotiation are framed quite broadly, such as *"let's talk about the possibilities for a long term collaboration,"* multiple issues are implicitly on the agenda for discussion. Narrower framing usually entails fewer issues, but therefore less scope for value exchange.

When the other party frames an issue in a way you cannot accept, a better way than arguing about it may be to reframe it. As William Ury has said, *"to change the game, change the frame."* A creative way to reframe is to respond to a proposition by saying something like: *"Let me understand what you are suggesting...."* and then repeat the proposition using different words and ideas that embrace your underlying interests while leaving the other party's basic idea intact, and then ask for confirmation of your understanding. Where the other party is trying to score points, resist the temptation to respond with counterpoints. Making good points is more effective than scoring cheap ones. Be tactful: Churchill once defined tact as *the art of telling someone to go to Hell in such a way that they look forward to the trip.* Tactful reframing is a smart way to get another party to subtly shift stance or style and open up to a discussion in an area that helps you achieve your goal.

In Chapter 3, we discussed how the brain, specifically the O/S2 social operating system, favors safe framing (e.g., when offered 50 and given the option either to "keep 20" or to "lose 30," most people opt to "keep 20" even though losing 30 produces exactly the same result). Using smart language that appeals to the other party's "safe" mode can influence how someone receives your frame or reframe and how the negotiation progresses from that point.

CONVEYING NEGATIVES

When you have to decline, or to tell the other party something they really do not want to hear, it can help to use a constructive frame. The more that a negative can be communicated within a positive framework, the more likely it will be accepted.

In The Power of a Positive No: How to Say No and Still Get To Yes (2008), William Ury offers a smart way to turn people down. He advises beginning with a Yes, some positive statement that aligns with your own values and interests. This initial Yes constructs half of the frame. Once done, communicate the No. Then complete the frame with a final Yes, another positive that may possibly envisage a productive next step, or an alternative or other constructive, supportive or mutually beneficial idea. This simple Yes-No-Yes maneuver is a compelling way to frame a negative in a convincing, meaningful, uncompromising and respectful way. And always try to give a credible reason for saying No. In a memorable speech, the banker J P Morgan remarked: *there are usually two reasons for anything: a good reason and the real reason.* Either works.

STAGING

Like theatre, and most other things outside the home, negotiation is a stage performance. The players need to consider the scenography and the choreography.

The place where parties meet to stage the negotiation can mean a great deal. You probably instinctively feel most comfortable on your home turf, which could be your office, or your counsel's office or somewhere else very familiar to you. More likely than not, the other party will feel that way too and prefer their own home ground. Research in 2011 by two North American business school professors, Graham Brown and Marcus Baer, summarized in the Harvard Business Review,[40] suggests that, in fixed pie distributive win/lose bargaining, parties conducting negotiations on home territory performed significantly better than the visiting party. The researchers ascribed this result mainly to the psychological effect of increased confidence generating a perceived home field advantage, but it may also have cultural roots.

The Brown and Baer results used undergraduate students as participants for their studies, and I wonder how realistic the study scenarios were and whether the results can truly be projected to mainstream commercial negotiations.

Experienced and savvy negotiators will likely ask themselves: *Do we really want the other party to feel uncomfortable from the start?* Although some will instinctively say yes to that question, let's think about that for a moment. Imagine you are the party with the greater, or at least equivalent, strength and the other party is in a difficult starting position. You are likely to be confident and the other party may be somewhat defensive, aggressive or uncommunicative. Are those ideal ingredients of a good negotiation? Where a successful outcome of an integrative negotiation would create a relationship for the future, think again about how you want to influence the mindset of the other party. The natural assumption that you have an advantage when the other party is less comfortable than you is often a dangerous illusion and you can easily adapt yourself to neutralize it. In fact, a party that is feeling uneasy is more likely to be difficult, cautious and negative, all of which are complicating factors in any negotiation.

The simple act of asking the other party where they would prefer to meet is itself a subtle power play on your part. If they suggest their place, and if you readily agree, you are signaling that you feel confident and see no danger. This may surprise, or perhaps even worry them. You are also being accommodating and respectful and therefore likely to arouse similar behavior in response. When the negotiation takes place on the other party's home ground, they are hosting, a role that carries certain implicit responsibilities towards you. As hosting is a social act, you, as the guest, have a privileged chance to witness the other party in their natural habitat. This insight can easily reveal clues about them: how they are established, what else is going on around them, how they behave at home, what the atmosphere is like, how they spontaneously present themselves and how they handle their staff. J.K. Rowling wrote that *if you want to know what a man's like, take a good look at how he treats his inferiors, not his equals*. There may be a great view, or interesting art, or in their office there may be personal things that illuminate their persona. Many of these things are possible social subjects for discussion before the negotiation begins, but they also help to build a character and gain an understanding. Quickly, you start to feel more (or less) comfortable about them than they may be feeling about you.

There are times when it is best to host a negotiation on your own patch, but the smart negotiator knows that the assessment needs to be made from the other party's standpoint. If they are coming a long way, offering to host can be a practical convenience, and another way to show respect. Like humility, hospitality can take the edge off hostility.

You can always propose a third, non-partisan, location. It is hard to find reasons to resist neutrality unless based on practicality or cost. Where there is tension or conflict between the parties, a neutral location may be the best solution all round. If all parties are willing to meet in a third location, try to influence the setting based not only on convenience and cost but also ambience and local facilities, such as interesting restaurants and other places to go to take a break, like proximity to a park or beach.

I once led my company to a negotiation with a major international competitor. We agreed to meet at the Crown Plaza at Munich Airport at 9am one day and both parties' delegations had to arrive by plane from abroad on the previous day. Just a short taxi ride from Munich Airport, overlooking the medieval town of Freising, is the Weihenstephan Abbey, a Benedictine Monastery that dates from 725. On the site is reputedly the oldest continuously-functioning brewery in the world, established in 1040. The Weihenstephan Brewery's large versatile dining room is perfect for informal gatherings and can also be adapted for business events. I missed the chance to suggest to the other party that we all dine together socially on the evening before our meeting. Instead, thoughtlessly, I invited my own group and external counsel to join me at Weihenstephan. I lost the golden opportunity to get to know my negotiating party much better in relaxed surroundings. We all make errors, but that was needless, careless and inexcusable on my part. I still kick myself when I think about it.

The significance of seating positions at negotiations are often trivialized or ignored, but they can make communications easier or more challenging. If two negotiating teams come into a room and see a rectangular table, they are likely to sit facing one another. An automatic physical juxtaposition of positions and interests is created at that very moment. It demonstrates that the participants are not part of the same group, but two camps, facing one another like the French and Russian armies at Borodino, prepared to do battle, win or lose, do or die. The perfect alignment for acrimony.

A round table, on the other hand, creates a different sense. Circles evoke notions of relationships and unity in the subconscious mind. Stone age henges are round, as are ancient amphitheaters. King Arthur, according to the Norman poet Wace, created a round table to enable his Knights to deliberate on equal terms leading to the chivalric order of the Knights of the Round Table. Yin and Yang are depicted in a circle. Because of the inclusive connotations, the flag of the European Union comprises stars denoting the Member States arranged in a circle. An extraordinary proportion of modern day logos feature circles: Alfa Romeo, Audi, BMW, Coca-Cola, Dell, Fiat, GE, Mercedes-Benz, NASA, Nissan, the Olympic Games, Saab, Starbucks, Volkswagen, my publisher Wolters Kluwer, and thousands more. Inter-State negotiations are often called Round Table Talks and WTO negotiations are referred to as Rounds.

Round tables help to camouflage power distribution because the seating positions promote informality and encourage the creation of the "in-group" scripts discussed in Chapter 3, freeing people up to relate to one another in a different, more communicative context. People are more socially adaptable at round tables.

If there are just two people negotiating, sitting together at the corner of a rectangular table or seated in a table-free environment effectively at right angles to each other, a more relaxed atmosphere exists. It is easier to avoid eye contact when appropriate, for example while contemplating, and is less confrontational than being seated opposite. Tense relationships can be converted into pro-social behavior by simple staging.

Taking proper breaks from the negotiating table can trigger new dimensions, and help to break deadlocks. As noted in Chapter 5, the simple act of going for a walk together can break tension. Walking side-by-side offers a very different dynamic from the typical confrontational meeting room. In his TED Talk, The Walk from No To Yes delivered in 2010, William Ury remarks that walking has a real power. You are moving in a common direction, taking in fresh perspectives. Even if you are not thinking along the same lines, the brains of the parties are noting some convergence. Walking can be a real tension-breaker.

E-NEGOTIATING

The type of communication medium can become part of the negotiation itself. Technology has come to the aid of negotiators in several ways, offering email and video conferencing as well as online data rooms and shared spaces, file sharing and tools for e-discovery and due diligence. In the conflict field, online dispute resolution, or ODR, although still in its relative infancy and focused on low-value dispute settlement has developed several functionalities that can help negotiators be more efficient and effective, including those discussed in Chapter 2.

Many governments are exploring how ODR can help reduce administration of justice costs. In April 2014, Professor Richard Susskind, an internationally-recognized authority on the future of technology in legal practice, chaired a UK advisory group on the development of ODR in dispute management. A working paper published on the judiciary.co.uk web portal in 2014 by Susskind and Matthew Lavy, a technology litigator, titled Likely Developments in ODR, predicts the arrival of systems that will help parties not only to analyze legal issues, but to convert them into rational decisions. While Susskind and Lavy note that existing ODR systems already provide useful functionalities for low-cost, non-adversarial negotiations, they say: *"tomorrow's systems may offer prompts on the tactics and strategy of negotiations. These prompts could be of two broad kinds. First, there might be systems that help to optimize one party's position, guiding on what is considered to be in the best interests of the user. Alternatively, in the spirit of game theory, the systems might make concrete recommendations for resolutions that constitute sensible outcomes for both parties (on the principle that rational decisions by individuals can lead to collective decisions that are irrational)."*

While this may be the exciting shape of the future, for the present we need to be aware of the benefits and dangers of using and abusing existing technology when negotiating. Electronic communications involve a range of settings, behaviors and processes that can affect a negotiation's efficiency and outcome, both positively and negatively.

Emails, for example, are a wonderful medium but their nature encourages highly spontaneous, and extremely brief reactions shared or sharable with numerous people. In an early (2004) article in the HBS newsletter Negotiation titled "How To Negotiate

Successfully Online"[41] by Professor Kathleen McGinn of HBS and Eric Wilson of Cogos Consulting, observed that negotiating online can easily start with a frenzy of activity, followed by a period of collective confusion. They emphasize the importance of first meeting face to face, or at least by video conference, to establish some basic rapport before relying too heavily on email interaction.

Emails can be great for low-hanging fruit and agreeing areas of common ground, but are often far less suited to mainstream negotiating where you really do need to see the whites of the other party's eyes. Nonetheless, when parties cannot negotiate physically, either at all, or all the time, how do the dynamics change?

This question is explored in You've Got Agreement: Negoti@ting Via Email (2009) by five negotiation educators, Noam Ebner, Anita Bhappu, Jennifer Gerarda Brown, Kimberlee Kovach and Andrea Kupfer Schneider.[42] They point out that negotiating while meeting face-to-face changes the kind of information that is communicated and how it is interpreted compared to meeting electronically

Professor Ebner and his co-authors suggest that the two dynamics that influence these changes are the richness of the communication medium in terms of communicating verbal and non-verbal signals (physical presence being rich in this regard while email is lean) and the level of interactivity. For example, where one of the parties has a high context culture where indirect communication exerts a major influence and the other a low context culture, email communication is likely to swing the negotiation pendulum more to favor the low-context, explicit, impersonal frame that can cause difficulties for the high context party and thereby render the negotiation more difficult for all. Because negotiators are less able to build an interpersonal relationship using email, the authors describe five main effects of email negotiating compared with face-to-face negotiation:

- increased contentiousness
- diminished information sharing
- diminished process cooperation
- diminished trust and
- increased effects of negative attribution.

The You've Got Agreement authors recommend a series of skills needed when negotiation by email:

- improved writing ability to enhance clarity and sensitivity
- message management to address the parties' anxieties
- building rapport and showing e-empathy, and
- managing the content in terms of clarity and appropriate framing.

And there's the security aspect. I make it a rule never to use the blind copy box on any email communication. It may save a few seconds by avoiding the need to forward a sent email to someone, but it excludes the risk that the recipient might accidentally respond by clicking *reply all* and potentially cause embarrassment, or compromise or destroy a negotiation or even expose you to liability.

In fact, it is wise to consider carefully who is added to the visible copy box of practically every email. The way the message is received and interpreted can change dramatically depending on who is copied on an email. As a rule, I only copy those who would be in the room if the negotiation is happening face-to-face, though you may need to copy someone else to make a point, or give reassurance to the recipient, or for another good reason.

The subject line is also important, and can help reframe an issue by how it is worded. Be wary of trying to negotiate internally by copying colleagues on an external email; almost inevitably, the words chosen will convey different or confusing messages. These may seem obvious points, but we have all witnessed the consequences of email sloppiness.

When planning a negotiation, consider the differences between face-to-face and electronic communications. It may make sense to meet at the outset to help establish the rapport and build trust, then defer to video conferencing and email at later stages, or for more minor issues. Email is such a ubiquitous way of negotiating that we need to consciously adapt our negotiating skills whenever using email, even where part or most of the negotiation is conducted in person.

KEEPING IN TOUCH

In Staying With Conflict: A Strategic Approach to Ongoing Disputes (2009), Bernie Meyer makes a strong pitch to go out of your way to stay in contact with the other party during a dispute. Where direct communication is inappropriate or officially blocked, find other ways to stay in touch. You could, for example, consider maintaining an open line via advisers. If you see the other party is due to speak at a conference or symposium, think about attending, and make an appreciative or positive comment at a coffee break or in a follow-up note. This implies you are not avoiding issues and have the perseverance and strength to confront them at the relevant moment.

IN A NUTSHELL

- Start as positively as the situation will allow.
- Listen first, speak later, unless making the first offer.
- Develop open questioning skills.
- Adopt an active speaking mode.
- Don't score points, make them.
- Know how to interpret non-verbal signals and communicate the right ones yourself.
- Use EI techniques to handle your own emotions and those of the other party.
- Release tension through meals, humor, venting and apologies.

Chapter 6

- Know how to frame and reframe productively.
- Say no positively – Yes-No-Yes.
- Do not underestimate the importance of staging negotiations well.
- Consider optimal seating arrangements.
- Technology has its place but also hidden dangers in negotiation.

CHAPTER 7
Process

When I was a kid 'bout half past three
My ma said "Daughter, come here to me"
Said things may come, and things may go
But this is one thing you oughta know...
Oh 't ain't what you do, it's the way that you do it
'T ain't what you do, it's the way that you do it
'T ain't what you do, it's the way that you do it
That's what gets results

Ella Fitzgerald, 1939

Six Sigma, the widely-used performance excellence system, is based on the simple principle that the quality of a goal, outcome or result is governed by the quality of the process used to achieve it. Generally in life, the right outcomes come much more easily if we improve how we go about reaching them. Negotiators ignore at their peril the advice given by the late Professor David W. Plant in We Must Talk Because We Can (2009) that: *We have to start by defining the process as part of the problem.*

Yet although just about every competent physician, engineer or scientist in any field will think very carefully about the process they employ for almost everything they do, negotiators all too often default to familiar, tried-and-true behavioral patterns and pay little conscious attention to process.

As negotiation is simply a structured form of communicating, the default format that most people instinctively adopt is simply to get together directly and just talk. Almost

Chapter 7

all negotiations are conducted using the straightforward process of bilateral direct-access. Negotiators often prefer some or all the dialogue to be conducted with or through agents, such as external counsel, but the underlying conventional one-on-one structure usually remains. That process works well for many deals, but can be a disaster for others.

Negotiation is more art than science. There is no one-size-fits-all way of handling a negotiation. The ideal process to employ will change from one situation to another. We need to consider what process would best be suited to each individual set of circumstances.

Shockingly, most negotiators seem to lose their imagination when it comes to process. If they prepare at all, they focus on the factual, economic and legal issues and, hopefully, on goals and ATNAs. Few think carefully about adapting the process through which the dialogue takes place to anticipate and manage predictable problems. With a flush of creativity and very little time or expense, a tailor-made process could be put in place that, in most cases, would vastly enhance the prospects of a successful outcome. The process chosen can be a catalyst to failure or success.

PREDICTABLE BLOCKAGES

Negotiation is inherently unpredictable. Hidden agendas, emotions, attitudes, assumptions, wrong information and partial knowledge all drive parties to make apparently illogical arguments, exhibit strange behavior and adopt unforeseeable positions. Despite all this, some circumstances point to the prospect of difficulties ahead that could be anticipated by selecting an appropriate process.

For example there may be a serious imbalance between the parties, based on size, financial power, sophistication, market position, political affiliations or other factors. Strongly conflicting cultures might cause timing, trust, communication and credibility problems, or negotiating styles may differ considerably. It may be clear from the outset that the parties' fundamental objectives do not coincide; there may be a conflict or other menace bubbling in the background, with or without the prospect or threat of litigation. Any kind of tension can inhibit communication; one or more negotiators may be stuck in a positional hole; deadlock may have been reached or is likely; there may be a history of poor communication or lack of mutual respect; physical distance can make face-to-face meetings difficult; or the negotiators in one party or another keep changing and causing instability and confusion. There may be deadlines that parties need to respect. The list of tripwires is endless.

Process

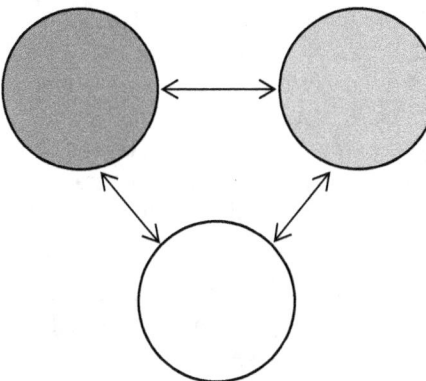

A 3-way negotiation involves 6 sets of rights, obligations and interests

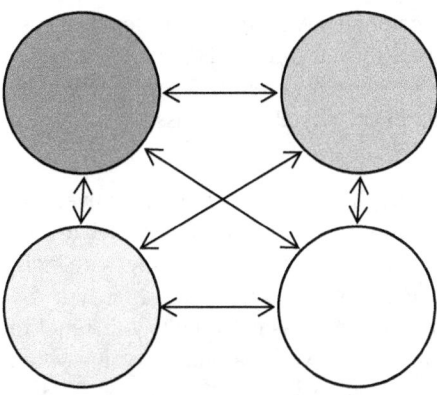

A 4-way negotiation involves 12 sets of rights, obligations and interests

Where more than two parties are directly involved in a negotiation, difficulties multiply. An integrative negotiation between two parties involves two sets of rights, obligations and interests. But a three-party negotiation involves up to six sets of rights, obligations and interests, and a four party deal can involve twelve. As more parties directly or indirectly engage in the negotiation, several things happen simultaneously. There are more negotiators in the frame. They are likely to have different styles and approaches to the deal and each may have a different agenda and motive. The negotiation will probably slow down and become more complex. Communications and logistics turn more intricate. Negotiators then find themselves spending more time trying to manage process than focusing on substance. Professor Plant's warning about process being part of the problem becomes a self-fulfilling prophecy.

The process challenge is not confined to integrative negotiations. In a two-party distributive bargain, where a gain for one means an equivalent loss to the other, negotiators can easily fail to reach agreement. Stand-offs and deadlocks are common.

PSYCHOLOGY AT WORK

Let's consider an actual example. But first some aviation stardust.

The Douglas DC-3 plane was a twin propeller workhorse. With a range of 2,400 km it could fly across the US or the Atlantic with just one refueling stop. Its short take-off and landing capabilities also made it ideal as a transporter. Over 600 DC-3s were produced between 1936 and 1942. This tough aircraft invoked a pioneering spirit from an age when pilots flew with their senses and muscles not their instruments. Steering them was like stirring concrete. Pilots took calculated risks, and were famed for seeking adventure and new frontiers. Some DC-3s are still airworthy today, mostly for thrill-seekers and scenic tourism.

Chapter 7

The romance ingrained in the iconic DC-3 is the historic marketing platform for a remarkable Dutch private company called PMEC. Led by Bob Bulder, the PMEC team had created a range of high quality, premium-priced aviator-style leisure gear aimed at the alpha-male. The signature item in PMEC's collection is a cargo pilot's sheepskin jacket, advertised with shots of tough-looking 30-year old flyers sporting three days of beard stubble, often against a backdrop of silver DC-3s parked in an airplane graveyard in Arizona, their noses projecting into the air like the aerial aristocrats they had become.

Many of PMEC's brand names and insignia, such as PME American Classic and a wings symbol were registered trademarks owned internationally by my employer for clothing and apparel. We had exclusively licensed these trademarks to PMEC. We had no expertise or commercial interest in the fashion field, and came to the conclusion that if PMEC would like to acquire the trademark rights for fair value, then we should sell them. It fell to me to approach PMEC to ask if they would like to buy the rights. Not surprisingly, Bob and his team much preferred to own the trademarks rather than license them – who wouldn't? The value of his company was largely represented by the brand names it marketed, and gaining full ownership and control of the IP rights would give added security to their business model for the long term. So we agreed the principle, and it was my job to negotiate the price with Bob. A classic distributive negotiation, but between friends.

Although there was not, and never had been, any dispute between my employer and PMEC, on this issue we had completely opposite interests. Bob naturally wanted to pick up the IP rights at the lowest possible cost, and, as a small company with tight operating margins, he did not have the financial resources to spend a lot. For my employer, a multi-billion multinational, the transaction was not remotely material to our core business. On the other hand, we had to deliver shareholder value when trading any of the company's intellectual property assets.

Bob and I met to discuss price, but it quickly became apparent that we were poles apart. Bob dropped anchor first. He noted, accurately, that my company was not using its position as IP owner and licensor to invest in the branding through marketing support, as PMEC had done. Yes, he said, the license generated a small annual royalty, but it was peanuts to a global consumer goods business like mine. Bob proposed that we assign the trademarks to PMEC for a price equal to the expected royalties for the next few years, discounted at present-day value.

I explained that much as we admired how PMEC had built a great business on the back of the license, that very success had made the trademarks really quite valuable if placed on the open market, even though we had not put them up for auction. I saw him wince the moment I made this remark. I simply said we had a duty to our shareholders to achieve a fair value in the sale price, and that value would inevitably have to be more than a few years' worth of royalties. We danced back and forth for a while but failed to make progress. I could see that Bob was getting frustrated. To try and break the cycle, we each agreed to ask our external accounting firms to value the trademarks, and then exchange the valuation reports before meeting again.

There are many ways to value IP rights and our respective accountants came up with vastly different figures. Bob asked PMEC's auditors to calculate a value range based on the royalties PMEC was paying under the license. We, on the other hand, asked our accountants to assess the value based on open market considerations, or what a third party might offer for them. Inevitably, the valuations came in at opposite ends of the spectrum. After exchanging the valuations, we were still in the same position. What to do? We met again to discuss how to swim out of the whirlpool.

Bob asked me a direct no-nonsense question. It was about the thought that was bugging him most. Was my company really willing to put the IP rights on the open market with the risk that the new owner would hike up the royalties or terminate the licence to PMEC when it next came up for renewal? That would seriously threaten the PMEC business because the cost of investing in new branding would be prohibitive.

I had already thought about this from a corporate social responsibility (CSR) standpoint, and discussed it internally. My view was that although we had to secure a fair value, "fairness" is a 360-degree evaluation. It included fairness to our shareholders, of course, but also meant not putting a small company's viability in jeopardy. My colleagues bought this rationale, and I was given negotiation flexibility to do the right thing.

From a negotiating standpoint, I wondered whether I should disclose this to Bob. Even though it would massively dilute my leverage, I quickly decided that I should do it – to inspire his trust and increase his confidence not only in my company and in me as a negotiator, but putting him out of his misery with regard to the possible Sword of Damocles hanging over him. It would hopefully also motivate Bob to reach a deal on the price. I was also appealing to Bob's sense of fairness. His eyes lit up when I told him. For the first time both of us felt a deal could be done on the price. But how?

This was a common predicament that confronts negotiators the world over. A distributive bargain, an anxious buyer and a willing seller, but an inability to agree on the price. Bob and I discussed going jointly to a third, this time independent, accounting firm for a valuation, but neither of us really favored that idea. What valuation criteria would we ask the new firm to use? We would be unlikely to agree. Then we had another process idea. What if we agreed minimum and maximum values, effectively a floor and ceiling, a preliminary ZOPA range as discussed in Chapters 2 and 5, and then see how far we were apart? I proposed a ceiling that was 50% lower than our accountants' initial open market valuation, and Bob proposed a floor that was 50% more than his accounting firm's valuation. Although this meant that I had come down much more than Bob had gone up, we had a ZOPA, even if it was a wide one. Bob said he could not afford to split the difference. We continued to discuss price, but made no progress. We were still at Square One. So, remembering Professor Plant's words, we put our heads together to develop a process more geared to the situation we were in.

What we envisaged was a simple three-step process. Step 1 would be an expert adjudication of the fair value for the IP rights which would be kept secret from the parties, followed by Step 2 – a facilitated negotiation to try and reach agreement, and

Chapter 7

if that failed, Step 3 would be the revelation of the adjudicated fair value in Step 1 that would bind both parties. This was a simplified version of an established dispute resolution process called Arbitration-Mediation or Arb-Med. It seemed like a possible, if slightly unconventional, way to enable us to reach an outcome.

We turned to a non-profit dispute resolution foundation in Amsterdam called ACB to assist us. Its executive director at the time, Manon Schonewille, was asked to identify a shortlist of six professionals having both commercial arbitration and mediation skills and experience. After researching the résumés she put forward, I was comfortable with the competency of them all, so I invited Bob to make the selection. Bob chose Willem Kervers, a Rotterdam-based full-time professional neutral handling around eighty business disputes a year. Bob asked me if I knew him; I did not, and nor did anyone in my company as far as I could find out. With ACB's help, we then prepared a short contract that spelled out the sequence of the three step process, the timing, the ZOPA, and committed both parties to accepting the adjudicated value if we were unable to reach a negotiated figure during the facilitated negotiation Stage 2.

On the agreed day, we spent the morning presenting our valuation arguments to Willem. Once he was happy he understood all the facts and arguments, Bob and I and our colleagues left to have lunch together, leaving Willem alone with a plate of cheese sandwiches to consider the fair value. We had arranged for Willem, at our joint cost, to have access by phone to an independent accountant who was an expert in intellectual property valuation to help him address methodologies and accounting principles used to value IP rights.

After lunch, we returned to the meeting room. Willem's sandwiches had been reduced to crumbs, and next to the water jug stood a white sealed envelope on which Willem had written: Confidential. We sat down, all of us transfixed by the envelope. Willem spoke, explaining that he had arrived at a fair value and had written the number on a piece of paper in the envelope. He then said his job now was to try and erase that number from his memory, and help us to arrive at a negotiated figure. It took him perhaps five or ten minutes to psyche himself from the adjudicatory mode into a facilitative one. He said he would like to have a conversation with each of us separately and confidentially. For several hours, Willem alternated twenty-minute caucuses with each of us. Each time, we felt we might be edging closer.

Eventually, Willem asked us all to convene in the meeting room. He outlined a short series of terms, including a price, for the sale of the IP rights that he suggested, based on his confidential discussions with each party, might be acceptable. They were in line with my private discussions with Willem and so I said that these terms were acceptable to my company. After a few clarifying questions, Bob confirmed acceptance for PMEC, and so we had a deal. Willem wrote a one-page non-binding deal sheet of the key terms and offered it to both of us to review and sign, which we did. We asked our lawyers, who were in the room, to convert the deal sheet into a formal draft agreement within a week. We all shook hands. Magically, a bottle of Champagne appeared and we toasted not only the completion of a difficult negotiation, but a successful process with the help of a genuinely neutral and expert facilitator. It was quite invigorating.

After the second glass, Bob said: *"Michael, I am curious to know whether I have negotiated a better or worse deal than if I had let someone else decide. Wouldn't you like to know too? Shall we open the envelope? It's just an academic number now."*

If I hesitated, it was for less than a second. *"Bob, if we open the envelope, and if it contains a number different from the one we agreed, then one of us will be unhappy. Do either of us want to inflict despondency on the other, or, just as likely, on ourselves? And if the envelope number is higher than the one we agreed, the armchair experts back at my corporate head office will simply mark me as a lousy negotiator. I would be crazy to hand them the evidence on a plate!"*

Bob said something like: *"Ah, but what if the number in the envelope is lower than what we agreed, then you go home a hero... Isn't it worth the gamble?"* My reaction was: *"Bob, if that turns out to be the case, you will be sad. There's an old English proverb: a hero is someone who is afraid to run away. Under that definition, we're both heroes already because we did not run away from a deadlock situation. The secret in the envelope will not prove it any further. Some things are better not knowing."*

Bob laughed and nodded: *"Anyway, what's important to me is that I can afford the price we have agreed."* I told him I was happy to hear that, and that my company will be equally satisfied, because, despite the much higher theoretical valuation at the start, the agreed price is fundamentally fair in the circumstances.

Willem, who had been listening to the conversation, silently reached for the envelope and slipped it into his bag. The secret stayed where it should remain, with him.

There are several reasons why this process helped lead to an agreement and how the lessons are transferable to many other negotiations where parties stumble to get to yes. Manon Schonewille, who had recommended Willem Kervers, in an article reporting on the case, summed it up:

> In any negotiation, whether in a dispute context or as a straightforward deal, there are dynamics and undercurrents that seal the deal. In this case, the deal sealer was the power of the envelope. Here we had two parties who wanted to do a deal but had different ideas about its value. Because Willem had made a decision, the parties knew they would end the day with a result. But would it have been palatable to both? The envelope represented the potential Worst Alternative to a Negotiated Agreement, or WATNA. Standing upright on the table for all to see, the envelope served as a constant reminder, a permanent reality check. It influenced both parties to listen more carefully to the other, and to be more inventive in seeking solutions, because opening that envelope could make them worse off. It was psychology at work.

In neurobiological terms, this negotiating experience was an application of the O/S 2 and O/S 3 Operating Systems described in Chapter 3. Willem represented an "out-group" force in O/S 2 because he had the power to impose an outcome on the parties. That encouraged each of us, as the parties, to view the other more through an "in-group" script as our joint preference was to forge an agreement rather than have an outside person impose it on us. We applied our rational operating systems, or O/S 3, with more vigor to come to an agreement.

Chapter 7

The process chosen for a negotiation can greatly affect how the brain conditions the parties' mindsets as they approach their dialogue. Just switching your perception of the other party into more of an "in-group" mode can help to resolve deadlocks that have been caused while in an "out-group" phase. *"Psychology at work"* really does sum it up.

DEAL FACILITATION: NEGOTIATE WHILE A NEUTRAL HANDLES THE PROCESS

Before embarking on any major negotiation, step back, take a deep breath and ask: *Is this likely to be a challenging one?* If the honest answer is a Yes, for whatever reason, a good follow-up question is: *Can a facilitated process help improve the prospects of an agreed outcome?*

Negotiations are collaborative or competitive, or a mixture of the two. There seems to be a view among many experts that those where the parties adopt a predominately collaborative approach are more integrative and focused on creating mutual value and therefore outside help with the process is not needed. They argue that parties to a typical collaborative negotiation, assuming they are rational, are usually able to handle process issues themselves because emotions are under control and options for mutual gain can be explored openly without too much difficulty.

I find this to be uncomfortably simplistic. The negotiation Bob and I had over the PMEC brand rights was very collaborative, but without the help of the Arb-Med process we would have faced a real problem. Collaborative negotiations involving more than two parties, situations where misunderstandings could easily arise caused by language or culture, and those that risk deadlock and turning competitive despite the best efforts of the parties, would also all benefit from process solutions.

Competitive, or positional, negotiations as they are often called, are typically dominated by manipulative strategies where negotiators try to claim value for themselves at the expense of the other party. Inevitably, that leads to tension, distrust, lack of respect, defensiveness, intimidation, stubbornness and deadlock.

Usually, but not always, the circumstances make the parties competitive. They may literally be competitors in the marketplace, or one party may be a government agency, or there may be some serious power imbalance. But competitive negotiations can arise simply because of the intransigent style of one or more of the negotiators. Whatever the reason, competitive negotiations breed disagreements, which, uncontrolled, escalate into disputes. Exchanging information to enable trade-offs and to find solutions becomes difficult. Competitive negotiations are virtually indistinguishable from those aimed at resolving formal disputes. To reach an acceptable outcome, the parties need some sort of joint external influence to ease the path to agreement via a facilitated process.

EXCUSES, EXCUSES

There are several reasons why negotiators do not seriously consider using neutral facilitators to help them make deals. They include habit, over-confident egos, fear, advisor protectionism and short-term cost constraints, mostly things that contribute to what Harvard Law School Professor Frank E.A. Sander once called *the deadening drag of status quoism*.

Typical reactions to the concept of involving a neutral facilitator include:

- *I don't need anyone to teach me how to negotiate;*
- *I have negotiated hundreds of deals and I can do it alone;*
- *An outsider will not know the details and will slow things down;*
- *This deal is confidential and market sensitive;*
- *Legal professional privilege may be compromised;*
- *The other party will see it as a weakness;*
- *It indicates that we anticipate major problems ahead;*
- *An extra person in the framework cannot possibly add value;*
- *It will make everything more complex;*
- *It will add cost and slow things down;* and
- *Too many cooks spoil the broth.*

These inhibitions mostly stem from lack of experience and insight into the use of competent facilitators to help negotiators by taking the process issues out of the problems.

All of these excuses can be countered, but there is another, more worrying reason that negotiators do not use neutrals to help negotiate deals: the possibility does not even occur to them. Their training and experience has made them so accustomed to a narrow set of behaviors that they fail to appreciate and consider alternatives.

Many agents, such as external counsel and other professional advisers, trade their services on the strength of their self-professed track record of deal-making mastery and intellectual rigor. They typically interpret a suggestion of using a neutral facilitator to assist negotiations rather defensively, as a challenge to their raison d'être. Some even prefer not to have their client present during certain negotiation phases and fear that a neutral facilitator will dilute their impact and control, and sideline their role. Some advisers discourage the engagement of neutral outsiders who, they fear, may influence their client behind closed doors. Their skepticism can express itself with derisive arguments like:

- *It's too early for a facilitator to come into the frame;*
- *Facilitation has a role in dispute resolution but not in deal making;*
- *It will be too difficult to find the right neutral facilitator;*
- *It is tactically unwise and will be misread by the other party;*
- *Disclosures to the facilitator may not be privileged;* and
- *The other party will never agree.*

These are all human reactions to something new and untried, but in most cases such concerns exhibit an excess of skepticism, self-interest and caution.

Chapter 7

In Getting To Yes With Yourself (& Other Worthy Opponents) (2015), William Ury explains that we are ourselves the source, or at least one of the sources, of many of the problems we encounter, and that we should have the courage and confidence to take responsibility for how we handle things and for what we say. Ury recommends stepping back, observing, thinking, listening and *going to the balcony*, as he puts it, to take a fresh perspective and to allow ourselves to consider options that may be counter-intuitive or that may depart from the well-trodden path.

In The New Lawyer: How Settlement is Transforming the Practice of Law (2008), Professor Julie Macfarlane condemns as outmoded the traditional lawyer-client model, in which the autonomous external counsel dictates strategy and tactics and in which the client, who may be represented by an internal counsel, essentially follows directions. This way to doing things is quickly being replaced by a more participatory and collaborative partnership, an effective role reversal in which the internal counsel pulls the strings regarding process and outcomes, and the external lawyer advises, executes and supports.

Top management expectations of the role of corporate counsel as captured in Chapter 1, combined with William Ury's wisdom and the changing dynamics of client/lawyer relationships, combine to open the door to the use of neutral facilitators in managing negotiations.

One thing that is largely missing is a proper appreciation of the benefits of facilitated processes in deals. The concept is not widely marketed and is therefore generally misunderstood. The value of facilitators currently seems confined to dispute resolution, where they are called mediators. Perhaps that is because most organizations that promote mediation and deliver mediation services do so in a purely dispute context.

RATIONAL APPRAISAL

First and foremost, parties need to understand that a neutral facilitator does not negotiate on behalf of the parties, but handles the process. Negotiating remains the exclusive preserve and responsibility of the parties. The facilitator's role is to make the process more conducive to a successful outcome, to help anticipate and avoid problems with process solutions, and generally to oil the wheels for forward motion. Second, in any major negotiation, the cost of the facilitator, shared equally between the parties, will be an infinitesimal fraction of the overall value of the deal. Third, never assume that the other party or parties will not agree. If you present the concept and explain the rationale objectively, and emphasize that the choice of facilitator must be made jointly, there is no obvious reason why they would refuse. Nor will the other party believe that the idea of hiring a neutral facilitator has its roots in weakness or fear provided the explanation given is true and complete. Finally, a facilitator can add huge value, not only by enabling the parties to negotiate a better, more sustainable deal, but by helping to implement subsequent interactions between the parties.

In The Global Negotiator: Making, Managing and Mending Deals Around the World in the Twenty-First Century (2003), Professor Jeswald Salacuse of The Fletcher School at Tufts University, one of the global thought leaders on deal facilitation, splits negotiating into three distinct stages: bringing the deal to fruition, managing and implementing the deal, and handling any conflicts that may ensue. Professor Salacuse calls these stages deal making, deal managing and deal mending. The third stage, deal mending, or dispute resolution, is addressed in Chapter 8 where facilitators (mediators) are increasingly used to help parties negotiate settlements. Curiously, as Professor Salacuse acknowledges, the same does not widely apply to deal making and deal managing, even though a facilitated process makes exceptional sense in very many negotiations and can bring huge additional value to all parties involved.

ADDED VALUE

The international conversation on the concept of deal facilitation has only really taken place since the Millennium but can be traced to the late Howard Raiffa, Professor of Managerial Economics at HBS in his classic work: The Art and Science of Negotiation (1982). Professor Raiffa sought mechanisms to achieve so-called Pareto efficiency, a situation first described by the early 20th Century Genoese economist Vilfredo Pareto, where it is no longer possible to make one party better off without making another worse off.

Deal facilitation was considered by Professor Raiffa as a process approach to mergers and acquisitions that could help parties to achieve Pareto efficiency. An article in 1989 by L. Michael Hager, then director general of the International Development Law Organisation in Rome, and Robert Pritchard, a commercial lawyer in private practice in Sydney, took up this idea. They summarized two case studies where parties negotiated commercial deals with the help of a facilitator. Their article presented a cogent case for using independent external facilitators to help parties negotiate deals, particularly where inter-cultural issues arise.

Professor Salacuse also followed up the Raiffa and Hager/Pritchard ideas. The Global Negotiator describes a major commercial deal facilitation role performed in 1990 by the late Robert Strauss, one of the founders of the Aikin Gump law firm, a former US Trade Representative and Ambassador to the Soviet Union and the Russian Federation. Japan's Matsushita (now Panasonic) sought to acquire Music Corporation of America (MCA) (now NBC Universal/Comcast). To help them come to terms, they together engaged Ambassador Strauss as *"counsellor to the transaction."* At the time, Strauss was on the Board of MCA and was also an advisor to Matsushita, so he was respected and trusted by both parties. Matsushita and MCA had previously tried, and failed, to agree the terms of the deal. Strauss facilitated the meetings that ultimately enabled the two companies to agree a USD 6.59 billion deal and complete the transaction.

More recently, former British Prime Minister Tony Blair was widely reported to have facilitated the completion of the merger in 2013 of mining giants Glencore and Xstrata. According to media reports at the time, the deal was consummated quickly after Blair become involved to break a deadlock over the merger price. He was called in because he was trusted both by Glencore's chief executive, Ivan Glasenberg and the head of Xstrata's largest independent shareholder, the Qatar Investment Authority, represented by then Qatari Prime Minister Hamad bin Jassim Al Thani.

Although these are examples of successful facilitation in mega-deal making, the principles apply to any important or complex deal negotiation. A neutral facilitator can do what negotiators often find very difficult or impossible to achieve – help them communicate through use of process techniques.

HOW DEAL FACILITATION WORKS

The operational nuts and bolts of deal facilitation are neatly explained in a 2011 article[43] entitled *Moving Beyond Just A Deal, a Bad Deal or No Deal: How a Deal Facilitator Engaged by the Parties as Counsel To The Deal can Help them Improve the Quality and Sustainability of the Outcome*. The authors, dispute resolution scholars and practitioners Manon Schonewille of the legal mediation office of Schonewille & Schonewille in Rotterdam and Kenneth Fox, Professor in the School of Business and Director of Conflict Studies at Hamline University in St Paul, Minnesota, explain that in addition to assuming the burden of being jointly delegated by the parties to configure the optimal negotiation process, the facilitator keeps the parties on track, improves communications, addresses face issues, preserves confidentialities and clarifies misunderstandings.

They also identify the potential benefits of using a deal facilitator, depending on the circumstances, to be:

- structuring an orderly process, providing a clear framework through professional management and ensuring a good preparation;
- promoting transparency and availability of objective information;
- increasing the chances of reaching an interest-based outcome within a pre-defined time frame;
- managing imbalances and neutralizing negative leverage;
- preventing negotiation breakdown caused by deadlocks, high emotions and communication and interpretation problems;
- supporting parties to maintain relationship building while still claiming value;
- neutralizing difficult negotiation tactics and managing conflicting personalities, styles or objectives;
- managing arguments between the parties' advisers (e.g., avoiding unproductive forays into irrelevant or tangential issues);
- enabling parties to explore new options and maximizing their underlying interests confidentially in a caucus;
- helping parties to deal with more extreme positions without derailing the negotiation;
- supporting parties in framing or reframing issues and generating clarity by reality testing;

- promoting understanding and communications in multi-cultural negotiations where incompatible values or languages are involved;
- assisting parties to deal with their constituency issues;
- being available after the deal is signed as a source of continuity to deal with potential people problems, tensions or unexpected issues that may arise during implementation.

Manon Schonewille and Professor Fox point out that while deal facilitation and dispute mediation are similar in nature, parties to a deal are typically more flexible in their positions or at least more open to exploring options for mutual gain than they tend to be when resolving a dispute with a mediator. ZOPA exploration best takes place early in a deal facilitation, enabling the parties to map out a framework for the outcome. In dispute settlements, parties often focus on the ZOPA rather later in the process. The parties to a prospective deal are usually more rational, optimistic and less emotionally wound up than disputants and they tend to be rather less negative about proposals made by the other party. Reactive devaluation is less of a problem than it often is when trying to settle a dispute.

On the other hand, they emphasize that in deal making, parties will routinely overvalue what they are selling and undervalue what they are buying, resulting in the special importance of anchors, ATNAs and reality-testing. But this also applies in dispute management.

AVOIDING TROUBLE

Perhaps the most substantial difference between deal facilitation and dispute mediation is the emphasis on problem avoidance and prevention.

In 1729, long before he became President of Pennsylvania, Benjamin Franklin bought the company that published his local newspaper, The Pennsylvania Gazette. He often contributed to the paper using an alias. In 1735, Franklin sent an anonymous letter to the paper under the pseudonym of *"an old citizen"* and pleaded for care to be taken about the risk of fire from hot coals. He began his exhortation with a statement that would go down in history and become a proverb: *"An ounce of prevention is worth a pound of cure."* Franklin incited the people to create firefighting stations, initially using leather buckets. The following year volunteers set up The Union Fire Company, Philadelphia's first firefighting organization. It came to be known as Benjamin Franklin's Bucket Brigade and as similar fire stations were created around the country, Philadelphia became known as the safest city in the world.

The Franklin philosophy lies at the root of deal facilitation. One of the greatest values of deal facilitation is its unique capacity to help negotiators craft long-term sustainable deals by preventing negotiations and concluded deals from degenerating into disputes. As Peppet, Salacuse, Schonewille, Fox and others have all pointed out, facilitators, a latter day Bucket Brigade, can also help parties avoid predictable deal implementation problems, long after the deal has been signed.

In some ways, the deal making phase is the easy bit. Although Professor Salacuse segments the issues into deal making, deal managing and deal mending, two-thirds of his book is devoted to deal making. Yet the deal managing or implementation phase can be even more challenging.

Involving a facilitator in the deal making stage brings into play a highly informed neutral resource who can help the parties consummate the deal into reality in the deal managing phase. The deal facilitator can be engaged by the parties on a jointly-funded retainer to stay in the frame long term. Management development programs in today's corporations are very sophisticated, aimed at providing key personnel with a well-rounded set of experiences and skills for further advancement. Progressive and valuable as these programs may be, a downside is that negotiators get moved around, severing relationships they may have generated with negotiation partners. Having a neutral facilitator engaged in the deal managing stage can be a very astute investment as a force of continuity.

GETTING AGREEMENT TO A DEAL FACILITATION PROCESS

Few people have direct personal experience of using a deal facilitator. The idea is rather unconventional. If you start explaining what a deal facilitator does, people are likely to reject the idea. They may dismiss it as a tactical maneuver, or a mechanism for disguising a vulnerability, or an unnecessary bureaucratic cost. Whatever the reason, because it is virtually unheard of, the proposition needs to be put forward differently to gain buy-in.

In Start With Why: How Great Leaders Inspire Everyone to Take Action (2009), management consultant Simon Sinek explains that to get agreement, you need to inspire by explaining your beliefs and your goals in ways that people can align with them. You do that by presenting the fundamental rationale, the why, behind your proposal before explaining the how and the what. The rationale needs to inspire. Then explain how the belief or goal can be materialized through action, and finally say what needs to be done to implement the action. First the WHY, then the HOW and finally the WHAT.

Although no two situations are the same, this simple sequence can be applied with great effect when persuading the other party to buy into a facilitated negotiation process, or, indeed, any other idea or proposition you want to seed in the mind of another person. Here is a basic example:

> *[Name], we both believe in exactly the same thing: a deal that both our organizations will not only be happy with, but delighted about. We both want a deal that will deliver intrinsic and holistic value for ourselves, that will stand the test of time, and will grow and lead to great things. We both want to emerge from this negotiation, which may get tough at times, with a sustainable relationship and jointly feel we*

> *have done a fine job. This is a well-trodden path, like negotiating prenuptial agreements, and actually, when you strip it down to its basics, our situation is not a lot different from a marriage contract! We believe, in spite of the obvious challenges, that together we can craft a deal that lasts because both parties have lots to gain. Right?* [the WHY]
>
> *To help manage the process, but not the substance, we could jointly engage a neutral person to act as kind of "counsel to the deal." The deal may be an inanimate thing, but we will give it a personality and character of its own! The facilitator's role will be to take responsibility for the process, remain entirely impartial and ensure the deal works equally well for both of us. I see the benefits as....... [articulate the main benefits]. And we might afterwards consider keeping the facilitator in the frame as the deal is implemented to help us build on it.* [the HOW]
>
> *The facilitator's impartiality is key, and we need to find exactly the right person, someone in whose personality, professionalism, knowledge and skills we both can have complete trust and confidence. We can discuss who, but there are lots of places where we can find suitable résumés. We can share the cost equally, and it will be a very small piece of the final value. We are just two parties wanting to forge a great deal without enduring process problems in getting us there.* [the WHAT]

This example sets out to explain the rationale and the thoughts underpinning the concept, and to start using a relevant metaphor or example that can easily be grasped to encourage understanding and buy-in.

In the WHY step, no detail is given, just the philosophy, motive and belief, a sense of purpose, which in this case is to craft a better, stronger, more successful and longer lasting deal for everyone.

The HOW plants another metaphor, "counsel to the deal" (a term coined by Professor Salacuse) and articulates the benefits.

The WHAT gets into a few key practicalities. It all hangs together, flows, has impact.

AN ALLEGORY

In 1961, Groucho Marx gave two pieces of advice to a prospective husband: *to keep his mouth shut and his chequebook open*. These days, the second has been partly replaced by prenuptial agreements, many of which are arrived at using a deal facilitator.

A prenup is a contract entered into by prospective spouses in contemplation of their marriage or civil union. It typically focuses on division of property, and its terms, assuming the contract is valid and enforceable, will usually override any statutory provisions to the contrary. Prenups can protect both spouses in the event of a marriage breakup or the bankruptcy of a partner.

If the future spouses were businesses or other organizations, the prenup might be called a JV agreement. From a process perspective, prenups and JV agreements have much in common. In both, the parties want to join together, not to become adversaries in some legalistic process. In both cases, the deal, whether euphemistically called a prenup or simply a JV agreement, is, in reality, a disguised divorce settlement. These things are often very hard for parties to get to grips with when termination is the last thing on their minds. They want to come together, but if they avoid addressing the toughest break-up issues, they are likely to end up with an unsuitable deal that does not stand the test of time.

A deal facilitator is in a unique position to table issues that the parties prefer not to raise, such as managing their emotions and dialogue about the risks of break-up and its consequences. The facilitator, being neutral, is ideally placed to draft a basic term sheet or memorandum of understanding for review by the parties' and their respective advisers that covers these hard-to-deal-with issues.

Prenups provide an excellent analogy for facilitated deal making by organizations because people can relate to them on a personal level.

IDENTIFYING THE RIGHT DEAL FACILITATOR

Deal facilitation is a real skill. The person selected needs to be neutral and impartial, but these are not the only relevant criteria. Above all, each of the parties needs to feel they can really trust the facilitator. To do that, you need to consider both the facilitator's competency and also their suitability from the standpoint of all parties.

Effectively, a deal facilitator needs to have the same fundamental competencies as a mediator of disputes. It therefore makes sense to consider experienced commercial mediators to take on the role of deal facilitators.

Suitability is a separate issue. Not all competent mediators may make suitable deal facilitators. Background experience, cultural considerations, language capabilities, location and other factors can affect suitability in the mind of one or more parties. They also need to be experienced negotiators. Competency and suitability of mediators, and where to find them, are covered in Chapter 8.

The parties will normally want to enter into an agreement with the deal facilitator before their engagement begins. An agreement would make clear the purpose of the engagement, the scope, role and responsibilities of the deal facilitator and such issues as confidentiality, impartiality and neutrality, fees and billing and termination of the appointment. A liability and indemnity clause may also be included.

IN A NUTSHELL

- Process directly affects the outcome of negotiation.
- More thought needs to be given to selecting the right process tailored to each negotiation.
- The process affects the parties' psychology.
- Keep process, relationships and substantive issues mentally separate.

- With deal facilitation, you and your negotiation partner lead the negotiation and determine the outcome, while the facilitator handles the process. You are then better able to negotiate by focusing entirely on the substance.
- Be intolerant of weak excuses for not using a deal facilitator.
- To persuade the other party to buy into your preferred process choice, always start with WHY before moving onto the HOW and the WHAT.

CHAPTER 8
Disputes

Do you have a conflict, or does the conflict have you?

Prof. Dr. Friedrich Glasl

In Diary of a Pilgrimage (1891), Jerome K. Jerome wrote: *If a man stopped me in the street and demanded my watch, I would refuse. If he then threatened me with violence, I would fight him. But if, instead, he threatened to sue me, I would take the watch from my pocket, give it to him, and feel I had got away lightly.*

Jerome was just repeating the wisdom of the ages. Confucius remarks in Analect 12.13: *In hearing lawsuits, I am just like others. What is necessary is to ensure that there are no lawsuits.* In The Art of War, his contemporary Sun Tzu says: *The greatest victory is that which requires no battle.* Abraham Lincoln told us *never to stir up litigation*, and that *a worse man can scarcely be found than one who does this*. Illustrating the illusion of litigation winners, Voltaire wrote: *I was never ruined but twice – once when I lost a lawsuit, once when I won one.*

More recently, the late Gore Vidal, master of the aphorism, observing that his lawyers were all contemporaries, concluded that *litigation takes the place of sex at middle age*. Apple's CEO, Tim Cook told financial analysts in April 2012, with passion: *I've always hated litigation, and I continue to hate it.* Irving Shapiro, a former Chairman of DuPont Company, pronounced that: *Litigation should be a last resort, not a knee-jerk reaction.* In similar vein, Microsoft's Corporate Vice President of Retail Sales, David Porter, has quipped that *litigation is the basic legal right which guarantees every corporation its decade in court.*

I was working in New York City leading the international legal group at Pfizer, when Wess Roberts' book Leadership Secrets of Attila The Hun (1987) topped the non-fiction bestseller list. Endorsed as "fantastic!" by author of In Search of Excellence, Tom Peters, it made me reflect on many aspects of my job as a corporate counsel. In a section entitled Attila on the Art of Negotiation, one piece of advice is: *Never arbitrate.*

Chapter 8

Arbitration allows a third party to determine your destiny. It is a resort of the weak. This really caught my attention, because I was doing a lot of arbitrating and litigating.

Up to that point, I had conducted myself as if litigation and arbitration really were the best, in fact usually the only, credible strategy to resolve disputes. To me, litigation was leverage on steroids. Sleepwalking, I had fallen into the trap identified by Abraham Maslow in The Psychology of Science (1966) that *it is tempting, if the only tool you have is a hammer, to treat everything as if it were a nail.* Leadership Secrets of Attila The Hun finally made me think of other tools. I began to realize that I could get much better results for my company more quickly and at lower cost by negotiation. But to do that, I needed to re-educate myself.

The National Conference on the Causes of Popular Dissatisfaction with the Administration of Justice in St Paul, Minnesota in April 1976 had kick-started a mini revolution in the history of dispute resolution in the US. The event has become known as the Pound Conference, in honor of Roscoe Pound, the reforming Dean of Harvard Law School for twenty years until his retirement in 1936. Supreme Court Chief Justice Warren Burger opened that seminal conference by urging the increased exploration and use of informal dispute resolution processes, a message strongly endorsed and amplified at the conference by Harvard Law School Professor Frank E.A. Sander in his paper at the event "Varieties of Dispute Processing."

Five years after the 1976 Pound Conference, Getting To Yes was published and the Harvard Negotiation Project was set up to improve negotiation and dispute resolution skills. Coincidentally, an extraordinary man, James F. Henry, was wearing out shoe leather trudging through the corridors of corporate America promoting assisted negotiation, that is, mediation, as the prime method for resolving business disputes. Jim created a small non-profit organization in New York City, a few blocks from my office, that he rather obliquely called the Center for Public Resources, as a platform for corporate counsel to come together to promote negotiation as the prime means for resolving business disputes, thereby reducing risk and cutting costs. It is now known as the International Center for Conflict Prevention and Resolution, or CPR Institute. Jim and CPR persuaded dozens, then hundreds and ultimately thousands of companies to sign a pledge to consider non-adversarial methods to resolve disputes. It currently reads*:*

> *Our company pledges to commit its resources to manage and resolve disputes through negotiation, mediation and other ADR processes when appropriate, with a view to establishing and practicing global, sustainable dispute management and resolution processes.*

Mediation skills courses began to spring up, initially around the US followed by Canada and then in parts of Europe and Asia, based on the work developed in the US.

My employer became an early signatory of the CPR Pledge, but to understand this concept better, I attended one of the mediation skills courses that were mushrooming all over the place. Only then did I fully realize the simple sense behind Attila The Hun's concept of not allowing a third party, like a Judge or arbitrator, to determine your destiny when, through negotiation, you could determine your own. And I discovered, to my amazement at the time, how much easier it is to negotiate effectively when a mediator is in the frame, and how much better the outcome can be.

By the early 1990s, I was convinced that, in most cases, there was more to gain by negotiating and mediating outcomes than by litigating and arbitrating them. Many other internal counsel agreed. Well ahead of me in this realization were corporate counsel peers in General Electric, a company whose motto is "Imagination At Work," and I began watching them carefully. In some countries, not just common law jurisdictions, this trend has taken sufficient root for important research studies to be undertaken to prove the value of having a mediator present when you negotiate.

THE NATURE OF DISPUTES

We argue when we disagree. We see the same basic facts, but we understand them in different ways. We apply different values and assumptions and we have different interests at stake that cause us to interpret the facts differently. We see the same situation in the way we want it to apply to others because that fits with our goals and needs. Then we craft positions to represent, even to distort, our interests. We embellish and exaggerate those positions, and argue about them, and gradually the positions take on an identity of their own. The positions detach from the interests and the dispute escalates. Minor or incidental positions get magnified out of proportion to their significance. Tactics come into play, contorting the positions by cloaking them in legal interpretations and new claims. Soon the dispute morphs entirely into a clash of positions and we start to lose touch with the underlying interests and needs. We no longer control the conflict, as Professor Friedrich Glasl observed, it controls us. It becomes a vortex, a whirlpool, and extracting oneself is difficult. That is the inevitable nature of most disputes, and the reason why they need to be resolved through mature negotiation, and as early as possible.

CORPORATE COUNSEL ATTITUDES TO DISPUTE RESOLUTION

There have been several studies, mostly in the US, that have vindicated the Attila The Hun philosophy that adversarial dispute resolution methods are increasingly falling out of favor, specifically because disputants desire control over the outcome in order to reduce risks and save costs.

In 1997, Professors David Lipsky and Ronald Seeber at Cornell University surveyed corporate counsel in 300 Fortune 1000 companies about their use of mediation and arbitration. The survey[44] found there were two main motivations for not litigating – economic and process control. The economic reasons were savings in cost and time. Under process control, typical incentives for preferring mediation were the parties' desire to control their own destinies, that mediation allows them to resolve disputes themselves, that the process was more satisfactory and, crucially, that the quality of negotiated settlements was higher.

In 2003, the American Arbitration Association (AAA) followed up the Cornell study with a research project[45] involving corporate counsel at 254 US-based companies to assess how they managed disputes. In particular, the AAA researchers wanted to discover whether it was possible to identify companies that were "dispute-wise" (i.e., preferring to negotiate outcomes rather than litigate them) and, if so, whether there was any relationship between "dispute-wise" business practices and favorable outcomes. The results of this research enabled analysts to identify eight attitudes and approaches to disputes adopted by internal counsel that, taken together, suggested that their companies were "dispute-wise," and concluded that these characteristics were associated with certain tangible business benefits.

Among the characteristics associated with "dispute-wise" companies, according to this research, are that internal counsel:

- Have a very good understanding of the business issues facing the company;
- Are highly integrated into the general planning process;
- Are focused on preserving relationships and settling disputes rather than just winning cases;
- Take a much less aggressive approach than the average; and
- Favor litigation over ADR much less often than the average.

LEVEL OF DISPUTE-WISE BUSINESS MANAGEMENT

	Total	Most	Moderate	Least
DESCRIBES LEGAL DEPARTMENT – VERY WELL				
The legal staff has a very good understanding of the broader business issues facing the company and industry	81%	93%	82%	68%
The legal department is highly integrated into the general corporate planning process	59%	81%	51%	42%
Senior management in this company is focused on preserving relationships and settling cases rather than just winning cases	48%	65%	45%	31%
A lot of our time is spent on highly complex and technical issues	41%	62%	37%	21%
A lot of our time is spent on international issues	12%	27%	7%	–
When disputes arise we usually take an aggressive approach	40%	28%	35%	59%
Our primary focus is on reviewing contracts and agreements	23%	14%	19%	36%
We often favor litigation over ADR	15%	3%	11%	31%

Reproduced with the permission of the AAA.

The research produced some fairly obvious findings, but also some that are quite surprising and thought-provoking. As you might expect, and in line with the Cornell study, the Legal functions in the most "dispute-wise" companies operated with significantly lower budgets than the least "dispute-wise" companies, and managed their legal costs more efficiently. Their companies also had stronger relationships with suppliers, customers, other third parties and with their own employees. Interestingly, the "dispute-wise" internal counsel were much less likely to describe their departments as "lean" or "stretched to the limits," suggesting higher job satisfaction and lower frustration rates among corporate counsel working for those "dispute-wise" companies.

The really headline-grabbing finding was that the price-earnings ratios of the most "dispute-wise" companies were, on average, 28% higher than the average for all publicly-held companies surveyed, and 68% higher than the average of the companies in the least "dispute-wise" category.

This survey was not sufficiently extensive to prove these statistics beyond doubt, but preliminary results like this, and from a source like the AAA, cannot be ignored. They suggest that internal counsel can make a significant contribution to the overall profitability of their companies by taking control of adversarial strategies and becoming more "dispute-wise." General Electric's CEO, Jeffrey Immelt, would no doubt call that "business savvyness."

Valuable research, at least from a US perspective, was carried out between 2011 and 2013 by the Straus Institute for Dispute Resolution at Pepperdine University in Malibu, California, with support from Cornell and CPR Institute in New York. Published in the Harvard Negotiation Law Review in 2014, a major part of the research was a follow-on survey[46] of corporate counsel in over 300 Fortune 1000 companies, almost half of them GCs.

Summarizing the findings in the Kluwer Mediation Blog,[47] Pepperdine Professor Thomas Stipanowich, who led the research, explained that companies were typically deploying strategies to control risk and cost in dispute resolution processes. To achieve this, they are using arbitration less and relying more on mediated negotiation and other approaches to resolve disputes informally, quickly and inexpensively. Paradoxically, the research also suggested that a hard core of internal counsel continued to rely on familiar litigation and arbitration as a means of applying leverage, even though most of them consciously *want to control their destiny* and admit that the tried-and-true adversarial processes do not offer them sufficient control over outcomes. They seem to chase the impossible, or at least are unsure quite how to break out of the vortex into which habit has incarcerated them.

In 2013, the International Mediation Institute conducted a survey[48] of seventy-six corporate dispute resolution counsel based in North America and Europe. When asked for their reaction to the proposition that parties to an arbitration should be actively encouraged by the arbitration provider to use mediation to settle their dispute, almost three quarters of responders felt that providers should be actively encouraging parties to use mediation, 22% were ambivalent and only 4% disagreed. Yet few arbitration institutions systematically encourage the parties to try and negotiate a settlement using mediation early in the process. Their rules often allow mediation, but the motivation behind it isn't there. As a result, almost half the respondents in the IMI survey wanted Courts and Tribunals to make mediation compulsory in both litigation and arbitration. About the same proportion considered their external counsel to be an impediment to the mediation process, and only 14% felt external counsel were not a barrier to mediation. Over 80% of internal counsel expected their external counsel to have been trained in mediation advocacy skills, though in reality very few actually are.

In A Scandal in Bohemia (1891), Sherlock Holmes proclaims: *it is a capital mistake to theorize before one has data. Insensibly, one begins to twist facts to suit theories, instead of theories to suit facts.* Eighty-five years later, in his paper Varieties of Dispute Processing tabled at the Pound Conference in April 1976, Professor Frank E.A. Sander of Harvard Law School echoed Mr. Holmes' wisdom when he asserted: *we need far better data...so that we can develop some sophisticated notion of where the main trouble spots are... And we need more data on the role played by some of the key individuals in the [dispute resolution] process e.g. lawyers.* Prof Sander proposed that *"alternative"* forms of dispute resolution, such as mediation, should be used to reduce reliance on conventional litigation, but recognized that impediments existed to the widespread uptake of mediation owing in part to *"the deadening drag of status quoism"* – the reluctance of external counsel to use other dispute resolution options than litigation and arbitration.

Global Pound Conference Series 2016-17

The essence of the 1976 Pound Conference was commemorated forty years later in the form of the Global Pound Conference (GPC) Series 2016-17, initiated by the charitable foundation, IMI. At the time of writing, the GPC Series is in mid-term. The aim of the Series is to convene all stakeholders in dispute resolution worldwide, to provoke focus and debate on existing tools and techniques for resolving disputes, stimulate new ideas, and generate actionable data on what commercial parties need and want, locally and globally. GPC events are being held in all continents and by the time the Series completes in mid-2017, thousands of stakeholders will have attended.

The GPC Series' Core Organizing Group is chaired by Michael McIlwrath of General Electric, who contributes the Foreword to this book. He notes that it was an ambitious project, never previously attempted in the legal field on anything like this scale. Each GPC Series event employs various real-time electronic data-collection methods ranging from multiple choice questions that are voted upon using a smartphone app (with the results, by stakeholder group, visible instantly), to open text comments and word clouds. This is generating a mass of reliable data on the causes of dissatisfaction and opportunities for improvement for all forms of dispute resolution services, ranging from litigation and arbitration to mediation, conciliation and hybrid processes.

At the heart of each event in the GPC Series are twenty core multiple choice questions, broken down into four sessions: (1) What parties, the demand side, need, want and expect; (2) The demand side's views on the services offered by the supply side; (3) What gaps and obstacles may exist to align supply and demand; and (4) Who can do what about making these improvements and when. The database of qualitative and empirical responses is being analyzed by the GPC's international Academic Committee, a group of impartial experts led by Professor Barney Jordaan at the Vlerick Business

School in Belgium. The raw results of each GPC event are published on the GPC website (globalpoundconference.org) and the full analysis and recommendations will be published in due course.

Once the GPC Series is complete, the data will reveal what gaps exist worldwide between the attitudes, needs and interests of disputants/parties compared to those of other stakeholder groups. Most exciting of all, the data analysis and recommendations will influence how the gaps can be bridged by changing attitudes, skills sets and practices to meet party needs more effectively.

CONFLICT ESCALATION

Unless they can be resolved through negotiation, formalized disputes easily take on a life of their own. The disputants start to lose control soon after litigation or arbitration begins. Lawyers, judges and arbitrators assume control because of the inescapable focus on the technicalities of process and procedural tactics. The disputants effectively become the audience in their own play.

When managing disputes, it is useful to identify, case-by-case, what point you have reached on a conflict escalation model, because that knowledge can prompt the best type of action needed to achieve an outcome.

In his book Konfliktmanagement: Ein Handbuch für Führungskräfte, Beraterinnen und Berater (1997) Professor Friedrich Glasl at the University of Salzburg contributed one of the best known escalation models used in civil disputes. The model was summarized in Professor Glasl's book Confronting Conflict (1999) and, with his approval, by Professor Thomas Jordan at the University of Gothenburg in an article[49] in October 2000. The Glasl Escalation Model, or simply "the Glasl Escalator" (because it is in constant motion), has nine steps spread over three distinct phases. In the first three-step phase, the parties are capable of resolving their dispute on a win-win basis. In the second three-step phase, litigation or arbitration begins, which will result in a winner and a loser. In the final steps, both parties typically lose, even if one technically wins. Parties gravitate from one step to another often without realizing that their direction of travel is leading them towards a mutually-destructive end.

The three steps in the first (win-win) phase can be summarized as:

(1) Tension, irritation and hardening of incompatible positions. More differences than common interests.
(2) Increasingly unpleasant debates and controversial exchanges. Inflexibility, exaggeration, tactics. Communication quality deteriorates.
(3) Actions, not words. Blocking maneuvers. Pressure exerted. Reduced communications. Preparations for adversarial action.

Disputes

In the second (win-lose) phase:

(4) In-group and out-group coalitions. Reactive devaluation. The other party is now an enemy. Litigation or arbitration. Communications very poor.

(5) Loss of face, constant negativity and entrenched positions. Strong and over-stated claims. Values predominate over issues. Complex process.

(6) Communication confined to the exchange of threats, counter-threats, ultimatums and deterring strategies.

In the final (lose-lose) phase:

(7) Limited destructive blows aimed at the other party's financial, legal or control elements. Defensive mechanisms deployed. Ethics set aside.

(8) Attempts to fragment and destroy the enemy. The will to win and make the other party lose is all-encompassing. Self-preservation.

(9) Together into the abyss. The drive to annihilate the other party is more important than self-preservation. Mutual self-destruction.

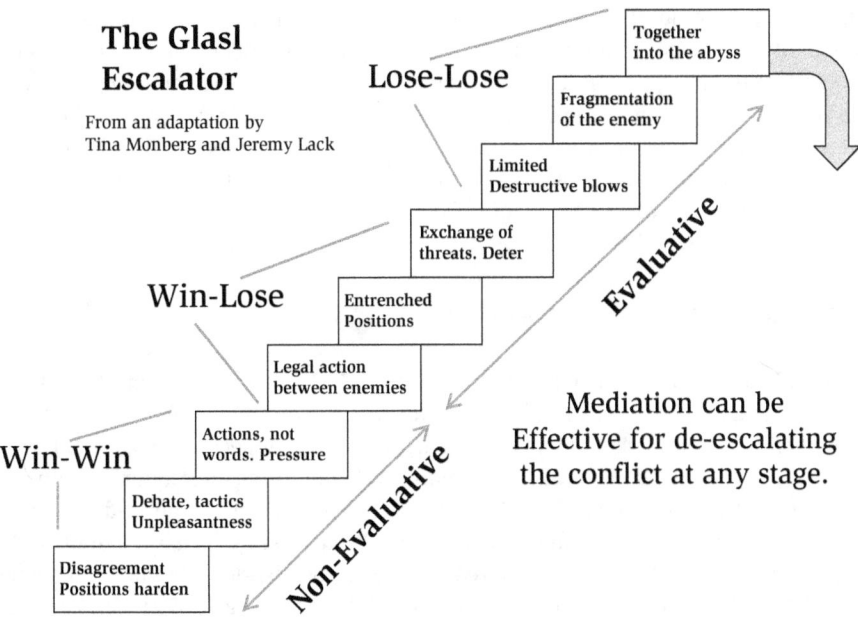

Of course the Glasl Escalator is illustrative and not an attempt to characterize the life cycle of all disputes. The principles, however, are valid. Up to and including phase 1 step 1, it should be possible for the parties to achieve a negotiated outcome. After reaching the threshold to step 2, the parties increasingly need outside help, such as a mediator, to achieve an outcome and prevent the dispute escalating further. By the time the dispute escalates to steps 4 to 6, if one party proposes a mediator, the other is likely to dismiss the idea if only because it was proposed by the other party, though if that problem can be overcome, for example by the proposal originating with a judge or arbitrator or some neutral source, mediation can result in a negotiated outcome or at least a de-escalation.

Litigation and arbitration certainly occupy an important place in the spectrum of dispute resolution options. If you absolutely must have a court judgment, for example because you need a formal precedent, or to make new law, or to establish a legal right beyond doubt, or to deter others, or because the other party flatly refuses to negotiate, then a negotiated settlement may not meet your needs.

But even in all those circumstances, I would not dismiss the negotiation route without careful analysis of the options. All litigation and arbitration is risky because you cannot control the outcome. All litigation and arbitration is a gamble in which your stake is your belief in your argument, one that the adjudicator may not share. If, for example, you own a patent for an invention that has never been tested in Court as valid and enforceable, it would be ideal to have a final judgment in your favor that forces the other party to stop using your invention, pay you damages, and above all that prevents others using the invention. But the judgment may not deliver all or anything you wish for. What if the judgment invalidates some of the patent's claims and weakens the patent? Might you end up worse off than negotiating a settlement in which the other party is seen by the market to step back and take a license, and publicly proclaim that it regards your patent as unassailable? Does everything really have to be black and white? There is power in shades of grey.

DESIGNER DISPUTE RESOLUTION

In his TED Talk in Chicago in October 2010, Getting To Yes author William Ury tells the story of a nomad whose Living Will left his flock of camels to his three sons. The Will provided that his oldest son would receive half the flock, his second son would have a third and the youngest son would have a ninth. After mourning their father's death, the three sons got together to split up the flock, which at the time comprised seventeen camels. They quickly realized they had a problem because seventeen is not divisible by two, three, or nine. If they slaughtered the flock and divided up the meat in the proportions provided in the Will, their livelihoods would be destroyed. They needed the camels alive. The amicable relationship the brothers had always enjoyed began to break down as they discussed the conundrum. To try and prevent the problem escalating into a full-blown dispute, they decided to consult an Elder, someone impartial, wise and respected, to guide them to a solution. The Elder thought about the problem, did not tell the boys what to do, but offered them her camel. Now the flock had increased to eighteen camels. The boys tried again to implement their father's Will. The first son took his half of nine camels, the second son had his third of six camels and the youngest son received his ninth of two camels. Since $9 + 6 + 2 = 17$ camels, they had one camel over which they returned, with appreciation, to the Elder.

Professor Ury, a professional neutral in geopolitical dispute resolution, explained that his life's work is directed at finding that eighteenth camel. The story illustrates how apparently intractable situations can move to a solution with the intervention of a neutral person.

Because every predicament is different, parties need to step back and consider how best to avoid escalation and break deadlock in disputes by using neutrals most effectively. The options are as diverse as human ingenuity. It just requires different thought processes and attitudes.

One day, senior people from two legal professional organizations approached me for help to resolve a dispute between them. They called me only because I was known to them both even though I was not a member of either institution. They explained that one of the institutions was about to sue the other, and there would also be a counter-claim. Legal proceedings had not yet begun, but the parties had exchanged copies of their draft claims. They asked if I could somehow assist them to find a solution that would prevent the dispute progressing to court. We agreed to meet to discuss the situation and they sent me the papers in advance.

Everyone in the room was a lawyer. The disputing institutions were led by lawyers and their internal and external counsel were also there. My first substantive question was to ask whether each party had read and understood the written claims of the other party. Everyone nodded emphatically. So I asked them if they would humor me by taking part in an experiment. Each party would retire to different rooms for twenty minutes to prepare and then come back and explain to me, the only neutral present, the other party's case in the first person, in no more than fifteen minutes each. No one would be allowed to start a sentence with "They say..." but as "Our position is..." or "We claim that...." I explained they would be acting, as if in the theater, with me as the audience, and that I would award an Oscar for the best performance. Jaws dropped open at the idea, but nobody declined. I told them I had borrowed the idea from experienced mediators and asked them to give it a try. *Consider it a bit of fun.* They agreed.

Trust me, I'm your mediator!

They peeled off into separate rooms, and I settled down to read the morning newspaper. Twenty minutes passed, then forty, then an hour. I was starting to read the small ads. I poked my head round the doors of their respective rooms and invited them back to get started, fully prepared or not. I thought it interesting that a bunch of top flight lawyers, who, an hour earlier, had professed deep familiarity with the other party's case, should need so long to figure out how to explain it in just 15 minutes.

Back in the meeting room, each party had chosen their external counsel to present the other side's case as if it were their own. Both counsel did a brilliant, convincing job, oozing passion and conviction in the merits of their opponent's case. Performances worthy of the Academy Awards. They even engaged in a humorous rebuttal exercise, prompting much hilarity. It is always striking how people's perceptions can change when they are invited to take up a role on the opposite side. I congratulated them and gave each counsel an image of the Oscar statuette.

When everyone had settled down, I told them I really did not think they now needed me and could find a solution under their own steam. Sandwiches were brought into the room and I took off to have lunch alone, promising to come back in two hours. When I did so, the parties had reached a settlement. I merely helped them frame the deal sheet summarizing the main terms.

Although this approach might not work for many dispute settlement negotiations, it does illustrate three important general aspects about resolving conflicts, and, for that matter, deal making in general. First, the presence of a neutral person in the room changes the dialogue's dynamics, even though all that person does is to fit the process to the problem. Second, the parties are the ones that do the negotiating, not the neutral. And finally, outcomes are easier to achieve if all the parties really do take the time to understand the other party's predicament and arguments, and really put themselves in the other's shoes.

So, when thinking about the best ways to manage a dispute with a view to achieving an acceptable settlement, be creative, even a little daring. Remember that disputes are easier to avoid than they are to resolve once they have arisen. Cast convention aside and think about the range of options available. Design the best route to a resolution having regard to the circumstances and the people you are dealing with. It could be an off-the-peg process or a hybrid of several tried and tested mechanisms. It just needs to be thought about in advance. It needs to be planned.

PEDR: PLANNED EARLY DISPUTE RESOLUTION

Fisher and Ury's Getting To Yes in 1981 was influential because it changed our prevailing attitudes from time-honored positional bargaining towards a more 21st Century interest-based negotiation. Thirty years later, Professor John Lande at the University of Missouri School of Law presented another important philosophical approach to dispute resolution in his book Lawyering with Planned Early Negotiation (2011), which is directed at external counsellors. He directly challenges the default approach to dispute resolution, which he calls *Litigation As Usual* or LAU. Professor Lande points to the paradox of the *Vanishing Trial*, that despite LAU, only about 10% of cases in State Courts and about 2% of cases in the Federal Courts actually get to a full-blown trial. Almost all are settled. The problem is that the 90% or 98% that settle are mainly resolved very late in the litigation life cycle, after most of the time and cost consumed in litigating have been spent.

There are numerous reasons for this phenomenon. First, as in all fights and contests, parties revel in the fantasy that the other party is a demon that will run out of steam, back off and eventually capitulate. They fail to fully anticipate counterclaims and other forms of revenge, both in and beyond the courtroom, and often underestimate the costs and stress involved until they are locked into the litigious spiral. They are goaded on by their counsel, who invariably want more information, if not all information, before advising on settlement strategies, and meanwhile want to keep the parties apart in case they say too much and compromise their case. External counsel remain acutely aware that the longer the case continues, the more fees it generates, and they all have budget targets to meet within their firms. Even if they do not deliberately place their own interests ahead of their client, which many consciously and genuinely do not, there is an irrepressible psychological force that encourages the case to continue along the winding adversarial path and follow the fixed process prescribed by legal rules for resolving disputes. Like a runaway wagon, the case is locked onto procedural railroad lines, gathering momentum. The parties cannot get off and become unable to think of another way to arrive at their destination until the courtroom steps, and the risks of losing, come into view.

Parties and their counsel often have unrealistic expectations, and it takes time for reality to kick in. Some parties just want to "have their day in Court" or to feel vindicated, or, since revenge is a dish best served cold, they simply want to inflict injury on the other party – until they realize how the costs are mounting for themselves. Or they fear expressing weakness if they take the initiative to propose settlement talks. All these motivations forcefeed calories into the expanding litigation waistline, until it is fit to burst.

Professor Lande calls this a *prison of fear* where parties dare not negotiate because doing so may appear weak; or the other party may take advantage of you in a negotiation; or you will give away too much. External counsel may fear their client will be disappointed in them if they are not seen and felt to be litigating relentlessly, that they may be sued by the client for incompetence, or that they will lose fee income if the case settles too early.

Lande's break-out concept involves psychologically re-orientating yourself to stop and plan for an early resolution. The goal is not winning, but resolving, and as early as possible. Lande recognizes that this philosophy is counter-intuitive, even revolutionary, for many lawyers, whose default solution is *Litigation As Usual*. How many external counsel, or for that matter corporate counsel, think hard about the spectrum of options for resolving a dispute? How many ask themselves how process might help reduce the risk of losing and limit the cost and time involved in singularly pursuing LAU? How many override the instinct to litigate to win, realizing it is a euphemism for losing it all?

With PEDR motivations in mind, in 2009 the Centre for Effective Dispute Resolution (CEDR) published CEDR Rules for the Facilitation of Settlement in International Arbitration.[50] These Rules were developed by a Commission led by former England & Wales Chief Justice Lord Woolf and Gabrielle Kohler Kaufman, Professor of Law at the University of Geneva. Internal counsel were represented on the Commission. The Rules are designed to supplement legal, institutional and ad hoc arbitration rules to increase the prospects of parties settling their disputes through negotiation and avoiding the need to press forward for an arbitral award. Take up of these Rules has been

Chapter 8

disappointing. Few arbitral institutions seem to promote or use them. Corporate counsel can, however, take the initiative to propose to the other party that they jointly apply to the arbitral institution administering their case to apply these Settlement Rules at any time during the proceedings.

The spectrum of possible dispute resolution options has more colours than the palette of an artist. Many enable the process to fit the problem rather than the problem being shoehorned into a conventional process. To help select the best process, parties have the benefit of Guided Choice, Referrers, Dispute Boards and professional case administrators to help them navigate the options. The options are not merely stand-alone. Many can be combined with others.

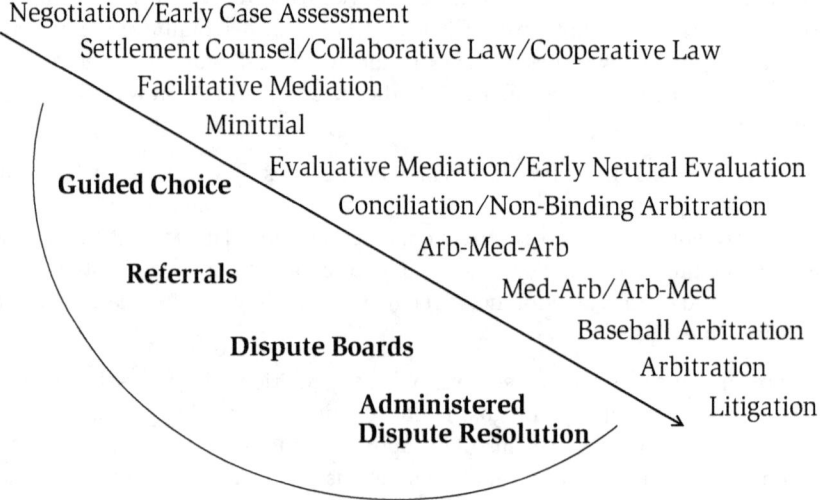

NEGOTIATION WITH ECA: EARLY CASE ASSESSMENT

During his time as British Prime Minister, Benjamin Disraeli chided a member of Her Majesty's Opposition, whom he considered ignorant and unprepared, with the remark: *My Learned Friend, as a general rule, the most successful people in life are those with the best information.* The same applies, in spadeloads, to negotiation and dispute resolution. Assessing information with a view to working out the best route to the desired outcome is the purpose of ECA tools described in Chapter 2, two of which are downloadable from IMI and CPR Institute.

DIRECT NEGOTIATION

If the parties are willing to communicate about their dispute and are in principle ready to find creative ways to resolve it, then direct one-on-one negotiation makes perfect sense. This is usually most likely if the dispute has not escalated past the first few steps on the Glasl Escalator. It gets increasingly challenging for the parties to get to the table in the right frame of mind and under their own steam as the dispute escalates into later steps.

Once the parties start communicating through external counsel, disputes tend to complicate beyond the point where direct one-on-one negotiation is likely. Formal litigation and arbitration are inevitably positional and confrontational, resulting in defensiveness and aggression. External counsel frequently advise clients that any negotiations should be delayed until more information emerges. This can be good advice, but it needs to be weighed against the inevitability of escalation, which will progressively inhibit the chances of negotiating a settlement without the intervention of a third party.

Corporate counsel frequently find themselves on the horns of this dilemma, torn between the desire to negotiate an outcome now and pressure from advisers to delay, and staying on the moving Glasl Escalator.

Right at the outset, internal counsel need to take the initiative to design the most appropriate and effective dispute resolution process, and assume a flexible, pragmatic, outcome-orientated approach. There are many different options to draw from. Each can be varied and combined to fit your circumstances. It is a great opportunity, not taken often enough, for corporate counsel to establish a relationship with the internal legal or responsible staff in the other party, to brainstorm the alternative approaches.

COLLABORATIVE LAW AND COOPERATIVE LAW

An option always worth considering, which does not entail the engagement of a neutral and impartial person, is Collaborative Law (CL), a direct interest-based negotiation process developed in the 1990s by family practitioners in the US, but equally applicable to most commercial disputes. Each party enters into a Limited Retention Agreement (LRA) with their own external counsel restricting their services to assisting them in resolving the dispute using non-adversarial methods and literally disqualifying them from handling any subsequent litigation or arbitration proceedings in relation to the dispute. The disqualification condition reflects the parties' common intent to settle, keeps each in total control of their negotiation, and provides their respective lawyers with a very strong psychological and economic motive to help their clients find an early amicable outcome. Effectively, the lawyers are switched from being litigation counsel trying to avoid settling a case, to settlement counsel trying to avoid litigation. Another common feature of Collaborative Law is that if the parties need an expert opinion, they can appoint a suitable person or panel on a joint basis, whose costs are shared equally and whose opinion is (usually) non-binding.

Chapter 8

A quarter of a century after the practice originated, CL is starting to become more widely practiced around the world, though still mainly in matrimonial and community disputes and family-type problems such as inheritance conflicts. CL is also, inexplicably, mainly used in common law jurisdictions. Slowly, but painfully slowly, CL is finding an application in civil and commercial dispute resolution, as more creative parties realize they need lawyers more to help them settle than as future litigators if the negotiations fail to reach a resolution.

There is no reason why CL should not be used in commercial dispute resolution. However, external litigation counsel in civil and commercial disputes outside the family and community fields are too often sceptical about the disqualification provision in the LRAs. To them, CL is counter-intuitive, applicable only to highly-charged emotional disputes and they see the introduction of a competing law firm as potentially threatening their position as custodian of their clients' interests. Many, often those with little or no experience of CL, steer their clients away from the idea, suggesting that it will be more costly in attorney fees if settlement is not reached. True, but the liklihood of settlement is greatly increased, so this is largely a non-argument.

To justify their opposition to CL, some US lawyers have scraped the bottom of the barrel and voiced concerns about whether LRAs violate ethical codes, particularly where a single pre-negotiation CL contract is entered into by all the parties together with their respective lawyers. Their ethical concerns arise from the implicit contractual restriction on the duty of any lawyer to advise freely on litigation or arbitration options. The ethical arguments only seem viable when lawyers are direct parties to the LRAs where a non-client is also a party. Professor Scott Peppett at the University of Colorado School of Law has usefully proposed a practical compliance path.[51] Ethical concerns do not seem to have been raised to a great extent in other jurisdictions where CL is practiced, such as Australia, New Zealand, France, Germany, Ireland and England & Wales.

To overcome these and other hesitations by lawyers, the US Uniform Collaborative Law Act is aimed at ensuring clients are properly advised about the implications of LRAs and the privilege aspects of a CL process. An alternative to CL, called Cooperative Law, has been proposed by Professor Lande. Similar to CL, the main difference is that parties' law firms are not contractually disqualified from handling litigation if settlement negotiations fail, but the parties themselves at least commit to taking a cooperative approach, and so instruct their external counsel with a view to settling the dispute. So Cooperative Law is a watered down version of Collaborative Law aimed at overcoming challenges to LRAs.

It is a sad reflexion on so-called professionalism that creative processes like CL need to be invented to overcome the resistance of litigation and arbitration counsel to press for early settlement strategies. Many external litigation lawyers need a firm hand from corporate counsel to get them to buy into a CL process with enthusiasm to help settle a dispute as early as possible. It's very depressing that such arm-twisting is necessary at all.

The International Academy of Collaborative Professionals[52] promotes the use of CL in most civil and commercial disputes. In a 2015 article in the journal Transaction Advisors,[53] Brian Slade, Associate Counsel at Coeur Mining Inc, one of the world's largest silver producers, and Christian Fabian, a partner at Mayer Brown, explained how CL has much to offer in resolving most post-closing disputes in mergers and acquisitions, such as claims for breach of representations & warranties, purchase price adjustments, earn-out disputes and covenant breaches. In M&A transactions, the parties typically want to maintain their relationship and avoid the risk of destructive dispute escalation. That goal is perhaps the most compelling rationale for using CL.

Corporate counsel should consider multi-step dispute resolution clauses in all contracts. A CL step is one that should be considered in such clauses, especially those where the parties are likely to have a continuing relationship.

MEDIATION

Lawyers the world over prize definitions in their quest for crystal clear interpretations, but most find things like mediation, that are not hidebound by familiar structural or process rules, hard to capture in legal terms. So what exactly is *mediation*? In two words: facilitated negotiation. Mediation is merely the application of deal facilitation, as discussed in Chapter 7, to the resolution of disputes.

The service supply-side of the dispute resolution market, made up of dispute resolution institutions, is so fragmented that it has been unable to come together and agree a commonly-accepted definition of mediation. Every service provider seems to define it differently, and many end up describing the form of mediation that they happen to favor or practice. Most definitions assume that mediation is an "alternative (or, more recently, 'appropriate') dispute resolution" (ADR) process, implying that mediation is a branch or sub-set of traditional process-driven dispute resolution like litigation or arbitration, which it is not. Some even go so far as to include arbitration within ADR, which, being private judging, it plainly is not. To the non-specialist, this is all rather confusing.

But wait: that cannot possibly be right. Mediation, like negotiation, is a social process, not a legal one. If it were a branch of law, mediators specializing in deal-making, like helping future spouses to finalize a prenuptial agreement, could not be *mediating*. But they are. As discussed in Chapter 2, mediation sits at the intersection of consensus and conflict and is a branch of negotiation, not of litigation or law. Mediation is often classified as an ADR process, but there is nothing "alternative" about it at all. In fact, negotiation, facilitated or otherwise, must surely be and remain the prime method of resolving disputes; litigation and arbitration are the alternative forms to which disputants turn if negotiations fail. A simple definition of mediation is: *Negotiation facilitated by a trusted neutral person.*

It's a pity that service providers cannot get together and agree such a short and sweet definition in the interests of clarity. If they were to do so, it would help corporate and other users to understand what the process is and how it works.

MEDIATION SUCCESS RATES

You have to approach mediation success rate claims with caution. What, for example, does "success" mean? A complete settlement? A partial one? Where one party capitulates, does that party consider that the process was a success? Data is hard to come by. Unlike litigation, mediation is informal and confidential, so there is a shortage of reliable public records of how many mediations take place and what outcomes they produce. There are few recognized national professional bodies for mediators, unlike the Bar Councils and Law Societies that represent lawyers. So in most countries, we have to rely on the unsubstantiated claims of mediators and service providers. But since they have motive to quote impressive, unprovable numbers to attract disputants to mediate, what should we believe?

Most mediation organizations claim that at least 80% of civil and commercial disputes settle when mediated. It's a startling figure. The AAA notes[54] that 85% of commercial disputes and 95% of personal injury claims result in written settlement agreements when mediated. Many practicing mediators say the same.

Fortunately, there is some objective credible data, to back up these claims from the world's fifth largest economy. The Centre for Effective Dispute Resolution (CEDR), a leading UK-based mediation service provider, conducts a biennial survey of the UK mediation market and publishes an audit report summarizing the findings. The Seventh CEDR Mediation Audit 2016[55] reflects the input of 319 mediators (which is more than half of all mediators registered with the UK's Civil Mediation Council). The Audit shows that 94% of mediated commercial disputes settle on the day of the mediation (75%) or shortly after (19%). CEDR estimates the size of the UK's civil and commercial mediation market to be about 10,000 cases per annum, representing £10.5 billion (about USD 13 billion) of claims, saving £2.8 billion (about USD 3.5 billion) in management time, relationship damage, productivity and legal fees. Looking back over the six previous CEDR Audits, there is a consistency to these statistics that lends the figures credibility. Anyway, this seems to be the best hard data available.

Nothing, however, beats personal experience. Over the years, I have been involved as a party negotiator or corporate counsel in over fifty cases around the world where a mediator or facilitator was used. Only three that I can now recall did not result in a settlement or deal. Two produced a negotiated settlement of most issues, but we needed an arbitral determination on several points of law. The third was an unusual situation where the other party was a government agency, there was a great deal of tension and distrust from day one, and the aim was not to resolve a specific dispute but to improve the quality of a complex web of relationships and to clear the air for mutually beneficial procurement and supply opportunities. If the other party and I were asked whether the transformative mediation process we used to help us achieve that objective was successful, I am confident we would agree that the process did achieve that goal, and to that extent was a "success."

Assuming the parties are rational and hire a competent mediator, the process is much more likely to help them resolve all or most of the disputes between them than prove to be a waste of time and effort. Mediation therefore merits being the default process for settling most disputes. The are exceptions. I would not necessarily favor mediation where I really need a judgment or award for technical purposes. I would not normally mediate when I need to create a compelling public deterrence, or set an important legal precedent or principle, or to make new law, where only a favorable court judgment would achieve that goal. I would probably not mediate really frivolous or vexacious claims where the other party is just trying to be a nuisance to get something, however small, because that just encourages copycats.

MEDIATION IS BETTER THAN ONE-ON-ONE SETTLEMENT NEGOTIATION

Although mediation is informal, the dynamic generates two vital over-arching advantages over a conventional one-on-one negotiation. First, the parties defer to the mediator on process matters, so automatically a mediated negotiation has a structure different from a non-mediated negotiation. Second, the quality of the negotiation increases – people behave themselves better. Negativity, cynicism and pessimism are reduced, or at least better managed. Parties are encouraged by the mediator to focus on needs and interests rather than demands and positions, and they can vent frustrations under the mediator's watchful eye, instead of bottling up or exploding uncontrollably.

Michael J. Roberts is an experienced commercial mediator in San Diego, having mediated over 4,000 disputes in thirty-five years with a cumulative settlement value exceeding USD 1 billion. In a 2002 blog piece[56] *Why Mediations Work When Negotiations Fail*, he put forward the following reasons. They exactly reflect my own experiences, and as I have not found a better elucidation, I asked Mike for permission to share them here:

> 1. *Effective negotiations have never really occurred in the first place. Effective negotiations require that the people issues be separated from the problem. I have often observed that the parties perceive the other side as being unreasonable and are suspicious of their desire to reach a settlement. As a result, the real problem is all but ignored and what is characterized as negotiation is really a series of personal attacks questioning the credibility, good faith and reasonableness of the other party. These negotiation sessions are often characterized by hard bargaining, unrealistic proposals and other tactics which only emphasize the differences between the parties. As a result, the parties become more defensive and entrenched in their positions, and refuse to make concessions. No common ground can be found in that environment. During mediation, the mediator controls the communication process so that unproductive discussions are avoided. When communications are skilfully directed by the mediator, the focus of the negotiations will gradually shift from the emotional issues to a constructive resolution of the real problem at hand.*

2. Mediation works when the ultimate decision makers sit at the bargaining table with the sole purpose of resolving their dispute. Many prior negotiations take place between parties who do not have the authority to make the settlement decision. For example, this is often the case when negotiations are with middle-management people who believe that their job is dependent upon looking strong in the eyes of their superiors. In a perfect mediation scenario, the CEO or another person with ultimate decision making authority is present. When this happens, settlement becomes almost a certainty.
3. During a mediation, the parties have the opportunity to hear directly from the opposition and in turn, are given the opportunity to directly educate and influence them. These direct communications allow for both sides to fully understand the other party's position and to eliminate misconceptions. Often, I hear parties comment that they have heard something for the first time and now understand where the other party is coming from. As a result, a mediation session provides each side with a more realistic view of the opposing position, allowing for the consideration of settlement proposals that otherwise would have been rejected as being "off the wall."
4. Mediation allows each side to "test market" a settlement proposal by privately conveying the proposal to the mediator. During the course of mediation, the mediator will often meet privately with the parties to confidentially discuss settlement proposals. Even if not authorized to convey a proposal to the other party, the mediator is able to determine whether the parties are in the same "ballpark" and whether or not a proposal is likely to be accepted by the other party. This allows each side to fully explore settlement options without negotiating against themselves, otherwise known as the "he who speaks first loses" method of negotiation. Everyone fears that any reasonable settlement proposal will be rejected by the other party and will then become the starting point for the next round of negotiations. This problem is eliminated in the mediation process.
5. Mediation offers each party a realistic look at their case and the result they are likely to achieve in court. As the parties become clear on what they can "realistically" expect to achieve absent a settlement, their positions on settlement often become more reasonable and flexible.
6. Mediation assists the parties in developing options for settlement. The more options that are developed, the greater the chances of success. In court, the only option available is normally an award of money damages. When engaged in a negotiation battle, the parties are likely to overlook creative settlement options that involve other types of consideration. It is the mediator's job to help identify and expand the menu of options so that less obvious solutions and alternatives can be explored. By pointing out the advantages of these suggestions and comparing them to the result that might be obtained in court, the mediator can often open the parties' eyes to the benefits of a solution which they have not seen before.

MEDIATION STYLES

There are three main mediation styles, each aimed at different user needs: facilitative, evaluative and transformative.

Facilitative mediators avoid making explicit recommendations to the parties, or giving advice or opinions, for example on the merits of the party's arguments, or predict what a court or tribunal would decide.

An evaluative mediator may express non-binding opinions if the parties ask for them. Both facilitative and evaluative mediation are used in solving specific disputes to achieve a negotiated settlement.

Transformative mediation has a different purpose and goal: to improve the relationship of the parties. Transformative mediation may be used, for example, when competitors need to find a more productive basis for working together in dealings with regulatory authorities, or public policy issues.

Many problem-solving mediators use facilitative or evaluative styles according to the nature and demands of the disputes they are mediating and the parties' preferences. If the most important tasks are to overcome communication blockages, identify hidden obstacles, develop options for mutual gain, and help the parties think creatively, the mediator may use mainly facilitative techniques. If deadlocks need breaking or there are unrealistic beliefs or expectations, or if the parties just need their heads banging together, a more evaluative style may be needed and wanted. Often the parties need both – facilitative and evaluative styles. No matter how mediation is practiced, it should observe the core principles of voluntariness, confidentiality, respect for the autonomy of the parties and the impartiality of the mediator.

Finding the right mediator is always crucial. That person needs to be acceptable to all parties. Some facilitative mediators refuse to be drawn into an evaluative mode, so it is important to determine alternative mediators' attitudes to evaluation before making a selection. This issue is included among the negotiating techniques in Chapter 10 and considerations that parties should take into account are neatly covered in International and Comparative Mediation: Legal Perspectives (2009) by leading dispute resolution scholar Professor Nadja Alexander, Academic Director of SIDRA.

TIMING

There is no single magic moment to mediate. Received wisdom from external counsel is usually to wait until the facts of the case and the other party's arguments are in the open, otherwise there is nothing to assess and no basis for meaningful settlement proposals. Coincidentally, of course, that usually means racking up most of the costs in the case. Where you absolutely need critical information in order to deal effectively with a dispute, and would be very unlikely to secure that information voluntarily in a negotiation, waiting may be essential. But in dispute management, increased delay usually accompanies increased risk. The Glasl Escalator does not stop moving, and nothing impedes its progress. So-called "cooling-off" periods in arbitration and Court processes are usually misused by one or more parties as "heating-up" opportunities. Invariably, the longer you wait to negotiate a settlement, the more complex and challenging the task becomes, and this needs to be weighed against the potential value of holding out for more information which may, or may not, have a bearing on settlement. With the passing of time, costs, complexity and the dispute's temperature all rise. Positions get exaggerated, entrenched and inflexible. Control is lost to external counsel. Problems proliferate. Whether the parties' relationship starts out well or badly, it is bound to deteriorate as the case progresses.

Chapter 8

MINITRIAL

Misnomers and malapropisms are common. Koalas are marsupials, but not bears; Panama hats are from Ecuador; French fries originate in Belgium (and taste better there, too) and Arabic numerals were invented in India. Jellyfish are not fish. Whoever uses a car's glove compartment for its professed purpose? And minitrials are not trials.

A minitrial is a structured negotiation, and one of the most effective and underutilized dispute resolution processes yet invented. One of the first recorded minitrials, in 1977, is described in a 1986 article[57] by Jethro K. Lieberman and James F. Henry in the University of Chicago Law Review. It involved two US companies, Telecredit Inc and TRW Inc (now part of Northrop Grumman). It was, from all accounts, quite a common patent infringement dispute, and the following summary is drawn from the Lieberman & Henry article and other reports.

In 1974, Telecredit had sued TRW for infringement of its patent rights, seeking an injunction to prevent further infringement, and damages of USD 6 million. Discovery involved the disclosure of over 100,000 documents incurring USD 500,000 in legal costs. By 1977, with no trial date in sight, and the looming prospect of more costs, delays, uncertainties and risks, Telecredit and TRW decided to try and resolve the dispute through a process they described as an "information exchange," but which a journalist's headline called a "minitrial" (and the term stuck).

What the two companies agreed was that Telecredit's President, Lee Ault III and TRW's Vice President, Richard Campbell would spend two days together, in the company of a neutral and impartial person, to try and agree a settlement. A retired patent judge was selected as the neutral. The two business leaders agreed that each would come to the information session with full authority to settle the dispute if terms could be agreed. It was also accepted that the content of the session would be confidential, that nothing stated would be admissible in subsequent legal proceedings, and that the neutral would not be called by either party to give testimony if the dispute progressed to a Court hearing.

The process agreed was that, at the start of the two days, the parties' external counsel would each be allowed four hours to present their arguments, followed by a two hour period for each side to reply and rebut. The lawyers would then withdraw, leaving the two business leaders to discuss, in the absence of the lawyers but in the presence of the neutral, to attempt to work out a settlement. If the case did not settle at the private session, the neutral would be asked to give the parties a non-binding opinion, and if they still could not settle, the information session would end and the litigation would continue.

According to one report, within thirty minutes of the completion of the legal presentations, the two business leaders had agreed the basic terms of a settlement. The neutral's non-binding opinion was not needed. The estimated savings, in further legal fees alone, were USD 1 million.

According to the New York Times on November 1, 1982, TRW used a similar process to resolve disputes with Automatic Radio and NASA. James McKee, GC of TRW's electronics and defense business, was quoted as saying: *Outside legal costs have just gone out of sight. And lots of times, the outside lawyers are the obstacle to quick settlement, because it is in their self-interest to keep the litigation going so they can get higher fees. With a minitrial or the other private hearings we've tried, you can get control back into the hands of the* [business people], *who will bring some common sense to bear.*[58]

For the business leaders – those with the full authority to settle – to hear both parties' arguments, rather than just the perspectives of their own external counsel, can be a salutory reality test. It can also prompt new ideas. By dispensing with the services of external counsel after the arguments have been presented, the decision makers feel less inhibited by legal considerations and more empowered to table broader business issues that can potentially offer solutions for mutual gain. Since the lawyers already have their arguments prepared for litigation, a minitrial would not normally incur significant additional costs, other than the time of the lawyers involved for the brief moment they come to present their arguments.

The minitrial format lends itself to more complex disputes that have crystallized to the point that the arguments of each party can be presented succinctly. The big cases involve the time and commitment of the parties' leaders, and their genuine desire to resolve if possible. But minitrial should not be dismissed as an option for resolving smaller disputes, and corporate counsel should always consider minitrial as a potential way to protect against the risk and cost of full blown litigation and arbitration.

EARLY NEUTRAL EVALUATION

Before settlement negotiations begin, if the parties have apparently developed divergent views of the prospects of success in a Court or tribunal, Early Neutral Evaluation or ENE may offer the basis for a solution.

In ENE, the parties select an appropriate impartial person, whose costs they agree to share, to offer them private or joint opinions on the strengths and weaknesses of their respective cases. ENE is a quick, informal reality-testing exercise that can be conducted in several ways. The neutral evaluator can meet with each party independently and offer each a private view of their case that is not disclosed to the other party. Or the parties can explain their cases to the evaluator in the presence of each other, and the opinion of the evaluator is then given to the parties jointly. The opinion of the evaluator is always non-binding, without prejudice and confidential.

The Centre for Effective Dispute Resolution CEDR, offers a basic model ENE agreement[59] and guidance notes for using the process. A more detailed ENE summary is available from the AAA[60] and a short book on the subject by former Judge Wayne D. Brazil, now a JAMS Panelist, entitled ENE (2012) is published by the American Bar Association's Section of Dispute Resolution.

Selection of the right evaluator is crucial to the effectiveness of ENE. The process depends on the parties having faith in the evaluator's impartiality, expertise and objectivity, as well as their willingness to listen, accept the evaluator's comments realistically, and negotiate with a view to settling, either one-on-one, or with the involvement of a separate mediator.

EVALUATIVE MEDIATION

Where the parties want an opinion on the merits, or the likely outcome of a trial, without the finality of a Court judgment or tribunal award, they can get this by selecting an evaluative mediator. Evaluative mediation, like ENE, is offered by many dispute resolution organizations.

But you need to be clear about what you want from the neutral. Evaluative mediation can be practically indistinguishable from non-binding arbitration. Are you really likely to trust and confide in confidence in a mediator, perhaps revealing your perceived weaknesses, if that person will later give the parties an opinion, even if non-binding, on the merits?

On the other hand, the parties may agree that they need a mediator who will crack open the outer shell of the dispute to resolve deadlocks on legal issues in order to access the value locked inside. It is likely to be a different process experience from traditional mediation, which works in a much more subtle, though no less effective, way.

It is possible for experienced mediators to tread the fine line between facilitative and evaluative processes, however. There is a practical review of this area in Using Evaluations in Mediation by Professors Dwight Golann and Marjorie Corman Aaron which forms Chapter 36 of the AAA Handbook of Mediation, third edition (2016).[61]

CONCILIATION/NON-BINDING ARBITRATION

In the spectrum of the leading methods of resolving disputes, conciliation occupies the space between mediation and arbitration. The big difference between mediation and conciliation relates to the parties' expectation of the neutral. A mediator is not expected to offer an opinion and propose settlement terms unless the parties ask. Evaluative mediators will do this, though facilitative mediators will not. A conciliator is engaged at the outset to offer the parties a non-binding opinion on how the dispute can be settled, including detailed settlement terms. Conciliation is a form of non-binding arbitration.

Although conciliation is less formal and usually much faster than binding arbitration, the process is often more structured and less flexible than mediation because the parties engage the conciliator to propose a possible outcome. The differences between mediation, whether facilitative or evaluative, and conciliation are more than subtle. Tactically, the parties are much less likely to take the conciliator into their full trust and confidence, privately revealing weaknesses, hidden agendas and skeletons in their closet, as they know the conciliator has the power to express an opinion on the case.

Many people are understandably confused about the difference between mediation and conciliation. The 2002 UNCITRAL Model Law on International Commercial Conciliation doesn't help. It defines conciliation as: *a process,* **whether referred to by the expression conciliation, mediation or an expression of similar import**, *whereby parties request a third person or persons ("the conciliator") to assist them in their attempt to reach an amicable settlement of their dispute arising out of or relating to a contractual or other legal relationship. The conciliator does not have the authority to impose upon the parties a solution to the dispute.* (emphasis added)

This only partly defines conciliation because it dodges the critical issue of non-binding settlement proposals. In China, mediation and conciliation are very widely used, but they are generally interchangeable terms because most mediators in China use an evaluative style. However, evaluative mediators differ in their approach. Some will only go so far as to challenge the parties' assumptions, "reality testing" as dispute resolvers call it, usually in private. Others will offer opinions only if the parties ask for them. And others automatically assume the object of the process is non-binding arbitration.

So conciliation is certainly an option, but ensure you know in advance how the process will work and assess whether it will meet the parties' needs.

ARB-MED-ARB

Arbitration is consensual private judging. Parties to a dispute have to agree to arbitration, something they mostly do contractually, long before a dispute arises, though they can decide to arbitrate a dispute once it has arisen. The important benefits of arbitration are that the parties control who will adjudicate over their dispute, and the proceedings take place in privacy and are generally confidential, so that details and reputations are unlikely to be covered in the media. Arbitration is great for face-saving. The parties get a single, unappealable, binding decision that in theory should be faster, cheaper, more flexible and less hidebound by technical complexities than litigation. And arbitration of international disputes has one huge, unique, overwhelming advantage over litigation: an arbitral award can be enforced in 156 countries under the 1958 New York Convention on the Recognition and Enforcement of Foreign Arbitral Awards.

But although local and national arbitration remains fairly efficient, international arbitration has become slow and, often, eye wateringly costly. It has been estimated that arbitration of disputes between international corporations and government agencies (known as ISDS – Investor-State Dispute Settlement) take on average 3.6 years to result in an award using recognized ISDS mechanisms at the World Bank's ICSID.[62]

One reason for the snail's pace is that arbitral awards are not appealable. This places a heavy burden on the arbitrator, and the institution administering the case, to ensure the full and proper application of natural justice and the Rule of Law. Arbitrators often err on the side of perceived fairness, permitting lengthy submissions on almost every possible point, and tolerating generous time limits. Arbitration can therefore be abused by timewasters and tacticians, resulting in what some critics have described as the "judicialization" of the arbitral process. To add to the speed problem, commercial disputes have become increasingly complex, often numerous parties and law firms are involved, and issues are increasingly legalistic as regulations multiply. The longer the process, the higher the costs.

Parties are often unable to agree on almost anything when a dispute erupts, and that includes choice of arbitrator. All too frequently, each party ends up nominating an arbitrator to a panel, and their nominated arbitrators are charged with selecting a third arbitrator, tripling panel fees and costs and adding to the complexity.

But in international disputes, there is a way to capture the enforceability benefit of an arbitral award while potentially overcoming the delay, cost and complexity problems of arbitral proceedings. That way is Arb-Med-Arb.

Arb-Med-Arb is a simple three-step process. First, the parties refer their dispute to arbitration. Once the tribunal has been formally constituted to hear the case, the arbitration is stayed for a short period. The second stage then happens during which a mediation takes place to try and resolve the dispute through assisted negotiation. The arbitrators in the first stage should not be the mediator, and, in fact, the best practice dictates that the mediator is affiliated to a separate organization. At the end of the mediation, the third stage is triggered when the case goes back to the arbitral tribunal. If the mediation has been successful, the tribunal can either conclude the proceedings or, if the parties wish, convert their settlement agreement into a consent award, which is enforceable under the New York Convention. If the mediation does not settle the dispute, the stay is lifted and the arbitration continues.

During 2013, I had the privilege, along with another corporate counsel, Josephine Hadikusomo of Texas Instruments, to be a member of a Working Group to make recommendations to develop the international commercial mediation space in Singapore. The Working Group was established by the Chief Justice of Singapore and the Ministry of Law and was co-Chaired by George Lim SC and Edwin Glasgow QC.

Singapore, one of the world's most successful economies, was already internationally recognized as a dynamic and forward-looking dispute resolution center. The Singapore International Arbitration Centre (SIAC), for example, is a world-class institution handling almost 300 cases a year at the time of writing. Although the Singapore Mediation Centre (SMC) was also an established success, its main focus was in domestic disputes. The Working Group's task was to recommend how that domestic achievement in mediation could be best applied on a global scale.

In 2014, to implement the Working Group's recommendations, the Singapore International Mediation Centre (SIMC) was created to stand alongside the SMC as a non-profit international mediation service provider. SIMC is affiliated to the SIAC and the two institutions launched a joint protocol and model clause for resolving disputes by Arb-Med-Arb if the parties choose this route. Under the protocol and model clause, stage 1 begins as a SIAC arbitration until the tribunal is formally constituted and the case is stayed; stage 2 then kicks in to revert the case to SIMC for mediation; after which in stage 3 the case returns to SIAC either for a consent award or for the stay to be lifted and the arbitral proceedings continue, depending on whether a settlement was reached.

The Singapore protocol and model clause for this pioneering procedure are set out in Appendix 5 and are reviewed in Contemporary Issues in Mediation (2016) edited by Professor Joel Lee and Marcus Lim. It is not necessary for the parties or the subject matter of their business to have any connection with Singapore in order to be able to adopt the Arb-Med-Arb clause in their contracts. SIAC is one of the most admired arbitration institutions internationally and SIMC has a panel of over sixty mediators from around the world and a similar number of technical experts with competency in over twenty technical fields.

A number of other arbitration institutions, among them the ICC International Court of Arbitration in Paris and the Hong Kong International Arbitration Centre (HKIAC) offer Arb-Med-Arb processes, and almost all institutions will provide an Arb-Med-Arb service if the parties ask for it, but SIMC, in partnership with SIAC, has made Arb-Med-Arb a strategic thrust. Until the Arb-Med-Arb process is more widely adopted and promoted by other arbitration institutions, parties anywhere in the world may choose the Singapore clause and protocol, or if they prefer, request a similar clause and process at another arbitration service provider, and adopt them into the dispute resolution section of their international contracts.

BASEBALL ARBITRATION

So-called because it is used to finalize the salaries that Major League Baseball clubs pay to some of their players, baseball arbitration is also called final offer arbitration or pendulum arbitration. It is an interesting, fast and effective way to settle zero-sum gain monetary issues.

In its simplest form, each party must table its best offer. A neutral arbitrator is appointed to choose the most reasonable offer. The arbitrator must chose one of the offers, and is not empowered to decide another figure. The parties are bound to accept whichever offer the arbitrator selects as the most reasonable.

It sounds simple, and it is, but it is also psychologically smart. The baseball arbitration process encourages the parties to present reasonable offers in the hope of having their figure chosen by the arbitrator, not the other party's. The process is therefore sometimes used in collective bargaining disputes between employers and unions to prompt both parties to make more reasoned, fair and anchored offers in the hope that their proposal is the one chosen by the arbitrator.

There is a variation on the process called night baseball where the parties table their best offers but do not disclose them to the arbitrator. They may, for example, seal them in envelopes and hand them to the arbitrator. The arbitrator then proposes a reasonable figure, the envelopes are opened, and whichever party's best offer is closest to the arbitrator's figure binds the parties.

Baseball or final offer arbitration can be used on a planned or ad hoc basis to resolve financial sticking points in negotiations, for example when trying to agree a price for a product or service or when setting a royalty rate in a license, or the value of an asset.

ARB-MED AND MED-ARB

Arb-Med is a variation on the arbitration process where the arbitrator makes an award but does not reveal it to the parties until the parties try to reach a mediated outcome, either with the arbitrator, or a different neutral, acting as mediator. If the parties do not reach an agreed outcome in the mediation session, the arbitral award is revealed and binds the parties. Arb-Med was the process we used in the PMEC situation described in Chapter 7. Arb-Med is suited to situations where the disputants are based in the same jurisdiction or would not need to enforce the award internationally.

Med-Arb, sometimes (but misleadingly) labelled with the oxymoronic term "binding mediation," is offered by some dispute resolution service providers to enable a mediator to impose an arbitral award on the parties if the mediation does not generate an agreed outcome. It is a dubious process if the same neutral acts as both mediator and then as arbitrator because parties are unlikely to be completely honest and disclose full information, including details that may prejudice their case, to someone who has the power of determination over them. It is a viable process where the mediator and the arbitrator are different people and do not engage in any private dialogue on the case. Med-Arb therefore often involves separate neutrals, as in Arb-Med, and has the merit of reassuring the parties that, one way or another, the process will result in an outcome, negotiated or adjudicated.

CREATIVE HYBRIDS

Many of these process options can be combined into hybrids in order to to fit a given situation. For example, mediation can be combined with baseball arbitration; if the parties cannot reach agreement on every issue during a mediation, the outstanding points can be resolved by each making a binding final offer on each of those points. Another neutral can then be asked to decide which offer is the most reasonable. Another example – instead of Arb-Med-Arb, the parties could agree an Arb-Con-Arb process where the neutral acts not as a mediator but as a conciliator and offers a non-binding settlement proposal that the parties can accept or reject. And if they reject it, there is nothing to prevent the parties asking the same or another neutral to follow the conciliation stage with a mediation session prior to the final arbitration stage, in an Arb-Con-Med-Arb process.

The permutations and scope for process creativity are endless. The main thing is to adapt the process to fit the problem, not the other way round.

GETTING THE OTHER PARTY TO NEGOTIATE

Even if you want to try an early dispute resolution option, you may hesitate to propose it. It takes two to tango. You may perceive that the other party would simply decline, or misinterpret the overture as weakness or some kind of trick to get them to capitulate or submit to pressure, or simply assume that you must somehow have more to gain than they do from negotiations. Reactive devaluation often results in one party flatly declining anything proposed by the other without any rational reason. They may not understand what early dispute resolution is, or why and how it works, or appreciate that exploring a settlement could be just as much in their interests as in yours. They may be set on recrimination, or want to have their day in court. Or their advisers may warn them against any non-adversarial strategy for any number of reasons: it's not the right time, or the exercise would be pointless, or a diversion, or costly.

There are various ways to anticipate objections to early dispute resolution or the fear that proposing mediation can be construed as an expression of weakness or doubt in your case. One is to sign a pledge as discussed at the beginning of this Chapter. Mediation organizations in several countries enable you to sign one, including in the US, France, the UK, Singapore, Poland and Brasil as well as the International Trademark Association. An additional option is to suggest your employer adopts its own written policy on conflict resolution that leaves you the discretion to litigate or arbitrate as necessary, but which you can use to explain to parties that by proposing settlement negotiations or mediation, you are merely following prescribed policy. Here is a policy statement adopted by Acre.com, an international executive search and recruitment firm that is a market leader in the sustainability, CSR, environment, health & safety and energy fields:

Conflict Resolution Policy

From time to time, all businesses experience conflicts. Although we protect and enforce our rights vigorously, it is our general policy to try and avoid and resolve any disputes that do arise through negotiation before they escalate into formal litigation or arbitration. In some cases, that is not possible or sensible. Where, for example, the other party cannot be relied upon to negotiate rationally or in good faith, or is being frivolous or vexacious, or we need immediate relief to protect our rights, or a court or tribunal decision to create a precedent or a deterrence, or to protect our assets, then we litigate or arbitrate as necessary.

However, in other cases, it is our policy to seek less expensive, more effective and faster methods to resolve disputes. There are many ways to do this that can create options for mutual gain, potentially addressing our needs and those of the other party. In those situations, whether we are in the position of claimant or respondent,

Chapter 8

> and regardless of how strong we perceive our case to be, we will propose settlement negotiations, using a non-adversarial process such as mediation, to try and reach an amicable settlement. We believe this is a more pragmatic and cost-effective approach for everyone. Our staff and [external counsel] are instructed to apply this policy wherever we do business.

Another way to get the other party to the table in the right frame of mind is to present yourself, personally, as a promoter of early dispute resolution processes. Leading blogs, such as the Kluwer Arbitration Blog, the Kluwer Mediation Blog and Mediate.com are normally willing to publish guest posts, particularly by corporate counsel, since the voice of disputants is expressed less frequently and is therefore sought after. If your Google profile shows a clear early dispute resolution inclination, any proposal you make to negotiate by any process option is much less likely to be misinterpreted by the other party as weakness. That's because the other party can see that you are merely practicing what you believe.

Identifying a referrer may be another option. If an appropriate third party, having no stake in the dispute, were to approach the parties jointly and propose an early dispute resolution option, this may be received positively by the parties simply because the idea originates with someone neutral. The referrer could be someone with a relationship with all the disputants but has not taken sides, or someone completely new and independent, for example a dispute resolution provider body.

There can be a lot more to being a referrer than simply proposing an early dispute resolution option to the parties. Judges and Court administrators often end up explaining the options to the parties and either requiring or urging them to mediate. The issues that referrers need to consider are set out in Referral To Mediation: A Practical Guide for an Effective Mediation Proposal (2008) by Machteld Pel, a former Vice President of the Arnhem Court of Appeal in the Netherlands.

In a contractual dispute, by far the most effective way to get the other party to negotiation and mediation is to include a dispute resolution clause that contractually binds the parties to negotiate in good faith before starting any formal legal action. Unfortunately, negotiators are very often thoughtlessly inclined to treat dispute resolution arrangements as a standardized boilerplate term in a contract that is simply drawn from a law firm's precedent file. Paradoxically, even though every contract is a disguised divorce settlement, negotiators like to avoid thinking about how disputes will be managed if they arise. They know a clause is needed, but don't think twice about it.

Many companies have a number of standard clauses that they insist on using whenever they enter into contracts. Dispute resolution is usually one of them, alongside choice of law, termination and other stuff that gets bundled in at the end. Usually, these terms are drafted by outside counsel, and almost invariably the dispute resolution clause is a straightforward reference to a Court or arbitral body.

My advice is – don't neglect this issue. The smart approach is a carefully-drafted multi-step dispute resolution clause that requires the parties, if a dispute arises, first to negotiate a solution in good faith, and if that fails, to go to mediation, and only if that fails, to resort to the last alternative of litigation or arbitration.

For many years now, I have flatly insisted on a multi-step clause whenever I negotiate. I tell the other party that we want to make every effort to negotiate a resolution either directly or with a mediator's help if a dispute arises, and I never accept excuses for why this is not prudent common sense. I have always responded to resistance with persistence, and cannot recall a single occasion in the past 15 years when I failed to get my way. The CPR Institute's Dispute Resolution Clause Selection Tool is a very helpful online facility to find the model clause you need, and the IMI web portal offers a neutral model clause and numerous links to dispute resolution institutions that publish their own model multi-step dispute resolution clauses (https://imimediation.org/model-mediation-clauses).

GUIDED CHOICE

External lawyers have a duty to identify the most suitable process to resolve their clients' disputes, but, as discussed, many default to Professor Lande's *Litigation As Usual* approach and lack the knowledge or experience of all the process options.

To fix this problem, Paul M. Lurie, a construction partner at Schiff Hardin in Chicago, developed a simple concept for disputants to engage neutrals specifically to help them design the most appropriate dispute resolution process for their particular conflict before any negotiations begin. The concept[63] envisages that, at a very early stage, the neutral would confidentially diagnose the dispute with the help of the parties and then suggest the most effective and customized settlement process. The neutral helps the parties make the most critical choices and approaches, including getting the most value from ECA tools, the pros and cons of particular process options, how and where to find the right expert, mediator or conciliator, and whether to use a dispute resolution service provider to administer the process.

To help promote this idea, Paul established a Guided Choice Interest Group made up of dispute resolution neutrals, corporate counsel, educators and litigators, mostly based in the US and Europe, all with the expertise to help parties to decide how best to manage their dispute. Innovations of this kind are badly needed, and although Guided Choice was initially applied in construction conflicts, it is applicable right across the spectrum of business disputes wherever in the world they arise.

In the same vein, the legal mediation firm Schonewille & Schonewille in Rotterdam has developed a useful way of analyzing whether mediation is likely to be suitable approach for resolving a dispute based on a comprehensive questionnaire and checklist (shown in Appendix 6, with the firm's consent).

Chapter 8

DRBs: DISPUTE RESOLUTION BOARDS

Until the bulldozers arrived in 1992, tiny and hilly Chek Lap Kok and Lam Chau islands, just off the coast of Hong Kong's Lantau Island, were known mainly as the habitat of Romer's Tree Frog, a tiny endangered species that thrived here, but practically nowhere else. The frogs were moved onto Lantau, the hills of Chek Lap Kok and Lam Chau were flattened, a giant polder was created, quadrupling the size of the islands, and one of the world's largest airports was constructed.

Opened in 1998, the new Hong Kong airport is a multi-billion dollar masterpiece, the world's largest construction project at the time. Terminal 1, designed by Sir Norman Foster, is 1.2 km long, the size of 35 football pitches. Breathtakingly, this monster took less than 3 years to build. The airport can accommodate 80 million passengers a year, more than JFK and Heathrow combined. There are almost 300 check-in desks and 80 customs booths, 160 shopping outlets and 40 restaurants. The 20-mile road and hi-speed rail link connecting Chek Lap Kok airport to Hong Kong Island includes the longest suspension bridge in the world. This place is an incredible feat of civil engineering and human ingenuity that was completed on time and within budget. On time and on budget? How?

Underpinning this project were the multi-step dispute resolution clauses that the Hong Kong Government and the Provisional Airport Authority mandated in all contracts with contractors and suppliers. Construction projects of any magnitude are often hotbeds of acrimony and recrimination as one contractor typically blames another for delays and other failures, egged on by insurers scampering to deny liability. There were 10 separate but connected mega-projects at Chek Lap Kok, involving 225 major construction contracts. A system of Dispute Resolution Boards, commonly called DRBs, was set up comprising neutral experts from technical and professional fields. Their roles were to oversee the progress of each project and to avoid disputes when they appeared to arise, or resolve them early if they had already crystallized. Mediation and conciliation were used as an obligatory precursor to arbitration, but other assisted negotiation techniques were also possible.

DRBs are a common feature of major multi-party infrastructure and engineering projects and the service is offered by many dispute resolution providers. They are normally contractual, and put in place before a project starts. Their purpose is dispute avoidance, even more than resolution. The DRB's panelists stay on top of events, receive progress reports, carry out site visits and often make their presence highly visible in order to build relationships even where there are no disputes to resolve. When a dispute does arise, the DRB is already in the loop, at least generally, and perfectly placed to act quickly. If ad hoc mediation does not lead to an amicable resolution, the DRB may make a non-binding recommendation, or follow it up with a binding decision, which may sometimes be appealable as a formal arbitration.

DRBs should be considered as a prime way to avoid any major multi-issue or multi-party deal from being de-railed by disputes and to help the parties negotiate settlements quickly and inexpensively. It is possible to use DRBs in other contexts too, for example regulatory compliance among members of an industry or profession, and in fact any major project. The cost can be a tiny proportion of the value derived from dispute avoidance.

ADMINISTERED OR NON-ADMINISTERED DISPUTE RESOLUTION

One of the first choices you have to make to resolve a conflict by any of the available options, other than straight one-on-one negotiation, is whether to engage a dispute resolution service provider to give the parties administrative support. If the conflict relates to a breach of contract, that choice may already have been made in the written agreement or in terms and conditions, though, even then, the parties can agree to change it.

Service providers vary in what they offer and what they cost. Their basic offering is case management, but many have expertise in additional services. Where the parties are barely on speaking terms, having a neutral service provider to handle logistical and administrative matters in setting up a dispute resolution process and ensuring that all participants understand the process constructively can be very valuable, in some cases even essential. Most service providers can propose established rules of engagement and model agreements to govern the process used to attempt to resolve the dispute. They deal direct with the parties, individually and jointly, and open lines of communication that may otherwise be difficult. Administered mediations can be particularly valuable where one or more of the parties is reluctant to mediate or to co-operate fully in an early dispute resolution process because the service provider can explain the process from an impartial standpoint.

But service provider levels and areas of expertise vary. Some are equipped only to handle a default dispute resolution format, such as mediation or conciliation. They may have little or no experience or capacity in some of the proven options, such as collaborative law or setting up a minitrial or the various hybrids of evaluative mediation or arbitral resolution. Their ability to give wise counsel to the parties on configuring the process to the problem may be restricted to the processes they promote and feel comfortable with. Where you believe you need more creativity and experience beyond the business model of a particular service provider, consider a Guided Choice service, check credentials of other providers, or consider using one of the larger international service providers that are more likely to have a broad track record of resolving disputes using hybrid processes.

There are some inconvenient truths that may not be a problem in some situations, but certainly can be in others. Most dispute resolution service providers have self-appointed panels of neutrals and may effectively limit your choice of neutral to those on their panel. The choice may not be broad enough for your needs.

Parties are not compelled to use a service provider to manage and administer their negotiation process. You can go straight to an individual neutral, decide on the process you want to use and self-manage. Where you are communicating well, everyone is motivated to resolve and the problem is not too complex in terms of issues or number of parties, service providers may have little value to add. Many individual mediators and other neutrals are willing to perform case management functions or share the tasks with the parties and their counsel. Some mediators have formed practice groups that replicate what service providers can offer.

The International Mediation Institute has devised a decision tree to help parties decide whether to delegate administration to a service provider. It is best viewed online at https://imimediation.org/decision-tree.

Always think first about what process would best suit your dispute. Do not hesitate to use a Guided Choice professional who is not selling their services as a dispute resolver but merely helping you and the other party identify the right process to adopt. Then think about whether you need an administered service. And then identify the right neutral.

FINDING THE RIGHT NEUTRAL

Phone-a-friend is the most common way to select a dispute resolution neutral, like a mediator. But it is fraught with problems.

People usually rely mainly on word of mouth to choose a lawyer, dentist, architect, accountant, surveyor, physician or any other professional. This phone-a-friend referral approach usually works reasonably well. You know the recommender, and they have favorable personal experience of the professional. You rely on the referrer's judgment and experience. There is something comforting and risk-free about that connection. It's not as if you are walking in off the street. The recommended professional owes a duty of care and responsibility to just one person, namely you. Only you need to decide whether you are happy with the professional's knowledge, experience and reputation. The choice is yours, and yours alone. If you decide the professional is not right for you, it is easy to walk away.

When trying to find the right mediator to help resolve a dispute, the situation is critically different. Dispute resolution neutrals owe an equal duty of care and responsibility to all parties, not just to you. While you may feel comfortable with a particular mediator, the other party may not, and vice-versa. In fact, in the midst of a dispute, the other party may react negatively to any mediator proposed by you for no better reason than that the suggestion originated from you.

There are other problems with phone-a-friend referrals to find mediators. A neutral who may have been just right for one dispute and one set of parties may be unsuitable for another situation. This may have little bearing on the neutral's competency as a dispute resolver, but be rooted in their nationality, culture, language proficiency, background, location, gender, age, past professional experience or other subjective factors that can influence your or the other party's perceptions of their suitability for your particular case. You and the other party need to decide on the mediator's style, facilitative or evaluative. Many mediators do both, but which style comes to them most naturally, and does it meet your joint needs?

Neutrals need to be trusted by all parties for their involvement to work. If one party feels that another party has some kind of special relationship or history with a proposed neutral, for example if the other party or their counsel has used that neutral previously, that may be dubious, even suspicious, and this can interfere with their willingness to trust the neutral.

And there is another problem. In most countries, anyone can set themselves up as a "mediator," whether trained and experienced or not. Many do not declare whether they adhere to a prescribed Code of Ethical Conduct, and if so which one, and what the consequences are of a claimed breach – such as an unauthorized disclosure of confidential information. This can cause some parties to approach mediation, and mediators, with caution, especially when the mediator is recommended by word of mouth. Directories and the personal websites of mediators are often too brief to help in the reassurance stakes. Hesitant parties need more comfort to address their often unexpressed fears or concerns.

You and the other party or parties need to be confident in the choice of mediator on two basic levels: competency and suitability. They are related, but mutually exclusive. A competent mediator is not necessarily a suitable one for the specifics of your situation. One party may feel a competent mediator who shares the cultural credentials or nationality of their opponent is automatically unsuitable. Conversely, a neutral person may be very suitable for the case, being a well-respected, expert in a particular field and seen as impartial by all parties, but may not be an experienced mediator. Competency in mediation, as in most other service fields, is very much related to experience levels.

Your external counsel may suggest a neutral. So may a service provider. Look behind the recommendation. Is external counsel making a choice from a tiny selection of possibilities that their firm has used? Is the service provider limiting its choice to mediators on its panel? If the answers are maybe, or perhaps, or yes, do further research. Like buying apples on a market stall, do not pick the first that comes within reach.

Many service providers publish detailed résumés of their panel members. The good service providers have careful competency selection methods and enable users to apply filters to narrow their choices based on certain parameters. But the suitability range may be very narrow. Most corporate counsel are passionately interested in the experience of parties who have used a particular mediator's services previously but many service providers do not publish that information about their panel mediators. Getting independent references can be difficult.

Most mediators simultaneously present themselves on their own websites. But that is often not enough. Many mediators' websites merely feature cryptic endorsements of prior users, almost always unattributed and always carefully cherry-picked. Even though this is intended to be a convincing objective endorsement of competency, and may actually represent a fair overview, you should not attribute much weight to them.

Look for organizations that have addressed this selection conundrum by giving users more objective and credible information about neutrals by offering independently-prepared summaries of prior user feedback. Preferably, look for neutrals who have posted video interviews of themselves, so that you can get a feel for their personae. Parties should ask themselves: can we vest our trust in this mediator? Where videos are not available, conduct personal interviews, preferably together with the other party, once you have discussed and agreed a shortlist.

The International Mediation Institute's (IMI) web portal includes a search engine[64] enabling users to identify mediators meeting their core requirements in terms of location, language capability, practice area and mediating style. The profile of each IMI Certified Mediator includes an independently-prepared Feedback Digest summarizing comments made about the mediator by parties in prior disputes. Details of the mediator's code of ethical conduct, disciplinary process and professional indemnity insurance are also included.

Where parties are not on speaking terms, consider using a service provider to help in the choice of neutral. Who you use will have a major impact on the likelihood of achieving a successful negotiated outcome. It is best not to cut corners on the selection of the neutral.

International Arbitration and Mediation: A Practical Guide (2010) by Michael McIlwrath, Global Chief Litigation Counsel at GE Oil & Gas and John Savage, a partner of King & Spalding, includes a wide range of advice on finding the right mediator and organizing a mediated negotiation as well as a model ECA template.

Toolkit Generating Outcomes (2009) by Manon Schonewille offers negotiation and dispute resolution advice, from preparation through process and dealing with problems, such as how to tackle risky questions. *See also* Appendix 6 for a checklist prepared by Schonewille & Schonewille on the issues the parties might consider when selecting the right mediator.

MEDIATION ADVOCACY

Most parties attending a mediation naturally want to be accompanied by someone they trust and who can contribute to the dialogue appropriately and positively. For example, if you are trying to resolve a dispute or make a deal, you may want your external counsel to join you. Selecting the right person to accompany you to a mediation is as important as selecting the right person to represent you in court or in an arbitration. They will, at least to some extent, speak on your behalf and support you.

The knowledge, skills, competencies and techniques needed to be an effective party advisor or representative in a mediation, or in any negotiation, are very different from those needed in an adversarial setting in a Court or tribunal. That person needs a solid familiarity with how mediation works, to counsel the party properly, to understand and define their underlying needs as opposed to their claims, to communicate effectively with the other side, to help break deadlocks, to develop creative options, to have problem-solving negotiation abilities, to prepare the party effectively so that they can make the right decisions and speak for themselves, to be able to help negotiate and craft a settlement agreement, to interact with the mediator efficiently, and to deal with the other party in the right way.

Statistics suggest that up to about 20% of mediated disputes are not settled by the end of the mediation session. Among fifteen reasons for failure advanced by two experienced US mediators, Jack G. Marcil and Nicholas D. Thornton in an article in the American Journal of Mediation,[65] most are related to lack of competency on the part of the mediator or mediation representatives and/or inappropriate or unrealistic expectations on the part of parties resulting from poor advice and guidance. Advocacy, or more accurately the ability to effectively represent parties in negotiation, including in a mediation, is not generally a discipline taught to lawyers. Many misperceive mediation as an opportunity for a debate where the mediator is a moderator, and fail to understand the need for real consensus-building and dialogue – a point made powerfully by Bernard Meyer in Beyond Neutrality: Confronting the Crisis in Conflict Resolution (2004).

There are several books devoted to the art of mediation advocacy. In Mediation Representation: Advocating as a Problem-Solver in Any Country or Culture (2010), Professor Harold Abramson covers not only the different skills, attitudes and approaches needed by anyone representing a party at a mediation, but also how to prepare for the mediation and how to prepare anyone accompanying you. The skills needed by mediation advocates are also explained in Toolkit Mediation Advocacy (2007) by Manon Schonewille, and in Effective Mediation Advocacy: A Guide for Practitioners (2016) by Andrew Goodman. Contemporary Issues in Mediation (2016) edited by Professor Joel Lee and Marcus Lim, provides a forthright overview of professional conduct by external counsel with regard to mediation, proposing a duty to consider mediation, a duty of independent judgment and a duty as a peacemaker.

The International Mediation Institute has established the criteria and system for certifying the competency of mediation advocates (as well as of mediators). Both systems are based on Qualifying Assessment Programmes (QAPs) implemented by provider, training, professional and educational organizations meeting specific criteria established by the IMI Independent Standards Commission (ISC).

THE DESTRUCTIVE FORCE OF DISPUTES

Companies are populated by people. They have egos and can negotiate on the basis of emotion and false perceptions of leverage. In the 1990s Litton Industries launched into an eleven-year litigation with Honeywell. There were two lawsuits, one based on anti-competitive behavior alleging misuse of a dominant position and bundling, the other alleging patent infringement. The claims exceeded USD 1.2 billion (the equivalent of USD 2.3 billion today). The lawsuits were motivated by the fierce competition that had taken place over decades between the two companies for control of the inertial navigation market. Once dominated by Litton since the 1960s, it had by the late 1980s increasingly seen market share decline in favor of Honeywell.

The management of both companies despised each other with a vengeance, and would do anything to get an edge over the other. When Honeywell bundled its cockpit setup to include inertial navigation equipment, effectively forcing commercial airlines to buy Honeywell's system if they wanted a good price, it was seen as an act of war by Litton. In addition, Litton believed that Honeywell had misappropriated key mirror technology patented by Litton for use in new ring laser gyros that both companies were developing. The knives came out.

Here were two Fortune 500 companies ready to go to war. Cost was no problem. The objective on Litton's part was to drive a competitor, seen as acting improperly, from the marketplace. The claims were strategically set at a sum that could have bankrupted Honeywell at that time. This became a main "business" objective of Litton throughout the 1990s. Tens of millions of dollars were spent on the litigation, lawyers and experts. Litton's real business took second place, its R&D suffered, and engineers were pulled off projects to assist with the litigation. Litton was initially successful in its actions, but Honeywell appealed. Cases were sent back for new trials. The validity of Litton's patent was challenged and then invalidated due to prior use. The reported cases in *Litton v. Honeywell* make stimulating reading for lawyers – a dramatic example, though by no means an exceptional one, of scorched earth litigation.

At one point half way through the various actions, Honeywell, apparently sensing that its survival might be at stake, offered to settle all the actions for a payment to Litton of USD 400 million. It was a pivotal point for Litton. Had it taken the settlement Litton would likely exist as an independent company today. Much of that USD 400 million could have been reinvested by Litton in R&D and in purchases of strategic acquisitions to grow the company. Litton, at that time, was practically the same size as the market leader, Northrop Grumman. However, ego, arrogance and a sense of having a competitor on the ropes combined to cloud business judgment, prevent a rational assessment of risk and exaggerated the leverage that Litton felt it had.

Litton turned down the settlement offer and continued the two lawsuits. In the process, Litton bled to death. It hemorrhaged financially and failed to maintain and expand its product base. At a time when competitors like Northrop were making strategic acquisitions to grow in the aerospace defense market, Litton lacked the resources to do so. A single minded demonization of a competitor drove Litton to continue with its win-at-all-costs litigation strategy. A classic example of a company making emotional rather than rational business decisions.

In the end it was Litton rather than Honeywell that folded. In 2001 Litton Industries was purchased by Northrop Grumman, a company it might itself have bought in 1997 when the Lockheed Northrop attempted merger fell through. Litigation had sapped Litton of its strength. Being bought out by a financially stronger competitor remained its last and only option.

Tellingly, when Northrop bought Litton and inherited the Honeywell lawsuits, it looked at them and considered the probability of a successful outcome from a new perspective. It had the opportunity to objectively and dispassionately, without ego or emotion, assess its ATNAs and apply new leverage. Northrop was a larger and stronger opponent that Honeywell now had had to face. Unknown to Honeywell at the time, Northrop, in its purchase price allocation, had allocated zero value to the lawsuits; it could afford to walk away and lose nothing.

Honeywell was approached to mediate the disputes and a settlement was quickly reached in December 2001. The benefits of a neutral facilitator, a willing defendant and a plaintiff who now had nothing to lose, made for the perfect ZOPA. Ironically, the number settled on was USD 440 million, virtually the same figure that Litton had turned down years earlier. The case will go down in corporate history as dramatic illustration of the uncontrollable destructive forces that litigation can unleash, as demonstrated in Professor Glasl's escalation ladder, and the unquestionable value of facilitated settlement negotiations.

Most of us have experienced the relentless emotional momentum that characterizes runaway litigation and arbitration. So often, formal dispute resolution processes reach a point, actually quite early in their life cycles, when no party is prepared to blink, imply doubt or weakness about their case, or reveal the agony of the cost and risk of losing. Part of our job, as corporate counsel, is the responsibility of taking the helicopter view, applying litmus tests to assess whether a particular dispute still makes business sense, and where doubt emerges, to take creative action to reach a negotiated outcome.

IN A NUTSHELL

- There is evidence to suggest that "dispute-wise" companies are more profitable and better parties to do business with.
- The Glasl Escalator warns of the consequences of not resolving disputes early through negotiation.
- Practice PEDR.
- Use ECA tools.
- Gain knowledge of all dispute resolution process options, including hybrids and mediator styles, and use Guided Choice support.
- Understand why mediation has crucial advantages over one-on-one negotiation.
- Adopt the creative ways to get the other party to negotiation in the right frame of mind, overcoming any misperceptions they may have.
- Know when to use service providers and how to find the right mediator.
- Always use a multi-step dispute resolution clause in every contract, and resist any attempt by the other party to impose a single step clause (litigation or arbitration without a prior mediation step).

Chapter 9
Ethics

> *We ought always to deal justly, not only with those who are just to us,*
> *but likewise to those who endeavor to injure us;*
> *and this, for fear lest by rendering them evil for evil,*
> *we should fall into the same vice.*
>
> Hierocles The Stoic
>
> from a fragment of Elements of Ethics, Second Century

Ethics overlay negotiations. Integrity underpins them.

Ethics are the unexpressed expectations of engagement that negotiating partners apply to each other, reflected in any written codes that the parties apply to their own conduct.

Integrity is the set of internal values and principles that you choose to guide your own behavior, such as truth, honesty, trust, respect, objectivity and understanding.

Sir Francis Bacon in 1621 honed in on the fact that *it is not what we profess, but what we practice, that gives us integrity*. In Shattering The Glass Slipper (2002) Charles W. Marshall wrote that *integrity is doing the right thing when you don't have to, when no one else is looking or will ever know, when there will be no congratulations or recognition for having done so*.

UNIVERSAL BASIC VALUES

Although people have different standards of ethics and integrity, some basic values are universal across mankind.

Professor Shalom H. Schwartz at the Hebrew University of Jerusalem conducted global research to identify ten of them, in four categories, in his Theory of Basic Values[66] that he believed generally transcend humanity:

Openness to Change

Self-direction: independent thought and action. Choosing, creating, exploring.

Stimulation: excitement, novelty, and challenge in life.

Self-enhancement

Hedonism: pleasure or sensuous gratification for oneself.

Achievement: personal success through demonstrating competence according to social standards.

Power: social status and prestige, control or dominance over people and resources.

Conservation

Security: safety, harmony, and stability of society, of relationships, and of self.

Conformity: restraint of actions, inclinations, and impulses likely to upset or harm others and violate social expectations or norms.

Tradition: respect, commitment, and acceptance of the customs and ideas that one's culture or religion provides.

Self-transcendence

Benevolence: preserving and enhancing the welfare of those with whom one is in frequent personal contact (the "in-group").

Universalism: understanding, appreciation, tolerance, and protection for the welfare of all people and for nature.

Although claimed to be universal, Professor Schwartz points out that the ways in which these values coincide or conflict, and how different people prioritize some at the expense of others, can vary, leading to different interpretations of both ethics and integrity.

Take leverage as an example, which we discussed in Chapter 5. It is an area which often challenges our integrity and ethics. Lord Acton, the Catholic historian, when opposing the Doctrine of Papal Infallibility during the pontificate of Pius IX in 1887, famously wrote that *power tends to corrupt, and absolute power corrupts absolutely*. Clint Eastwood was being serious when he remarked that *it takes tremendous (self)discipline to control the influence and power you have over other people's lives*.

How do we behave in line with the ethical standards that govern us professionally, and our personal standards of integrity, when negotiating? These are not only academic or theoretical assertions; they have important applications in everyday practice when negotiating.

Jan Eijsbouts, for many years GC and Director of Legal Affairs of AkzoNobel NV, the world's largest paint and coatings company, now Professor of Corporate Social Responsibility (CSR) at Maastricht University and President of the World Legal Forum, draws a distinction between *ethics in* and *ethics of* negotiation.

Ethics in negotiation refers to the duty to take into account relevant substantive and accepted norms of CSR applicable to the subject matter of the negotiation. These could include, for example, human rights implications or any natural justice aspects.

The *ethics of negotiation,* on the other hand, concerns norms regarding the way we conduct negotiations and arrive at the outcomes we are seeking, such as fair play, no bribery, no price fixing or other anti-trust behavior and no inappropriate financial recording).

Business ethics comprise all CSR norms, which have increasingly become part of accepted corporate governance. Most of these aspects are likely to have crystallized in a company's Code of Business Conduct or in legislation. Some exist as self-regulatory norms for certain industries, or in international norms such as the OECD Guidelines for Multinational Enterprises 1976 (revised in 2011)[67] which are technically non-binding but entail political and reputational consequences that can be much more severe than a fine or other conventional sanction.

We will focus here more on the *ethics of* category, but it is essential for corporate counsel involved in negotiations to keep both the *ethics in* and the *ethics of* negotiation, top of mind. Dilemmas involving both are not rare.

CODES OF CONDUCT, CORPORATE GOVERNANCE AND CSR

Most companies operating internationally have a code of business conduct and adhere to international principles of both corporate governance and CSR. They differ in levels of detail and sophistication. Some merely implement legal requirements, others go well beyond into voluntary standards that far exceed the requirements of law, often reflecting the so-called Triple Bottom Line business principle of people, planet and profit (or prosperity). Ethics, good governance and CSR are all crucial to an organization's reputation, which most business leaders rightly prize as one of their most valuable assets.

As a negotiator, you represent your employer in an outside environment. Your negotiating behavior is inevitably measured against the reputation of your organization. Conversely, when you are negotiating with a party whose ethical standards are lower than yours, there is a risk that they will try to take advantage of the limitations they know inhibit you. That is when you need to be firm, focusing on your ATNAs and on leverage, letting the other party know you have options, and being willing to let the deal fall through purely on ethical grounds. CSR principles can be useful anchors in negotiation because they are objective public standards from which you cannot compromise, that usually you can readily explain, and if you are convincing in expressing your lack of wiggle room, third parties have little choice but to play by your rulebook if they want a deal.

Many corporate counsel seem to have a weak grasp of their organization's CSR commitments, which are often managed by a separate compliance or corporate affairs staff function. But for corporate counsel, a thorough understanding of these norms and how and why they are applied is essential. In his 2011 inaugural lecture[68] as Professor at Maastricht University, Jan Eijsbouts provided a practical overview of the CSR scene and its relationship to corporate governance and company law under the title Corporate Responsibility, Beyond Voluntarism: Regulatory Options to Reinforce the Licence to Operate. It is a helpful overview for any internal counsel engaged in negotiations of both deals and settlements.

THE COALFACE

Two examples of the many situations where I have experienced the interplay of ethics, integrity and power are described in earlier pages.

My employer's reaction to a bribery attempt by a Court appointed expert who tried to secure a payment in return for a favorable opinion to the Judge, is mentioned in Chapter 5. Our ethical values viewed the request for a professional fee as a bribe, but the expert, having leverage over the situation, clearly did not see it that way, and your perception of your own leverage can cloud your vision. For us to have conceded would certainly have violated the company's Code of Business Ethics, even though the payment could have been camouflaged as an external counsel fee, and nobody would have known. But we were able to turn the leverage tables and get the expert to surrender his appointment. In that case, our integrity and our Code of Conduct were in alignment and all we had to do was change the balance of bargaining power to protect our interests.

But what if my colleagues had acceded to the external counsel's suggestion to uplift his fees and take care of the bribe? The risks of being found out were minimal and the benefits were great. If it was your job to implement such a managerial instruction, what would you do? Decline? Go along with it? Duck out and let someone else handle the situation?

In Chapter 7, I described the PMEC negotiation, where an assignment of intellectual property rights was being negotiated with a small licensee who had built its business based on those rights and made them valuable. It would not have violated my company's ethical code if we had put these rights up for auction in the market and let PMEC bid for them. However, being a small business, PMEC most likely would not have been able to afford a freely determined open market price, and if the rights had gone to someone else merely in the interests of making money, it could have severely wounded the PMEC business. Our personal values found that prospect untenable. So we voluntarily excluded the option of an open market bidding process, even though we would most likely have made more money by doing so. Number three of Stephen Covey's 7 Habits of Highly Effective People (1989) is: *the main thing is to keep the main thing the main thing.* The main thing in many negotiations can be to do the right thing, and to stick to your values.

But what if my internal colleagues had taken a hard-nosed approach and instructed me to go and find another buyer for the IP rights, even if that meant putting PMEC and its small staff in jeopardy? Would I have tried to persuade them otherwise? Yes, certainly. What if I failed? Would I refuse, go against my employer's instructions, and do what I considered to be right? Would I have asked someone else to conduct the negotiation and erase the memory? Would I have gone higher up in the organization to get the unreasonable approach reversed? Yes, certainly. Would I have enlisted other staff support that respects a code of professional ethics, such as the Finance function, to back my stand? Yes, again. What if all those options were unsuccessful? What if I would be fired if I did not comply? What would I have done? What would *you* have done?

At the coalface, you can be very severely tested. Achieving your goals while maintaining your integrity is sometimes impossible. It's not just that there are corporate, organizational and often industry ethical codes to respect and apply; in addition, lawyers have to abide by professional ethics codes. And above that, *you* have to contend with your own integrity standards.

Naked ambition, personal pride, bonus targets, key performance indicators and managerial pressures can be such powerful forces that the only way forward can seem to entail compromising your integrity and ethical standards. Something has to give. You find yourself in a cold sweat, wrestling with the horns of a dilemma. It happens.

ETHICAL COURAGE

Lawyers are by far not the only professionals facing the consequences of ethical risk taking. We all know that in 2002 the Arthur Andersen auditing and consulting firm was indicted on criminal charges over its unethical handling of Enron's accounting, and forced to surrender its licenses. In her book Final Accounting: Ambition, Greed and the Fall of Arthur Andersen (2003), Barbara Ley Toffler, formerly the partner in charge of Ethics and Responsible Business Practices in the consultancy arm of Andersen (she left before the firm collapsed after Enron, and went on to teach at Colombia Business School) quotes from the funeral eulogy for Arthur E Andersen, who had started as a mail boy and by his death in 1947 at the age of 61 had built his firm into one of the largest accounting firms in the world:

Chapter 9

> Mr. Andersen had great courage. Few are the men who have as much faith in the right as he, and fewer still are those with the courage to live up to their faith as he did... Those principles upon which his business was built and with which it is synonymous must be preserved. His name must never be associated with any program or action that is not the highest and best. I am sure he would rather the doors be closed down than that it should continue to exist on principles other than those he established... Your opportunity is tremendous; your responsibility is great.

The word courage is used twice, but is rarely mentioned in ethical codes. Often cynically misused as a euphemism for dangerous or stupid, courage in the ethical context means the willpower to do the right thing in full knowledge of the consequences.

The Arthur Andersen collapse spectacularly illustrates what can happen when a few people lack ethical courage. Clients of Andersen paid the firm vast fees for consulting services that far exceeded the firm's standard charges for comparatively low margin auditing services. There was tremendous pressure from certain notorious clients for the firm to engage in creative auditing in order to retain their highly profitable consulting business. Key members of the firm's leadership lacked the ethical courage to risk the consulting fees by insisting on good accounting practices and principles. The firm had developed a culture based on greed, blame and fear that placed their own interests above those of their clients' stakeholders.

Corporate counsel, among other professionals, need ethical courage. Looping back to Chapter 1, we need to be sufficiently *tough-minded* to endure the extreme loneliness often associated with making ethical choices. Responsible business leaders are well aware that they are custodians and stewards of other people's assets and livelihoods, and, unless you are working for an unprincipled organization, you should find that ethical conundrums can be resolved at the top of the tree. It is worth reminding ourselves of what GE's CEO Jeff Immelt hinted at in October 2012, reported at the start of Chapter 1: *Companies these days are so exposed, and there is no way we can run a company like GE unless we have trust – unless you have people around you that you can trust, that you know are going to do the right thing, and that you can just rely on their judgement – even, sometimes, when you don't like it, and you know it's the right thing to do.*

The most inspiring work that aims to address these extremely difficult issues, though largely from a Western perspective, is the 500+ page compilation What's Fair: Ethics for Negotiators (2004) edited by Carrie Menkel-Meadow, Professor Emerita at Georgetown Law and Michael Wheeler, Professor of Management Practice at HBS. It is a book that deserves to be at the elbow of every corporate counsel. The forty or so leading contributors touch on many of the toughest ethical conundrums and dilemmas you are likely to encounter in the real world that stretch your values and your ethics. It remains one of the first and most important books any negotiator should read from cover to cover.

THREE ETHICAL THEORIES

In Bargaining For Advantage: Negotiation Strategies for Reasonable People (1999), G. Richard Shell, Professor of Legal Studies and Business Ethics and Management at Wharton, describes three schools of negotiation ethics that he calls Poker, Idealist and Pragmatist.

Poker negotiators are rule-driven, complying with the law but not afraid to bluff, exaggerate, deceive and mislead provided that doing so does not give rise to illegality. They are inclined to interpret the law creatively if it suits them. They automatically distrust the other party, and it usually shows.

Idealist negotiators apply their personal as well as professional ethical codes to negotiating just as they do when they are not strictly negotiating. They will allow the other party to make erroneous assumptions, provided they have not actively and consciously misled them into doing so, and will also not voluntarily declare or admit their weaknesses. Idealists are more easily trusted and respected, but can be exploited by unscrupulous parties unless they are canny enough to recognize the risks and know how to handle them.

Pragmatic negotiators have one leg in each school, with more weight on the leg in the idealist camp. They consider themselves pragmatic idealists. They will not mislead or lie if there is a realistic option for not doing so, because they thereby are more likely to generate trust, credibility and respect and build sustainable relationships. But they will adopt poker characteristics and mislead or lie if forced and provided they can justify doing so on ethical grounds. They will observe ethical codes and strongly prefer options that accord with their standards of integrity.

TRUTH AND LIES

In Chapter 6 when dealing with communication, we touched on the importance of listening and questioning. You are less likely to mislead or lie if you are silent or in questioning mode. The more you listen and question, the more information you acquire and the more contextual vibrations come across to you from the other party to help you interpret what they are saying. Questioning is relatively safe from an ethical perspective, and how you phrase a question can communicate a point you want to get across. Silence, like inaction, can be a form of dishonest communication in some situations when it would be necessary to reveal information or to clarify and correct, but in most situations saying nothing is a valid way to avoid a lie.

ETHICS OF BARGAINING TACTICS

Professor Roy J. Lewicki at the Fischer College of Business at the Ohio State University (OSU) and Professor Robert J. Robinson at the University of Hawaii Shidler College of Business conducted two studies, one among 320 OSU MBA students and the other among 736 MBA students at HBS, the latter of which included a large proportion of non-US participants. Their studies assessed the extent to which eighteen negotiation tactics were viewed by the survey participants as ethical, unethical or marginal, and from this they developed a scale of Self-reported Inappropriate Negotiation Strategies, or "SINS." The tactics on the SINS scale, all of which raised at least a theoretical question of ethical appropriateness, were grouped in four categories:[69]

Misrepresentation of Information

- Intentionally misrepresent factual information to your opponent to support your negotiating arguments or position.
- Intentionally misrepresent the nature of your arguments to the press or your constituency in order to protect delicate discussions that have occurred.
- Intentionally misrepresent the progress of negotiations to the press or your constituency in order to make your own position or point of view look better.
- Intentionally misrepresent factual information to your opponent when you know that they have already done this to you.

Bluffing

- Threaten to harm your opponent if they do not give you what you want, even if you know you will never follow through to carry out that threat.
- Promise that good things will happen to your opponent if they give you what you want, even if you know that you can't (or won't) deliver those good things when the other's cooperation is obtained.
- Lead the other negotiator to believe that they can only get what they want by negotiating with you, when in fact they could go elsewhere and get what they want cheaper or faster.
- Hide your real bottom line from your opponent.
- Make an opening demand that is far greater than what one really hopes to settle for.
- Gain information about an opponent's negotiating position and strategy by fishing in a network of your friends, associates and contacts.
- Make an opening offer or demand so high (or low) that it seriously undermines your opponent's confidence in his/her own ability to negotiate a satisfactory settlement.
- Convey a false impression that you are in absolutely no hurry to come to a negotiation agreement, thereby trying to put more time pressure on your opponent to concede quickly.

Manipulation of the Other Party's Network

- Talk directly to the people whom your opponent reports to, or is accountable to, and tell them things that will undermine their confidence in your opponent as negotiator.

- Talk directly to the people whom your opponent reports to, or is accountable to, and try to encourage them to defect to your side.
- Threaten to make your opponent look weak or foolish in front of a boss or others to whom they are accountable.

Inappropriate Information Gathering

- Gain information about an opponent's negotiating position by paying friends, associates and contacts to get this information for you.
- Gain information about an opponent's negotiating position by trying to recruit or hire one of your opponent's key subordinates (on condition that the key subordinate bring confidential information with him/her).
- Gain information about an opponent's negotiating position by cultivating his/her friendship through expensive gifts, entertaining, or "personal favors."

The results are summarized in Chapter 16 of What's Fair. Most (twelve) of the tactics were considered ethically inappropriate. Just four tactics, all of them in the bluffing category, were considered ethically appropriate. Only two, also both in the bluffing category were rated marginal. Overall, 22% of participants classified themselves as aggressive negotiators, and 78% considered they were cooperative in negotiation settings. The significant proportion (almost 28%) of non-US MBA students participating in the HBS study highlighted a suggestion that, in some, but not all, instances, US negotiators may be regarded as less ethical than their foreign counterparts, which is an interesting observation of a culture that openly prides itself on high standards of ethical behavior.

Although these two studies were restricted to the opinions of MBA students, they do suggest that most people are pragmatic negotiators and will bluff to some extent, but draw the line at deceptive and underhand tactics. They are also broadly consistent with the Schwartz Theory of Basic Human Values.

ETHICAL NEGOTIATION POKER

Reassuring though that may be, we have all met poker negotiators who disregard ethical considerations with impunity. How do we maintain our ethical standards when other parties resort to cheating, lies, threats, subversion and blackmail?

First, stand firm on your ethics and consciously resist the temptation to react at the same low level. As Professor Shell has advised: *aim high where ethics are concerned.* This enables you to be consistent, trustworthy, respected and true to yourself as well as the organization you represent. Second, defy the other party's expectations and do the opposite. Be firm in the face of hostility and aggression, but politely, as discussed in Chapter 4. Where possible, walk away, until the other party relents. Where not possible, consider whether a change of process can help.

Poker negotiators tend to be hostile, or at least to use the more malevolent tactics of those who are in conflict. It makes sense, therefore, to consider deal facilitation. Negotiators are much less likely to adopt poker tactics quite as aggressively when there is a neutral person in the frame. This is because the neutral can manage the process so that the negotiation switches away from a positional debate to an interest-based dialogue that promotes good faith (or at least less bad faith) exchanges. The dynamic of having a neutral in the frame naturally changes the negotiation paradigm from contest to cooperation. Of course, it requires the other party to agree to jointly engage a neutral, but if approached correctly, as discussed in Chapter 8, this may be achievable. Even so, mediators frequently encounter ethical dilemmas. Many illustrations are contained in Mediation Ethics: Cases and Commentaries (2011) edited by Professor Ellen Waldman at Thomas Jefferson.

Where engagement of a neutral is resisted, rewind. Liars are often inconsistent. Asking the same questions more than once over a period of time can elicit different responses, surfacing contradictions that you may be able to exploit. If you doubt something the other party is saying, consider a reality check. It serves no purpose to contradict something without substance. One option may be to ask the opinion of an expert.

Playing along can also be a viable strategy at times. Declining to argue a point and parking it out of the way, avoiding further discussion for the moment, can clear the way for a more productive dialogue. Some poker negotiators use positional statements and threats because they assume they can shift your stance. When they realize this is not going to work, they can change tack. You need to allow them space to conveniently "forget" an earlier statement or claim that may be causing them to perpetuate a lie they told earlier by the simple technique of conducting yourself as if you have forgotten about it.

Playing along can also work in other ways. By not challenging the other party's contorted belief, it may become possible to reason it out. For example, the other party may claim that their BATNA is litigation or arbitration, but instead of challenging the merits, you may be able to demonstrate that a litigated or arbitrated victory may be Phyrric and achieve nothing practical or that by winning a battle they may lose the war, or simply incur pointless costs.

THE CORPORATE COUNSEL'S DILEMMA

What if the business people ask you to participate in a deliberately deceiving strategy during a negotiation, for example to settle litigation, one that, if acted upon by the other party, would favor your company at their expense? Given that business "ethics" may not be the same as legal ethics, which prevails?

Professor Marc Galanter at the University of Wisconsin coined the word "litigotiation" in the 1980s to mean the pursuit of settlement in the context of the Court process. As mentioned in Chapter 8, 90% or more of cases typically settle in most jurisdictions, and corporate counsel frequently drive those settlements. What if no litigation is involved and you are simply engaged in a straightforward JV negotiation? Are the ethical rules different?

One of the problems is that any lawyer, whether external or internal, is likely to be governed by more than one set of ethical conduct rules. One may be binding while another may be a guideline with no sanctions. For example, in addition to your own organization's standards, values and principles, there are likely to be relevant national and state or provincial codes of professional ethical conduct, violation of which can get you disbarred, fined or condemned in some other way. There may also be ethical guidelines such as the International Bar Association's (IBA) Principles on Conduct for the Legal Profession 2011 and the American Bar Association's (ABA) Model Rules of Professional Conduct 2016, and the ABA's Ethical Guidelines for Settlement Negotiations 2002.

Although these and other professional rules and guidelines are directed at external counsel, they are generally applicable to corporate counsel, even when not acting in a strictly advisory capacity.

The IBA Principles are just that, principles. They are important because they are intended to apply globally, regardless of culturally-driven ethical standards. The ABA's Ethical Guidelines are more detailed and practical in the context of American litigation and are annotated with useful interpretative guidance. They prohibit such practices as making false statements of material fact, exploiting the other party's mistake over material facts, extortionate tactics and repugnant client strategies, and cover other ethical areas. Whether or not you are governed by US ethical standards for lawyers, these codes and guidelines are important for any lawyer-negotiator to comprehend.

Do not assume that counsel representing the other party, even if governed by the ABA Rules and Guidelines, will necessarily abide by them. In Mediation Ethics' chapter on Mediating with Lies in the Room contributed by Professor Dwight Golann at Suffolk University in Boston and Melissa Brodrick, the Ombudsperson at Harvard Medical School, it is noted that studies of attorneys in Arizona and Missouri found that 19% would knowingly hide crucial information in a given scenario even though it would lead to the commission of a fraud.

When I have faced ethical dilemmas, I have rarely just said no. Instead, I have tried to propose another, viable, route to the same goal. It may be less attractive, or less certain, but there usually are, as Mark Twain wrote in 1889 in A Connecticut Yankee in King Arthur's Court, *more than two ways to skin a cat.*

Disclosures, specifically how much to disclose, often present dilemmas for corporate counsel. Let's say you are selling a business and you stumble across a copy of a document dated many years earlier that suggests another party still has a substantial claim on the business that is not time-barred. You have no evidence that the potential claim is invalid, or that the potential claimant knows about the apparent right to claim, and all enquiries have drawn a blank. The claim, if it exists, is so large that it exceeds the value of the business. Do you disclose this particularly unsavory skeleton in the cupboard that nobody else knows anything about, and which is little more than a suspicion? Personally, I would do so, but perhaps accompanied by a request for a non-disclosure undertaking and an offer to give an indemnity that expires on the date the claim would become time-barred. It would place my company in a no-worse situation than if the business had not been sold, and would avoid any theoretical post-closing claims.

NOT TOUCHING THE VOID

I have implemented my own seven personal principles that seem to have worked effectively: fairness, good faith, honesty and truthfulness, refusal to misrepresent, transparency to the extent necessary not to mislead, clarity and simplicity.

But nothing beats a litmus test, a rule of thumb that you can use every day. One of the best on ethics is that offered by Professor Michael Wheeler of HBS in his book The Art of Negotiation: How to Improvise Agreement in a Chaotic World (2013):

> Acting responsibly doesn't require a doctorate in moral philosophy, but it does mean knowing your core values before negotiation begins. There are tried-and-true tests that can help you not cross the line separating right and wrong:
>
> – Universality check. Could you recommend that everyone in your situation act this way?
> – Reciprocity check. Would you want others to treat you this way?
> – Publicity check. Would you be comfortable if your actions were fully and fairly described in a newspaper or online?
> – Trusted-friend check. Would you be comfortable telling your best friend, spouse or children what you are doing?
> – Legacy check. Is this how you want to be known and remembered?

AN INTERNATIONAL CODE OF NEGOTIATION ETHICS?

I believe there would be great value in having a published statement of ethical principles that people may choose to adopt or be guided by when negotiating internationally. Currently, such a statement or code does not seem to exist, nor does there seem to be a suitable global body that could credibly promulgate an International Code of Negotiation Ethics in numerous languages and promote its voluntary adoption, not only for lawyers but all negotiators. But such a body and such a code would not be difficult to establish.

IN A NUTSHELL

- Some basic values are universal, across cultures, but are applied unequally.
- Ethics and integrity are not the same thing.

- There are three (Shell) ethical approaches to negotiation: Poker, Idealist and Pragmatist.
- Studies suggest most people prefer cooperative bargaining and pragmatic ethics.
- Lawyers, whether internal or external to corporations, need to abide by ethical codes and guidelines.
- When facing a dilemma, search for other, practical, ways around it that respect ethics and integrity.
- Apply the Wheeler six-point litmus test.
- We need an International Code of Ethics for negotiators.

CHAPTER 10
Techniques

It is not because things are difficult that we do not dare,

it is because we do not dare that they are difficult.

Seneca

Landscape painters have a dizzying array of tools and methods that they are adept at using instinctively to create the results they want to achieve. They need to match their brush to the chosen medium. Short handle or long? Mink, squirrel, hog or synthetic bristles? Round, pointed, flat, bright, filbert, angular or fan tips? Then comes the choice of oil, acrylic, gouache, pastel or watercolor. Paper, canvas or board? Primary colors or blends? There are hundreds of permutations. Artists need to be adaptable, creative and willing to experiment and take risks, always able to step back, correct errors, change their minds and try something new.

Negotiators are artists, because negotiation is an art form. Deals share much in common with paintings and other works of art. They capture a predicament, tell a story, convey messages. Deals, like art, are skillfully constructed using a mix of tools and techniques that lie invisibly behind the final image, but were essential to the crafting of it, because human actions and responses cannot be reliably foreseen. Negotiating a deal, like creating a piece of art, is inherently unpredictable and risky.

It is worth spending a few moments to collect some of the best and lesser-known techniques that negotiators use in their art. Some have been mentioned in earlier pages. Others are obvious, but perhaps too obvious and often overlooked. Yet others are inspirational and creative, suitable only in certain situations, but always worth keeping in the toolbox.

There are twenty techniques that I would like to highlight from the many that could be recited here. Many are captured in the great negotiation books included in the Bibliography.

Chapter 10

TEAM LEADERSHIP

Negotiation can be an iceberg. The bit above the water is the dialogue with the other party, but handling your own people can be an even more challenging task. Various business and support functions are likely to have a stake in the matter, and not everyone may share the same view about the goals and components of success. There may even be disagreement about whether a negotiation should be taking place. Politics can impede traction, even kill the deal.

Recognize these realities and assume a central coordinating role by taking command of preparation. Corporate counsel are well positioned and qualified to do this. Because preparation is central to success, and if you are coordinating the prep work through interaction with all internal parties, you quickly acquire an unassailable influence over the negotiation. Become familiar with the preparation tools suggested in Chapters 2 and 7 and use them to forge internal stakeholder buy-in. Ensure that the front line negotiators know their goals, ATNAs and any red lines, and have clear authority to close the deal on or above the agreed baseline or walk-away terms. Build in enough flexibility and wiggle room. Nobody likes surprises, but they are endemic in negotiation. When unpredictable things happen, have a clear understanding about your level of discretion.

In the Preface, I mentioned an important book - Getting It Done: How to Lead When You're Not In Charge (1998) by Professor Roger Fisher and management consultant Alan Sharp. For me, this is the ultimate source of servant team leadership skills for corporate counsel.

Control external counsel. Forge a clear understanding with them about their role and level of participation. They can be an indispensable help, but also a monumental hindrance. Where the other party's external counsel fronts their negotiating team, this does not necessarily mean you need to have your external counsel do the same. External counsel are crucial advisers, but they are also valuable tools. You control, and need to be seen to determine, how those tools are used to maximize their value. Perception is everything.

In Negotiating Life: Secrets For Everyday Diplomacy and Deal Making (2013) Professor Jeswald Salacuse reminds us that the other party is also empowered and constrained by the limits of their authorization, and it is important, if at all possible, to discover the extent of their mandate. They may be coy about revealing it, or, in exchange, ask you to disclose yours. A perfectly reasonable first step is to ask the other party's negotiator whether they have settlement authority without ratification. If they don't, tell them you will also need to seek ratification of any deal (even if, privately, that step is unnecessary because you already have approval).

I believe team leadership is a kind of golden key for corporate counsel, not just leading their own team but leading their colleagues, not as a power play, but in a servant capacity, and mostly without them necessarily feeling they are being led.

PROCESS

Usually, little or no thought is given to process options when preparing to negotiate. Yet the wrong process quickly compounds the problem, sometimes even becoming the main problem, impeding and even preventing agreement being reached.

Most negotiators operate a subconscious creed, a knee-jerk assumption that they can handle both the substance and process without outside help. The very suggestion of a neutral facilitator to help the parties handle the process aspects, freeing up the negotiators to focus on their job, is strangely anathema to them.

In Chapter 7, we looked at how process can unlock the door to the outcome. Negotiators need to shake off their inexcusable antipathy towards the importance of process and consider what process options may suit the specific negotiation dynamics. There is an unspoken, perhaps egoistical, sentiment that engaging a neutral person to handle process somehow smacks of failure, of being unable to deal with the situation alone. This belief can be fueled by external counsel if they fear loss of influence and control when facilitators and mediators enter the frame. Parties need to take a firm hold, dare to be a little creative and realize that delegating process and administration to an impartial neutral is very likely to enable them and the other party to perform their negotiating job more effectively.

ROLEPLAY

Negotiation trainers are fond of game theory to improve strategic thinking and to sharpen negotiation skills. Game theory examples, most famously The Prisoner's Dilemma and the X-Y Game Win As Much As You Can (but there are many others), do help negotiators plan whether in given circumstances and assuming rational participants, they should act cooperatively or competitively. It is important for negotiators to experience these games, but there is an even more practical, but equally engaging, way to prepare for certain specific negotiations.

Where you are facing a particularly difficult or important negotiation, consider the following prep work as part of what you might call a *pre-mortem*:

- Prepare a roleplay that, as closely as possible, mimics the factual circumstances of the deal or settlement you are trying to achieve. The roleplay should consist of a general description of known facts and confidential information for each of the parties (your own party and, as best as you can envisage it, the other party). The confidential instructions for the other party should be based as much as possible on what you know about their situation, but you may have to use some intelligent projection and guesswork.
- Then, allocate roleplayers for each party, preferably involving actual stakeholders within your own party. Some will have to be nominated to play the other party's role; try to enlist your lead negotiators to play the role of the other party.

- Give each party their own confidential instructions, plus the general description. Do not let each see the confidential instructions of the other party.
- Appoint a moderator, whose role is to manage the negotiation process in a way that is as close to anticipated reality as possible.
- Hold a post-mortem engaging the players and anyone invited to watch. Capture their comments.

It would be dangerous to make firm assumptions about the other party's motivations and any hypothetical hidden agendas that may have been ascribed to them, but the great value of roleplaying the negotiation in advance is that you consider more carefully where the other party is likely to be coming from, and how, if those assumptions are correct, you may want to behave. A sample roleplay is included in Appendix 7 as an illustration.

Roleplays are just one way to conduct a pre-mortem - an attempt to envisage all thethings that could go wrong in a negotiation, leading to failure. If you can identify thosethings, you may be able to anticipate and, if possible, address them in advance.

DEFROSTING

If you are not familiar with the other party's negotiators, create an opportunity to get to know them personally. Suggest getting together for a meal before the negotiation begins. Propose sharing the cost if that is appropriate, not for frugality reasons but to let them feel they have a stake in the motivation behind the occasion. If not appropriate, cover the cost yourself. It will be a minor investment that will pay substantial dividends. You can agree not to talk shop and just take some time out. I have gone so far as to attend a conference in another country where I knew my prospective negotiating partner is due to speak, simply for the chance to meet and possibly dine together.

POWER SEATING

Think carefully about where you sit. If there are several of you attending a negotiation session, agree in advance who will take the lead. If you are hosting the negotiation, try to choose a round table, or, better still, no table at all. For more on seating, *see* Chapter 6.

HANDS-FREE

Most people entering a room to negotiate automatically set themselves up with a laptop, tablet and/or papers. More often than not, this is a mistake, unless the session has been planned to discuss written materials. You exude confidence and authority and generate subconscious respect by staying visually connected to everyone in the room, actively listening and engaging, and not taking notes. For as long as possible, keep the space before you uncluttered by paraphernalia you are unlikely to use.

POLITENESS

Rarely viewed as a technique in negotiation, politeness is a powerfully disarming phenomenon. Touched on in Chapter 4, Politeness Theory is a mechanism for addressing face issues. It takes the wind out of the sails of aggressors with alacrity. Although I have not found convincing statistics on the effect of politeness in negotiation, it stands to reason that polite negotiators are more respected, listened to and trusted, and likely to achieve their goals more quickly. Politeness does not imply weakness any more than rudeness suggests strength. It does not imply weakness to remain polite in the face of acrimony or attack; in fact it indicates confidence and control.

I have noticed that literally all the most effective negotiators I have encountered, regardless of their cultural attributes, have shared several politeness-related characteristics. Among them, they are all respectful, witty, self-deprecating, *tough-minded*, warm, relaxed, charming, amusing and skilled in etiquette.

FIRST MOVER

Some negotiation experts advocate caution about making the first offer, arguing that if the other party quotes their terms first, you can counter-offer or, if they have been too aggressive, walk away. If you are a buyer, this is what normally happens anyway. But what if you are a seller, or neither a buyer nor a seller because the negotiation is a lot more complex than that? What if the other party either moves first, or waits for you to do so, resulting in a Mexican Standoff?

A first offer is an anchor. In distributive (fixed pie) negotiations, be ready, willing and able to make the first move, but be able to "anchor the anchor" – that is, support it with an objective justification. Think in advance exactly what that anchor will be. It needs to be better than your BATNA, but if you over-state, you may prompt a no-ball response, even a refusal to consider it, or a walk-out, or an attempt to force you into an embarrassing climb-down.

The reason why first moves are anchors is that they psychologically condition the other party to negotiate in your territory. There is plenty of empirical evidence to back this up. But if you justify the reasonableness of the first move by providing credible, objective data to support it, you can stand your ground with confidence.

Where the negotiation is more complex and integrative, it may make more sense first to explore the issues holistically and assess how they interact. Moving too fast may undershoot the maximum value available.

MESOs

Making multiple equivalent simultaneous offers, or MESOs, is a technique described in 2005 by Professors Victoria Medvec of the Kellogg School of Management at

Northwestern University and Adam Galinsky of Columbia Business School. Smart MESOs can be a useful deadlock breaker when parties are close to a deal, but where the details of several elements having different value remain outstanding. One party (or possibly more than one) puts forward two or three variations of their offer, each totaling the same, or approximately the same, value to the party putting forward the MESO, but which may have different values to the party receiving it.

The idea behind MESOs is to sweeten the offer by providing alternative connected values so that the receiver of the offers can chose the one that is best for them.

An example given by Professors Medvec and Galinsky is where, in a hiring situation, the prospective employee makes three offers simultaneously, treating salary, bonus and location in different ways, but each amounting to the same thing financially to the employee. The cost and precedent implications to the employer may be different, and they then have the ability to select which they prefer.

In order to be confident that the MESO offers are worth roughly the same to you, ascribe in your own mind how you value and prioritize each component. Although they may amount to the same value to you, the other party may prioritize them differently, and therefore the prospect of a deal on one the options increases.

SALAMI SLICING

Controlling the negotiation agenda without the other party feeling railroaded or cornered, which would erect barriers to progress, requires some subtle footwork. Many negotiations comprise multiple issues. Some are easier to agree than others. Some favor you more than the other party and vice versa. Some have higher priorities than others or are dependent on others.

In those situations, you can build momentum by dissecting the issues into digestible pieces that are more likely to be agreeable to the other party on an individual basis than if swallowed as part of a larger whole. Sometimes, it is appropriate to list all the perceived issues up front, get the other party's ideas and support for the list in principle, and then agree an order for addressing them. On other occasions, when you believe the other party may feel threatened or could react negatively to a list of what they might consider barriers or conditions, an advance listing may not be the best approach.

Either way, you need a clear plan of action to salami slice successfully, with a logical progression that connects the issues into a coherent whole. If you have prepared properly, that should not be a problem. Always consider how the other party is likely to view the approach, not just how you mean it. If they feel manipulated, because the slices merely favor you at their expense, the approach could be unproductive at best, even damaging or catastrophic. But dare to do it if the circumstances are right. Salami slicing can build cooperation and alignment quite quickly if done artfully in the right sequence.

LOW-HANGING FRUIT

If there is tension or hostility in the air before you start a negotiation, for example because you are trying to settle a dispute, or a conflict is simmering in the background, you need to try and extract negatives from the situation. Where several relatively minor issues are involved that can potentially be exchanged and where agreement appears achievable, consider addressing these issues first. Harvesting low-hanging fruit can improve sentiment on all sides if everyone perceives they are starting to address their interests at the outset. It needs to be reciprocal to work properly. Improved mindsets open parties up to exploring creative solutions to the more difficult issues.

Select the issues with care. Ensure they appear capable of swift agreement and, taken together, result in roughly equivalent benefits for each party.

WHITEBOARDING

Rather than leaving issues as spoken words recorded in the negotiators' heads or in their private notes, where they may be remembered or expressed differently, consider the benefits of using a whiteboard, flip chart or a projected electronic equivalent to capture them as a jointly-constructed medium. This becomes a shared experience to which every party can contribute. Psychologically, each negotiator can see and appreciate their input reflected. Buy-in can become easier. Shared notes can be photographed by the negotiators on smartphones.

Always try to be the scribe that writes the words. Seat yourself close to the whiteboard or flip chart, or, before the session begins, hook your laptop to the meeting room's projector, making it look more natural for you to assume the publicly humble but privately crucial role of transcribing. This enables you to frame the words used to reflect your interests but in a way that is also acceptable to the other party.

Mastering mind mapping software can be an important skill in complex negotiations, especially those with a brainstorming element. Mind maps enable information to be clustered and presented in the form of diagrams, such as cycle wheel spokes on a shared screen or in tree branch style. Mind mapping can be traced to the Roman philosopher Porphyry who plotted out the Categories in Aristotle's Organon, and is a brilliant technique for accommodating positions and demands while expressing them as interests and needs. Completed mind maps can then be shared electronically as a record of the dialogue.

PARKING

Where progress can be made on some issues but not others, parking those that are problematic and returning to them at a later moment can be a wise move. It helps to steer around potential deadlocks, deferring them until a moment is reached when they can be reassessed in light of progress made in the meantime.

Chapter 10

Where one party clearly feels particularly strongly about a difficult issue, but the time is not right for addressing it, note it on the whiteboard, flip chart, mind map or other shared record. This gives that party the comfort of knowing that their concern is not being sidelined, derogated or downplayed but is genuinely being stored as a future agenda item. Where the issue is more of a position than an interest, parking can be an extremely effective way to manage it because when you reach the moment to bring it back into discussion, the other party's attitude towards it may have changed for the better. There may be a reduced appetite for it at a later stage because other factors have a bearing on the issue's importance, and they may be more willing to compromise or find another way to address their needs.

ANCHORING

We discussed anchors in Chapter 5. Always think of a convincing rationale for the value you are trying to claim. It could be in the form of objective standards, precedents, facts or authorities that the other party would find difficult to deny or argue. Where there is no credible anchor, state why you need what you are claiming and why you set the anchor the way you did.

A compelling reason, especially one that does not just benefit you, can be the next best thing to a strong anchor. You do not need to give the real or most important reason, but it has to be a good one that the other party will buy.

Negotiation is persuasion. Anchors help you to influence the judgment of the other party to the point that they are convinced they can and should agree. It will not necessarily lead to agreement, but it is an essential tool in the task of changing disagreement and doubt into concession and agreement.

PRINCIPLES

Lawyers have a natural and understandable tendency to focus on detail. It is one of their most important strengths, but the expression of this inclination often needs to be curtailed. Keep your goals top of mind at all times, together with your ATNAs and any boundaries or red lines that would cause the negotiation to collapse. Keep your eyes on the prize. These principles – the goals, ATNAs and red lines – form your negotiation framework and everything else should fit comfortably within them.

When artists buy a canvass, and before they start painting, they first apply a solid paint as a toned ground. Then they are likely to sketch a light outline. Only when happy with the composition and balance do they start to complete the detail. Negotiation is an art form.

TIME OUT TO REFRAME

When the going gets tough, things are getting heated, frustrations are surfacing and you appear to be making little or no progress, relax. Take a break. There are many ways to do this. You can split into your respective groups for a while. Or, better still, get out of the negotiating environment and take a breath of fresh air.

In Getting Past No: Negotiating With Difficult People (1991), William Ury proposes five steps of breakthrough negotiation. First, take control of yourself, focus on your goals and your ATNAs, and, as he puts it *"go to the balcony."* Second, defuse the situation and disarm any aggression and tension by not arguing; instead, find things you can support or at least accommodate. Third, *to change the game, change the frame* and rework the other party's statements in the context of the wider shared issues. Fourth, save the other party's face by giving them a way out, a line of retreat, a face-saver, or what Ury, quoting Sun Tzu's Art of War, called *a golden bridge.* And finally, persuade the other party that their best interests are served by a deal that addresses everyone's needs. If necessary, hint at your BATNA.

Time out gives you and the other party the opportunity to reflect, reconsider and reframe. You can do all these things on a short walk in the sun, or even in the rain or snow, ideally together with the other party.

RECIPROCITY

Negotiations require give and take, which is not necessarily the same thing as compromise. In Chapter 4, we reviewed the importance of reciprocity from a cultural perspective. But reciprocity is wired into all human DNA. Primates and other animals have long been known to exhibit cooperative reciprocal behavior that generates mutual trust and in-group inclusiveness.

In his bestseller Influence: The Psychology of Persuasion (1984), Professor Robert Cialdini at Arizona State University identifies six core principles of influence, the first of which is reciprocation. Humans are pre-conditioned to feel that if they are offered a concession, then a concession should be returned to them. Of course, we can override this instinct quite easily by willpower, but with what consequences? There is another, more subtle result. The receiver of the concession will be naturally inclined not to exploit the concession giver in the interests of gaining more concessions, so a reciprocal concession is offered and the process becomes circular.

Reciprocity is a powerful form of persuasion. You can use it to ameliorate the impact of out-group dynamics, generate trust and respect and improve the negotiation climate. Consider what elements are suitable for reciprocal trading, both those that you have to trade and those that you wish from the other party. Consider the sequence of the things you trade or any concessions you make and ensure at least equivalent value in return.

Occasionally, you need to make a concession without a trade in return. When you need to bring about a dramatic change in negotiation dynamics, just giving something away, particularly something of more value to the receiver than to you, can bring great rewards later. Ensure there is a rationale behind it that you can express to the other party, and to your own constituency.

CONTRA-FLOW

In an episode of the internationally successful 1990s comedy sitcom Seinfeld, set in an Upper West Side Manhattan apartment, George Costanza, Seinfeld's best friend, proclaims himself a loser because every time he follows his gut instincts, things lead to disaster. On a whim, he decides on a contrarian strategy, consciously doing the exact opposite of his instinctive choices. It works spectacularly and hilariously well.

There are times when negotiators, and particularly lawyer negotiators who are likely to be naturally cautious and reluctant to dare, should consider the Costanza Contra-Flow Principle and be counter-intuitive.

If the other party proposes to host your first negotiating session at their office, most negotiators would instinctively resist. There is a human preference for home turf. It seems to pay dividends in sport, where the local crowd will urge you on vocally and inject new impetus into your veins, but that does not happen in negotiation, so homeland preferences can be irrational. You can learn many things about the other party by being at their place, observing them, and assessing their surroundings, staff and facilities. Although contextual, context always matters.

If your intuition drives you to focus on the areas of disagreement, because those are what impede progress, first spend time on common ground, appreciating the value and significance of issues you agree upon. This conditions both parties' minds more positively.

If you have a lot to say, consider staying silent, listening and probing. If the other party is formal, consider informality. If they are hostile, be disarmingly friendly. When you are not sure about something, ask the other party for advice. Of course you would not choose to do these things all the time, but at least consider what surprising benefits they may bring to the negotiation.

Years ago, my company decided to terminate a contract with a large Japanese corporation. It was a fixed ten-year contract, with eight years still to run. There was no early termination clause and the contract was governed by Japanese Law. It fell to me to negotiate an immediate end to this agreement for commercial reasons. I asked our external counsel in Tokyo to advise. They said there was no way out, that the other party could insist on performance, or the net present value of their likely profits for the next eight years, plus any consequential losses. I asked external counsel to cook up a force majeure argument. Reluctantly, they did so, but emphasized it only worked academically, and would never fly in a Japanese Court.

I made an appointment to meet the GC of the Japanese corporation in Tokyo, alone (I did not invite external counsel to join me – there was no point). He received me graciously, clearly having guessed at the purpose of my visit, but was too polite and too smart to ask. He was not joined by his external counsel. After several hours of enjoyable exchanges that were unrelated to the contract, and after he had hosted me to a truly memorable private lunch, he signaled that the floor was mine. The first words out of my mouth were: *"I need to terminate our agreement, and I have no contractual right to do so. I am in a totally weak position. I need your help."* This went against all my instincts, but it had the merit of being the naked truth. Japanese are often hard for Westerners to read, but I am certain I saw an invisible smile. A few hours later, I had a deal, within the mandate my employer gave me. The contrarian Costanza Principle really can produce excellent results.

EXPRESS WHY

In Chapter 7, we considered the importance of starting with the rationale for any proposition we make, in order to attract buy-in. But we lawyers are implementers by training – wired to think more in terms of what and how.

A thread that weaves through most expert writing on negotiation is the importance of keeping the parties' shared objectives in sharp focus by frequent repetition. They make up the why, or what the Boston-based negotiation strategy consultancy Lax Sebenius calls the *social contract* or *the spirit of the deal* – the factor that underpins the arrangement.

Giving convincing reasons for each proposition you want the other party to agree builds the spirit of the deal. The more credible your reasons, the less likely the other party will be able, credibly, to resist.

The Express Why principle should flow through the negotiation and into the final deal.

THE DRAFTING INITIATIVE

Wherever feasible, be the one to prepare document drafts. You are in a much stronger negotiating position if you are the party preparing the versions for review and comment by the other party. It's rather like the art of controlling meetings – the person with the most influence in a meeting often appears to be the Chair, or the most persuasive speaker, but is actually the one who writes the minutes or meeting notes.

In order to retain the respect of the other party, always make drafts balanced, and not inappropriately favorable to yourself. Construct drafts so that they objectively represent the flavour and conclusions of the negotiation. Where you include elements that were not specifically agreed, do not slide them in, be honest enough to highlight them. Capture the reciprocity of the negotiation. Where possible, construct the document using plain, not legalistic, language. Begin with a background statement that frames the content of the document, trying to avoid obvious bias. Document recitals may have little or no legal significance, but can help parties to bridge differences, save face and can be very valuable for those who have to interpret the contract in years to come.

Often, deal or term sheets, or memoranda of agreement, are a useful precursor to a full draft. They snapshot the deal, and can be brief and simple, merely summarizing the core points negotiated, but are generally non-binding and subject to the final agreement. It is really important to be the party to prepare this document. Put in a non-binding clause but get the parties to sign it, or at least write their initials, which imports a psychological commitment to something that has no technical legal bearing. An important stepping stone to final closure.

In the main agreement, focus particularly on the dispute resolution clauses and resist the temptation to draw them from a previous contract or a precedent model. Favor multi-step approaches to dispute resolution, beginning with negotiation, then mediation, and only if that fails, arbitration or litigation. Discuss the value of these clauses with the other party before presenting the draft, and make them a red line. If the other party (or, most likely, their external counsel) objects, explain the rationale and preferably be in a position to quote such a clause as your policy in order to avoid disputes; if that doesn't work, be prepared to walk away from the deal. It is hard to envisage circumstances where a party can reasonably refuse a multi-step dispute resolution clause, and if they do, bad faith, unreliability or stupidity must lie behind it – a bad omen for any deal.

Where you are unable to assume the drafting role, at the very least insist on sharing the task in some way, or if that is refused, go ahead and produce your own draft anyway and present it to the other party before they have a chance to send theirs to you.

How you present a draft agreement can be as important as its substance. In Negotiating The Impossible: How to Break Deadlocks and Resolve Ugly Conflicts Without Money or Muscle (2016), Professor Deepak Malhotra at HBS emphasizes the importance of *the optics of the deal*. Usually, the draft agreement will have to be reviewed by people not directly involved in the negotiation and sometimes by others, such as the final decision makers, antitrust authorities and other regulators and indirect stakeholders, Courts, and tax people. Ensure that the way it is framed is appropriate from their standpoints and does not unwittingly cause alarm or defensiveness.

NEGATIVE TECHNIQUES

There are also things you should avoid doing at all costs. Many are simply the opposites of the things you should be doing. In Winning Negotiations (2011), a Harvard Business Review compilation, Professor James Sebenius of HBS contributes a chapter entitled Six Habits of Merely Effective Negotiators. In it, he lists six common negotiating errors:

- Neglecting the other side's problem
- Letting price bulldoze other interests
- Allowing positions to drive out interests
- Searching too hard for common ground
- Neglecting BATNAs, and
- Failing to correct skewed vision

Professor Sebenius' point about common ground is that it is a mistake to assume that all deals are based on shared interests. The solution may arise not just in spite of their differences, but because of them. His analysis of all six errors is important to keep in mind.

3-D Negotiation: Powerful Tools to Change the Game in your Most Important Deals (2006) by Professor Sebenius and Dr. David Lax encourages an approach to negotiation based on the three dimensions of deal tactics, deal design and deal setup. This inspires ways to consider negotiation techniques in a more refined and targeted way.

I have selected here just 20 of the scores of techniques that could have been mentioned. If you would like to see additional techniques described in a further edition of this book, I would be grateful if you will please contact me at the email address shown on page vii.

Tomorrow

> *Many of the things you can count, don't count;*
> *many of the things you can't count, really count*
>
> Albert Einstein

The Danish physicist Niels Bohr was awarded the Nobel Prize for Physics in 1922, the year after Einstein. He warned that *prediction is difficult, especially if it is about the future*. It may seem like a malapropism when related as a soundbite, but he was emphasizing that, to predict, you need to identify both the elements of the past that cannot be expected to continue, and the new factors that are likely to fundamentally change existing dynamics. And then connect them. One person who has done just that in recent years in relation to legal practice and the role of lawyers is Professor Richard Susskind.

In The Future of the Professions (2015) Richard Susskind and Daniel Susskind emphasize that: *"clients of the future will be inclined to pay for output rather than input, for the value delivered rather than the effort expended."* Richard Susskind has written several books about the future of lawyering, many of them international bestsellers. They explain why and how the demand side's needs and expectations are rapidly changing for both internal and external counsel, and what must happen if you are to add continuing value. In The End of Lawyers? Re-Thinking the Nature of Legal Services (2010) and in Tomorrow's Lawyers: An Introduction to Your Future (2013, 2017), both of them controversial, well-argued and credible, Susskind predicts that many traditional sources of work for lawyers will become redundant, replaced by technology, done by others, or simply not needed. Rather than become unemployable, Susskind says lawyers will redeploy. In Tomorrow's Lawyers, Susskind suggests that it is possible to break down, or as he calls it, *decompose* the lawyer's work on deals and disputes into a set of constituent tasks. He identifies nine areas in which lawyers will need to apply existing and new skills in order to survive. Transactional work will revolve around *negotiation*, research, legal advice, due diligence, transactional management, template selection, one-off drafting, document management and risk assessment. Dispute resolution will call for skills in *negotiation*, strategy, tactics, project management, advocacy, document review, research and disclosure.

Conspicuously, negotiation features in both of Susskind's decomposed lists of transactional and dispute resolution legal competencies. Many, including negotiation, are not widely taught as part of law courses. Law, like finance, has always been viewed as a "hard" skill. But negotiation is generally considered a "soft" skill, and so rarely taught in law courses. The pernicious categorization of knowledge and skills as "hard" and "soft" has had a pejorative effect on negotiation education, for lawyers and for others.

Hard skills are generally considered to be those for which knowledge and practice can be effectively learned through teaching, not just acquired by experience, and can readily be independently and objectively assessed using objective measurement criteria. All traditional professional practices for which competency can be credentialed are regarded as hard skills, as well as foreign language fluency and anything requiring detailed factual knowledge.

Soft skills are generally a function of personality and experience in which competency is more subjective and can only be taught to a limited extent. Competency in soft skills is difficult to assess independently owing to a lack of consistent objective measurement criteria. Leadership, positivity, self-confidence, persuasion, teamwork and work ethic are widely considered to be soft skills.

Of course, real-world competency in most activities is a combination of hard and soft skills. To be an effective lawyer, you must possess the knowledge that makes law a hard skill, and you also need soft skills to apply and leverage that knowledge. The reverse is also true: to be an effective leader, which is considered a soft skill, you also need hard skills both to do the right things and to inspire others to do them right.

NEGOTIATION IS MAINLY A HARD SKILL

I have asked scores of people from different countries and cultures whether they consider negotiation to be a hard skill or a soft one. Almost everyone's immediate reaction when presented with this question viewed negotiation as a soft skill. Perhaps they had been subliminally influenced by popular assumptions. For example, the Division of Graduate Studies at Brandeis University seems to classify negotiation as a soft skill.[70] The same conclusion is assumed in the subtitle of Simon Horton's book The Leader's Guide to Negotiation: How to Use Soft Skills to Get Hard Results (2016). These, and many other examples can unwittingly convey a mildly derogatory connotation to negotiation – that it is somehow less tangible, substantial and definable than traditionally-taught abilities, and somehow less capable of being appraised.

To a second and equally international group, I put the question differently. I asked whether they considered negotiation to be a skill that can be taught and assessed. Interestingly, almost everyone I asked considered that negotiation could indeed be taught and assessed, and when I asked if they would therefore classify negotiation as a hard skill, all said yes. It all goes to show that the answer you get depends on the question you ask.

The differences between the two questions were clear. I defined hard and soft in terms of ability to teach the skills and assess competency, and the word "predominantly" hinted that negotiation was a combination of hard and soft skills.

There are many negotiation skills that are teachable and objectively assessable. The ability to prepare effectively is one. So is knowledge and application of culture, leverage, communication abilities, process options, dispute management skills, ethics and negotiation techniques. Various systems, checklists and other technical applications can be used to enhance this bank of knowledge and skills. There are soft skills that also need to be deployed: the ability to persuade, to listen actively to what is being said, to understand correctly and reframe appropriately, EQ, adaptability, teamwork and many others. These can all be tested and assessed in role play scenarios.

Both hard and soft negotiation skills are needed in the appropriate proportion depending on the situation. Excellence in all the hard negotiation skills and many of the soft ones can be gained by being taught effectively in classes, role plays and other behavioral learning activities. These skills can also be assessed against pre-set objective competency criteria that cross language, cultural and other boundaries.

Yes, competency as a negotiator can be taught and objectively assessed. Negotiation, unquestionably, is a hard skill.

TEACHING AND ASSESSMENT

The proof can be found in the many outstanding negotiation courses and workshops around the world, usually lasting between three and five days, that teach the basics and many advanced skills. Most provide a certificate of completion and professional development credits. The Harvard Program on Negotiation's (PoN) regular Negotiation and Leadership course has over 35,000 alumni. It lasts three intensive days, with an add-on one-day in-depth treatment of a specific area, such as dealing with difficult people and problems, or conflict negotiation. Many faculty members are world leaders in negotiation. The PoN also holds a three-day Negotiation Master Class and periodic one-day author seminars. Many business schools, professional organizations, negotiation trainers and dispute resolution programs around the world offer executive education courses on negotiation skills. A few law schools do, too.

However, although most courses are costly in terms of fees and time, most people walk away with little more than a certificate of attendance. There are a few exceptions, such as TNI The Negotiation Institute in New York. If negotiation courses offered a skills assessment and a negotiation competency accreditation, providing evidence of having achieved a visible high standard, participants would have something that others would recognize and respect. It would help corporate counsel to be admitted to the business front line, to be more readily trusted as the lead negotiator for their organizations.

Some mediation skills courses long ago recognized the need to qualify people formally as accredited or certified mediators. Mediation knowledge and skills that a participant acquires during the course, which usually lasts three to five days, can be assessed at the end, usually in a role play setting. Those that pass the assessment are awarded a formal accreditation. For example, mediator training courses run by some professional bodies and training institutions, such as the Chartered Institute of Arbitrators and the Centre for Effective Dispute Resolution CEDR in the UK, the ADR Institute of Canada and the Maryland Center for Dispute Resolution in the US, all set high level competency criteria for mediation skills and offer assessments leading to accreditations for those who pass. In Australia, the National Mediator Assessment Standards are applied by Recognized Mediation Accreditation Bodies. The Singapore International Mediation Institute (SIMI) and The Hong Kong Mediation Accreditation Association Limited (HKMAAL) have published mediator competency criteria that enable trainers to grant assessed accreditations. Similar competency criteria for mediators apply in the Netherlands, Argentina, Nigeria and Austria. The International Mediation Institute has developed internationally-applicable competency criteria for mediators and for mediation advocates and has developed inter-cultural competency criteria for mediators. These assessments cover hard skills and also those considered soft, such as empathy, listening, emotion and persuasion.

The Singapore International Dispute Resolution Academy (SIDRA), launched by the Chief Justice of Singapore in March 2016, has an integrated program of training, research and consultancy that provides thought leadership in both negotiation and dispute resolution. These, and other initiatives need strong encouragement and support. Looping back to the very start of Chapter 1, and the Dell Technologies slogan, they give us The Power To Do More.

If knowledge and skills competency criteria can be a success in mediation, which is merely assisted negotiation, one has to ask: why have negotiation courses not done the same?

THE NEED FOR AN INTERNATIONAL NEGOTIATION INSTITUTE

When it was created in 1983 as a research project, the Program on Negotiation was a collaboration of several leading US-based educational institutions, initiated by Harvard and MIT, in which several others now participate. The PoN quickly inspired numerous negotiation teaching and training courses around the world.

Negotiation needs to be recognized as a vital skill required by everyone, regardless of their professional focus, to enable deals and settlements to be conducted and concluded more efficiently and effectively.

As negotiation is a post-qualification discipline, the key to encouraging more people to become trained in negotiation is to give them a recognizable global qualification that can, over time, be widely respected and valued. This will vest us with the trust of our stakeholders and the respect of our negotiating partners. It will empower us to negotiate effectively.

Now is the time for the world's leading negotiation skills educators, in partnership with major companies, law and consulting firms, professional bodies and business associations, to give birth to a new initiative, a platform that builds upon the value that has already been created. It would be born international and not have a national identity or a specific national culture. While not providing training or any other services, it would have a very clear main mission: *to convene stakeholders worldwide to develop and publish high level assessable criteria for advanced interest-based negotiation skills that are globally applicable.* This platform could develop the assessment methodology that could be used by educators and trainers around the world as a common basis for negotiation skills accreditation. With input from all the outstanding institutions that back its mission, it could also prepare and publish an International Code of Negotiation Ethics to serve as a guide for responsible negotiators worldwide.

This new entity would need a small inter-cultural staff but need have no single physical office. It would have an inspiring multilingual interactive web portal. Its governing body would be drawn from the institutions and organizations that support and fund its work.

It could attract funding for a scholarship program for critical candidates, especially in developing countries, to enable them to be trained in world class negotiation knowledge and skills in the top negotiation training programs, and return home with an internationally-recognised qualification.

It could simply be called the *International Negotiation Institute.*

Endnotes

1. For example, Rule 3.7.1 of the Charter of core Principles of the European Legal Profession and Code of Conduct for European Lawyers provides: *The lawyer should at all times strive to achieve the most cost-effective resolution of the client's dispute and should advise the client at appropriate stages as to the desirability of attempting a settlement and/or a reference to alternative dispute resolution.*
2. https://www.youtube.com/watch?v = szwp2MfrURI.
3. http://www.americanoutlook.org/reagan-and-the-midwest.html.
4. http://www.fastcompany.com/3049913/know-it-all/7-habits-of-tough-minded-leaders.
5. http://www.gcleaderscircle.org/wp-content/uploads/2014/07/GCLC-Target-Topic-GC-Corp-Governance-final-July-2014.pdf.
6. https://global.oup.com/academic/product/the-generalist-counsel-9780199892358?cc = gb& lang = en&.
7. http://papers.ssrn.com/sol3/papers.cfm?abstract_id = 2218855.
8. https://info.bgllp.com/40/459/uploads/justice-dept-memo-on-corporate-wrongdoing.pdf.
9. http://www.globallegalpost.com/publications/732553b59c50ba66c5f233141ee9226f.
10. http://www.terralex.org/publication/p2a4016ca5e/2015-general-counsel-excellence-report.
11. http://www.danpink.com/books/whole-new-mind/.
12. https://law.ubalt.edu/academics/pdfs/Carnegie%20Report%20article_final.pdf.
13. http://www.cleaweb.org/Resources/Documents/best_practices-full.pdf.
14. http://www.icicte.org/Proceedings2013/Papers%202013/13-2-Neuland.pdf.
15. This example is a slightly adapted version of one used by Michael McIlwrath, Global Chief Litigation Counsel, GE Oil & Gas at a presentation in Rome in October 2006 entitled Leadership Tools – GE's Early Dispute Resolution System. The author is grateful to Mr. McIlwrath for his consent to use this example.
16. http://gpi.sagepub.com/content/5/1/35.short.
17. www.IMImediation.org.
18. This chapter has been prepared with contributions from Jeremy Lack and François Bogacz of Neuroawareness, an international neuroscience training academy in the fields of negotiation and conflict resolution, and Dr. Olga Klimecki, a neuroscientist at the Centre for Interdisciplinary Affective Sciences in Geneva. The ideas that follow are expressed in more detail in a talk given by Jeremy Lack at the Strauss Institute at Pepperdine University in Malibu, CA on November 9, 2015. A written version is available in the Pepperdine Dispute Resolution Law Journal Vol. 16 and at www.neuroawareness.com.
19. http://scholarship.law.cornell.edu/cgi/viewcontent.cgi?article = 2027&context = facpub.
20. http://journals.plos.org/plosone/article?id = 10.1371/journal.pone.0001128.
21. http://www.mediate.com/articles/cloke8.cfm.
22. https://editorialexpress.com/cgi-bin/conference/download.cgi?db_name = EEAESEM2016& paper_id = 398.
23. "Stories Mediators Tell," (Eds. Eric R. Galton and Lela. P. Love), American Bar Association, 2012, p. 257.
24. https://www.geert-hofstede.com/tools.html.
25. http://www.forbes.com/2006/10/25/carrefour-china-chereau-qanda-biz-cx_pnc_1025mckinsey.html.
26. These dimensions are related in more detail in Hofstede, Geert; Hofstede, Gert Jan and Minkov, Michael *Cultures and Organizations: Software of the Mind* Third Revised Edition, McGrawHill 2010 ISBN 0-07-166418-1 © Geert Hofstede BV, quoted with permission.
27. http://www.ocai-online.com.
28. The research methodology and results are explained in detail in the journal Organizational Behavior and Human Decision Processes 39, 84–97 (1987).
29. http://kluwermediationblog.com/2013/08/14/ramblings-of-a-neuro-linguist-the-impact-of-voice-on-communication/.
30. http://kluwermediationblog.com/2012/06/14/ramblings-from-a-neuro-linguist-non-verbal-communication-and-rapport/.

Endnotes

31. http://www.ted.com/playlists/171/the_most_popular_talks_of_all?gclid = CIzmhPTUh88CF bIV0wodehQIKA.
32. https://www.psychologytoday.com/blog/the-personality-analyst/200909/what-emotional-intelligence-is-and-is-not.
33. http://www.mhs.com/product.aspx?gr = io&id = overview&prod = msceit#top.
34. http://atrium.haygroup.com/ww/our-products/ei-quiz.aspx.
35. http://www.pon.harvard.edu/daily/negotiation-skills-daily/the-limits-of-emotional-intelligence-as-a-negotiation-skill/.
36. http://onlinelibrary.wiley.com/doi/10.1111/nejo.12045/abstract.
37. https://hbr.org/2013/01/should-you-eat-while-you-negot.
38. http://courses2.cit.cornell.edu/fit117/documents/samples_planning/OnHumorAndIrony.pdf.
39. http://www.nyulawreview.org/sites/default/files/pdf/NYULawReview-72-5-Levi.pdf.
40. https://hbr.org/2011/09/negotiate-where-you-want.
41. http://www.people.hbs.edu/kmcginn/pdfs/publishedarticles/negotiate-successfully-online.pdf.
42. http://papers.ssrn.com/sol3/papers.cfm?abstract_id = 1392474.
43. Chapter 5, ADR In Business: Practice and issues across countries and cultures, Volume II (2011).
44. http://digitalcommons.ilr.cornell.edu/icrpubs/4/.
45. https://www.adr.org/aaa/ShowPDF?doc = ADRSTG_004327.
46. http://papers.ssrn.com/sol3/papers.cfm?abstract_id = 2221471.
47. http://kluwerarbitrationblog.com/2013/03/14/what-does-the-fortune-1000-survey-on-mediation-arbitration-and-conflict-management-portend-for-international-arbitration/.
48. https://imimediation.org/imi-international-corporate-users-adr-survey-summary.
49. http://www.mediate.com/articles/jordan.cfm.
50. https://www.cedr.com/about_us/arbitration_commission/Rules.pdf.
51. https://lawweb.colorado.edu/profiles/pubpdfs/peppet/newEthics.pdf.
52. https://www.collaborativepractice.com/.
53. https://www.transactionadvisors.com/insights/collaborative-law-option-resolving-ma-disputes.
54. https://www.adr.org/aaa/ShowPDF?doc = ADRSTG_004315.
55. http://www.cedr.com/docslib/The_Seventh_Mediation_Audit_(2016).pdf.
56. http://www.mediate.com/articles/roberts4.cfm.
57. University of Chicago Law Review, Volume 52, Issue 2, March 1, 1986.
58. http://www.nytimes.com/1982/11/01/business/new-alternatives-to-litigation.html.
59. https://www.cedr.com/about_us/modeldocs/?id = 9.
60. https://www.adr.org/aaa/faces/services/disputeavoidanceservices/earlyneutralevaluation?_afrLoop = 503824377001301&_afrWindowMode = 0&_afrWindowId = qdvethr1e_64#%40%3F_afrWindowId%3Dqdvethr1e_64%26_afrLoop%3D503824377001301%26_afrWindowMode%3D0%26_adf.ctrl-state%3Dqdvethr1e_108.
61. http://www.jurispub.com/Bookstore/United-States/AAA-HANDBOOK-ON-MEDIATION-3RD-ED-.html.
62. https://icsid.worldbank.org/apps/ICSIDWEB/Uncitral/C3765/Claimant's%20Response%20to%20the%20Respondent's%20Requests%20under%20ICSID%20Arbitration%20Rules%2028(1)%20and%2039(1)/Legal%20Authorities/CL-13.PDF.
63. http://www.schiffhardin.com/Templates/Media/Files/Publications/PDF/CLInt_March_2014_Lurie.pdf.
64. https://imimediation.org.
65. Avoiding Pitfalls: Common Reasons for Mediation Failure and Solutions for Success by J.G Marcil and N.D. Thornton. http://www.americanjournalofmediation.com/docs/Avoiding%20Pitfalls%20-%20Common%20Reasons%20for%20Mediation%20Failure%20and%20Solutions%20for%20Success.pdf.
66. http://scholarworks.gvsu.edu/cgi/viewcontent.cgi?article = 1116&context = orpc.
67. http://www.oecd.org/daf/inv/mne/48004323.pdf.

Endnotes

68. http://www.l4bb.org/articles/OBS_7885_-_Eijsbouts_digitale-1.pdf.
69. Items from the Self-Reported Inappropriate Negotiation Strategies (SINS) scale, developed by Robert Robinson, Roy J. Lewicki and Eileen Donahue, 1998, used with permission of the developers.
70. http://projectmgmt.brandeis.edu/downloads/BRU_MSMPP_WP_Feb2012_Balancing_Project_Management.pdf.

Bibliography

Abramson, Harold *Mediation Representation: Advocating as a Problem-Solver in Any Country or Culture* (2010).
Alexander, Nadja *International and Comparative Mediation: Legal Perspectives* (2009).
Alexander, Nadja and Howieson, Jill *Negotiation: Strategy Style Skills* (2010).
Axtell, Roger *Dos and Taboos Around the World* (1991).
Axtell, Roger *Dos and Taboos of Humor Around the World* (1999).
Bennis, Warren *On Becoming A Leader* (1989).
Brazil, Wayne *Early Neutral Evaluation* (2012).
Brodow, Ed, *Negotiation Boot Camp: How to Resolve Conflict, Satisfy Customers and Make Better Deals* (2014).
Brown, Penelope and Levinson, Stephen *Politeness: Some Universals in Politeness Usage* (1987).
Cialdini, Robert *Influence: The Psychology of Persuasion* (1984).
Cloke, Kenneth *Mediating Dangerously: The Frontiers of Conflict Resolution* (2001).
Costantino, Cathy and Sickles Merchant, Christina *Designing Conflict Management Systems: A Guide to Creating Productive and Healthy Organizations* (1996).
Deardorff, Darla and Berardo, Kate – Building Cultural Competence: Innovative Activities and Models (2012).
Dobelli, Rolf *The Art of Thinking Clearly* (2013).
Dubey, Prashant and Kripalani, Eva *The Generalist Counsel: How Leading General Counsel Are Shaping Tomorrow's Companies* (2013).
Ebner, Noam; Bhappu, Anita; Gerarda Brown, Jennifer; Kovach, Kimberlee and Kupfer Schneider, Andrea *You've Got Agreement: Negoti@ting via Email* (2009).
Falcão, Horatio *Value Negotiation: How to Get the Win-Win Right* (2010).
Fisher, Roger and Ertl, Danny *Getting Ready To Negotiate: A Step-by-Step Guide to Preparing for Any Negotiation* (1995).
Fisher, Roger and Sharp, Alan *Lateral Leadership: Getting it Done When You're Not the Boss* (2004).
Fisher, Roger and Ury, William *Getting To Yes: Negotiating Agreement Without Giving In* (1981).
Fraser, David *Relationship Mastery: A Business Professional's Guide* (2015).
Fraser, Véronique and Roberge, Jean-François – Legal Design Lawyering: Rebooting Legal Business Model With Design Thinking (2016).
Gardner, Howard *The Theory of Multiple Intelligences* (1983).

Bibliography

Gates, Steve *The Negotiation Book: Your Definitive Guide to Successful Negotiating* (2011).

Gefland, Michele and Brett, Jeanne *Handbook of Negotiation and Culture* (2004).

Glasl, Friedrich *Confronting Conflict: A First-Aid Kit for Handling Conflict* (1999).

Golann, Dwight and Corman Aaron, Marjorie *Using Evaluation in Mediation* AAA Handbook of Mediation (2016).

Goleman, Daniel *Emotional Intelligence: Why it Can Matter More than IQ* (1995).

Goodman, Andrew *Effective Mediation Advocacy: A Guide for Practitioners* (2016).

Hall, Edward *Beyond Culture* (1976).

Harvard Business Essentials *Negotiation* (2003).

Harvard Business Review *Winning Negotiations* (2011).

Heineman Jr, Ben *High Performance with High Integrity* (2008).

Hofstede, Geert; Hofstede, Gert Jan and Minkov, Michael *Cultures and Organizations: Software of the Mind* (2010).

Honeyman, Christopher; Coben, James; De Palo, Giuseppe (Eds) *Venturing Beyond The Classroom* (2010).

Horton, Simon *The Leader's Guide to Negotiation: How to Use Soft Skills to Get Hard Results* (2016).

Ingen-Housz, Arnold *ADR in Business: Practice and Issues Across Countries and Cultures* (2011).

Kahneman, Daniel *Thinking Fast and Slow* (2011).

Karsaklian, Eliane *The Intelligent International Negotiator* (2014).

Kinsey Goman, Carol *The Nonverbal Advantage: Secrets and Science of Body Language at Work* (2008).

Lande, John *Lawyering with Planned Early Negotiation: How You Can Get Good Results for Clients and Make Money* (2011).

LeBaron, Michelle *Bridging Troubled Waters* (2002).

Lebaron, Michelle; McLeod, Carrie; Floyer Acland, Andrew (Eds) *The Choreography of Resolution: Conflict, Movement and Neuroscience* (2013).

Lee, Joel and Teh, Hwee Hwee *An Asian Perspective on Mediation* (2009).

Lee, Joel and Lim, Marcus (Eds) *Contemporary Issues in Mediation* (2016).

Lempereur, Alain and Colson, Aurélien *The First Move: A Negotiators Companion* (2010).

Lewis, Richard *When Cultures Collide: Managing Successfully Across Cultures* (1996).

Lewis, Richard *Cross-Cultural Communication: A Visual Approach* (1999).

McIlwrath, Michael and Savage, John *International Arbitration and Mediation: A Practical Guide* (2010).

Macfarlane, Julie *The New Lawyer: How Settlement Is Transforming the Practice of Law* (2008).

Malhotra, Deepak and Bazerman, Max *Negotiation Genius: How to Overcome Obstacles and Achieve Brilliant Results at the Bargaining Table and Beyond* (2007).

Malhotra, Deepak *Negotiating the Impossible: How to Break Deadlocks and Resolve Ugly Conflicts Without Money or Muscle* (2016).

Menkel-Meadow, Carrie and Wheeler, Michael *What's Fair: Ethics for Negotiators* (2004).

Meyer, Bernard *Beyond Neutrality: Confronting the Crisis in Conflict Resolution* (2004).
Meyer, Bernard *Staying with Conflict: A Strategic Approach to Ongoing Disputes* (2009).
Meyer, Erin *The Culture Map: Decoding How People Think, Lead and Get Things Done Across Cultures* (2014).
Mnookin, Robert *Bargaining with the Devil: When to Negotiate, When to Fight* (2010).
Mnookin, Robert; Peppet, Scott and Tulumello, Andrew *Beyond Winning: Negotiating to Create Value in Deals and Disputes* (2000).
Monberg, Tina *Serve to Profit: Butterfly Leadership* (2014).
Morrison, Terri and Conaway, Wayne *Kiss, Bow or Shake Hands: Doing Business in More Than 60 Countries* (1995).
Movius, Hallam and Susskind, Lawrence *Built to Win: Creating a World-Class Negotiation Organization* (2009).
Navarro, Joe *What Every Body Is Saying: An Ex-FBI Agent's Guide to Speed-Reading People* (2008).
Neale, Margaret and Lys, Thomas *Getting More of What You Want: How the Secrets of Economics and Psychology Can Help You Negotiate Anything in Business and Life* (2015).
Nisbett, Richard *The Geography of Thought: How Asians and Westerners Think Differently and Why* (2003).
Pel, Machteld *Referral to Mediation: A Practical Guide for an Effective Mediation Proposal* (2008).
Plant, David *We Must Talk Because We Can: Mediating Intellectual Property Disputes* (2009).
Raiffa, Howard *The Art and Science of Negotiation* (1982).
Roberts, Wess *Leadership Secrets of Attila The Hun* (1987).
Salacuse, Jeswald *The Global Negotiator* (2003).
Rosen Svensson, Charlotte *Sweden CultureShock!* (2009).
Salacuse, Jeswald *Negotiating Life: Secrets for Everyday Diplomacy and Deal Making* (2013).
Schonewille, Manon *Toolkit Mediation Advocacy* (2007).
Schonewille, Manon *Toolkit Generating Outcomes* (2009).
Schonewille, Manon and Fox, Ken *Moving Beyond Just A Deal, A Bad Deal or No Deal* (included in Ingen-Housz, Arnold (Ed) *ADR in Business: Practice and Issues Across Countries and Cultures* (2011).
Sebenius J and Lax, David *3-D Negotiation: Powerful Tools to Change the Game in Your Most Important Deals* (2006).
Shapiro, Daniel *Negotiating the Non-negotiable* (2016).
Shell, Richard *Bargaining for Advantage: Negotiation Strategies for Reasonable People* (2001).
Susskind, Lawrence *Good for You, Great for Me: Finding the Trading Zone and Winning at Win-Win Negotiation* (2014).
Susskind, Richard *The End of Lawyers? Re-thinking the Nature of Legal Services* (2010).
Susskind, Richard *Tomorrow's Lawyers: An Introduction to Your Future* (2013).
Susskind, Richard and Susskind, Daniel *The Future of the Professions: How Technology Will Transform the Work of Human Experts* (2015).

Bibliography

Svensson, Charlotte Rosen – Culture Shock! Sweden (2009).

Trompenaars, Fons and Hampden-Turner, Charles *Riding The Waves of Culture: Understanding Diversity in Global Business* (1997).

Ury, William *Getting Past No: Negotiating with Difficult People* (1991).

Ury, William; Brett, Jeanne and Goldberg, Stephen *Getting Disputes Resolved: Designing Systems to Cut the Cost of Conflict* (1988).

Ury, William *The Power of a Positive No: How to Say No and Still Get to Yes* (2008).

Ury, William *Getting To Yes with Yourself (and Other Worthy Opponents)* (2015).

Volkema, Roger *Leverage: How to Get It and How to Keep It in Any Negotiation* (2006).

Waldman, Ellen (Ed) *Mediation Ethics* (2011).

Weeks, John *Unpopular Culture: The Ritual of Complaint in a British Bank* (2004).

Wheeler, Michael *The Art of Negotiation: How to Improvise Agreement in a Chaotic World* (2013).

Williams, Greg and Williams-Washington, Kristin *Mastering Negotiations Through Body Language and Other Nonverbal Signals* (2015).

Zetik, Deborah and Stuhlmacher, Alice *Goal Setting and Negotiating Performance: A Meta-Analysis* (2002).

APPENDIX 1
IMI Olé! Case Analysis and Evaluation Tool

This tool is downloadable as a Word document at www.IMImediation.org where it can also be completed online. Reproduced here with the kind permission of the International Mediation Institute

International Mediation Institute
www.IMImediation.org

Olé!
Concise Case Analysis & Evaluation Tool

Olé is a process to help you to analyze and assess specific disputes in order to determine the best possible way forward - potentially reducing risk, uncertainty, cost and time.

- Olé can be used by a disputant and legal counsel.
- Olé is simple to use.
- Olé prompts the right questions and encourages concise answers.

Olé! is also available to complete online at: www.imimediation.org/ole

It is not necessary to complete all sections of Olé! and there are no mandatory sections.

Appendix 1

Olé! is an excellent aid to evaluating a particular case historically and prospectively, and for determining the best management strategy for each dispute.

What Olé! covers

1. **Basic Facts of the Dispute**

An opportunity to summarise the key facts, claims made and positions taken by each side both formally and off-the-record, an opportunity to consider which stakeholders have most to gain or lose as a result of the case, and how far the dispute has escalated.

2. **Case Analysis**

An aid to analysing the future interests of both sides separately from the past and present positions, and to focus on the historic and prospective costs for both sides.

3. **Strategy Analysis**

A series of questions that can impact on the strategy behind the dispute.

4. **Financial Loss Analysis**

A simple method for assessing the financial impact of the claims made in the dispute by each side.

5. **SWOT Analysis**

Assessing the Strengths, Weaknesses, Opportunities and Threats for each side.

6. **BATNAs, WATNAs and PATNAs**

Identifying the best, worst and probable outcomes if the dispute does not settle.

7. **Way Forward Options**

A scorecard for comparing the relative attraction of the alternative ways forward for the dispute.

8. **Future Strategy Summary**

Based on the Olé! analysis, this is a chance in a few words to summarise the strategy for each dispute looking to the future, and to identify the action steps and options to implement them.

9. **Ongoing Review**

An option to reconsider the strategy depending on certain trigger events.

10. **Performance Measurement**

Identifying how to measure success.

Appendix 1

1. Basic Facts

1.1 Description of the dispute

1.2 Value of the dispute

1.3 Relevant Countries

1.4 Extent of communications between parties to date (in quality/number)

1.5 Main claims made/positions taken formally to date <u>by us</u>

1.6 Positions taken/offers made off-the-record <u>by us</u>

1.7 Main claims made/positions taken formally <u>by the other party</u>

1.8 Positions taken/offers made off-the-record <u>by the other party</u>

Appendix 1

1.9 Our main stakeholders in this dispute (Consider who has most to gain/lose from the outcome of the dispute, who may raise or remove obstacles for you, both internal and external.)

1.10 What stage has the dispute reached on the Escalation Ladder? [Footnote 1]

1.11 Any other significant considerations? [Footnote 2]

2. Case Analysis

2.1 Our present and future interests, concerns, needs and motives as distinct from our past and present positions. [Footnote 3]

Our Positions...	Our Interests...

2.2 Our guess at the other party's past and present positions and their present and future interests, concerns, needs & motives

Other Side's Positions...	Other Side's Interests...

2.3 A comparison of both parties' present and future interests, concerns, needs and motives

Our Side...	Other Side...

2.4 Our legal and expert fees and costs to date

Appendix 1

2.5 **Our non-legal costs to date**

    2.5.1 Cost of management time on this dispute ☐

    2.5.2 Lost opportunity costs ☐

    2.5.3 Cost of being unable to use funds for other purposes ☐

    2.5.4 Other potentially hidden costs ☐

2.6 **Our guess at the other party's legal and expert fees and costs to date** ☐

2.7 **Our guess at the other party's non-legal costs to date**

    2.7.1 Cost of management time on this dispute ☐

    2.7.2 Lost opportunity costs ☐

    2.7.3 Cost of being unable to use funds for other purposes ☐

    2.7.4 Other potentially hidden costs ☐

2.8 **Estimate of our legal and expert fees and costs in the future** ☐

2.9 **Estimate of our non-legal costs in the future**

    2.9.1 Cost of management time on this dispute ☐

    2.9.2 Lost opportunity costs ☐

    2.9.3 Cost of being unable to use funds for other purposes ☐

Appendix 1

    2.9.4   Other potentially hidden costs

2.10 Our guess at the other party's legal and expert fees and costs in the future

2.11 Our guess at the other party's non-legal costs in the future

2.11.1   Cost of management time on this dispute

2.11.2   Lost opportunity costs

2.11.3   Cost of being unable to use funds for other purposes

2.11.4   Other potentially hidden costs

3. Strategy Analysis

3.1 Is there a strategy in place for this dispute?

3.2 Has the strategy changed over time?

3.3 To what extent have negotiations been positional?

3.4 To what extent have negotiations been interest-based?

Appendix 1

3.5 Which side has been dominating the agenda

3.6 How many discussions have there been between business principals?

3.7 Why did they not succeed?

3.8 How may you have contributed to their not succeeding?

3.9 What intentions did you attribute to the other side?

3.10 What intentions do you think they attributed to you?

3.11 In what way are you a victim?

3.12 In what way has the other party been evil/inconsistent with your values?

Appendix 1

3.13 In what way has the other side been a victim?

3.14 In what way have you been evil/inconsistent with your values?

3.15 What are the other party's values?

3.16 What did you expect from the other party?

3.17 What did you think the other party expected from you?

3.18 What effect has each party's strategy had on the relationship between the parties?

4. Financial Loss Analysis

4.1 Indicate on the table how losses are calculated, both for Us and the Other Side.

The way in which damages may be calculated can vary from jurisdiction to jurisdiction. The quantum of damages can vary greatly, depending on the theory that is to be applied and the evidence in support. The assessment of quantum is sometimes left until late in proceedings, after issues of liability have first been determined. However, this can lead to unsatisfactory situations, where the costs of the proceedings become disproportionate to the damages that can be obtained. An early understanding of the likely theoretical bases on which damages may be claimed and their approximate assessment is an important step to be done at the beginning when a conflict arises.

Appendix 1

These calculations should be revised continuously throughout the case. Complete the chart:

Financial Analysis of Loss	For Us	For the Other Side
Restitution Damages		
Expectation Damages		
Unjust Enrichment Damages		
Industry-specific norms		
Value of any additional remedies		
What, realistically is the best claim		

5. SWOT Analysis

5.1 Our main strengths

5.2 Our main weaknesses

5.3 Our main opportunities

5.4 Main threats to our case

5.5 Other side's main strengths

Appendix 1

5.6 Other side's main weaknesses

5.7 Other side's main opportunities

5.8 Main threats to the other side's case

5.9 Now summarise on the charts:

SWOT Analysis for Us

Positive	Negative
Strengths:	Weaknesses:
Opportunities:	Threats:

SWOT Analysis for the Other Side

Positive	Negative
Strengths:	Weaknesses:

Appendix 1

Positive	Negative
Opportunities:	Threats:

6. BATNAS, WATNAs & PATNAs

Effective negotiators and dispute strategists evaluate BATNAs, WATNAs and PATNAs.

BATNA = Best Alternative To a Negotiated Agreement now - ie the most favourable realistic scenario if there is no settlement (e.g. we win on all significant points at trial)

WATNA = Worst Alternative To a Negotiated Agreement now - ie the least favourable realistic scenario if there is no settlement (e.g. we lose on all significant points at trial)

PATNA = Probable Alternatives To a Negotiated Agreement now - ie the most likely realistic scenario if there is no settlement (e.g. what the Court or Tribunal is likely to decide)

6.1 Assess our BATNA, WATNA and PATNA, and, assess them hypothetically on four levels:

- The amount of time it is likely to take to arrive at a **final** judgment or award (i.e. taking into account all possible appeals and tactical delays).
- The total cost involved in getting to the **final** judgment or award.
- What the **final** Judgment or Award will be - i.e. the final outcome.
- What the consequences of that outcome would be.

6.2 Then assess the Other Side's BATNA, WATNA and PATNA on the same four levels.

6.3 Capture these with keywords on the chart:

		Us	Other Side
BATNAs	Time		
	Cost		
	Award/Outcome		
	Consequences		

Appendix 1

		Us	Other Side
WATNAs	Time		
	Cost		
	Award/Outcome		
	Consequences		
PATNAs	Time		
	Cost		
	Award/Outcome		
	Consequences		

7. Way Forward Options

After completing sections 1-6 of Olé!, score each of the following options in terms of relative attraction as a process for delivering the PATNA. 1 = low; 5 = high

Bear in mind the practical aspects such as risk, costs, time. Also consider enforceability of outcomes, in particular that negotiated and mediated settlements are usually contractual and can also often be converted into a legally binding and enforceable judgment or award.

Option	Score				
	1	2	3	4	5
Negotiation (including collaborative law)	○	○	○	○	○
Neutral Fact Finding	○	○	○	○	○
Facilitative Mediation	○	○	○	○	○
Evaluative Mediation	○	○	○	○	○
Mini-Trial	○	○	○	○	○
Arbitration	○	○	○	○	○
Litigation	○	○	○	○	○

Negotiation by parties personally. No neutral involved, parties negotiate directly with one another. Some negotiations use lawyers who are Collaborative Practitioners - meaning that if the negotiations do not result in a settlement and the dispute is pursued in litigation or arbitration, then the practitioners will step aside and the disputants must use other law firms to pursue their case.

Neutral Fact Finding utilises a third party neutral with expertise to examine disputed facts central to the case. Usually a step in a settlement process.

Facilitative Mediation is a non-binding and voluntary assisted negotiation process where a third party neutral, agreed by the parties, and who has no power to impose a solution, helps them to elicit their respective interests and helps the parties to reach a mutually acceptable settlement based on their subjective and future interests. For more on facilitative mediation see www.IMImediation.org

Evaluative Mediation (sometimes called Conciliation or non-binding arbitration) is an evaluative, non-binding and voluntary assisted negotiation process where a third party neutral, agreed by the parties, and who has no power to impose a solution, helps them to understand objective parameters based on which an outcome would be reached using specific norms (e.g., the applicable law of the contract). The Evaluative mediator helps the parties to identify the zone of possible agreement using norms-based criteria (e.g., what a court is likely to rule) and is encouraged by the parties make proposals of his/her own as to where a possible solution may lay. For more on evaluative mediation, see www.IMImediation.org

Mini-Trial involves the parties' lawyers presenting their cases to a panel comprising senior executives of each of the parties plus a neutral. The neutral helps clarify the issues and evaluate the case.

Arbitration is litigation in private, using party-appointed neutrals, based on an arbitration organisation's Rules or rules agreed between the parties. There is normally no appeal from such as process save for serious cases of error or bias.

Litigation/Opposition Proceedings are the conventional methods for resolving disputes and conflicts in formal actions. They entail using national court systems and using civil servants or former advocates that have reached the status of judges. These courts can be appealed and can have procedural rules that the parties are not free to deviate from.

8. **Future Strategy Summary**

Summarize future preferred strategy for this dispute.

Based on that strategy, what are the action points needed to implement it, by whom, by when and within what cost constraints. Complete the chart:

Action Point	Implementer	Due Date	Max Budget

Appendix 1

9. Ongoing Review

Indicate the most appropriate moments to review the case strategy again. Complete the chart:

Trigger Event / Review Description	Date for review

10. Performance Measurement

Indicate what future milestones would help to measure success. For example:

> Containing future costs below a certain level?
> Concluding a settlement on acceptable terms?
> Concluding a settlement by a certain date?
> Securing other advantages (perhaps beyond the scope of the dispute)?
> Meeting defined business objectives?
> Improving the relationship between the parties?

Complete the chart:

Milestones	Measurements

This completes your Olé case evaluation and analysis.

Appendix 2
CPR Corporate Early Case Assessment Toolkit

Reproduced with the kind permission of the International Institute for Conflict Prevention and Resolution (CPR Institute) www.cpradr.org. This Toolkit is available at: https://www.cpradr.org/resource-center/toolkits/...0/CPRECAToolkit2010.pdf

**RESOURCES FOR NAVIGATING COMPLEX BUSINESS DISPUTES
CORPORATE EARLY CASE ASSESSMENT TOOLKIT**

Produced by the Corporate Early Case Assessment Commission
of the International Institute for Conflict Prevention and Resolution

Appendix 2

CPR assembled a commission of leading corporate counsel, attorneys and academics to collaborate in the production of an Early Case Assessment tool which could be used across a broad spectrum of commercial disputes. The organization gratefully acknowledges the individuals who contributed their expertise and insights to this project.

Lawrence N. Chanen
Senior Vice President & Associate General Counsel *JPMorgan Chase*

Dan S. Dunham
Senior Corporate Counsel
Pfizer, Inc.

Anurag Gulati
Assistant General Counsel
General Mills, Inc.

J. Andrew Heaton
Associate General Counsel
Ernst & Young LLP

Paula A. Johnson
Senior Counsel
ConocoPhillips

Janet S. Kloenhamer
President, Discontinued Operations
Fireman's Fund Insurance Co.

Patrick Lamb
Valorem Law Group

Prof. John Lande
Director, Program in Dispute Resolution
University of Missouri School of Law

Melanie Lewis
Director, Solutions Program
Coca-Cola Enterprises, Inc.

Duncan R. MacKay
Assistant General Counsel, Dispute Resolution
Northeast Utilities

Deborah Masucci
Vice President & Director of Dispute Resolution
American International Group Inc.

Julie S. Mazza
Senior Counsel
Citigroup Inc.

Barbara McCormick
Assistant General Counsel
Johnson & Johnson

Richard N. Papper
Vice President &
Senior Litigation Counsel
Bank of New York/Mellon

Roland Schroeder
Senior Counsel, Litigation & Legal Policy
General Electric Company

Beth Trent
Legal Director
Schering-Plough Corporation

Patricia Caycedo-Smith
Associate General Counsel, Litigation
Duke Energy Corporation

Nancy L. Vanderlip
Vice President & General Counsel Electronic Components
ITT Corporation

Jennifer Boyens Victor
The Victor Law Firm

Thomas R. Woodrow
Holland & Knight LLP

Appendix 2

CPR Staff: Cathy Cronin-Harris Senior Consultant
Kathy Bryan President & CEO   Thomas L. Aldrich Senior Consultant

Titles and affiliations reflect participants' positions at the time of drafting (2009).

The views expressed in these ECA Guidelines do not reflect the views of the participating CPR Members' companies.

© 2009 International Institute for Conflict Prevention & Resolution. All rights reserved

Appendix 2

FUNDAMENTALS OF EARLY CASE ASSESSMENT

CPR Definition: Early Case Assessment

CPR's Early Case Assessment Toolkit (ECA) outlines a simple conflict management process designed to facilitate more informed and expedited decision-making at the early stages of a dispute. The process calls for a team working together in a specified time frame to gather the key facts of the dispute, identify the key business concerns, assess the various risks and costs the dispute poses for the company, and make an informed choice or recommendation on how to handle the dispute.

While one of the possible recommendations could be to settle or resolve the dispute, CPR wishes to emphasize that these Guidelines are not about settlement, although that could be one possible outcome of Early Case Assessment. Instead, these Guidelines focus on evaluating the dispute so that an appropriate strategy can be formulated, whether that is settlement, full-bore litigation, or something in between, with an eye toward reducing or eliminating disputes as soon and as inexpensively as possible.

Benefits of Using Early Case Assessment

In today's highly litigious business climate there are numerous business and legal trends supporting the use of Early Case Assessment. These trends include an increasing volume of claims and litigation, the increasing complexity and protraction of claims, and the resulting higher legal fees and settlements. In this climate, many legal departments have worked to develop new definitions of "value" and "win" by treating disputes as a business process, and protracted litigation as a defect to be remedied. One effective tool for controlling disputes and reducing or eliminating litigation is the ECA process.

There are numerous potential benefits of implementing an Early Case Assessment program, including:

- Enhanced, early case analysis
- Enhanced, early risk identification and analysis
- Enhanced, early evaluation of potential end-game solutions
- Enhanced ability to gauge business needs and solutions, and improved client relations
- A reduction in legal costs and expenses
- A reduction in settlement and resolution costs
- A reduction in the "claim-through-resolution" cycle time

Appendix 2

Setting the Stage for Successful Early Case Assessment

The growing adoption of Early Case Assessment programs arises from the mandate of in-house legal departments to better and more effectively manage litigation, in terms of outcome and cost, and to do so with better calculation of the business interests and objectives implicated by that litigation.

In addition, in-house legal departments have at their disposal more and better tools for gathering necessary data to assess litigation risks and solutions, measure progress, communicate lessons learned, and track successful strategies and solutions. Early identification of risks, business prerogatives, likely outcomes, and potential alternative resolutions should be a part of every Early Case Assessment program.

Using CPR's ECA Toolkit

CPR's ECA Guidelines provide a structured approach for conducting early evaluation of a dispute. It is intended to be a flexible tool that may be adjusted by in-house counsel to meet the particular needs of their business. It can be applied in whole or part depending on dispute circumstances to conduct early, rapid and consistent analysis of a dispute to find the most effective resolution path geared toward limiting corporate expenditures, serving business concerns and utilizing the most appropriate conflict resolution process.

Many companies employ a computerized matter management system for purposes of tracking litigation, claims, government investigations, and related legal matters. The ECA is not intended to take the place of a matter management system; however, one may usefully become a component of the other. Therefore, corporate users are encouraged to tailor these guidelines and tools to their particular needs and requirements.

CPR's ECA Toolkit comprises:

- A detailed, step-by-step guide for users who are less familiar with the concept of ECA and seek a comprehensive analytical model.
- A short Executive Summary form for sophisticated users who are familiar with the elements of the ECA process. See Appendix A.

For more assistance with your ECA process, contact info@cpradr.org. To download materials in an electronic format, please visit CPR's website at www.cpradr.org.

Appendix 2

About CPR

The International Institute for Conflict Prevention and Resolution (CPR) is an independent, nonprofit think tank that promotes innovation in commercial dispute prevention and resolution. By harnessing the expertise of leading minds in ADR and benchmarking best practices, it is the resource of choice for multinational corporations with billions of dollars at risk. CPR is also a trusted and respected destination for lawyers seeking superior arbitrators and mediators and cutting-edge ADR tools and training. Our elite membership includes General Counsel from global corporations, attorneys from the top law firms in the world, sitting and retired judges, highly-experienced neutrals and ADR practitioners, and leading academics.

CPR **ECA Step-by-Step Analysis**
1. Capture Matter Information & Assemble Team
2. Informal Factual Review
3. Business Concerns
4. Forum & Adversary Analysis
5. Risk Management Analysis
6. Legal Analysis
7. Cost / Benefit Analysis
8. Determine Settlement Value
9. Establish Settlement Strategy
10. Develop Preliminary Litigation Plan

Post-Resolution: Loop-Back Process (Prevention)

Appendix 2

STEP 1 CAPTURE MATTER INFORMATION & ASSEMBLE TEAM

Describe the Matter

- Parties: Claimant/Plaintiff; Respondent/Defendant; Third Parties
- Nature of dispute
- Apparent amount at risk
- Background and relationships of parties
- How company learned of matter
- Status of insurance and any related indemnity agreements
- Identification of other applicable contracts, pre-dispute agreements, and agreements regarding how disputes may be handled

Identify the Stage of Development and Contractual Requirements

Note: Do not duplicate matter management system which may contain some of this data.

- Status of negotiations
- Review relevant dispute resolution provisions of contract
    - Negotiation
    - Two-tiered negotiation in company
    - Mediation
    - Arbitration
    - Other
- If arbitration will commence, identify
    - ADR provider
    - Applicable arbitration rules
    - Arbitrators
    - Commencement date
    - Causes of action
    - Damages/remedies
- If litigation filed, attach the complaint and identify:
    - Court/Location
    - Judge
    - Docket no.
    - Date filed *(By whom)*
    - Cause(s) of action
    - Damages/other remedies sought *(Claim for Injunctive/Prelim.Relief)*
    - Court-ordered mediation required/completed

- Dispositive motions filed (*When/Outcome?*)
- Filing deadlines approaching
- Jury trial matter

Note: May be omitted if the Complaint is attached or if the matter is a repeating matter, such as a class action or mass tort.

Identify Counsel and Team for Company, Other Party and Third Parties

- Inside counsel
- Outside counsel
- Business unit/person(s) involved/affected
- Insurance representatives

Assign Duties and Time Frame to Complete ECA Process

The key benefit of a systematic ECA review is to assemble the information and focus the team on the issues that may be most relevant to settlement before the astronomical costs of discovery and motion practice begin.

How early can it be done? Depending on the complexity of the case, the lawyers who use these methods regularly believe that the review should be completed within the first 30-90 days.

The purpose of the ECA is not to conduct an exhaustive legal and factual analysis, but to collect essential information, understand the basic strengths and weakness of the legal positions and use that information to conduct an early cost/benefit analysis. The ECA redefines what the essential information is in order to value the case quickly and as effectively as possible.

With an ECA policy in place, it is even better if all the parties can agree to stay discovery and the filings in the case until the ECA is complete. In pattern cases, or situations where both sides are willing to have further discussions before discovery, an agreement to postpone discovery may be more likely.

Appendix 2

STEP 2 INFORMAL FACTUAL REVIEW

Conduct Internal Interviews

- Information gathered from discussions with company, law firm, and other lawyers with knowledge of the matter
- Information gathered from client business contacts with knowledge of the matter

Collect Internal Documents

- Hard copy documents
- Electronic documents, including number, type, format, media, cost of storage and production, and possible role for e-discovery expert

Identify Witnesses and Experts

- Identify the fact witnesses and their location
- Evaluate role of experts, if any
- Provide a summary of the interviews with witnesses
- Assess witness capability and credibility

Contacts with Opposing Counsel

- Information garnered
- Agreements on informal discovery or information exchange

Review Relevant Company and Industry Historical Information

- History of similar claims in the company (if any)
- Average number of days to resolution of such claims
- Special circumstances differentiating this case from other similar cases
- In-house, law firm, and other lawyers with relevant experience on similar matters
- Business client contacts with knowledge of similar matters

- Relevant company files and/or databases
- Similar matters in the industry/industry concerns/history
- Damages awards and settlements
- Length of litigation process and procedural issues
- Other relevant public data/records or information that might be available

Identify Essential Information Needed

- If key information is currently unavailable that is essential in selecting resolution strategy, describe informal routes to acquire that information

STEP 3 BUSINESS CONCERNS

Identify Client's Priority Business Concerns and Interests

- Protecting sensitive data
- Legal *(E.g., Need new precedent; need TRO or PI; etc.)*
- Economic: short term, long term
- Timing
- Relationships (including confidentiality)
- Publicity and reputation
- Psychological *(E.g., understand occurrences; receive apology; be heard by authority figures; vindicate action; clear name; change policies for others in similar situation; etc.)*
- Other special/unique/sensitive concerns affecting disposition strategy:
    - Corporate survival/treasury at risk
    - Business relationship at stake
    - Reputation/public relations/stock price
    - Repetitive claim/floodgates issue/class action
    - New product under scrutiny
    - New or existing legal precedent
    - Technical issue, e.g. intellectual property
    - Location of proceedings: forum, venue, jury issues
    - Industry concerns; possible co-defendants
    - Possible criminal liability; corporate governance; compliance; government oversight; RICO
    - International matter, FCPA, or foreign political concerns
    - High level executive testimony required

Appendix 2

Assess Opponent's Likely Priority Business Concerns and Interests

- Protecting sensitive data
- Legal *(E.g., Precedent; PI; etc.)*
- Economic: short term, long term
- Timing
- Relationships (including confidentiality)
- Reputation
- Psychological *(E.g., understand occurrences; receive apology; be heard by authority figures; vindicate action; clear name; change policies for others in similar situation; etc.)*
- Other

Define Successful Resolution from a Business Perspective

NOTE: Identification of mutual concerns and interests may lead to dialogue with opponent and possible Early Case Resolution through collaborative negotiation.

A good ECA process should evaluate the business interests of both parties in the resolution of the dispute. Interest-based questions, which typically give rise to opportunities to find common ground, are often not explored until actual settlement discussions were underway. Lawyers using the usual adversarial practices often fail to uncover elements of the dispute that might be relevant to settlement but may be unrelated to the legal claims in front of them. For example, considerations which focus on the relationship of the parties and business strategy and goals should be analyze and reviewed.

STEP 4 FORUM & ADVERSARY ANALYSIS

Forum Analysis

- Judge's profile *(including circuit or state court rulings out of sync with majority on relevant issues)*
- Potential jury pool
- Mediator's profile
- Arbitrator's profile

Appendix 2

Opposing Counsel Analysis

- Reputation or experience of opposing counsel:
  - Negotiation reputation
  - Trial reputation
- Counsel's incentives to settle early
- Similar claims litigated against the opposing lawyer? What was outcome and what approach was used by opponent?

Opposing Party Analysis

- Any continuing business relationship with adversary *(Anything over $_____requires business or other higher level approval of case strategy)*
- Specify financial and legal resources of the adversary
- Immediate needs of adversary that might support use of an early settlement process *(E.g., financial crisis; etc.)*
- Signatory to CPR Pledge©?

STEP 5 RISK MANAGEMENT ANALYSIS

Legal Hold Notice Issuance, Date and List of Recipients

- Documents
- E-mails
- Length of hold; renewal reminders
- Expansion of document custodians

Insurance

- Is the claim insured or self-insured?
- If insured, has the carrier been notified? Has the carrier accepted coverage, disputed coverage or issued a reservation of rights?
- If the carrier has not been notified, who is responsible for giving notice and when will notice be given?
- Have all potentially applicable policies been located?
- Who is responsible for locating all potentially applicable policies?

Appendix 2

STEP 6 LEGAL ANALYSIS

Ascertain and Narrow Scope of Claims and Defenses

Conduct Risk Assessment of Each Claim and Defense

Estimate Possible Damages Spectrum

Identify Additional Information Necessary to Evaluate Damages

Determine Whether and Type of Damages Experts that will be Required

Estimate Costs to Completion

- Outside counsel fees
- Other litigation expenses and "hard" costs
- Anticipated expenditure of internal resources and "soft" costs, including
    - In-house lawyer time
    - Business professional time
    - Witness time

Appendix 2

STEP 7 COST/BENEFIT ANALYSIS

DISPOSITION STRATEGY AS APPLICABLE	Percentage Likelihood of Success/Loss	External Legal Costs	Internal Costs High (H); Medium (M); Low (L)	Time to Complete	Does Strategy Advance Priority Business Concerns or Not?
Dispositive Motion					
Negotiate (without any mediator)					
Mediate (with a mediator)					
Arbitrate					
Discovery or E-Discovery & E-Discovery Vendor Use, if any					
Experts					
Trial					
Other: Dual Track; Appeal; etc.					
TOTALS					

STEP 8 DETERMINE SETTLEMENT VALUE

Identify the range of monetary settlement that would be a good result and identify any non- monetary solutions with the potential to resolve the dispute. Consider attaching a decision-tree or similar analysis. A detailed overview of Decision- Trees can be found here.

Appendix 2

STEP 9 ESTABLISH SETTLEMENT STRATEGY

Review Negotiation History and Current Demand/Offer

Assess Settlement Barriers to Determine if Mediation is Warranted

- The following common settlement barriers can be effectively addressed via mediation:
  - Unassisted negotiations have already failed
  - Communication difficulties and past history foreclose dialogue
  - Emotional barriers to settlement exist between parties or counsel
    - Psychological barriers exist such as partisan perceptions, attribution biases, face-saving needs, reactive devaluation, etc.
    - Process barriers exist such as no settlement event, lack of settlement authority, positional bargaining limitations, etc.
    - Cultural barriers to effective dialogue exist
    - Merit barriers exist such as unrealistic expectations, insufficient key information to settle, etc.
- The following more difficult settlement barriers often foreclose settlement. However, even these barriers have been overcome in mediation:
  - Fundamental corporate or other principle at stake that cannot be settled
  - Need for new precedent is critical
  - Managerial responsibility at center of matter including corporate finance or reorganization cannot be settled
  - Public message needed including defending claims that may open the floodgates to similar claims
  - Public vindication sought
  - Extreme power disparities between parties foreclose ability to bargain
  - Absence of resources that can be used for trade-offs in negotiation

Determine Form of Early Resolution Best Suited to Advance Interests and Business Concerns

The final step is to use the information and analysis gathered through the process to evaluate whether the matter can be settled through one of many ADR techniques, which can include any of the following, alone or in combination:

- Negotiation by:
  - management
  - in-house counsel

Appendix 2

      – outside litigation or settlement counsel
      – collaboratively trained lawyer(s)
      – other third-party skilled or technical facilitator
- Early Neutral Evaluation
- Early Discovery Exchange
- Competitive Mock Trial
- Shared Focus Study
- Mediation
    - Court conducted mediation
    - Private mediation
        - General or technically trained mediator
- Summary Jury Trial
- Arbitration
    - Non-binding
    - Binding for all or some of the claims

Alternatively, the case could simply be kept on a litigation track heading toward a court trial on the merits.

Secure Resolution Authority

STEP 10 DEVELOP PRELIMINARY LITIGATION PLAN

Plan Adjudication Route if Settlement Path is Not Successful

Identify Future Opportunities to Reconsider Settlement

Establish Initial Budget and Timeline of Activities

Appendix 2

POST-RESOLUTION LOOP-BACK PROCESS (PREVENTION)

Once a dispute is resolved, the collaborative team may well benefit by engaging in a "lessons learned" exercise, not only to capture the valuable insights gained from any dispute for application to another, but also to identify appropriate business practice corrections, which may include contract or policy or procedure revisions, enhanced training programs or revised business processes to prevent recurrence.

Appendix A:
Executive Summary

Date prepared: _____   Date last updated: _____

Matter/Dispute
Claimant
Type of Claim
Amount of Claim
Business Unit(s) Affected
Current Status: ☐ *Court* ☐ *Arbitration* ☐ *Mediation* ☐ *Unassisted Negotiation* ☐ *Other (specify):* _____
Assessment of Issues and Outcomes including Rationale (Include goals and objectives for all parties to the dispute)
Identification of Interests: Ours/Theirs/Joint
Assessment of Settlement Value (Identify the range of monetary settlement that would be a good result and identify any non-monetary solutions with the potential to resolve the dispute)
Proposed Resolution Strategy and Rationale including Special Circumstances Affecting Strategy
Use decision tree analysis or summarize: – Resolution phases – Time frames – Preliminary litigation management plan – Budget/costs including counsel fees, forum fees, and liability estimates   (Total budget for short matters; 12 month budget with "ballpark" totals for prolonged matters) *(Optional: Attach Decision Tree Analysis, if appropriate)*

© *2009 International Institute for Conflict Prevention & Resolution. All rights reserved.*

APPENDIX 3

Article: Dealing With 'Selective Perception' and Bad-Faith Allegations in Commercial Settlement Discussions

Reproduced with the kind permission of the author, Michael McIlwrath and the publisher of Alternatives, the International Institute for Conflict Prevention and Resolution (CPR Institute) www.cpradr.org.

Mel Brooks reportedly said, "Tragedy is when I cut my finger. Comedy is when you walk into an open sewer and die."

Experienced litigators know too well that the same reasoning can be applied to perceptions of good and bad faith in disputes. Because a party inevitably will view its own position as fair or at least sensibly advanced, the inexorable conclusion is that a far-off position taken by the other side can only be explained as unrealistic or even bad faith. How else to account for outrageous demands or denials of reality in the face of one's own reasonableness?

That question is at the center of "International Dispute Negotiation," a full-day simulation of an international commercial dispute held regularly for the past four years at the author's employer, GE Oil & Gas in Florence, Italy. The course's goals include helping managers and front-line employees better quantify the cost or value of disputes, and identify and overcome impediments to resolution.

The author is based in Florence, Italy, where he is senior counsel for GE Oil & Gas, and litigation counsel to the GE Energy companies in Europe. He is a member of CPR's European Advisory Committee, and has acted as CPR's delegate to the European Commission's Working Group in drafting an ADR Code of Conduct. Special thanks to Laura Stipanowich, whose father is publisher of this newsletter, and who was a legal intern at GE Oil & Gas during the summer of 2004, for her assistance in preparing this article.

Appendix 3

Not surprisingly, the course reveals the biggest and usually only impediment to resolution is a significant divergence in valua-tion—that is, the number each party is willing to accept as a fair value or an accurate estimate of what a judge or arbitrator will award. What has been surprising, however, is how easily participants will conclude the other side is acting in bad faith when all participants share similar professional backgrounds, have access to the same information about the dispute, and even started out on the same side in the negotiations.

Indeed, it's amazing at how quickly, consistently, and radically participants' valuations change when they take up a role on the opposite side.

To follow Mel Brooks' definition about comedy and tragedy, whether a party will

NEGOTIATION

perceive the other as unrealistic or as acting in bad faith depends far more on where the party sits than on access to or awareness of the underlying facts.

SETTLING A CATASTROPHE

The course starts with teams of four to five participants playing different roles on a British-led international consortium, with the common task of preparing for settlement negotiations with an Italian equipment supplier the consortium blames for a "cata-strophic explosion" at its Egyptian project site—one that the supplier later will refer to as a mere "equipment failure."

Through a detailed claim statement sent by its lawyer, the consortium—which is referred to in this article as the Claimant—has informed the supplier of $66 million in losses. These consist of $600,000 in damage to the equipment itself, more than $3 million in project costs that can no longer be recouped, and about $62 million in business lost after the project's cancellation. Counsel for the consortium has invited the supplier to attend a meeting in Cairo, with a warning about litigation that will follow unless an acceptable settlement can be reached.

Always a challenge in any complex dispute, valuation in the international context must address the additional uncertainties of legal and cultural differences injected into the mix of factors to be considered. In considering all possible factors, the Claimant groups are asked to provide their (1) opening offer in negotiations, which cannot be more than the $66 million already demanded, (2) settlement goal, and (3) best alternative to a negotiated agreement, better known as "Batna," which in the training's context is the point at which arbitration under the contract's dispute resolution clause becomes the preferred option.

The results of this preliminary goal-setting session, from a simulation held with 30 participants in May in Florence, Italy, are set out in Table 1 at the top of the next page, with the overall averages in the left column in millions of Euros.

Although the numbers vary greatly among the groups, the Claimants' expectations run uniformly high in seeking all out-of-pocket costs plus several million dollars of loss-of-business damages. These expectations remain high until the claim is answered, which occurs when the groups

> **Valuation in international cases must address additional legal and cultural uncertainties.**

are divided and at least two participants from each Claimant group move to form a Respondent team. Both Claimants and the newly formed Respondent teams receive a copy of a four-page detailed letter from the Respondent's counsel raising a number of defenses, including information about events leading up to the "explosion" that suggests the possibility of the Claimant's contributory negligence.

Table 1: Claimant Opening Offers, Settlement Goals, and Batna Based on Unanswered Claim

	\multicolumn{8}{c}{Group}							
	Avg	1	2	3	4	5	6	7
Opening offer	42.47	62.3	40	32	20	66.0	17.0	60
Settlement goal	13.36	34.0	22	12	6	6.5	6.0	7
Batna	4.30	6.0	7	6	5	2.5	2.17	2

The Respondent's letter has the predictable effect of immediately lowering the Claimant team valuations. The impact is even more pronounced among Respondent teams, however, where valuations drop to levels irreconcilably below Claimant assessments.

Table 2 below, from the same May 2004 session, shows the parties' valuations following receipt of the detailed claim response from Respondent's counsel. It is evident at this stage, which is just before face-to-face negotiations are set to begin, that valuations are not only far apart but across the Claimant and Respondent teams there is an expectation that the other side agrees with their own assessment.

Table 2's Column 1 (far left) provides the Claimants' revised estimates of their losses. Taking into account the potential difficulties introduced by the Respondent's

> **Participants may be receiving the same information but filtering it in a way that best fits their interests.**

counsel, the Claimants now believe they can prove an average of only €2.9 million in damages, compared with an earlier average settlement goal of nearly €13.4 million and a Batna of €4.3 million. They have promised their management to recover between 75% and 100% of these provable losses (Column 2). This internal commitment roughly tracks what they believe to be the Respondent's valuation of the dispute

Appendix 3

(Column 3, middle). The Claimants, obviously, have comfortably set their settlement goals for an amount they perceive to be within the Respondent's reasonable valuation of litigation risk.

If only life was so easy. The Respondents, as the chart above shows, no longer value the dispute at levels even approaching what the Claimants have predicted, and have set aside financial reserves to cover a potential adverse judgment that range from 50% down to just 3% (Column 4) of what they would need to settle within the different Claimant groups' financial expectations. The reserves are an even smaller fraction of the Batna the same participants had established when they were on the Claimant teams (Table 1).

Table 2: Reaction to Detailed Claim Response—Claimant and Respondent Loss Estimates and Perceptions of Opposing Party's Valuations

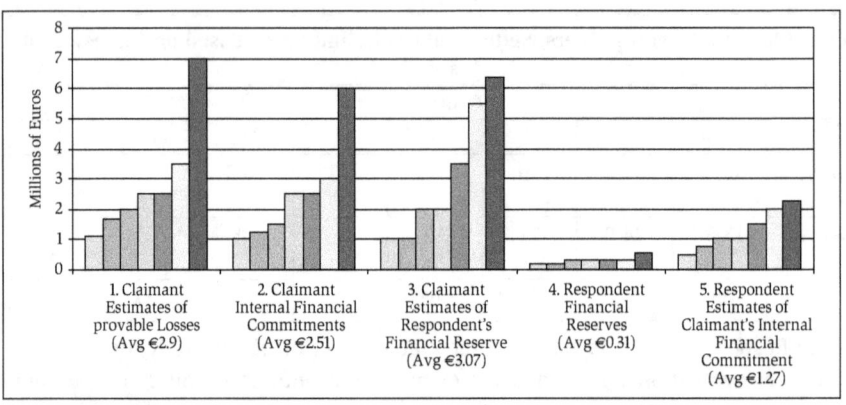

And the Respondent groups do not fare much better in predicting the other side's new valuation of the dispute. Although the Respondent groups are slightly more generous in their efforts to guess the Claimant's financial commitment, they still miss the mark by an average of 50% (Column 5).

BAD START

And now settlement negotiations begin, and with these distant expectations they generally begin badly. As one Claimant participant noted, "We know our claim has problems, but we believe we will recover at least a portion of what we genuinely lost. Although our last offer was $15 million, we are willing to accept $2.5 million as settlement, which we view as more than fair under the circumstances and certainly less than [the] Respondent knows [it] will have to pay." For their part, most Respondent teams have now assessed a nearly zero value to the claim and remain willing to settle for a much lower amount, an average of only $310,000. Clearly, if the Respondent is willing to pay at most $310,000 and the Claimant will not settle for less than $2.51

million, then an expectation gap of $2.2 million, or roughly seven times the Respondent's best offer, must be addressed. It does not help that the parties' positions, based as they are on technical and legal information provided to both parties, already have begun to crystallize.

WHAT'S THE EXPLANATION?

And herein lies the rub: how to explain the gap, and then address it? In the real world, it would be easy to at least partially blame the different valuations on imperfect access to information, or an imperfect technical or legal capacity to assess it. But in our course, and at this stage of the simulation, both sides are operating from the same information about the underlying dispute and, as noted above, they share similar professional backgrounds.

Instead, what appears to be pushing the parties in different directions is simply their selective perception of the data, i.e., participants may be receiving the same information but filtering it in a way that best fits their interests, giving greater importance to favorable data and discounting or ignoring what is unfavorable. Information that each participant would in other circumstances treat as arguable opinions or doubtful facts becomes, in the context of taking sides to a dispute, irrefutable truth. Each side is as likely as the other to attribute unrealistic expectations to the other side or, as is often the case, "bad faith" in demanding something that is much more or much less than one deserves. Do participants themselves realize that just switching sides is the reason for the startling valuation differences? We have not seen this; in fact, even when presenting the stark

THE CLAIMANTS HAVE COMFORTABLY SET SETTLEMENT GOALS FOR AN AMOUNT PERCEIVED TO BE WITHIN THE RESPONDENTS' VALUATION. IF ONLY LIFE WAS SO EASY.

data above we have difficulty convincing participants that they were selectively interpreting the facts, although most are ready to believe this of the other side. A common reaction was expressed by one recent participant, who said it was "frustrating to suddenly switch sides and experience obstinacy where you feel the situation is clear."

In the face of such tenacity, how is the gap to be closed? In the context of the dispute negotiation course, it almost never is. Once the parties become enamored of their positions and have staked out clear goals and immovable bottom lines, settlement on pure valuation terms is nearly impossible.

So if there can be no agreement based on a fair valuation of the disputed matter, how does the course conclude? Notwithstanding ferocious and bitter disagreements, most participants over the years have been able to find overriding commercial interests that provide a way for the parties to bury the hatchet and move on to new projects. The rare failure has resulted in the occasional arbitration hearing at the end of the course day, with an award—and legal bill—that is bound to leave both sides feeling they could have done better.

In fact, disappointment with arbitration outcomes has led the program's designers to strongly encourage even the bitterest of opponents to pursue mediation—also held within the course—so that participants can leave the day with a greater sense of accomplishment.

Do the results of this course affect the way GE Oil & Gas conducts its disputes? In reinforcing the company's preference for early settlement, very much so. By providing an opportunity to experience and reflect upon the same dynamics that commonly thwart efforts to settle in the real world, the dispute negotiation course helps managers understand the importance of documenting their contractual rights, encourages early identification of disputes and promotes de-escalation, introduces managers to the basic concepts and benefits of mediation, and helps keep the company's aim—and, to the extent possible, our adversary's aim—on commercial interests rather than the win/lose results of litigation.

The course probably has little impact on how the company conducts itself in those few instances it is unable to avoid going to court or arbitration. But at least when an adversary takes a completely unrealistic position, we know they probably think the same about us.

And that's the tragedy of litigation.

DOI 10.1002/alt.20035
(For bulk reprints of this article, please call (201) 748-8789)

APPENDIX 4

Article: Culture and its Importance in Mediation

Joel Lee[1]

This is Chapter 7 of Mediation in Singapore: A Practical Guide.
General Editors Danny McFadden and George Lim SC.
Published in 2015 by Sweet & Maxwell.
Reproduced here with the kind consent of the author, editors and publisher.
The copyright belongs to Thomson Reuters.

1.	Introduction	266
2.	Culture – The Blind Men and the Elephant	266
3.	Culture: Much Ado About Nothing?	271
	3.1. A contextual segue	271
	Meanwhile, Back at the Ranch ...	273
4.	Status, Belonging, Communication and Face	279
	4.1. Definitions	280
	Status	280
	Belonging	280
	Communication	281
	Face	282
	4.2. Interaction of notions of status, belonging, communication and face	283
5.	Conclusion	286

---

1. Associate Professor, Faculty of Law, National University of Singapore. The writer wishes to thank Ms Teh Hwee Hwee (Supreme Court of Singapore) without whom *An Asian Perspective on Mediation* may never have seen the light of day. The writer would also like to thank Mr Nigel Yeo for his assistance in editing this chapter.

Appendix 4

CHAPTER 7 CULTURE AND ITS IMPORTANCE IN MEDIATION

1. INTRODUCTION

[7.001]   It is said that a fish cannot know what water is because it is all-pervasive. Water is all the fish knows and the fish cannot distinguish water from the fabric of its existence.

[7.002]   So it is with culture. Culture is so deeply ingrained within us by the processes of socialisation that we often do not realise we are affected by it. We simply swim through it like a fish through water. It is how we perceive, and interact with the world.

[7.003]   Of course, we are different from fish. We have the ability to "go meta" and to reflect upon our behaviours, thoughts, beliefs, values and identity.[2]

[7.004]   This chapter seeks to take the reader on this "meta-journey". It will first explore definitions and frameworks about culture, before looking at how culture is important in mediation. Specific attention will be placed on the context of Singapore, and we will look at Singapore's journey to dealing with the intersection between culture and mediation. This chapter will then look at formulating a working model to traverse the intersections between status and belonging on one hand, and modes of communication and face concerns on the other.

2. CULTURE – THE BLIND MEN AND THE ELEPHANT

[7.005]   When talking about culture and trying to define it, this writer is reminded of the story of the Blind Men and the Elephant. For readers unfamiliar with this story, one telling of the story goes like this.[3]

> Once upon a time, there were six blind men in a village. One day the villagers told them, "Hey, there is an elephant in the village today."
>
> They had no idea what an elephant is. They decided, "Even though we would not be able to see it, let us go and feel it anyway." All of them went where the elephant was. Every one of them touched the elephant.
>
> "Hey, the elephant is a pillar," said the first man who touched his leg.
>
> "Oh, no! It is like a rope," said the second man who touched the tail.

---

2. This is of course an opinion based on conventional scientific views and anecdotal evidence. The writer cannot say with absolute certainty that a fish is unable to "go meta". That would be an interesting experiment to explore.
3. Modified from "Elephant and the Blind Men" (last accessed March 17, 2014), http://www.jainworld.com/literature/story25.htm.

Appendix 4

"Oh, no! It is like a thick branch of a tree," said the third man who touched the trunk of the elephant.

"It is like a big hand fan" said the fourth man who touched the ear of the elephant.

"It is like a huge wall," said the fifth man who touched the belly of the elephant.

"It is like a solid pipe," said the sixth man who touched the tusk of the elephant.

They began to argue about the elephant and every one of them insisted that he was right.

[7.006] This teaching tale is often used to illustrate notions of relativity, multiple perspectives, harmonious living or even wave-particle duality. For the purposes of this paper, it also illustrates that what culture is, depends on what we focus on.

[7.007] One could seek to define culture via academic definitions. There is of course neither dearth of nor agreement about academic definitions. A sampling follows:

(a) "patterned ways of thinking, feeling and reacting, acquired and transmitted mainly by symbols ...; the essential core of culture consists of traditional ideas and especially their attached values";[4]
(b) "the collective programming of the mind that distinguishes the members of one group or category of people from another";[5] or
(c) "the unique character of a social group; the values and norms shared by its members [that] set it apart from other social groups."[6]

[7.008] The problem with academic definitions is this: those definitions that seek to be encompassing may over-generalise and seem simplistic, while those seeking comprehensiveness must cope with so many variations and exceptions that their usefulness is undermined.

[7.009] What is clear from the above definitions is that any perspective on culture is always in reference to a particular community or group. It simply depends on the boundaries that we draw to identify that community or group.

[7.010] Sometimes, we equate the culture of a particular community or group with its rules, etiquette and customs. It is trite, of course, that culture is more than rules,

---

4. Clyde Kluckhohn, "The Study of Culture" in Daniel Lerner and Harold D Lasswell (eds), *The Policy Sciences* (Stanford University Press, 1951), p 86.
5. Geert Hofstede, *Culture's Consequences* (Sage Publications, 2nd edn, 2001), p 9. See also generally "The Hofstede Centre" (last accessed March 17, 2014), http://www.geert-hofstede.com.
6. A Lytle, J Brett, and D Shapiro, "The Strategic Use of Interests, Rights and Power" in *Negotiation Journal,* Vol 15 (1999), p 31.

etiquette and custom.[7] These rules, etiquette and customs are usually the outward manifestation of the cultural iceberg that lies beneath.

[7.011] It is also trite that culture is a generalisation and cannot be attributed to all other members of that community or group. It may be that a particular member of that community or group is a complete exception to the general rule or that s/he may share some characteristics, but not others.

[7.012] To be fair to those attempting a comprehensive academic definition (in the writer's opinion, this is akin to quantum physicists attempting to construct a "grand theory of everything"[8]), the task of delineating culture communities or groups is made more complicated by a shrinking world and the segmentation of cultures.

[7.013] In the past, one could delineate a cultural community or group along national or ethnic lines. These would be the days when cultural anthropologists like Margaret Mead could observe a group or community like the Samoans, and identify their cultural traits.[9] Of course there would be exceptions but in those days, one could be fairly sure it was an exception and not the norm.

[7.014] This was possible because there was very little cross-grouping "contamination" or influence: the Samoans had very little exposure to other cultural influences, whether through travel or other means. There was therefore the illusion of sameness, which in that time was relatively reliable.

[7.015] With the advent and development of modern travel, communication and, of course, the Internet, this is no longer true. The lines between cultural communities and groupings are blurring. It is now possible for a Chinese to be born in Singapore, grow up in New York, be educated in the UK and end up living and working in Hong Kong. It would be a mistake, then, to assume that one was dealing with a Singaporean Chinese. This individual may not manifest any characteristics of what it might mean to be Singaporean Chinese. Further, exposure to movies, music and other forms of media could also mean that any individual that we look at could manifest different sub-cultures depending on the context s/he is put in. In the context of business, the person may manifest characteristics of typical "western" business values. However, when in a martial-arts context, we may see the manifestation of a sub-culture that may be very different from the behaviours and values that are typical of that individual. Put simply, the illusion of sameness is gone.

[7.016] The writer finds that thinking about culture in terms of frameworks is far more satisfying and useful. A framework essentially takes certain cognitive or

---

7. Kevin Avruch and Peter Black, "The Culture Question and Conflict Resolution" in *Peace and Change*, Vol 16(1) (1993), p 22.
8. "Theory of everything" (last accessed March 17, 2014), http://en.wikipedia.org/wiki/Theory_of_everything.
9. For information relating to Margaret Mead and her work, see generally "Margaret Mead", (last accessed March 17, 2014), http://en.wikipedia.org/wiki/Margaret_Mead.

behavioural characteristics or traits, and tracks them over cultures. When using frameworks, it is important to make some preliminary points.

[7.017] First, it is trite that there are many diff erent frameworks available to measure culture. It is not a matter of which framework is right (or wrong) or which one is better. The appropriate question is which framework is more useful in the context that we are choosing to use them in. Put another way, no single framework is superior to another.

[7.018] Secondly, frameworks may overlap. For example, how cultures respond to hierarchy and authority in society is captured in the frameworks of Hofstede,[10] Brett[11] and Salacuse[12] even though they may have diff erent names for this characteristic or trait.

[7.019] Thirdly, when using frameworks, it is important to remember that characteristics and traits are not digital i.e. one or the other, but are better measured on a continuum. This allows measurements to be more nuanced.

[7.020] Finally, just as it is important to select a framework that is most appropriate for one's purpose, it is also not necessary to accept a framework in its entirety. Since the cultural traits within each framework are, by and large, represented as separate traits, it is permissible then to select only certain traits from various frameworks to measure and discuss.

[7.021] As an example, the writer has chosen to refer to Geert Hofstede's Dimensions of Culture.[13] By way of background, Hofstede initially identifi ed four cultural dimensions that could be used to describe important diff erences between cultures.[14]

[7.022] These fi rst four cultural dimensions were:

(a) *Power distance*. This dimension measures how society handles inherent inequalities which may result from prestige, wealth and power.[15] Cultures with high power distance tend to be comfortable with hierarchical structures and clear authority fi gures. Cultures with low power distance tend to be comfortable with fl at organisational structures and shared authority.[16]

---

10. Hofstede, note 5 above.
11. Ibid.
12. Salacuse places each factor on a continuum and locates where a particular culture is on that continuum: see Jeswald Salacuse, "Negotiating: The Top Ten Ways Culture Can Aff ect Your Negotiation" (last accessed March 17, 2014), http://iveybusinessjournal.com/topics/the-organization/negotiating-the-top-ten-ways-that-culture-can-affect-your-negotiation#.UyfWR466_dk.
13. Hofstede, note 5 above.
14. This was as a result of studying IBM employees from over 53 countries and cultures.
15. Hofstede, note 5 above, p 79.
16. Michael Carrell and Christina Heavrin, "Negotiating Essentials: Theory Skills and Practices" (Pearson, 2008), p 224.

(b) *Individualism/collectivism*. This dimension measures the relationship and extent of integration between the individual and the group that prevails in a given society.[17] Cultures which rate high on the individualism scale tend to play down relationships and focus more on the individual, as well as individual rights. Cultures which rate low on the individualism scale tend to be collectivist and focus more on close ties between individuals.[18]

(c) *Masculinity/femininity*. This dimension measures the degree to which the traditional masculine or feminine traits are reinforced in any given society.[19] Cultures characterised as masculine reinforce control and power with a high degree of gender diff erentiation. Cultures characterised as feminine reinforce nurturing and co-operation with a low degree of gender diff erentiation.[20]

(d) *Uncertainty avoidance*. This dimension measures a society's tolerance for uncertainty and ambiguity.[21] Cultures high on uncertainty avoidance tend to be rule-oriented, with regulations and controls to minimise the amount of uncertainty. Cultures which are low on uncertainty avoidance tend to have fewer rules, and can more readily cope with change and taking risks.[22]

[7.023] After surveys conducted with Chinese employees and managers, a fifth dimension was added.

(e) *Long-term orientation*. This dimension measures the degree to which a society is forward-looking and with long-term objectives in mind. Cultures high on this scale, value long-term commitments, cultivate a respect for tradition and look towards future rewards. Cultures low on this scale look towards immediate results and are more amenable to change.[23]

[7.024] In an earlier work, the writer has looked at the possible impact these dimensions can have on mediation.[24] For the purposes of this chapter, the writer will only focus on two dimensions, Power Distance and Individualism/Collectivism and consider how the interaction between these dimensions aff ect how we choose to communicate and manifest face concerns. Before doing so, we will fi rst turn to consider whether and how culture is important to mediation.

---

17. Hofstede, note 5 above, p 209.
18. Carrell and Heavrin, note 16 above, p 225.
19. Hofstede, note 5 above, p 279.
20. Carrell and Heavrin, note 16 above, p 227. Of course, this presupposes that one buys into these stereotypes of gender.
21. Hofstede, note 5 above, p 145.
22. Hofstede, note 5 above, pp 224–225.
23. Carrell and Heavrin, note 16 above, p 227.
24. See generally Joel Lee and Teh Hwee Hwee (eds), *An Asian Perspective on Mediation* (Academy Publishing: Singapore, 2009).

3. CULTURE: MUCH ADO ABOUT NOTHING?

[7.025] It would be very odd and politically incorrect for one to suggest that, in relation to mediation, culture was unimportant or insignificant. However, looking at this question in the cold light of day, it is a fair question. Does culture really have such a significant impact on human interactions, specifically mediation?

[7.026] There has always been a tension between two schools of thought, the "Universalists" and the "Culturalists". The "Universalists" believe that all conflicts are fundamentally universal in nature. Humans manifest universal patterns of behaviour, and a general and universal model of conflict resolution applies by recognising universal human needs and addressing them. Culture plays a minimal, if not non-existent, role in the resolution of disputes.

[7.027] The Culturalists, on the other hand, believe that we are more different than we are similar. While group characteristics and traits do exist, culture is complex, dynamic and multi-dimensional. It is personal to the individual and any model of conflict resolution can only be a generalisation, which is at best, a guide.

[7.028] Of course, it is important to note that the "Universalists" and the "Culturalists" form two extreme ends of a continuum and where one stands within that continuum determines how one approaches conflict resolution theory and practice.

[7.029] This was precisely where Singapore found itself in 2003. The commonly used model of conflict resolution in Singapore (and many other jurisdictions) at the time was the facilitative interests-based model. The question posed was whether this model of conflict resolution was appropriate in the Asian context. If it was, what modifications, if any, needed to be made to take into account relevant cultural differences? If it was not appropriate, then what model should replace it?[25]

3.1 *A contextual segue*

[7.030] Before looking at how Singapore dealt with this question, it is useful to make a contextual segue. Singapore is a small island state, with an area of approximately 700 square kilometers and a population that is 5 million people strong. Its population is made up of many ethnicities consisting of Malays, Chinese and Indians among others.[26] Modern-day Singapore was founded by Sir Stamford Raffles in 1819, colonised by the British in 1824 and subsequently occupied by Japan during the Second World War. After the Japanese surrender, Singapore reverted to British rule and remained a British colony until its independence in 1965.

---

25. Joel Lee and Teh Hwee Hwee, "The Quest for an Asian Perspective on Mediation" in Joel Lee and Teh Hwee Hwee (eds), *An Asian Perspective on Mediation* (Academy Publishing: Singapore, 2009), paras 1.35-1.39.
26. "Singapore", (last accessed March 17, 2014), http://en.wikipedia.org/wiki/Singapore.

Appendix 4

[7.031] Singapore has since become a developed country with all the trimmings of modernity, and a robust economy. The country is governed by a democratically elected unicameral parliament and the legal system is based on the English common law system.

[7.032] Historically, there are indications that disputes were resolved through indigenous forms of mediation practiced among the ethnic groups. The mediators were often religious and community leaders who had standing and credibility in their respective circles.[27] Under British infl uence, these traditional methods of dispute resolution eventually gave way to litigation in the courts as a primary way to resolve disputes, which brought with it the attendant tangible and intangible costs.

[7.033] The modern history and development of mediation in Singapore has been explored elsewhere, both inside and outside this volume.[28] The writer will not seek to repeat any of that here, save to say that since 1994, mediation has taken root in the form of the Primary Dispute Resolution Centre in the Subordinate Courts, Community Mediation Centres and the Singapore Mediation Centre. In each of these contexts, disputes between parties of diff erent races, ethnicities and, increasingly, nationalities are mediated regularly.

[7.034] In particular, the writer would like to highlight the work of the Community Mediation Centres, which were the fruit of the eff orts put in by the Committee on Alternative Dispute Resolution. This committee was set up by the Ministry of Law to explore ways of resolving community disputes in order to preserve religious, racial and community harmony.[29] This is an understandable priority in a small, racially-diverse country with a densely packed population. The main idea was to replicate the traditional and indigenous mechanisms for resolving community disputes, and to foster community spirit.[30] Culture clearly plays an important role in these types of mediation.

[7.035] This segue was important for two purposes. First, it was to provide those unfamiliar to Singapore with some contextual background. Secondly, it was to illustrate that in the melting pot of races that is Singapore, it would be absurd to say that culture was not important. If it is sometimes perceived that culture is not often discussed in Singapore, this is due to the fact that it is so much a part of Singapore life that talking about it would be odd; as if it were something unusual.

---

27. Joel Lee and Teh Hwee Hwee, n 24 above, paras 1.3-1.6; 1.16-1.19.
28. See generally Joel Lee and Teh Hwee Hwee, note 24 above; Joel Lee, "The Evolution of ADR in Singapore" in Wang Guigo & Yang Fan (eds), *Mediation in Asia-Pacifi c: A Practical Guide to Mediation and Its Impact on Legal Systems* (Wolters Kluwer, Hong Kong, 2013), pp 397-421; Joel Lee, "Singapore" in Carlos Esplugues & Silvia Barona (eds), *Global Perspectives on ADR* (Cambridge: Intersentia, 2014), pp 383-420.
29. Teh Hwee Hwee "Mediation Practices in ASEAN: The Singapore Experience" (paper presented at the 11th General Assembly of the ASEAN Law Association, Bali, February 15 to 18 2012), p 8.
30. Report of the Committee on Alternative Dispute Resolution, July 4, 1996.

Appendix 4

Meanwhile, Back at the Ranch ...

[7.036] From 1994 to 2003, mediation training and practice overseas, in particular "Western sources" such as those in the United States, Australia and the United Kingdom, had a heavy influence on modern mediation practice (including training and accreditation).[31] As mentioned, this is the facilitative interests-based model and while it worked well enough most of the time, there was no denying that it was not always a comfortable fit.

[7.037] Considering that one view is that mediation has its roots in the Asian culture,[32] this irony was not lost on the former Chief Justice Dr. Yong Pung How who remarked that Singapore had to relearn mediation from the West.[33] It is therefore not surprising that the Singapore Mediation Centre was tasked with looking at whether the facilitative interests-based model was appropriate for the Asian context.

[7.038] A working group was convened to study this question and was faced with the dichotomous choice of "West versus East".[34] The working group rejected this distinction and proceeded from the assumption that the interests-based model of conflict resolution provided a functional paradigm that was universal to the human condition.[35] What sometimes caused an uncomfortable fit with cultures outside the West were the cultural assumptions inherent within the model that had their origin in the West.[36]

[7.039] These assumptions were:[37]

1. The primacy of the individual and the individual's expectation of autonomy.
2. The priority of the interests of the individual.
3. The premium placed on direct and open communication for constructive conflict management.
(d) The importance of maintaining a good working relationship for constructive conflict resolution.

---

31. Joel Lee and Teh Hwee Hwee, note 24 above, para 1.20.
32. Teh Hwee Hwee, note 29 above, p 2.
33. Speech at the launch of DisputeManager.com (July 31, 2002), (last accessed March 17, 2014), http://app.subcourts.gov.sg/Data/Files/File/eJustice/Archives/CJSpeech_ LaunchDisputeManagerDotCom.pdf.
34. In writing this paper, the author is well aware of the dangers of using sweeping terms like the "East", "West" or even "Culture". It is outside the scope of the paper to explore the problems of this definitional minefield. Suffice it to say that this issue is explored thoroughly in the book by Joel Lee and Teh Hwee Hwee, note 24 above.
35. Joel Lee and Teh Hwee Hwee, "Appropriateness of the Interests-Based Model for the Asian Context" in Joel Lee and Teh Hwee Hwee (eds), *An Asian Perspective on Mediation* (Academy Publishing: Singapore, 2009), paras 2.52-2.59.
36. See generally the discussion in Joel Lee and Teh Hwee Hwee, note 24 above.
37. Joel Lee and Teh Hwee Hwee, note 35 above, paras 2.37-2.51.

Appendix 4

[7.040] The operational behaviours that flowed naturally and unconsciously from these assumptions are:[38]

Western-oriented Cultural Assumptions of the Interests-based Model	Resulting Features/Strategies of the Interests-based Model
Primacy of the individual and the individual's expectations of autonomy	Western-oriented assumption puts disputing parties first and in the centre. Mediator is an external neutral party who facilitates the process and has low substantive authority. Parties know best and are therefore most well placed to decide on the form of mediation process and shape of mediated outcome. Interactions are kept informal to encourage parties to negotiate and take decisions.
Priority of interests of the individual	Western-oriented assumption gears mediation process towards helping parties maximise and satisfy individual interests. Interests include those of self and immediate family members.
Direct and open communication constructive for conflict management	Open debate and confrontation acceptable. Explicit expression of feelings, views and concerns encouraged to "air" grievances. Joint sessions perceived to be beneficial as flow of information may create new levels of understanding and create options for settlement. Mediator facilitates process by asking questions to surface underlying interests and hidden emotions and turn them into issues for joint discussion.
Unconditionally constructive approach to maintaining good relationship for optimal outcome	Cultivation and maintenance of good relations to facilitate securing a good outcome. In view of objective, same approach to relationship building generally taken for one and all.

[7.041] These assumptions were by and large invisible when the model was used in a context that had compatible cultural assumptions. There is no clear distinction between the functional and operational paradigms of the facilitative interests-based model. This is of course not surprising and illustrates the point this chapter began with. These cultural assumptions are the water we swim within and until the water goes

---

38. Joel Lee and Teh Hwee Hwee, note 35, para 2.51.

missing or is corrupted to the extent that it causes discomfort, we generally do not realise that it is there. The problem is that, by not making a distinction between the functional and operational paradigms, what is sometimes conveyed in mediation training and practice (e.g. encouraging direct communication) is an operational matter, which may not fit the cultural context one is operating within.

[7.042] By identifying these "western" cultural assumptions and replacing them with cultural assumptions appropriate to the context of Singapore (and other cultures which share its heritage),[39] it was possible to preserve the usefulness of the interests-based model of conflict resolution (its functional paradigm) and harmonise it with the culture of Singapore in application (its operational paradigm).

[7.043] These "Asian" assumptions (in juxtaposition to the ones earlier identified) were:[40]

1. The primacy of social hierarchy and the individual's expectations to fulfill roles in any hierarchical relationship.
2. Priority is given in observing proper conduct.
3. Communication and conduct is geared towards preserving harmony, relationships and face.
4. One approaches context-dependent relationship maintenance as a way of life.

[7.044] Before looking at the impact these assumptions have on the operational aspects of implementing the interest-based model, it is important at this point to highlight two observations.

[7.045] First, there is no suggestion that these assumptions represent the values system of all Asians, nor is there any attempt to prescribe any "Asian Model" of mediation. That would be an absurd proposition. It simply offers *one* Asian perspective, that of Singapore, and provides a methodology by which academics and practitioners of mediation in other contexts may choose to contextualise the interests-based model for their own cultures.

[7.046] Secondly, it is important to highlight here that by inserting these "Asian" assumptions into the conflict resolution model, the functional paradigm of using "interests" to resolve the dispute remains untouched. What changes are the operational aspects of implementing the interests-based model.

[7.047] The operational behaviours that flow naturally and unconsciously from these assumptions are:[41]

---

39. See generally the discussion in Joel Lee and Teh Hwee Hwee, "Asian Culture: A Definitional Challenge" in Joel Lee and Teh Hwee Hwee (eds), *An Asian Perspective on Mediation* (Academy Publishing: Singapore, 2009).
40. Joel Lee and Teh Hwee Hwee, ibid, paras 3.46-3.60.
41. Table modified from Joel Lee and Teh Hwee Hwee, ibid, para 3.62.

Appendix 4

Suggested Asian-oriented Cultural Assumptions	Resulting Features/Strategies of the Interests-based Model
Primacy of social hierarchy and the individual's expectations to fulfill roles in hierarchical relationships.	Asian-oriented assumption requires mediator to be at the heart of the mediation.
	Mediator has high social status and is expected to lead and guide.
	Parties expect guidance from mediator, and are expected to value and respect his opinions.
	Interactions with an authority figure in the form of mediator may be expected to be formal.
Priority in observing proper conduct.	Interests include those of self, immediate family members and wider groups, and group interests may have priority, especially in a dispute with another in-group member.
Communication and conduct gearing towards preserving harmony, relationships and face.	Disputants may be more reserved and reticent, and prefer to communicate through non-verbal cues or in more subtle ways.
	Unearthing issues that should be left unspoken may lead to embarrassment and disengagement from the process.
Context-dependent relationship maintenance a way of life.	Cultivation and maintenance of good relations with in-group members a matter of priority and an end unto itself.
	Any interest in cultivating or maintaining relationships with out-group members is similar to the original Western interests-based model.
	Nature of relationship (in-group/out-group) dictates appropriate approach to issues of relationship.

[7.048] By juxtaposing the operational behaviours from both values system, it is clear that certain tensions can arise. It can be illustrated thus:[42]

---

42. Joel Lee and Teh Hwee Hwee, ibid, para 3.62.

Appendix 4

Resulting Features/ Strategies of the Interests-based Model –Western Assumptions	Resulting Features/ Strategies of the Interests-based Model – Asian Assumptions	Tensions Created in the Asian Context due to Incompatible Cultural Characteristics
Western-oriented assumption puts disputing parties first and in the centre.	Asian-oriented assumption requires mediator to be at the heart of the mediation.	A party-centric process may leave mediator and parties feeling out of place.
Mediator is an external, neutral party who facilitates the process and has low substantive authority. Parties know best and therefore most well-placed to decide on form of mediation process and shape of mediated outcome. Interactions are kept informal to encourage parties to negotiate and take decisions.	Mediator has high social status and is expected to lead and guide. Parties expect guidance from mediator, and are expected to value and respect his opinions. Interactions with an authority figure in the form of mediator may be expected to be formal.	A mediator who does not assume position of authority may be deemed ineffective. A mediator who holds back on giving guidance may be viewed to have abdicated his responsibilities. Individuals not accustomed to being the sole locus of decision-making. They may be frustrated if prompted to take decisions without any assistance in the form of inputs from an authoritative source. Interactions with the mediator on egalitarian terms may be a breach of social etiquette and cause discomfort.
Western-oriented assumption gears mediation process towards helping parties maximise and satisfy individual interests. Interests include those of self and immediate family members and these take priority above all else.	Interests include those of self, immediate family members and wider groups, and group interests may have priority, especially in a dispute with another in-group member.	Satisfying and maximising individual interests may not be considered "proper conduct".

Appendix 4

Resulting Features/ Strategies of the Interests-based Model –Western Assumptions	Resulting Features/ Strategies of the Interests-based Model – Asian Assumptions	Tensions Created in the Asian Context due to Incompatible Cultural Characteristics
Open debate and confrontation acceptable. Explicit expression of feelings, views and concerns encouraged to "air" grievances. Joint sessions perceived to be beneficial as flow of information may create new levels of understanding and create options for settlement. Mediator facilitates process by asking questions to surface underlying interests and hidden emotions and turn them into issues for joint discussion.	Disputants may be more reserved and reticent, and prefer to communicate through non-verbal cues or in more subtle ways. Unearthing issues that should be left unspoken may lead to embarrassment and disengagement from the process.	Pursuit of individual rights and search for collaborative solution to problems do not justify open confrontation. Open confrontation disrupts harmony. Joint sessions for open discussion may be perceived as face threatening. There may be a preference for private sessions.
Cultivation and maintenance of good relations to secure a good outcome or facilitate future dealings. In view of objective, same approach to relationship building generally taken for one and all.	Cultivation and maintenance of good relations with in-group members a matter of priority and an end unto itself. Any interest in cultivating or maintaining relationships with out-group members is similar to the original Western interests-based model. Nature of relationship (in-group/out-group) dictates appropriate approach to issues of relationship.	Requiring a one-size fits all approach to relationships is a blunt instrument with no nuance. Requiring parties to build a relationship where none is valued can cause discomfort. Not recognising that the relationship is the substance can give rise to a conflict of expectations between the mediator and the parties.

[7.049] As an aside, it is interesting to note that what has typically been referred to as the "facilitative interests-based model", is a descriptive amalgam of the functional paradigm (interests-based) and one aspect of the operational paradigm (facilitative). Therefore, it stands to reason that, where the circumstances call for it, it is possible to manifest the interests-based model in a less facilitative, if not non-facilitative, manner. In fact, one could even practice directive/authoritative (not authoritarian) interests-based mediation. It should be made clear that this means that mediators may take on more of a leadership role but without depriving parties of their power to decide how to resolve their dispute.

[7.050] At this point, some may wonder how this is different from the proposition that when resolving conflicts in "Asia", one should, for example, use indirect speech. The writer submits that this is too blunt an instrument. This presupposes a dichotomous choice of direct vs. indirect speech based on whether we have characterised the context as "East" or "West". As long as one has characterised the context to be "East", this view prescribes the use of only indirect speech. However, this cannot be right – in the "East", direct speech is often used.

[7.051] Expressed metaphorically, imagine a large corkboard that is divided into various segments. Some of these segments are red, others green. The idea is to throw and land a dart at only the green segments. However, the task is made more challenging because the corkboard is covered with paper and the person throwing the dart has no idea where the segments are. If the entire board represents every context in Asia, the segments indicate the contexts that are appropriate to use indirect or direct language and the paper covering the board is our ubiquitous reference to the "East", then the metaphor is complete. Any dart thrown would essentially be a wild guess and whether the dart lands on a red or green segment is left up to chance. The dart will sometimes land appropriately and other times not. This is therefore akin to using only indirect language in every context in the "East".

[7.052] The methodology presented above provides us with a sharper tool by which to cut away the paper so that the segments on the corkboard can be seen, identified and analysed. One would still need some skill to land a dart on the correct segments but less is left to chance. By identifying and understanding the assumptions underlying any cultural context in which we are seeking to apply the interests-based model, one has a framework to accurately determine when to use indirect or direct language.

4. STATUS, BELONGING, COMMUNICATION AND FACE

[7.053] As mentioned earlier, it would be inaccurate to make a general assertion that in an "Asian" context, one must use indirect language and that face concerns are prevalent. There are many instances in Asia where parties communicate directly and do not seem concerned about helping the other party preserve "face". While one could dismiss these instances as anomalies, the writer submits that there is coherence and consistency in these behaviours and a framework underlies and guides them. This section seeks to formulate this framework so as to assist readers in traversing this challenging area.

Appendix 4

4.1 Definitions

[7.054] As a preliminary point, it is useful to define some of the terms that the framework will revolve around.

Status

[7.055] The first is the notion of *status*. This is expressed by Hofstede as Power Distance and is measured by the Power Distance Index (PDI). This is a measurement of how society handles inherent inequalities, which may result from prestige, wealth and power.[43] Put simply, some cultures are more hierarchical than others. Hierarchical societies i.e. societies with a high PDI have a more defined sense of roles and obligations and there are clear decision makers (usually at the top of the hierarchy). Status, seniority, age and even gender therefore matter. Societies which are more "flat" i.e. societies with a low PDI tend to be comfortable with shared authority, more diffused roles, and have a preference for consensus.

[7.056] It is important to note that the PDI is, as with many other things, contextual. Within a society that that has a low PDI e.g. the USA, there are certain contexts within that society that may exhibit a higher PDI. The military and the legal profession are two examples of groups that generally exhibit a higher PDI. Conversely, within a society that has a high PDI, some contexts within that society may manifest a lower PDI.

Belonging

[7.057] The second is the notion of *belonging*. This is expressed by Hofstede as Collectivism/Individualism and is measured by the Individualism Index (IDV). This is a measurement of the relationship and extent of integration between the individual and the group that prevails in a given society.[44] Put simply, cultures that have a high IDV tend to play down relationships and focus more on the individual and individual rights. Conversely, cultures with a low IDV tend to be collectivist and focus more on close ties between individuals. As with the PDI, there may be contexts within a high IDV culture where they may manifest a lower IDV and vice versa. Individuals within the same collective or grouping can be referred to as being "in-group". Those that are not within the same collective or grouping can be referred to as being "out-group". Of course, these are static snapshots of the relational belonging between two individuals. It can be that the relational belonging is in transition i.e. two individuals are moving from an out-group relationship to an in-group relationship (or vice-versa) either by design or circumstances.

---

43. Hofstede, note 5 above, p 79.
44. Hofstede, note 5 above, p 209.

Appendix 4

Communication

[7.058] The next notion to consider is *communication*. For the purposes of this paper, this amorphous concept can be split into direct and indirect communication.[45] Direct and indirect communications are often associated with low-context and high-context communication respectively. Put simply, a direct or low-context communicator derives meaning primarily from the words that the speaker uses. Similarly, they will seek to transmit meaning primarily with words. Very little meaning, if any, is derived or transmitted via the context, hence the reference to low-context communication. A direct communicator who does not feel able to commit to the deal that is on the table may simply say, "This is not a good deal for me. I cannot agree".

[7.059] On the other hand, an indirect or high-context communicator derives meaning from and transmits meaning not just from words but also through contextual cues and clues. Taking the same message from the previous paragraph, an indirect communicator may say, "Let me take this proposal back to consider it" but gives off non-verbal cues indicating that he is just being polite.

[7.060] At this point, it is useful to make three points about the nature of direct and indirect communication. First, it is important to be clear that both forms of communication seek to convey the same message. Those that engage in direct communication will simply say what they mean. Those who engage in indirect communication will fi nd some other way to convey this message that requires the listener to read between the lines. This could even be expressed as a metaphor.

[7.061] Secondly, because we have a preference for our own style of communication, this often leads to each type of communicator attributing negative intentions to the other type of communicator. Direct communicators may perceive indirect communicators to be "shift y", "evasive" and "unwilling to communicate". On the other hand, direct communicators are perceived as "insensitive", "abrasive" and "brash".

[7.062] Thirdly, direct and indirect communication is not a digital either-or distinction. Instead, it is an analogue distinction that traverses a continuum. Put another way, it is not useful or easy to say whether any piece of communication is "direct" or "indirect". One can more usefully say that one piece of communication is more direct or more indirect than another piece of communication.

[7.063] Fourthly, accepting the preceding point will aff ect how we think about our communication styles. While there are "tests" or survey instruments that one can take to determine whether one is a direct or indirect communicator, it is probably more useful to think of these as indicators of one's communication style preferences. Instead

---

45. These ideas have been explored previously in Joel Lee, "Thoughts on Direct and Indirect Communication" (May 14, 2012) (last accessed March 17, 2014), Kluwer Mediation Blog, http://kluwermediationblog.com/2012/05/14/thoughts-on-direct-and-indirect-communication.

Appendix 4

of being a single point on the direct-indirect communication continuum, our communication style preference is more of a range within this continuum. Put another way, our communication style preference is a continuum within a continuum; for some, their range could be greater or narrower than someone else's.

[7.064] Fifthly, diff erent people will perceive the same phrase diff erently depending on their communication style preferences. A person who is closer to the indirect end of the direct-indirect continuum would likely consider phrases, that are considered indirect by those on the other end of the continuum, to be direct Therefore, even when a person who was closer to the direct end of the continuum restated a phrase more indirectly, it may not be heard by one on the indirect end of the continuum as being indirect.

[7.065] Finally, since we are able to operate inside a range within the direct-indirect continuum, most people exercise some discretion and choice about where within their range they will communicate. What guides this choice can be the values they have about communication (it is important to be open and direct) or the model of mediation being used (in the interests-model of mediation as practiced in many western jurisdictions, direct communication is prescribed) or the context and conditions that the mediation is being conducted in (where there is a concern about preserving the harmony of the collective and saving face of individuals, indirect communication may be prescribed).

Face

[7.066] The final notion to look at is the concept of *face*. This is a diffi cult concept to defi ne. It is sometimes expressed in some western contexts as ego or pride and can include the concern for dignity, honour and status.[46] Some provide a four quadrant framework encompassing face saving, asserting, restoration and giving.[47] For our purposes, it is not necessary to delve into the intricate complexities of face.[48] It is suffi cient to make two observations.

[7.067] First, a person can either save one's own face or give the other person face. While it is possible to say that one "saves the other person's face", for the purpose of this piece, we will take this to mean the same thing as giving the other person face. Further, while it is possible to say, although admittedly an uncommon formulation,

---

46. John Ng, "The Four Faces of Face Implications for Mediation" in Joel Lee and Teh Hwee Hwee (eds), *An Asian Perspective on Mediation* (Academy Publishing, Singapore, 2009), para 7.3.
47. Stella Ting-Toomey, "Intercultural Confl ict Styles: A Face Negotiation Theory" in Young Yun Kim and William Gudykunst (eds), *Theories in Intercultural Communication* (Sage, 1988), pp 213–235; Stella Ting-Toomey and Mark Cole "Intergroup Diplomatic Communication: A Face-Negotiation Perspective" in Felipe Korzenny and Stella Ting-Toomey (eds), *Communicating for Peace: Diplomacy and Negotiation Across Cultures* (Sage, 1990), pp 77–95.
48. For a discussion on face, see generally John n 46 above.

Appendix 4

that one "asserts one's own face", for the purposes of this piece, we will take this to mean the same thing as saving one's own face.

[7.068] Secondly, what does it mean exactly, in behavioural terms, to save or give face? The starting point is the assumption that where there are no face considerations, two parties will communicate with each other in a direct manner and can reasonably expect and assert for what they are entitled to in terms of, inter alia, respect, behaviour or rights. We will take this to be the norm.

[7.069] When face considerations come into play, based on the first observation above, two scenarios arise. In the first scenario, Party A may feel a need to give Party B face. Behaviourally, this means that Party A may communicate indirectly, manifests patterns of deference and asserts for less than what s/he is entitled to. In the extreme, Party A may even completely refrain from asserting for his/her entitlement. In the other scenario, Party A may feel the need to save face. Behaviourally, this means that Party A may communicate directly, manifest patterns of dominance/ authority and assert for exactly what s/he is entitled to. In the extreme, Party A may even assert for more than his/her entitlement, perhaps to the point of seeming unreasonable. Essentially, in this context, deviating from the norm can be seen as a manifestation of giving or saving face.

[7.070] In the context of mediation, the need to give or save face may also manifest as a reluctance to talk about certain things in joint session. Put another way, a private session can be a very useful tool to manage face considerations.

[7.071] Now that we have considered the four notions of status, belonging, communication and face, this chapter will turn to how they interact with one another.

4.2 *Interaction of notions of status, belonging, communication and face*

[7.072] In the proposed framework, status (PDI) and belonging (IDV) form the two variables that determine which communication and face strategies to engage in. For example, if we were to isolate the status variable and examine its effect on communication and face, a number of possible variations exist.

[7.073] The table below seeks to capture, admittedly imperfectly, the various permutations that might occur.

Appendix 4

		X	PDI High		PDI Low	
Y			**High Status**	**Low Status**	**High Status**	**Low Status**
PDI High	*In-Group*	*High Status*	β Indirect Communication, Face Play	Indirect Communication, Face Play	Indirect Communication, Face Play	Indirect Communication, Face Play
		Low Status	Direct Communication, Norm	Indirect Communication, Face Play	Direct Communication, Norm	Direct Communication, Norm
	Out-Group	*High Status*	α Direct Communication, Norm	Indirect Communication, Face Play	Direct Communication, Norm	Direct Communication, Norm
		Low Status	δ Direct Communication, Norm	χ Direct Communication, Norm	Direct Communication, Norm	Direct Communication, Norm
PDI Low	*In-Group*	*High Status*	Indirect Communication, Face Play	Indirect Communication, Face Play	Direct Communication, Norm	Indirect Communication, Face Play
		Low Status	Direct Communication, Norm	Direct Communication, Norm	Direct Communication, Norm	Direct Communication, Norm
	Out-Group	*High Status*	Direct Communication, Norm	Direct Communication, Norm	Direct Communication, Norm	Direct Communication, Norm
		Low Status	Direct Communication, Norm	Direct Communication, Norm	Direct Communication, Norm	Direct Communication, Norm

[7.074] It is important to make a number of observations at this point. This table captures a communication from someone delineated in bold (the x-axis) to a person delineated in italics (the y-axis). The x-axis captures two variables, the PDI and the level at which one is at their respective hierarchies. The latter is expressed as "high status" or "low status" and only makes sense when matched with the status of their counterpart on the y-axis. The y-axis captures these two variables as well. In addition, it captures whether "Y" relative to "**X**" is considered to be in-group or out-group.

[7.075] Secondly, the various intersection points capture the mode of communication that can be expected from X to Y, taking into account the corresponding variables. The intersection points also capture whether "Face Play" is engaged in. While this is arguably descriptive, it can also be prescriptive. The reader can use this table to guide his/her actions when faced with similar circumstances. For example, in the box indicated by "δ", where X (High PDI, High Status) is communicating to Y (High PDI, Low Status, Out-Group), it is fairly safe to assume that X will communicate with Y in direct language and not be very concerned about giving the other person face.

[7.076] Thirdly, some boxes have been shaded. This is to capture the nuance that the behaviours described in that box are to be expected as a starting point but that the opposite set of behaviours may be engaged in, depending on the judgment call of the speaker. For example, in the box indicated by "α", X (High PDI, High Status) is communicating to Y (High PDI, High Status, Out-Group). The assumption is, *ceteris paribus,* that X will engage in direct communication and not be too concerned with face play. However, if X prioritises the fact that both of them are from high PDI contexts and are both of high status, X may choose to depart from the default mode indicated.

[7.077] Finally, this table does not take into account situations in which parties may be in transition from in-group to out-group and vice versa. For example, in the box indicated by "β", X (High PDI, High Status) is communicating to Y (High PDI, High Status, In-Group). As indicated in that box, one would ordinarily expect X to engage in indirect communication and engage in face play. However, if the relationship between X and Y was transiting to that of an out-group, then X might engage in the opposite set of behaviours of direct communication and little concern for giving the other party face. Similarly, in the box indicated by "X", where X (High PDI, Low Status) is communicating to Y (High PDI, Low Status, Out-Group), X may nonetheless engage in indirect communication and face play rather than direct communication and little concern for face play if the parties are in transition.

[7.078] This writer does not propose to elaborate on all the possible variations depicted in the table. Some variations have been explored elsewhere.[49] How might this be helpful to mediators? First, it can help the mediator determine what mode of communication to use with the parties. If both parties prefer communicating in a particular mode, it would behoove the mediator to match that mode. A mismatch between parties who prefer indirect communication and a mediator preferring direct communication would lead to the mediator being perceived as being insensitive, pushy and unable to understand the nuanced complexity of the problem and relationship between the parties. In turn, the mediator would perceive the parties as being unwilling to communicate and evasive. Conversely, where the parties prefer direct communication and the mediator prefers indirect communication, the parties may perceive the mediator as being wishy-washy, ineffective and not really getting to the point. In turn, the mediator may perceive the parties as being impatient and pushy.

[7.079] Secondly, if parties prefer different modes of communication, the mediator must be careful not to let his/her preferred mode of communication give the impression that s/he is partial and siding with the party with whom his/her communication preference matches. In addition, the mediator plays an important role in bridging the gap. The mediator can do this by playing the role of a translator. This will usually be in relation to a piece of indirect communication as the party who is a direct communicator is not likely to "get it". Another way of bridging the gap is for the mediator to address the labels (which may be unspoken) that one party has attributed to the other party by reframing the behaviours in question. The mediator may have to reframe more direct instances of communication (which have a clear meaning but may come across as abrasive) so that the message is more palatable and not lost. Yet another way is for the mediator to play the role of a coach, and assist one party (preferably in private session) to communicate in a manner that better fits the other party.

---

49. Joel Lee, "In Praise of Private Sessions" (April 14, 2012) (last accessed March 17, 2014), Kluwer Mediation Blog, http://kluwermediationblog.com/2012/04/14/in-praise-of-private-sessions.

[7.080] Thirdly, where face play is important to both parties, the mediator can use this information to help parties construct agreements that both save and give face. These may involve symbolic gestures that may otherwise not surface if one were to focus purely on substantive interests. Further, being aware of status and belonging issues can help the mediator decide on when to shift into private sessions so as to get parties to communicate more openly. Where face play is important to one party only, as with the preceding point, the mediator can bridge the gap by playing the role of a translator, coach or reframer.

[7.081] Finally, an understanding of the issues relating to belonging can assist the mediator in reframing an out-group situation as one of being in-group. Alternatively, it may assist the mediator to find some way to assist parties who are out-group to transit to being in-group. This can assist in the creation of options that parties can agree upon and comply with in sustainable ways.

5. CONCLUSION

[7.082] Speaking as a recovering Universalist, it is easy for this writer to answer the question "is culture important?" – of course it is. The challenge is to not fall into the trap of thinking that the generalisations we draw represent reality. Generalisations are useful in that they give us shortcuts through which we can more easily navigate our world. However, the sin is to forget that they are generalisations and that the map is not the territory. It is therefore important for us to have a framework from which we can create our own generalisations when we meet with a situation that does not fit with the generalisations that we presently have.

[7.083] This piece has offered a limited framework to think about the interaction between status, belonging, communication and face. While it is hoped that it will have contributed somewhat to mediation thinking and scholarship, more importantly, it is hoped that it offers mediators a practical way to traverse the sometimes difficult territory of communication and face.

APPENDIX 5

Singapore Arb-Med-Arb Clause and Protocol

This clause is available at: http://simc.com.sg/the-singapore-arb-med-arb-clause/ and is reproduced here with the kind permission of the Singapore International Mediation Centre

Any dispute arising out of or in connection with this contract, including any question regarding its existence, validity or termination, shall be referred to and finally resolved by arbitration administered by the Singapore International Arbitration Centre ("SIAC") in accordance with the Arbitration Rules of the Singapore International Arbitration Centre ("SIAC Rules") for the time being in force, which rules are deemed to be incorporated by reference in this clause.

The seat of the arbitration shall be [Singapore].*

The Tribunal shall consist of _____** arbitrator(s).

The language of the arbitration shall be _____.

The parties further agree that following the commencement of arbitration, they will attempt in good faith to resolve the Dispute through mediation at the Singapore International Mediation Centre ("SIMC"), in accordance with the SIAC-SIMC Arb-Med-Arb Protocol for the time being in force. Any settlement reached in the course of the mediation shall be referred to the arbitral tribunal appointed by SIAC and may be made a consent award on agreed terms.

* Parties should specify the seat of arbitration of their choice. If the parties wish to select an alternative seat to Singapore, please replace "[Singapore]" with the city and country of choice (e.g., "[City, Country]").

** State an odd number. Either state one, or state three.

Appendix 5

SIAC-SIMC ARB-MED-ARB (AMA) PROTOCOL ENGLISH | BAHASA INDONESIA| 华语 | 日本語 | 한국어

This Protocol is available at: http://simc.com.sg/siac-simc-arb-med-arb-protocol/ and is reproduced here with the kind permission of the Singapore International Mediation Centre

1. This AMA Protocol shall apply to all disputes submitted to the Singapore International Arbitration Centre ("SIAC") for resolution under the Singapore Arb-Med-Arb Clause or other similar clause ("AMA Clause") and/or any dispute which parties have agreed to submit for resolution under this AMA Protocol. Under the AMA Protocol, parties agree that any dispute settled in the course of the mediation at the Singapore International Mediation Centre ("SIMC") shall fall within the scope of their arbitration agreement.

2. A party wishing to commence an arbitration under the AMA Clause shall file with the Registrar of SIAC a notice of arbitration in accordance with the arbitration rules applicable to the arbitration proceedings ("Arbitration Rules"), which Arbitration Rules shall be either: (i) the Arbitration Rules of the SIAC (as may be revised from time to time); or (ii) the UNCITRAL Arbitration Rules (as may be revised from time to time) where parties have agreed that SIAC shall administer such arbitration.

3. The Registrar of SIAC will inform SIMC of the arbitration commenced pursuant to an AMA Clause within 4 working days from the commencement of the arbitration, or within 4 working days from the agreement of the parties to refer their dispute to mediation under the AMA Protocol. SIAC will send to SIMC a copy of the notice of arbitration.

4. The Tribunal shall be constituted by SIAC in accordance with the Arbitration Rules and/or the parties' arbitration agreement.

5. The Tribunal shall, after the exchange of the Notice of Arbitration and Response to the Notice of Arbitration, stay the arbitration and inform the Registrar of SIAC that the case can be submitted for mediation at SIMC. The Registrar of SIAC will send the case file with all documents lodged by the parties to SIMC for mediation at SIMC. Upon SIMC's receipt of the case file, SIMC will inform the Registrar of SIAC of the commencement of mediation at SIMC (the "Mediation Commencement Date") pursuant to the SIMC Mediation Rules. All subsequent steps in the arbitration shall be stayed pending the outcome of mediation at SIMC.

6. The mediation conducted under the auspices of SIMC shall be completed within 8 weeks from the Mediation Commencement Date, unless, the Registrar of SIAC in consultation with the SIMC extends the time. For the purposes of calculating any time period in the arbitration proceeding, the time period will stop running at the Mediation Commencement Date and resume upon notification of the Registrar of SIAC to the Tribunal of the termination of the mediation proceeding.

Appendix 5

7. At the termination of the 8-week period (unless the deadline is extended by the Registrar of SIAC) or in the event the dispute cannot be settled by mediation either partially or entirely at any time prior to the expiration of the 8-week period, SIMC shall promptly inform the Registrar of SIAC of the outcome of the mediation, if any.

8. In the event that the dispute has not been settled by mediation either partially or entirely, the Registrar of SIAC will inform the Tribunal that the arbitration proceeding shall resume. Upon the date of the Registrar's notification to the Tribunal, the arbitration proceeding in respect of the dispute or remaining part of the dispute (as the case may be) shall resume in accordance with the Arbitration Rules.

9. In the event of a settlement of the dispute by mediation between the parties, SIMC shall inform the Registrar of SIAC that a settlement has been reached. If the parties request the Tribunal to record their settlement in the form of a consent award, the parties or the Registrar of the SIAC shall refer the settlement agreement to the Tribunal and the Tribunal may render a consent award on the terms agreed to by the parties.

Financial Matters

10. Parties shall pay a non-refundable case filing fee as set out in Appendix B of the SIMC Mediation Rules to SIAC for all cases under this AMA Protocol.

11. Where a case is commenced pursuant to the AMA Clause and where parties have agreed to submit their dispute for resolution under the AMA Protocol before the commencement of arbitration proceedings, this filing fee is payable to SIAC upon the filing of the notice of arbitration. Otherwise, the portion of the filing fee remaining unpaid in respect of the mediation shall be payable to SIAC upon the submission of the case for mediation at SIMC.

12. Parties shall also pay to SIAC, upon request, an advance on the estimated costs of the arbitration ("Arbitration Advance") as well as administrative fees and expenses for the mediation ("Mediation Advance") in accordance with SIAC and SIMC's respective Schedule of Fees (collectively "the Deposits"). The quantum of the Deposits will be determined by the Registrar of SIAC in consultation with SIMC.

13. Where a case is commenced pursuant to the AMA Clause and where parties have agreed to submit their dispute for resolution under the AMA Protocol before the commencement of arbitration proceedings, the Mediation Advance shall be paid with the Arbitration Advance requested by SIAC. Otherwise, the Mediation Advance shall be paid upon the submission of the case for mediation at SIMC.

14. Without prejudice to the Arbitration Rules, any party is free to pay the Deposits of the other party, should the other party fail to pay its share. The Registrar of SIAC shall inform SIMC if the Deposits remain wholly or partially unpaid.

15. SIAC is authorised to make payment of the Mediation Advance to SIMC from the Deposits or the Arbitration Advance held by SIAC without further reference to the parties.

APPENDIX 6
Mediation Suitability Scan

Reproduced with the kind permission of legal mediation office Schonewille & Schonewille, Rotterdam, the Netherlands, www.schonewille-schonewille.com.

I. **GENERAL ASPECTS TO CHECK**

1. Business and legal: Expected value of outcome esp. considering the interests.
2. Expected costs of resolution process (money time, risk, (un)certainty, stress, precedent).
3. Relationship: Expected psychological value of resolution process (recognition, getting attention, day in court, excuse, confidentiality, being 'heard', proof one's right).
4. Expected procedural aspects of resolution process (empowerment | staying in charge vs. delegation of responsibility and predictability).
5. BATNA | WATNA | RATNA & leverage for both parties.
6. Expected compliance with legal ruling? How likely is it to recover/enforce the claim? Ease of enforcement of ruling?
7. Convincing (objective) Criteria, hard & fast rules vs., fairness and reasonableness?

II. **EDR SCAN |MAX SCORE = 100 POINTS. 0 – 50 = ARBITRATION OR LITIGATION WORTH EXPLORING; 50 – 100 = MEDIATION OR SETTLEMENT NEGOTIATIONS WORTH EXPLORING**

A. Parties involved	0	1 point	2 points
1. Are there more than 2 parties involved?	N	Maybe	Y
2. Do you see options for offering a proposal or can you negotiate about a solution?	N	Partly	Y

Appendix 6

A. Parties involved	0	1 point	2 points
3. Are you under (time) pressure to reach a solution fast or do you want to end the dispute quickly?	N	Partly	Y
4. Would you or the other party benefit from time delay while not being prepared to let this interest surface during the process (hidden agenda)?	Y	Partly	N
5. Is there a longstanding relationship between you and the other party?	N	Partly	Y
6. Will you (have to or want to) do business with the other party in the future again or is there a dependency or on going relationship?	N	Partly	Y
7. Is the other party a foreign entity or does it concern an international case (with potential jurisdictional or enforcement issues)?	N	Partly	Y
8. There is an extreme imbalance of power and/or one party cannot represent or protect their own interests sufficiently or is unwilling to take responsibility for decisions?	Y	Partly	N
points			
Total A:			

B.1. My Interests, Concerns, Needs, Motivators	0	1 point	2 points
1. Is it a matter of principle or NIMBY case for you?	Y	Maybe	N
2. Will a decision made by an independent party make consulting with your constituency or 'selling the result' back home easier?	Y	Partly	N
3. Is privacy or confidentiality important? Does sensitive information that you prefer not to disclose play a role?	N	Partly	Y
4. Do you (also) want to achieve changes in future attitude, behaviour, communication, recognition, an excuse or anything else that cannot be provided for in a legal ruling?	N	Partly	Y
5. Are you particularly concerned with publicly asserting or proving you are right (for example to send a wider message)?	Y	Partly	N
6. Is it a matter of utmost importance, high risk, potential huge impact on business, precedent, or anything else that would make it important to stay in control of the outcome yourself?	N	Partly	Y
7. Do you have a desire to reach settlement yourself and on your own terms?	N	Partly	Y
8. Is it important to you that the other party understands and listens to your point of view?	N	Partly	Y

Appendix 6

B.1. My Interests, Concerns, Needs, Motivators	0	1 point	2 points
9. From a tactical/strategic point of view it is important to initiate talks first.	N	Partly	Y
points			
Total B.1:			

B.2. Their Interests, Concerns, Needs, Motivators	0	1 point	2 points
1. Is it a matter of principle or NIMBY case for them?	Y	Maybe	N
2. Will a decision made by an independent party make consulting with their constituency or 'selling the result' back home easier?	Y	Partly	N
3. Is privacy or confidentiality important? Does sensitive information that they prefer not to disclose play a role?	N	Partly	Y
4. Do they (also) want to achieve changes in future attitude, behaviour, communication, recognition, an excuse or anything else that cannot be provided for in a legal ruling?	N	Partly	Y
5. Are they particularly concerned with publicly asserting or proving they are right (for example to send a wider message)?	Y	Partly	N
6. Is it a matter of utmost importance, high risk, potential huge impact on business, precedent, or anything else that would make it important to stay in control of the outcome themselves?	N	Partly	Y
7. Do they have a desire to reach settlement themself and on their own terms?	N	Partly	Y
8. Is it important to them that you understand and listen to their point of view?	N	Partly	Y
9. From a tactical/strategic point of view it is important to initiate talks first.	N	Partly	Y
points			
Total B.2:			

C. Dispute & Conflict Dynamics Analysis	0	1 point	2 points
1. The dispute involves several claims | conflicts and/or all issues cannot be addressed in one legal procedure.	N	Maybe	Y
2. Is the core of the matter solely about money or division of goods?	Y	Partly	N

Appendix 6

C. Dispute & Conflict Dynamics Analysis	0	1 point	2 points
3. Is the core of the matter disagreement about interpretation of new legislation (e.g. to establish a new principle of law) or similar legal issue; or is a precedent needed (e.g. an explanation of General Terms?)	Y	Partly	N
4. Are there other issues that caused the conflict like treatment issues, disrupted communication, misunderstandings, emotions, lack of clear understanding, data conflicts?	N	Partly	Y
5. Is the case technically and/or substantively complex or requires specialist knowledge or are there several issues that play a role at the same time for which an integrated solution is necessary?	N	Partly	Y
6. A legal ruling will not (fully) resolve the dispute or the underlying conflicts.	N	Partly	Y
7. Is it important to also include business aspects into the solution?	N	Partly	Y
8. The dispute is escalated beyond repair, meaning that the parties cannot even sit in the same room, do not want to talk with each other or the dispute is meanwhile not about the disagreement but about destroying each other and bringing about harm.	Y	Partly	N
points			
Total C:			

D. Legal & risk analysis	0	1 point	2 points
1. Can the ruling in this case negatively affect other cases and will that (potentially) have a major impact?	N	Partly	Y
2. Is it relatively easy for you to proof your position and point of view and/or are there hard and fast rules / objective criteria applicable that support your case?	Y	Partly	N
3. Is there a high probability (>80%) that you would win if you go to court?	Y	Partly	N
4. Do you expect your constituency and the other party to comply easily with a legal ruling? Is a ruling easily enforced?	Y	Partly	N
5. Is there a high probability that the other party would win if you go to court?	N	Partly	Y
6. Is the other party |(probably) acting in bad faith or are they on a fishing expedition or trying to delay resolving the case?	Y	Partly	N
7. Would you qualify this as a high risk (= high probability of occurrence) and high impact (= much potential damage) case?	N	Partly	Y

Appendix 6

D. Legal & risk analysis	0	1 point	2 points
8. Would a very unhappy counterparty | negative outcome for them potentially cause damage to your image?	N	Partly	Y
points			
Total D:			

E. Procedural preferences	0	1 point	2 points
1. Do you prefer a formal procedure with clear and prior-fixed timelines?	Y	Maybe	N
2. Do you prefer a flexible, custom-made procedure?	N	Partly	Y
3. Do you want to have maximum process control?	N	Partly	Y
4. Do you want to have maximum outcome control?	N	Partly	Y
5. Is it important to you that at the end of the process there is the guarantee of an outcome that parties have to accept?	Y	Partly	N
6. Is it important to you that you can reach the best possible outcome and/or a win-win solution?	N	Partly	Y
7. Is it important for you to control the costs of the proceedings and/or do you have the financial means and time necessary to support prolonged procedures including appeals?	N	Partly	Y
8. Is there a mediation or negotiation clause in the contract | corporate ADR policy?	N	Partly	Y
points			
Total E:			

III. SELECTING THE MEDIATION PROCESS AND THE MEDIATOR

1. General criteria in selecting a mediator

Applicable	Mediator selecting criteria	Priority
☐	Cultural skills	
☐	Language skills	
☐	Gender	
☐	Location | nationality	
☐	Deadline | availability within desired timeframe	
☐	Costs	
☐	Applicable code of conduct | Mediation Rules | Mediation law	
☐	No conflict of interest	
☐	Specialization and practice area	

Appendix 6

Applicable	Mediator selecting criteria	Priority
☐	Mediation expertise	
☐	Substantive knowledge | Professional background	
☐	Mediation style | approach (see 2. below)	
☐	Caucus | joint session or mixed approach (see 3. below)	
☐	Co-mediators or solo-mediator (see 4. below)	

2. Selecting a mediation style | mediation process

It is important for users of mediation services to select a mediator with a style or number of styles that meet the needs of their specific case – suitable both for all the parties involved and for the situation that needs to be resolved.

As in the choice of any professional service, you first need to identify your and the other parties' likely needs, discuss the details of the process and then ensure your choice of a professional meets those needs.

The type and style of mediation can be defined by focusing on <u>two axes:</u>

a) how directive or facilitative the neutral will be on matters of process (e.g., time management, whether to caucus or not, written submissions if any, opening presentations, etc.); and

a) how evaluative or non-evaluative | facilitative the neutral will be on matters of substance (e.g., ranging from refusing to express any views, to doing tough reality-testing and preparing to give a media-tor's proposal if the parties do not reach an agreement).

This leads to four different main types mediation process, which can vary greatly also within the same quadrant, depending on the degree of emphasis on process and/or substance. Mediators ideally should be flexible & able to operate in each of the quadrants according to the needs of the situation and stage of the mediation process.

A general rule of thumb is that unless parties are experienced in mediation a mediator can be more directive on the process at the outset to avoid that a discussion on what process to follow becomes another disputed issue. During the exploration stage the parties and their advocates can take on a more directive role in managing | driving the process themselves. During option generation and negotiation it mainly depends on the sophistication of the parties and the power balance as well as whether it is a caucus (only) mediation or mediation in joint session (mainly).

Appendix 6

Quadrant A: (Facilitative on Process & Non-Evaluative on Substance).

Starting the process: 4 types

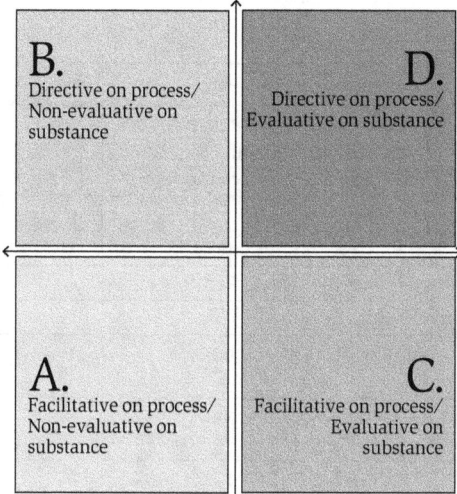

Mediator = convener | facilitator, mediation = interest-based negotiation and social process. Facilitative, interests-based mediation, where the role of the mediator is to generate choices, both on procedural options and on substance to enable the parties to find solutions themselves. Parties are given the opportunity to explore their relationship, recognise and express emotions, and discuss their fears and hopes, misunderstandings, intentions and motivations. The neutral avoids expressing views, or using any substantive knowledge and will not be making any proposals to the parties as to possible outcomes.

Quadrant B: (Directive on process and non-evaluative on substance).

Mediator = manager of process, mediation = efficient interest-based negotiation process to work through any substantive issues for which the parties bare the responsibility. Directive, interests-based mediation, where the role of the mediator is similar to that of the mediator in Quadrant A, regarding substantive issues but where the mediator is expected to take more of a leadership role and direct the process itself.

Quadrant C: (Facilitative on Process and Evaluative on Substance).

Mediator = conciliator, mediation = process to solve substantive issues based on objective norms and expert opinions. This can be described as a form of facilitative, norms-based mediation where mediators are chosen for their substantive knowledge of the norms that would normally apply to this sort of dispute (e.g., the applicable laws, case law or industry standards that would apply if a tribunal were to decide the matter).

Quadrant D: (Directive on Process and Evaluative on Substance).

Mediator = conciliator and process manager; mediation = positional negotiation managed by a conciliator. This can be described as a form of directive, norms-based mediation where the role of the mediator is to be efficient in generating outcomes, and to set and control the process. The mediator is expected to be able to form a view as to

Appendix 6

what would settle the dispute and to possibly propose it to the parties if they do not reach an agreement within a set period of time.

Rules of thumb for choosing a mediation approach

Quadrant A

Applicable	Quadrant A features:	Priority
☐	In mediation experienced & sophisticated parties that can agree on process decisions: (e.g. time management, to caucus or not, written submissions, opening presentations, role division, etc.).	
☐	Power and leverage in relative balance.	
☐	Important to (re)build relationships, trust and affiliation.	
☐	Emotions and/or relationship issues need to be worked through.	
☐	Recognition and empowerment are beneficial.	
☐	It is important to overcome communication issues and identifying blocking issues.	
☐	Business solutions, options for mutual gain or creative approaches are desired.	
☐	Sufficient time for exploration of underlying interests is useful.	
☐	(Voluntary) Compliance is important.	

Quadrant B

Applicable	Quadrant B features:	Priority
☐	Highly escalated conflict (Glasl main stage III)	
☐	Parties do not want to spend time discussing how the mediation process should be managed or have very different preferences and cannot agree on a joint approach.	
☐	Large power imbalance with risk of one party to potentially dominate the process.	
☐	Time is of the essence, however relationship issues, emotions, recognition and empowerment are important and need to be addressed.	
☐	Sufficient time for exploration of underlying interests is necessary.	
☐	Voluntary) Compliance is particularly important.	
☐	No need for continuous support of intermediary to set communication rules after closing of mediation.	
☐	Parties are able to work through substantive issues and generating (legal) norms themselves and do not need substantial guidance on (legal) norms from the mediator while generating options (e.g. because they are ably represented by legal advisors).	

Appendix 6

Applicable	Quadrant B features:	Priority
☐	Mediator support of directing a discussion towards topics that are sensitive or that none of the parties want to address may be helpful.	
☐	Underlying interests and/or hidden agenda's need to be worked-through.	
☐	It is important to overcome communication issues and identifying blocking issues.	
☐	Business solutions, options for mutual gain or creative approaches are desired.	
☐	(Voluntary) Compliance is important.	

Quadrant C

Applicable	Quadrant C features:	Priority
☐	In mediation experienced and sophisticated parties that can agree on process decisions: (e.g. time management, to caucus or not, written submissions, opening presentations, role division, etc.).	
☐	Conciliation type of mediation is desired.	
☐	Need for breaking deadlocks by non-binding mediator opinions, thorough reality testing questions, comments and facts and law actively discussed and commented by the mediator.	
☐	Guidance on settlement through norms, objective criteria (e.g. industry standards, law, etc.) or bench-marks is useful.	
☐	Expert opinion can help with constituency issues.	
☐	Future relationship more important than being in control of the substantive issues.	

Quadrant D

Applicable	Quadrant D features:	Priority
☐	Highly escalated conflict (Glasl main stage III).	
☐	Parties do not want to spend time discussing how the mediation process should be managed or have very different preferences and cannot agree on a joint approach.	
☐	Large power imbalance causing one party to potentially dominate the process and substantive issues.	
☐	Conciliation or informal arbitration type of mediation is desired.	
☐	Guidance on settlement through norms, objective criteria (e.g. industry standards, law, etc.) or bench-marks is useful.	
☐	Expert opinion can help with constituency issues.	

Appendix 6

☐	Future relationship, working through emotions | misunderstandings and being in control of the substantive issues less important than reaching an outcome.	
☐	Deadlines and fast solution are essential.	
☐	Expert (legal) opinion will help to settle the issues at stake.	

3. Caucus, joint sessions or mixed approach

Caucus

- ☐ Thorough reality testing is likely to be necessary.
- ☐ Exploration of underlying interests | hidden agenda's.
- ☐ Efficiency | limited time.
- ☐ Settling monetary issues | numbers discussion.
- ☐ When emotions are running so high that adequate communication is not possible.
- ☐ Explore specific options that parties do not want to bring up themselves and/or explore options in confidence.
- ☐ A discussion with an (unwilling) advisor or participant who is not experienced in mediation about how things can be better handled or reality testing of an involved manager or client is likely to be necessary.

Joint sessions

- ☐ On-going or future relationship.
- ☐ Exploration of joint interests.
- ☐ Empowerment of the parties, mutual understanding and recognition are important.
- ☐ A mutual gain, win-win outcome is desired.
- ☐ Sophisticated parties who are able to constructively communicate and represent their own interests.
- ☐ Direct communication is desired.
- ☐ Relationship or communication issues need to be addressed and solved.
- ☐ If parties want to leave open the option of a mediator's advisory opinion in a later stage of the mediation, especially if it may be binding.
- ☐ The parties expertise is essential for brainstorming and crafting a settlement, e.g. if a business solution is desired.
- ☐ A creative outcome is desired.

Mixed joint session | caucus model

Appendix 6

Combines most of the pro's and con's. A joint session model base where caucus is used as a tool is advisable in most cases.

4. Co-mediators or solo-mediator

Co-mediators

- ☐ In a complex dispute, for example many parties (rule of thumb: more than two) or with many participants at the mediation table (rule of thumb: more than four).
- ☐ When the case is technically complex, or deals with complicated substantive issues so a combination of facilitative and evaluative approach is beneficial.
- ☐ When the parties are deadlocked for example because the conflict is psychologically or emotionally challenging or concerns a protracted or exceptionally escalated conflict.
- ☐ When different kinds of expertise or skills are required, for example substantive expertise or multilingualism, different mediation experience or mediators with different nationalities to bridge cultural differences in an international setting.
- ☐ When parties are in different locations most of the time and it is impractical for them to meet regularly or at all.
Co-mediation teams are particularly beneficial in cross-border and complex commercial disputes.

The advantages of co-mediation:

- ✓ Greater efficiencies for multi-party disputes.
- ✓ Better balance and complementary skills.
- ✓ Less tendency to seek coalitions and try to influence the neutrals as a team.
- ✓ A greater ability to address difficult emotional and/or social issues.
- ✓ A greater ability to identify and analyze possible impasses and adapt the process to the dispute.
- ✓ An enhanced ability to take into account personal feelings and identify non-verbal communication issues.
- ✓ Better observation of the dispute and personalities involved (two mediators can focus on different things and see, hear and perceive more than one).
- ✓ Can serve as an example of teamwork: helping the partners in the negotiation to work more collaboratively both in joint sessions and in separate sessions.
- ✓ Enhances perceptions of impartiality and balance.
- ✓ Can provide non-binding evaluative input on positions (if one neutral is requested to do so), without compromising the facilitative and collaborative nature of the process
- ✓ Can provide hybrid processes, if useful to the process at any stage.
- ✓ Can help the parties to generate more ideas, options and alternatives, which often leads to better solutions and outcomes.

Appendix 6

- ✓ Can increase the efficiency of caucuses (separate meetings) if both mediators meet separately with different groups of people at the same time.
- ✓ Increases creativity and provides greater outcome satisfaction, leading to higher settlement rates.

Co-mediation improves the effectiveness of a facilitated settlement process, especially if different mediation styles are expected by each negotiation partner. It leads to better outcomes by improving the quality of the process as well as the quality of the result. Studies have shown that the settlement rate is higher in co-mediations as compared to solo-mediations, and legal counsel tend to give higher satisfaction ratings regarding the outcomes of co-mediations. A mixed gender and cross-cultural team also adds diversity and can better address intercultural issues, capable of designing culturally appropriate interventions into the process.

Appendix 7

Sample Roleplay

This Roleplay was prepared by Michael Leathes together with Manon Schonewille. It is not copyright protected and is freely downloadable as a Word document for use in training programs from www.michaelleathes.com.

Axel and Marie-Claire married in 1999. In 2001, they quit their jobs (they both were working for an international headhunting firm) and together started an internet-based business called Ozone Agency. The company operates in executive recruitment, placing people experienced in the climate change, corporate responsibility and sustainable development fields, and Ozone is the only niche recruitment firm operating internationally in this area of expertise. In 2001, it was just the two of them, but the business started growing immediately, and they now have a staff of 40 located in 30 countries. Ozone's clients include many multinational companies and they now have a database of 100,000 people working in this professional field worldwide. Turnover has been increasing by an average of 20% per annum, and now stands at $40m of gross billings. Axel and Marie-Claire each own 50% of the business. The pre-tax gross profit is 10% of turnover and each is expecting to collect $1m in dividends this year, much of which they reinvest.

Blue Sky Green (BSG) is a large American recruitment agency based in New York but with offices in many countries. BSG is wholly owned by a private equity group called Mama Mia who bought BSG two years ago and have been investing and expanding its business each year. BSG is a general recruitment firm, specializing in senior executives but make their money mainly from searching for and placing executives in corporate affairs, PR and lobbying departments of international corporations. Mama Mia is owned by former insurance brokers Marta and Martin, who have been in partnership for over 10 years. They hold the key positions on the Board of BSG. Mama Mia has assets exceeding $2 billion and numerous investments and shareholdings in many service fields in different countries.

Appendix 7

Marta & Martin approached Axel & Marie-Claire saying they were interested in expanding BSG into the areas in which Ozone is operating, and to do so on a broader geographic basis. They asked if Axel & Marie-Claire might be interested in having a discussion about incorporating Ozone into BSG, and if so, whether a meeting to explore the prospect might be in order. Marie-Claire replied saying they always listened to serious proposals and would be happy to meet, but that the Ozone business was going very well and selling out at this time was not top of their agenda.

Martin responded that dialogue is always a good thing, even it led nowhere, but when exploring potential options for mutual gain, it can help to engage a neutral person to facilitate discussions. Martin said he knew from Mama Mia's lawyer that there was an expert deal facilitator in the same city as Axel and Marie Claire, and asked if they would agree to take this path. If so they could share the cost of the facilitator, just for a day. After consulting their external counsel Marie-Claire and Axel thought there was no downside, and so they agreed.

The meeting is about to take place in a hotel with the deal facilitator present. Both parties attend with their counsel.

PRIVATE INSTRUCTIONS FOR

Axel & Marie Claire, co-owners of Ozone

Coincidentally, a month before Mama Mia/BSG made contact, you agreed to split up. You have been together since 2001 and you had both worked like crazy in the business. It placed strains on your relationship, you drifted apart emotionally, and you both feel like a complete change. You are on good terms, there are no children, and you want to stay platonic friends. Axel wants to go exploring to see more of the planet before it gets destroyed by pollution and global warming, but Marie-Claire cares about the 40 Ozone staff and enjoys being in business – though not the long hours. However, you both agree that now might be the ideal moment to sell Ozone. The business is still expanding, there were no credible competitors yet, and you are both still youthful. You decided to seek a professional valuation.

The accountancy firm's valuation of Ozone in the present market, given the absence of debt and the positive prospects for the business was x2 to x3 gross billings for 100% of Ozone shares – ie $80m-$120m. Talking about it later, Axel said that anything over $50m was fine with him for a quick sale. It would generate at least $25m for each of them and they could both live comfortably for the rest of their lives. If a deal was on the table at that amount, Axel wanted to take it.

Marie-Claire does not agree to sell at a discount under any circumstances. After tax, the number is suddenly not so attractive. In fact Marie-Claire wants over €100m for all the Ozone shares. This will enable them to enable the staff to share in the value of the business. Anything less is, for her, out of the question. Axel says she is being greedy, but this is typical of how the relationship had gone out of control. In the past, they had agreed everything. Now, it has become so much more difficult.

Before going into the meeting, you agree not to let the Mama Mia/BSG people know your relationship is breaking up otherwise they may try to divide and rule. You both agree to play it cool and project to Mama Mia as a picture of perfect harmony, continuity and optimism. You also agree to do more listening and questioning than talking and proposing. But you don't want to lose them, because nobody else has expressed interest in Ozone - although, of course, someone might come along later.

Axel has $20m a gambling debt from reckless bets over the Internet. This started as a recreational hobby, but is now a serious problem. He received a call last week from someone describing what he had been wearing and where he had been the previous day, and insisting that he pay this debt in the next 30 days. Yesterday, he received a threatening reminder that he has only three weeks left. It is one of the factors that have driven Axel and Marie-Claire apart, as Axel previously tried to hide his gambling from Marie-Claire. Axel, is scared and needs cash quickly.

Marie-Claire wants to invest in a new business in another field. This will cost over $30m. She wants Ozone's employees looked after, and will not sell at any price. Marie-Claire feels she has worked too hard to see someone else take the profit.

You trust your joint external counsel, a friend for years, who has been aware all along of Axel's gambling and your marital problems. Be honest about everything, in private, with both the facilitator and your lawyer.

PRIVATE INSTRUCTIONS FOR

Marta & Martin, co-owners of Mama Mia/BSG

You are business partners. And that's it. It's worked really well. You are both very wealthy and tough-minded, and you are also both charming and gregarious.

You have done your due diligence on Ozone. The business is doing well, and the sector they are in is exploding internationally. They are not leveraging their position well, and if they don't do it soon, someone else will eat their cake. Remarkably, although other recruitment firms have tried to get a slice of the action in Ozone's market, none has succeeded, mainly because of Axel's and Marie-Claire's reputations and their high public profile. Their candidate database and client list are a gold mine.

Ozone is a really attractive proposition. Al Gore's Nobel Prize in 2007 and his movie *An Inconvenient Truth* began a momentum where climate change and sustainable development became a "must-have" staff resource for any major company, and there is a buzz that you want to benefit from in the future. You were eagerly searching for expertise in this emerging profession, and kept hearing about Ozone. You can see that accessing Ozone's international database will enable you to leapfrog into this market

Appendix 7

and develop the field worldwide. You will be able to expand the business globally with a bit more investment and lead this sector, internationally.

Although you are known to be cash rich investors, you didn't succeed by overpaying value for your investments. You bought BSG a few years ago for half of its real value because the owners were poorly advised and focused more on risks than opportunities. BSG is now worth five times what you paid for it.

You worked out that the value of Ozone, which has no debt and is increasing its billings by 20% per annum, is x2 to x3 annual gross billings, or $80 to $120m. You also know the business is expanding and worth a premium. But you don't want to spend that kind of money. Paying fair value is almost against your principles! But this is a unique little opportunity. There's nothing else like it out there, and the window of opportunity is now. The price would be greater in a year or two.

You agree to pitch an offer of $50m, pointing out that you would have to spend at least another $50m to penetrate new markets. These investment costs are actually exaggerated but cannot be contested.

Your goal is get Ozone for no more than a total of $100m. You would consider paying $60m now but with an earn-out for Axel & Marie-Claire if they stay with the business and if it expands as indicated at a 20% rate in its current markets for at least 3 years. Then you would pay a further $40m bonus. Only with extreme reluctance will you pay more. You want to snap a deal in principle at this first meeting, and you don't want to lose it. You are leaving town the day after the meeting. You want a deal in principle by the end of the day, that will be summarized in a signed Deal Sheet for lawyers to work on the full agreement afterwards.

Be honest about everything, in private, with the facilitator and your counsel.

PRIVATE INSTRUCTIONS FOR EXTERNAL COUNSEL OF OZONE

(please also read the private instructions for Axel & Marie-Claire)

You have advised Ozone and its two owners for around 10 years now, and you have come to know both Marie-Claire and Axel, and their business, very well. The personal relationship between Axel and Marie-Claire became strained about a year ago, and you were not really surprised when they told you that they had decided to get divorced. It was poor timing, however.

Marie-Claire is more level-headed than Axel, particularly right now when he has dubious debt collectors harassing him. Axel is capable of doing something irrational, driven by his need for immediate cash.

You regard Ozone as your client. You want what's best for both the Ozone shareholders but you cannot favour one over the other even if you think Axel is starting to go off the rails.

Appendix 7

It is obvious to you that something needs to be done to fix things between Axel and Marie-Claire if there is any realistic prospect of concluding a favorable deal with Mama Mia/BSG.

Cooperate with the facilitator though obviously your first duty is to your clients. Retain the trust of both your clients. Step carefully, but decisively. Also consider your relationship with the lawyer of Mama Mia/BSG. Play a role in this negotiation – don't just sit on the sidelines and give legal advice if requested – your clients have asked you to participate because they value your wise counsel and creativity and want you to tie up all the loose details if a deal can be worked out. Participate as a constructive solution provider.

PRIVATE INSTRUCTIONS FOR EXTERNAL COUNSEL OF MAMA MIA/BSG

(please also read the private instructions for Marta & Martin)

Last year, for another client, you participated as an adviser in a deal negotiation that was done with the help of a deal facilitator. It worked very well indeed. Given that Marta and Martin have allocated only a day to try and meet the owners of Ozone and persuade them to sell their business, you thought that cutting through the positional dance as quickly as possible to get to the bottom line interests was critical, and that's why you urged them to negotiate with the help of a facilitator. You do not know the facilitator personally.

You have been legal counsel for Marta and Martin for a good number of years. They are classic new-age entrepreneurs – they move fast and instinctively, make quick concessions, say they are throwing their cards on the table, expect instantaneous reactions and want to cut a deal right away. They get impatient when they meet resistance or hesitation. They don't like legalistic or prudent thinking, but it is nevertheless part of your role to remind them of any risks they take.

Acquiring Ozone is exactly the right opportunity for Mama Mia right now. Combined with the infrastructure they have built into BSG, this would be a very shrewd investment. You hope they don't trip because of their quest for speed and their notorious black-and-white, bottom line approach to things.

Cooperate with the facilitator, though obviously your first duty is to your clients. Retain the trust of your clients. Step carefully, but decisively. Also consider your relationship with the counsel of Ozone. You will need to work cooperatively in drafting a purchase contract if an agreement in principle is reached, and you cannot afford to be too aggressive (which, admittedly, has been your style in the past). Play a role in this negotiation – don't just sit on the sidelines and give legal advice if requested – your clients have asked you to participate because they value your wise counsel and creativity and want you to tie up all the loose details after they have worked out the general principles. Participate as a constructive solution provider.

Appendix 7

PRIVATE INSTRUCTIONS FOR THE DEAL FACILITATOR

You are an experienced dispute resolution mediator, but you have never acted as a deal facilitator before. Assume the process principles are similar.

Take the initiative to lead on the negotiation process, but let the parties do the actual negotiating. Explain this to everyone. Explain that the goal of the meeting is to explore whether Mama Mia/BSG and Ozone can make a deal of some kind, and that you are impartial, there to assist as necessary.

Raise the possibility that you may suggest private sessions between you and the parties and their counsel if you think that makes sense at any point. Explain that since it was Marta & Martin who suggested the discussion, you propose to invite them to start. Then give the floor to Marie Claire and Axel so they have a chance to comment, then feel your way from there.

Emphasize confidentiality, including and in particular anything you are told in private, unless the disclosing party releases you from confidentiality.

Index

A

Abramson, Harold, 173
Achievement-ascription scale, 64
Active speaking, 99–100, 117
Actives scale, 60–65
Administered or non-administered dispute resolution, 169–170
ADR Institute of Canada, 208
Adventure learning, 7
Agassi, Andre, 100, 101
Ahmadi, Sheila, 39
Alternative (or Appropriate) Dispute Resolution (ADR), 20, 29, 138, 141, 153, 208
Alternatives To a Negotiated Agreement (ATNAs), 24, 26, 85–86, 91, 105, 120, 131, 175, 180, 192, 198, 199
American Arbitration Association (AAA), 140–142, 154, 160
American Bar Association (ABA), 160, 187
Anchors, 22, 25, 78, 86–91, 100, 106, 122, 131, 164, 180, 195, 198
Andersen, Arthur, 181, 182
Arb-Med, 124, 126, 164
Arb-Med-Arb, 161–164

B

Baer, Marcus, 112, 113
Baseball arbitration, 163–164
Becker, Boris, 100, 101

Bennis, Warren, 73
Best Alternative To a Negotiated Agreement (BATNA), 26, 30, 85, 90, 91, 186, 195, 199, 202
Bhappu, Anita, 116
Bias, 25, 37–40, 42, 43, 47, 84, 94, 96, 201
Bogacz, François, 34, 46
Brazil, Wayne, 160
Brett, Jeanne, 19, 55, 65
Brown, Graham, 112, 113
Brown, Penelope, 68

C

Cameron, Kim, 71
Carnegie Foundation for the Advancement of Teaching, 6
Caruso, David, 104
Centre for Affective Sciences (CISA), 34, 46
Centre for Effective Dispute Resolution (CEDR), 149, 154, 160, 208
Chek Lap Kok Hong Kong Airport, 168
Child, Peter, 65
Cloke, Kenneth, 18, 39
Coben, James, 7
Collaborative Law (CL), 151–153, 169
Colson, Aurélien, 90
Conciliation, 70, 143, 160–161, 165, 168, 169
Conflict resolution policy, 18–20, 165–166, 173
Cooperative Law, 151–153

Index

Corman Aaron, Marjorie, 160
Corporate Social Responsibility (CSR), 123, 165, 179–180
Costantino, Cathy, 20
Covey, Stephen, 28, 181
CPR Institute, 29, 138, 142, 150, 167
Cuddy, Amy, 103
Culturology, 53–56, 58, 75

D

Danziger, Shai, 42, 43, 47
Deal facilitation, 126, 129–135, 153, 186
Denniston, Brackett, 1
De Palo, Giuseppe, 7
Dierdorff, Erich, 6
Dispute Resolution Boards (DRB), 168–169
Dispute Systems Design (DSD), 19–21, 29
Dispute-wise study, 140–142, 175
Dobelli, Rolf, 25
Drafting initiative, 201–202
Drucker, Peter, 22
Dubey, Prashant, 2

E

Early Case Assessment (ECA), 29–31, 150, 167, 172, 175
Early Neutral Evaluation (ENE), 159–160
Ebner, Noam, 116
ECA toolkit, 233
Ego-social, 57, 59
Eijsbouts, Jan, 179, 180
Emotional Intelligence (EI), 4, 6, 24, 104–107, 109, 117
E-negotiating, 115–117
Ertl, Danny, 20, 25
Ethical courage, 181–182
Ethics, xix, 2, 10, 43, 78–80, 98, 99, 105, 145, 152, 171, 172, 177–189, 206, 207, 209

F

Fabian, Christian, 153
Facework, Face, 54, 67–69, 71
Feedback Digest, 172
Fisher, Roger, xvii, 19, 20, 23, 25, 85, 148, 192
Forester, John, 108
Fox, Kenneth, 130, 131
Fraser, David, 96
Fraser, Véronique, 9

G

Galanter, Marc, 186
Gardner, Howard, 104
Gefland, Michele, 55, 65
General Electric (GE), 1, 4, 10, 47, 48, 114, 139, 142, 143, 172, 182
Gerarda Brown, Jennifer, 116
Glasgow, Edwin, 182
Glasl Escalator, 145
Glasl, Friedrich, 137–175
Global Counsel Leaders Circle, 2
Global Pound Conference 2016-17, 143–144
Golann, Dwight, 160, 187
Goldberg, Stephen, 19, 20
Goleman, Daniel, 104
Goodman, Andrew, 173
Greenleaf, Robert, xviii
Guanxi, 54, 69, 70, 76
Guided Choice, 150, 167, 169, 170, 175

H

Hager, L. Michael, 129
Hall, Edward, 55, 56
Hampden-Turner, Charles, 55, 63
Handy, Charles, 54
Hard skills-soft skills, 206–207
Harvard Program on Negotiation (PoN), 7, 105, 207, 208
Heineman, Ben, 10
Henry, James, 138, 158

Hofstede Centre, The, 60
Hofstede, Geert, 55, 57–60, 70
Honeyman, Christopher, 7
Hong Kong International Arbitration Centre (HKIAC), 163
Horton, Simon, 206
Howieson, Jill, 24
Humour, 72
Hybrids, 40, 55, 101, 143, 148, 164–165, 169, 175

I

ICC International Court of Arbitration, 163
Immelt, Jeffrey, 1, 2, 142, 182
Individualism-collectivism scale, 57, 58, 64
Individualism-communitarianism scale, 64
Indulgence-restraint, 55, 58–60
International Code of Negotiation Ethics, xix, 188, 209
International Mediation Institute (IMI), 29, 142, 143, 150, 167, 170, 172, 173, 208
International Negotiation Institute, xix, 208–209
Investor-State Dispute Settlement (ISDS), 162

J

JAMS, 160
Jordan, Thomas, 144

K

Kahneman, Daniel, 40–42, 88, 111
Kalowski, Joanna, 39
Kervers, Willem, 124, 125
Kindler, Jeff, 2
Kinsey Goman, Carol, 103
Klimecki, Olga, 34
Kluwer Arbitration Blog, 166
Kluwer Mediation Blog, 102, 142, 166

Kovach, Kimberlee, 116
Kripalani, Eva, 2
Kupfer Schneider, Andrea, 116

L

Lack, Jeremy, 34, 46, 48, 145
Lande, John, 148, 149, 152, 167
Lavy, Matthew, 115
Lax Sebenius, 201
Lee, Joel, 55, 69, 75, 102, 103, 163, 173
Legal Design Lawyering, 9
Lempereur, Alain, 90
Leverage, 6, 10, 12, 21, 25, 27, 28, 46, 49, 77–91, 95, 97, 98, 123, 130, 138, 142, 173–175, 178, 180, 206, 207
Levi, Deborah, 109
Levinson, Stephen, 68
Lewicki, Roy, 183
Lewis, Richard, 55, 60–63, 76
Ley Toffler, Barbara, 181
Lieberman, Jethro, 158
Lieberman, Matthew, 40–42
Liebman, Carol, 47
Lim, George, 162
Lim, Marcus, 163, 173
Linear-active scale, 55, 60–62
Lin, Yutang, 67
Lipsky, David, 140
Listening, 125, 128, 183, 194, 200, 208
Litigation As Usual (LAU), xvii, 148, 149, 167
Litigotiation, xix, 186
Litov, Lubomir, 3
Long, Carlton, 47
Low-hanging fruit, 26, 41, 86, 116, 197
Lurie, Paul, 167

M

Macfarlane, Julie, 28, 128
Malhotra, Deepak, 25, 202
Maryland Center for Dispute Resolution, 208

Mayer, John, 104
McDuff, Ian, 72
McGinn, Kathleen, 116
McIlwrath, Michael, 4, 47, 143, 172
Mediate.com, 166
Mediation, 4, 20, 21, 29, 55, 69, 70, 102, 109, 124, 128, 130, 131, 138, 140, 142, 143, 145, 146, 153-157, 160-173, 175, 186, 187, 202, 208
Mediation Advocacy, 143, 172-173
Mehabrian, Albert, 101, 102
Menkel-Meadow, Carrie, 182
Meyer, Bernard, 173
Meyer, Erin, 56, 65-67
Minitrial, 158-159, 169
Minkov, Michael, 71
Mnookin, Robert, 95, 99, 101
Monberg, Tina, xviii, 145
Movius, Hallam, 31
Multi-active scale, 55, 60-62

N

Navarro, Joe, 103
Negotiation Framework (NF), 21-28, 30, 31, 198
Neutral-affective scale, 64
Nisbett, Richard, 54

O

OECD Guidelines for Multinational Enterprises, 179
Olé Online evaluation, 219
Online Dispute Resolution (ODR), 115
Outcome-Based Education (OBE), 6, 7
Oxytocin, 38, 39, 46

P

Pareidolia, 40, 41
Pareto efficiency, 129
Pel, Machteld, 166
Peppet, Scott, 99, 131, 152
Peter, Laurence, 77

Philotimo, 70
Pink, Daniel, 4
Planned Early Dispute Resolution (PEDR), 148-150, 175
Plant, David, 119, 121, 123
Politeness Theory, 68, 195
Positions and interests, 114
Pound Conference 1976, 138, 143
Power distance, 58, 69
Prisoner's Dilemma, 193
Pritchard, Robert, 129
Probable Alternatives To a Negotiated Agreement (PATNA), 26, 30
Prospect Theory, 111

Q

Quinn, Robert, 71

R

Rachlinski, Jeffrey, 34
Raiffa, Howard, 129
Reactive devaluation, 21, 25, 50, 84, 90, 131, 145, 165
Reactive scale, 84, 90, 131, 145, 165
Realistic Alternatives To a Negotiated Agreement (RATNA), 26, 85, 91
Reciprocity, 69, 188, 199-201
Reframing, 95, 109, 111-112, 130
Roberge, Jean-François, 9
Roberts, Michael, 155
Roberts, Wess, 137
Robinson, Robert, 183
Role profiles, 8
Rowling, J.K., 74, 113
Rubin, Robert, 6

S

Salacuse, Jeswald, 129, 131-133, 192
Salovey, Peter, 104
Sander, David, 34
Sander, Frank, 127, 138, 143
Savage, John, 172

Schiphol Airport, 87, 88
Schonewille, Manon, 124, 125, 130, 131, 167, 172, 173
Schwartz, Shalom, 178, 185
Sebenius, James, 202, 203
Seeber, Ronald, 140
Self-reported Inappropriate Negotiation Strategies (SINS), 184
Sepe, Simon, 3
Sharp, Alan, xvii, 192
Shapiro, Daniel, 109
Shapiro, Irving, 137
Shell, Richard, 78, 79, 83, 183, 185
Shulman, Amy, 2
Sickles Merchant, Christina, 20
Sinek, Simon, 100, 132
Singapore International Arbitration Centre (SIAC), 162, 163
Singapore International Mediation Centre (SIMC), 163
Six Sigma, 8, 9, 119
Slade, Brian, 153
S-M-A-R-T, 22
Specific-Diffuse scale, 64, 65
Stanton, Angela, 39
Stipanowich, Thomas, 142
Straus Institute for Dispute Resolution, 142
Straus, Robert, 129
Stuckey, Roy, 6
Stuhlmacher, Alice, 22
Susskind, Daniel, 205
Susskind, Lawrence, 31, 87
Susskind, Richard, 115, 205
SWOT analysis, 30

T

Theory of Basic Human Values, 185
Ting-Toomey, Stella, 67

TNI The Negotiation Institute, 207
Todorov, Alexander, 74
Training, xix, 4-9, 18, 36, 37, 41, 72, 84, 105, 127, 173, 201, 208, 209
Tri-O/S, 34, 46-49
Trompenaars, Fons, 55, 63-65
Trump, Donald, 78
Tversky, Amos, 111

U

UNCITRAL Model Law on International Commercial Conciliation, 161
Ury, William, 19, 20, 46, 85, 111, 112, 115, 128, 146, 147, 199

V

Volkema, Roger, 78, 79, 83

W

Weeks, John, 71
Wheeler, Michael, 182, 188
Williams, Greg, 102
Williams-Washington, Kristin, 102
Wilson, Eric, 116
Wistrich, Andrew, 34
Worst Alternative To a Negotiated Agreement (WATNA), 26, 30, 85, 90, 91, 125

Z

Zak, Paul, 39
Zero-sum gain, 26, 86, 163
Zetik, Deborah, 22
Zone of Potential (or Possible) Agreement (ZOPA), 26, 86-87, 89, 91, 123, 124, 131, 175

www.ingramcontent.com/pod-product-compliance
Lightning Source LLC
Chambersburg PA
CBHW050837230426
43667CB00012B/2034